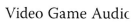

Video Game Audio

MW00580324

Video Game Audio

A History, 1972–2020

CHRISTOPHER HOPKINS

McFarland & Company, Inc., Publishers
Jefferson, North Carolina

All illustrations are from Wikimedia Commons.

ISBN (print) 978-1-4766-7435-3
ISBN (ebook) 978-1-4766-4605-3

LIBRARY OF CONGRESS AND BRITISH LIBRARY
CATALOGUING DATA ARE AVAILABLE

Library of Congress Control Number 2022031741

© 2022 Christopher Hopkins. All rights reserved

*No part of this book may be reproduced or transmitted in any form
or by any means, electronic or mechanical, including photocopying
or recording, or by any information storage and retrieval system,
without permission in writing from the publisher.*

Front cover images: EKKAPHAN CHIMPALEE/ Antrakt2/Shutterstock

Printed in the United States of America

*McFarland & Company, Inc., Publishers
Box 611, Jefferson, North Carolina 28640
www.mcfarlandpub.com*

To my family.
To my mom, LuAnne, and my father, Frank.
To my brothers, Stephen and James.
And to my fiancée Mariane and daughter Milagros.

Table of Contents

Preface

"SOUNDS Like Fun and Games" and "History of Video Game Music." These were the first two university courses I developed to promote video game audio. Long Island University commissioned me to create the course "SOUNDS Like Fun and Games" for the university's summer game course offerings in 2010. The course was the start of my research into the presentation of video game audio history for this book. The contents of this book arose from a commission by Five Towns College to design and teach an undergraduate university course, "History of Video Game Music." I developed the course for Five Towns College as a blended course with multimedia examples online. The students used class time to play video games and critically discuss the period's musical sound and style characteristics. The course consisted of 15 modules covering audio from commercial arcades to the Xbox One (from 1972 to 2015). Five Towns College ran the course for two semesters. When I began teaching the university course at Five Towns College, I published an article in the *Journal of Literature and Art Studies* promoting music composition through gaming software. "Mario Paint: An Accessible Environment of Musical Creativity and Sound Exploration" analyzes the pros and cons of seven games and online interfaces and how they use gaming culture to facilitate musical creativity and composition. After the courses in video game music

and the article for the academic journal, I wrote this book to present video game audio history, showing a history that, unlike traditional history studies, can be experienced through listening to and playing video games.

Welcome to *Video Game Audio: A History, 1972–2020*. I am a scholar, author, and professor of video game music studies. Growing up in the 80s and 90s, I have fond memories of playing video games in my house with my brothers, particularly on the NES and Genesis. The melodies were very catchy, and they became the soundtrack of my afternoons and evenings after school.

The first exposure to video game music that I can remember was *Super Mario Bros.* for the NES. My grandmother bought for me and my older brother *The Miracle Piano Teaching System* for Mac computers. This game was how I first learned to play the piano. Using the *Miracle*'s musical keyboard connected to the Mac computer, I was able to "shoot ducks" in a shooting gallery using the correct musical notes of a song and assist parachuters in safely landing by playing the correct notes of a triad together. After completing the 40 lessons of the *Miracle*, I took formal private piano lessons. As a result of an excellent musical education, I make a living as a church organist and pianist, using my piano expertise in a positive way. Games that use musical instruments, whether they be educational or playful experiences or both, appear in this book.

During my middle school and high school years, I composed music in the style of video game music for local school and university music competitions. My earliest programming experience was with Greg Ewing's Wolfedit level editor for Wolfenstein 3D for Mac. I played the shareware version of Wolfenstein 3D from the CD for *Mario Teaches Typing*. My favorite game was *Sonic the Hedgehog 3 for the Genesis*. For over a decade, I asked Santa Claus for a Sega Nomad for Christmas. One year, my older brother Stephen, on Christmas Day, opened a present and exclaimed, "I got the Nomad!" However, much to my despair, it was not the Sega Nomad but the Creative Nomad MP3 player. I finally received a Sega Nomad from an eBay auction a few years later. I had much fun with my brothers hooking up Xboxes with crossover ethernet cables to play *Halo* on multiple TVs in the house. My younger brother James was the champion of my household.

Once I entered college, I found opportunities to incorporate video game studies into my coursework. During my undergraduate music studies at Boston College, I wrote my honors music thesis on "The Role of Music in Video Games." In a course on "Technology and Culture," I wrote "The Implications of the Ratings System in Video Gaming." During my doctoral music studies at Five Towns College, I composed video game music on the Korg M3 keyboard. Finally, in a course on college teaching, I created and gave a mock class on "The Art of Video Game Music," a proposed 15-week course exploring the influences of art, television, and film with video game music.

On a whim, I took a course in computer science at Boston College. The experience was fulfilling, and I double majored in music and computer science, earning two bachelor's degrees in four years. I took graduate courses at Long Island University in information technology education and game design and development. I was the lead programmer for *Beam Master* and *Orbital Round Bits*, two mobile games. My friend Keith Jordan and I presented *Orbital Round Bits* at Playcrafting NYC Summer Expo, IndieCade East, and the New Jersey Arcade independent gaming festivals. I completed certification as an end user of Wwise, audio middleware software, from Audiokinetic. After searching for an academic program for video game music, I earned a specialist certificate from Berklee College of Music in Orchestrating and Producing Music for Film and Games. At Long Island University, I completed an independent study in game audio with Dr. Elena Bertozzi. Over 15 weeks, I read and outlined all of the chapters in *Game Sound: An Introduction to the History, Theory, and Practice of Video Game Music and Sound Design* by Karen Collins and *Audio for Games: Planning, Process, and Production* by Alexander Brandon. In addition, I composed seven pieces of video game music, collecting them into an online portfolio promoting my skills as a video game composer.

Before teaching at Five Towns College, I earned a doctorate from Five Towns College in Music History and Literature. I devoted two years of my studies to my doctoral dissertation, *Chiptune music: An exploration of compositional techniques as found in Sunsoft games for the Nintendo Entertainment System and Famicom from 1988–1992*. I gained a deeper appreciation for video game music when I spent an entire summer transcribing all of the musical tracks of eight NES and Famicom video games by developer Sunsoft to musical notation. I also contacted and interviewed past and present composers of NES and chiptune video game music from North America, Europe, and Japan. When interest grew in the academic world about my doctoral dissertation, I accepted invitations to present my findings as a guest speaker at the North American Conference on Video Game Music and the Spring meeting of the New York Chapter of the American Musicological Society. These experiences helped me formulate the trends in video game music, having discovered musical traits developed in the late 80s and early 90s that modern composers still employ to evoke the NES chiptune style.

The interest in ludomusicology (the study of music in games) has increased dramatically in the 21st century. The primary focus of ludomusicologists is in musical analysis, which is a valid method of determining the value of video game music. I believe with conviction that video game music is a gateway for musical expression for all ages. Video game music is an art form worthy of study, appreciation, and respect. Those who program sounds and music, compose music, record audio samples, build sound engines, and design audio hardware are masters of the interplay of man's imagination and creativity and technology's potential and limitations. I hope you find the creative results of this interplay within this book.

Introduction

What are the best examples of video game audio and music? *Video Game Audio: A History, 1972–2020* examines historical trends in video game sound and music in North America, Europe, and Japan across arcade, computer, home, handheld, and mobile games, from the first sounds of *Pong* in the arcades to the Sony PlayStation 5. Some of the trends spanning gaming systems and periods are game systems as multimedia devices, synthesized to sampled sound, pre-recorded to dynamic audio, and mono to stereo to surround sound. Game systems are evaluated by their audio capabilities and their industry competition. Some factors affecting a system's audio include backward compatibility, discrete or multifunctional soundchip, storage media, audio programming documentation, and analog or digital outputs. The timeline organizes all of the events in the video game industry in chronological order, including games, gaming systems, music albums, and events. Some of the game systems discussed include the PC, NES, PlayStation, Dreamcast, Xbox, Wii, Game Boy, PSP, and iOS and Android devices. Some games include *Dance Dance Revolution, Monkey Island 2: LeChuck's Revenge, Rez, Lumines*, and *Monument Valley*. This book is the gateway for those who want to explore the most significant moments of audio from the video game industry.

The book's structure takes inspiration from the three books in the *Classic Home Video Games* series by Brett Weiss. In the books, Weiss identifies each game from a home console's library with basic information and a paragraph or more describing what makes the game good or poor. For my book, I sought to give equal attention to the games of video game audio. I spent significant research time finding accurate or valid release dates in North America, Europe, and Japan in an attempt for historical accuracy. Considering the lack of precise records before internet press releases, I feel that the timeline events are not in conflict with one another.

I am proud that this book encompasses international influences. My personal experience is limited to game releases in the United States. The book includes some games and gaming systems exclusive to Europe and Japan from additional resources and contacts. I discovered instances in which a publisher released a game in one region years before another region. Such instances become significant when identifying changes in game audio between regions.

Chapter 1 is an exploration of major achievements in video game audio hardware and software. The organization of this chapter is based on new developments in video game audio. Some of the topics found include audio cable hookups, audio waveforms, voice sampling,

MIDI, digital audio, live orchestral music, surround sound audio formats, and industry awards.

Chapter 2 is the timeline of video game audio history from the perspectives of hardware, software, and events. This section includes the audio abilities of each gaming system and fascinating audio elements in many video and computer games. The organization of this chapter is chronological from the first release, whether in North America, Europe, or Japan.

Chapter 3 is the expanded universe of video game audio. This section includes avenues of further exploration in various topics of video game audio. Some of the descriptions of notable musical tracks from Chapter 2 were lengthy, so they appear in this section for those who want to begin musical analyses second by second. Games that I removed from the book for brevity's sake appear as "honorable mentions." Lastly, I included a bibliographical section of print and online resources of other topics in ludomusicology with greater detail, notably composer and audio staff interviews and composing music for video games.

The appendix, "Commercial Video Game Music Soundtracks," provides the resources to listen to and buy the official soundtracks of the games listed in the book. I compiled the titles of all of the officially released video game soundtracks of the games listed. The production of the official soundtracks involved creative input from the composers and game developers.

The glossary contains definitions of audio industry terms. Contrasting words with specific meanings include track vs. song, soundtrack vs. official soundtrack, CD-DA vs. CD-quality audio, ROM vs. RAM, game vs. software, audio channel vs. sound channel, and cover vs. master recording. These

definitions avoid ambiguity in video game audio history.

The bibliography collects all of the sources used in the making of this book into one section. The sources are taken from internet articles, online videos, online forums, console manufacturer websites, interviews, magazines, books, newspaper articles, game manuals, game guides, hardware, and programming documentation. I am impressed at the many dedicated online users who scanned computer and game magazines, game manuals, and strategy guides, direct paper sources reflecting the attitudes of the period.

The history of video game audio is just the starting point for a greater discussion of music contributions to video games and culture. This book specializes in the temporal placement of game console releases, game releases, and other events in video game audio history. This book does not explore the histories and backgrounds of prominent composers and game audio staff in great detail. Additional resources are thorough on this subject and appear in Chapter 3. The course I developed at Five Towns College included background information on game audio industry leaders, particularly their early lives and their pathway into the video game industry.

This book does not offer a tutorial in composing music for video games. Such a tutorial requires a deeper analysis of the musical structures of video game music and the tools to compose efficiently and integrate music into a format for video game engines. I dissected NES musical soundtracks for my doctoral dissertation, explaining how to produce the desired chiptune effects used in NES games.

This book does not provide the resources to play the games listed in the book. A few games are exclusive to their original gaming system. However, most games have ports and releases on modern gaming systems. I compiled the game platforms of all of the games listed, but they do not appear in this book. If there is an interest in this information, I am happy to share it.

Each book in ludomusicology contributes to preserving video game audio, building on older research to uncover new insights. My hope for this book is that my readers will discover new and exciting audio accolades in video game audio, then perhaps pick up and play a game from the book in which audio plays a crucial part in the gameplay. Video game audio is internationally relevant to the industry. Its history relies on audio development teams, ludomusicological scholars, and video game preservation groups. Like others before and others to come, this book preserves video game audio history, adding further validation to significant games and video game audio awards.

CHAPTER 1

An Exploration of Major Achievements in Video Game Audio Hardware and Software

Overview

Electronic audio technology has dramatically advanced since the early days of consumer video games. The history of video game audio began as early as 1951 when a computer produced a piece of music to conclude a game of checkers. Video games with audio for consumer use started in 1972 with the arcade game *Pong* by Atari in North America. At least eight years after, game audio consisted of sound effects with the occasional musical jingle, a musical track of only a few seconds. The graphics of the games of the '70s, which to modern gamers seem primitive and even unviewable, were just enough to offer the player an abstract idea as to the games' objectives. In the decade of the 1970s, computer graphics were the driving factor in the gaming experience. When game developers had more resources for audio,

they had to make new considerations. Game audio considerations include the type of audio hardware, its audio capabilities, and the effect of sound on the player's enjoyment. When audio hardware choices were lacking, game developers were at the mercy of the system hardware. They relied solely on their creative processes to devise expert programming and electronic tricks to work around design limitations. There were only a few individuals who possessed audio programming skills and participated in audio hardware design. Sound effects and music that supported better gameplay and more fully immerse players in the gaming experience arose from these creative decisions. These creative decisions are the impetus for exploring significant achievements in video game audio hardware and software.

Motivating Factors Affecting Game Audio

Three motivating factors have directed the audio experience in games. The hardware of the game systems is the first factor. In the present day, the hardware of all home gaming consoles supports uncompressed LPCM audio in 7.1

surround sound. Much of a game's data size is from the large audio files. While the audio is of high quality and supports seven surround speakers and a subwoofer, the audio files are larger than those of compressed audio formats like mp3 and m4a. Handheld gaming systems, in contrast, support many compressed file formats. While game sizes are increasing on the handheld systems, it is neither feasible nor logical to support advanced surround sound formats when most players listen to game audio from the systems' stereophonic internal speakers. The go-to gaming device is the smartphone for many people. For smartphone owners, having the power of a computer in pocket size is convenient, and so are the audio needs. As a convenience to smartphone users, games are downloaded and purchased as apps through the internet. Compressed audio formats are standard for devices with limited RAM (random-access memory) and ROM (read-only memory). Using the phone's internal speakers or using headphones, the difference between compressed and uncompressed audio quality is not noticeable. The common thread between these gaming devices is that their hardware is designed with purpose and intent by hardware manufacturers. The goal could be for the ultimate home theater experience (home consoles) or a convenient on-the-go time drain (smartphones). Nevertheless, developers work within the ecosystem of the device for which they design their games.

The second motivating factor is financially successful games. Whenever a game achieves big sales, other developers and console manufacturers in the video game industry notice. It is economically risky to experiment with something new in audio, especially if it be disorienting for veteran players. Harmonix is a video game company that founded its business on games focusing on music and gameplay. When *Guitar Hero* was a success in the video game market, a craze for music and rhythm games emerged in the video game industry. Over time, players become disenfranchised from

the release of similar music/rhythm games. Music games attracted the video game industry when *Guitar Hero* introduced a plastic-guitar controller as a fresh way to interface with the music. Subsequently, the next logical step in the evolution of the music genre was to add drums and vocals. The combined instrument group formed a video game rock band, resulting in the *Rock Band* series. However, this industry trend ebbed and flowed. The games in the series play similarly, except for changes in song selections and minor adjustments to graphics and gameplay.

The third motivating factor is the development team. Currently, video game development is a big business. Game developers and publishers spend millions of dollars on developing, publishing, and marketing video games. There are numerous tiers of developers, from triple-A companies to an independent company of one person. Yet anyone can make a mark in the industry. Toby Fox is the developer, publisher, writer, and composer of *Undertale*, released on PC in 2015. The game was a critical success upon release, with popular original characters with a life of their own among fans. The music is retro and chiptune-based, inspired by the sounds of the SNES (Super Nintendo Entertainment System). No matter the technical capabilities of game systems, the imagination of the game is in the minds of the development team. Until 1980, the game development staff expected the programmer to work as the audio designer and composer. When game production budgets increased, employees became specialized in each task of game development. What is common across video game history is that, whether a one-person team or a team of thousands, ideas must be communicated and shared. The group brings ideas to fruition through their imaginations and skillsets.

Trends in Game Audio

The three motivating factors, game system hardware, financially successful games, and the development team, propel exciting aural possibilities, which the video game industry recognizes for aesthetic quality and financial potential. These factors assist in identifying trends in video game audio and music. Audio trends are interpreted from the perspectives of sound generation, design choices, and creative applications. The yearly breakdown that follows is an initial passthrough of video game audio history, ordered by the audio trends when they were first introduced. To be considered a trend, rather than an isolated event, the trend must span across at least one decade and have a cause-and-effect relationship in creating and applying other game audio.

1972

AUDIO SPEAKER

Video games for consumer use first supported audio in 1972. This year, Atari released *Pong* as an arcade game in North America. Before *Pong*, there were only electromechanical arcade machines with electronic sounds (*Periscope* by Sega in 1966). *Pong* was the first video game machine to have an electronic video screen with an internal speaker. Internal speakers are speakers that are part of the machine. Consumer-grade television sets always had internal speakers so that people could hear the relevant audio with the video. Internal speakers are a common feature for handheld and mobile gaming devices. Some home consoles include internal speakers in their controllers. The Wii Remote for the Nintendo Wii and the Wii U Gamepad for the Nintendo Wii U contains internal speakers. In 1989, the Game Boy was the first handheld game system to include monaural audio from an internal speaker and stereophonic audio from a 3.5mm audio-out port. In 2004, the Nintendo DS was the first handheld game system to include stereophonic internal speakers with virtual surround sound. Mobile phones, whether smartphone or otherwise, have a monaural internal speaker. Tablets have either monaural or stereophonic internal speakers. In 2015, the Apple iPad Pro was the first tablet to have two sets of stereophonic internal speakers. When placed in small devices, it is not easy to distinctly hear the audio panning difference between monaural and stereophonic internal speakers. The speakers are too small to produce a sound loud enough to matter. Internal speakers are more of a convenience for players.

SOUND EFFECTS

Pong was the first game with sound effects. The game lacked music of any kind. Sound effects are often short, not necessarily musical, and reflect recent activity. They need to be immediate, unlike music, which can adapt more smoothly. Music and sound effects compete for player attention in video games. When a game system's hardware has sound channel limits, sound effects are programmed to take precedence over musical parts. In modern games, music without sound effects appears in the credits and sometimes during dramatic cutscenes. Music-only versions of game soundtracks are available on CD releases and YouTube videos. The creation of sound effects has changed over time. When using the sounds generated by a PSG (programmable sound generator), the programmer must be highly creative to create a sound that somewhat reflects the intended sound effect. The programmer could manipulate a waveform's ADSR envelope (Attack Decay Sustain Release), which was the best attempt to give the illusion of the intended sound effect. Once game systems could interpret audio samples, audio designers could record sounds on a sound stage and manipulate them in a sound editor to create much more realistic and even supernatural sound effects.

Audio Waveforms

The manipulation of basic waveforms forms the sounds of *Pong*. A waveform is a curve that shows the shape of a sound wave. Each shape corresponds to a unique musical timbre. A PSG generates sound using basic waveforms. The basic waveforms found in early game systems are square, pulse, triangle, sawtooth, sine, and white noise. The appearance of the waveforms under an oscilloscope dictates the waveforms' names. Unlike the other waveforms with a regular pattern, white noise is a form of random sound with many frequencies at equal intensities. The duty cycle defines a pulse wave, determining how often the wave is on. The square wave is a subset of a pulse wave with a 50 percent duty cycle. The square wave has a unique timbre in video game music history, as it was one of the first sounds used in video games. Whenever a broad audience speaks on video game sounds, it usually recognizes these sounds, a staple of the industry. Sound effects relied upon the square wave while music explored timbres through other audio generation methods. The square wave is the primary soundwave in most sound channels in the Sega Master System and Sega Game Gear. Percussion and sound effects effectively use white noise.

1977

Soundchip

In 1977, Atari released the Atari 2600, the first home console with a discrete soundchip. The first microprocessor and consumer computer were released before 1977. A soundchip is a computer chip or microprocessor part of a gaming system's audio hardware. A discrete soundchip is a chip that is dedicated solely to audio. Most early soundchips were discrete and dedicated within a game system. Some manufacturers of soundchips are Texas Instruments and Yamaha. Multifunctional chips not dedicated to a single purpose can generate sound and other computational or mathematical functions unrelated to sound. The chip found in the North American version of the NES (Nintendo Entertainment System), the Ricoh 2A03, is a modification of the MOS Technology 6502 processor. Within the NES, the 2A03 contains both a CPU (central processing unit) and a custom sound unit. When regular chips could process the audio themselves, software programming resolved audio functions. The N64 (Nintendo 64) lacks a discrete soundchip. An N64 programmer creates audio routines in software that the CPU chip understands.

Coaxial Cable

The Atari 2600 was the first video game system to send an audio signal to a television. The Atari 2600 connected to a TV set using the included RF (radio frequency) adapter and coaxial cables. A coaxial cable is an analog video and audio solution. The earliest home consoles connected to a television via coaxial cable (Atari 2600, NES, Genesis). The Atari 2600 needed an RF switch or RF modulator as an intermediary between the console's output and the television. The last home console to support a coaxial connection via RF adapter was the Microsoft Xbox in 2001. The coaxial cable transmits video and unbalanced monophonic audio. Until the introduction of HDMI, the coaxial cable was the original one-cable solution. Of all the cable solutions, the coaxial cable (as used for video and audio) offers the most inferior quality in video and audio. However, all home consoles until 2001 support a coaxial connection using an RF adapter.

DAC (Digital-to-Analog Converter)

When the Atari 2600 console transmitted video and audio to be shown and heard through a TV set, the RF converter box acted as a DAC (Digital-to-Analog Converter). A DAC is a computer chip that takes digital audio stored as PCM and converts it to an analog signal that a set of audio speakers can output. The DAC is necessary to hear digital sound. The analog signal that comes from the DAC goes into an amplifier. The amplifier uses electricity to boost the sound and send it to the audio speakers. A DAC needs to be able to handle the audio fidelity of the PCM data. Human hearing has a limit of audio data at roughly a maximum bit depth of 21 bits and a sampling rate of 42 kHz. For the best sound, a DAC needs to convert a digital audio signal of at most that quality to an analog signal. Most DACs support either 2 or 8 channels (stereo or multichannel). A DAC outputs the audio as an analog signal. The output port of a DAC is either an internal speaker or an analog cable (RCA, coaxial, 3.5mm headphone, XLR, TRS). Each game system or controller with an audio microprocessor requires a DAC to send the audio to an internal speaker or an analog audio port.

PSG (Programmable Sound Generator)

The Atari 2600 generates sound using the TIA (Television Interface Adapter), which, in addition to controlling the system's graphics and input, managed the system's audio. The TIA contained a PSG (Programmable Sound Generator). A PSG generates basic waveforms and noise, the most basic being the square wave. All PSGs support the square wave. Other waveforms include sawtooth, triangle, and pulse (variable duty cycle). Each waveform can be adjusted using an envelope to adjust the amplitude of the attack, decay, sustain, and release portions of the waveform. The earliest discrete soundchips contain PSGs. Before PSGs, discrete audio circuits generated the sound, built on a case basis.

Some successful PSG soundchips include the General Instruments AY-3–8910, the Texas Instruments SN76489 (SMS, Game Gear), and the Yamaha YM2149 (a licensed AY-3–8910). Other PSG soundchips include the LR35902 (Game Boy, GBC [Game Boy Color], GBA [Game Boy Advance]), Mikey (Lynx), PC Speaker, SID (C64 [Commodore 64]), TIA (Atari 2600, 7800), AY-3–8914 (Intellivision), SN76489A (ColecoVision, Genesis), 2A03 (NES), and Sunsoft 5B (uses YM2149).

PSG is a form of sound generation used by the Atari 2600, POKEY

(Potentiometer and Keyboard Integrated Circuit) chip for the Atari 7800, Atari Lynx, Intellivision, ColecoVision, Nintendo NES, Game Boy, Game Boy Color, Game Boy Advance, VRC6 chip for the Famicom (Family Computer), Sunsoft 5B chip for the Famicom, Sega Master System, Sega Game Gear, Genesis/Mega Drive, TurboGrafx-16, C64, and the arcade game *Gyruss* (1983).

Sound Channels

The Atari 2600 was the first video game system to support two sound channels of audio. A sound channel is similar to a musician capable of playing only one sound at a time. In early games, this was the limiting factor in how good video game music could be. With one sound channel, the audio could either be a sound effect or a musical tone, one or the other but not both simultaneously. Programmers had to consider writing a monophonic musical line knowing that a sound effect would take precedence over the music. Limitations in sound channels were a concern for music and audio until no longer limited with the Sega Dreamcast in 1998 for home consoles and the Sony PSP (PlayStation Portable) in 2004 for handheld systems. While there are many examples of great video game music that worked with less than 10 sound channels, music comprised of 20 sound channels is no longer hindered by other audio constraints. When CD Digital Audio became an option, developers took advantage of creating authentic sounds and playing them back without compromise. Like the Atari Jaguar and Nintendo 64 (N64), some systems did not have sound channel limits in hardware. For those systems, the software takes responsibility for creating sound channels. Depending on how taxing the audio is for a game on these systems, there may

very well be a variable number of sound channels available.

Storage Media

The Atari 2600 was the first home console to store each game on storage media inserted into a video game system. Interchangeable games allowed video game systems to be more versatile in the number of games they can play. Before storage media, the video game system stored all of the game's programming, which could neither be altered nor removed nor added. The media used to store a game affects the audio that can be stored and played. Game developers initially stored game ROMs (read-only memory) on cartridges. A cartridge consists of a plastic shell that houses the ROM. A ROM chip is attached to a circuit board along with other small chips. There is a part of the board that protrudes so that the system reads the information from the ROM when connected. Cartridges are durable and protect the contents inside. Only the edge that makes contact with the cartridge port of a game system receives some wear and tear. The primary value of cartridges was that gamers could interchange games using the same gaming system.

CD media became appealing to developers for its large memory and its CD-DA (Compact Disc Digital Audio). Hardware add-ons brought the first CD-based game systems to market as early as 1991. However, the Sony PlayStation in 1994 effectively harnessed and popularized CD media. In addition to expanded memory for game programming and assets, the economic value for mass-production was significantly less than cartridges. The ROM boards inside cartridges contained many individual parts, whereas a CD is one piece. The tradeoff, however, would come from loading times and piracy. Game systems can scan ROM data, and games are hard to duplicate. Game systems need to read CD data more slowly, and one with the right CD-burning equipment can easily copy games.

Interestingly, Nintendo designed the N64 around cartridges when other console manufacturers designed their systems around CD media. For Nintendo, piracy was a concern. Even when Nintendo released the GameCube, it read proprietary discs smaller than the standard CD or DVD. Games continue to use disc-based media with some assistance from hard drives. Dual-layer DVDs and Blu-ray discs hold much data on a disc. However, the size of games has ballooned, and reading data from a disc is too slow for smooth gameplay. The solution is for the system to download most of the art and audio files from the disc and onto an internal or external hard drive. The assets can be read faster from a hard drive over a disc.

Games distributed through online services have always existed. The Atari 2600 had the first dial-up game distribution service called GameLine in the early '80s. The Master Module was a unique cartridge with a phone jack that could receive data through a modem. Users could select from a library of games to download and play a few times for a fee. The company that provided the service eventually became America Online. Online distribution services found reasonable success with the Sega Channel, released in North America in December of 1994. Users place the adapter in the cartridge slot of the Genesis and connect a coaxial cable to the back of the adapter. Each time the user connected to the Sega Channel, a menu would load and offer games to download. When the user turned off the Genesis, the system lost the downloaded games. The Sega Channel rotated the available games monthly or biweekly and offered anywhere from 50 to 70 games at a time. The online distribution of games was notable as some games never saw a cartridge release in North America but were available exclusively on the Sega Channel. It also offered demos so players could try out games without needed to purchase the game cartridge. The infrastructure and user interface were innovative at the time. However, due to being released late in the Genesis' life and its high subscription cost, it did not catch on as Sega had hoped.

Sega learned from the Sega Channel when it released the Dreamcast in 1998. The Dreamcast was the first game system to be online-ready with a built-in modem and offered downloadable content for its games. Since the Dreamcast included all of the equipment needed to play multiplayer games and view online content internally, all that a user needed to do was purchase a subscription to SegaNet.

On November 15, 2002, the launch of Xbox Live for the Microsoft Xbox allowed players to download and store small games on the system's internal hard drive. In 2009, handheld game systems received full downloadable games with the Nintendo DSi and Sony PSP Go, both upgrades to earlier models. Since the smartphone era heralded by the Apple iPhone in 2007, mobile devices with Internet capability have online marketplaces with free and paid games available for download. Home consoles allow players to hook up external hard drives to download games and to keep their saves.

PWM (Pulse-Width Modulation)

When Apple released the Apple II computer in North America on June 10, 1977, it introduced the PC Speaker, an internal speaker capable of producing sound via PWM (Pulse-Width Modulation). PWM is similar to PCM (Pulse Code Modulation). It is a digital representation of audio data in bit values of 0s and 1s. The bits of PCM audio represent an analog signal's amplitude at sampled moments in time. In contrast, the bits of PWM audio data represent the width of the pulse (duty cycle) of an analog signal at sampled moments in time. The amplitude remains constant.

Bit depth is a way to understand PWM data. For example, suppose the PWM data has a bit depth of 16. In that case, each group of 16 bits represents a duty cycle of the audio signal. For example, a 16-bit value of 0b1000000000000000 (0x8000) translates to a 50 percent duty cycle. This value signifies that the digital signal is "on" for 50 percent of the time and "off" for the remaining time. The sampling rate of the PWM data determines the amount of time each data sample represents. Continuing the example, if the PWM data is 16-bit, 44.1 kHz, then each sample of PWM data represents a time of 0.00002 seconds (1 second divided by 44,100 samples). Beyond the field of audio, electrical devices favor PWM over PCM when regulating power.

PWM is a means of sound generation in the PC Speaker, Sega 32X, and the VMU of the Sega Dreamcast. The PC Speaker is a good candidate for PWM. As a simple device, it only recognizes when a voltage is on (5V) or off (0V). All devices that playback PWM can play crude audio samples.

STEREOPHONIC (STEREO) AUDIO

Atari expanded its brand in 1977 with *Atari Video Music*, the first commercial music visualizer and the first consumer device supporting stereophonic audio. In a stereo audio output, after audio production, the game system mixes all sound channels into left and right audio channels, transmitted to the speakers. The speaker to the left of the player gets the left signal, and the speaker to the right of the

player gets the right signal. The speaker placement is the origin of the designations for the "left" and "right" speaker. If additional speakers were available, they could only receive one of the two audio signals, being left or right, regardless of placement. *Dragon's Lair* in 1983 was the first arcade game to support stereo audio. The Sega Genesis in 1989 was the first home console to support stereo audio. Stereo audio remains a simple analog option for almost all video game systems made after 1987.

HANDHELD GAMES

Handheld video games began in 1977 with Mattel's *Auto Race*, which included sound effects. Since then, handheld games have evolved significantly. With the release of the Nintendo Switch in 2017, home consoles and handheld game systems have merged. Until the 2010s, the technology of handheld game systems lagged behind home consoles by about 10 years.

The Sega Nomad in 1995 was an early attempt to merge home console and handheld game systems. The Sega Nomad is a handheld version of the Sega Genesis with a small backlit screen with a cartridge port for Genesis games. It contains all of the hardware needed to play Genesis games. Also, the Nomad has a controller port for a second player to hook up a Genesis controller. Using a special A/V (audiovisual) cable just like the Genesis, a player can use the Nomad with a television. Although the Nomad could play almost the entire Genesis gaming library without fault, the Game Boy remained the dominant handheld game system. Sega already had the Game Gear as its primary handheld game system. Sega also released numerous hardware add-ons to the Genesis in the early to mid–'90s.

Most importantly, however, the Nomad's battery life was low: 6 AA batteries for two hours. That is a high price to pay for the home console experience on the go. Regarding audio, the Nomad has a monophonic internal speaker. It sounds much better when using headphones plugged into the headphone port. Although the Nomad maintained the Genesis hardware in a handheld form factor, it still was a marketing flop.

The Game Boy Color, released in 1998, can be compared to the NES, released in 1985. *Super Mario Bros. Deluxe* is a version of the NES game *Super Mario Bros.* for the Game Boy Color with some new features. The main difference between both games is the smaller screen size of the GBC. The music on the GBC closely recreates the music on the NES despite the two systems having different soundchips. The advantage of the GBC was that the memory size of games was much larger than NES games. *Super Mario Bros. Deluxe* takes up 348 KBs of memory, whereas *Super Mario Bros.* takes up 32 KBs.

The Nintendo Game Boy Advance, released in 2001, can be compared to the SNES, released in 1991. This comparison is made stronger through all of the SNES games ported to the GBA. Looking at the *Mario Advance* series, *Super Mario World: Super Mario Advance 2* is a port of *Super Mario World*, and *Yoshi's Island: Super Mario Advance 3* is a port of *Super Mario World 2: Yoshi's Island*. Unlike the GBC, the GBA soundchip works differently than the soundchip of the SNES. The SNES contains the S-SMP by Sony. When designing the GBA, Sony no longer

worked with Nintendo. The GBA contains the ARM7TDMI. Audio designers and composers had to make changes to SNES audio to work with the audio capabilities of the GBA. The GBA also supports the legacy sounds of the Game Boy and GBC, so games of NES quality sound satisfactory.

Sony supported its handheld game systems that brought some of its home console experience to the handheld market. The PSP (PlayStation Portable), released in 2005, can be compared to the PS2 (PlayStation 2), released in 2000. An example of a game that was first released for the PS2 in 2001 and later released for the PSP in 2006 is *Gitaroo Man*. The PSP port plays like the original and adds an exclusive two-player Duet mode with two new stages. The PSP had a lot of processing power and was known for bringing 3D gaming to the handheld market. The audio and music are identical in audio fidelity on both systems. The only aspect holding back handheld systems is the internal speaker, which is too small to be truly immersive.

The PS Vita (PlayStation Vita), released in 2011, is comparable to the PS2 and PS3 (PlayStation 3). The PS3 was released in 2006. Using the Remote Play feature on the PS Vita, it can play PS3 games remotely. *Uncharted: Golden Abyss*, released in 2011 for the PS Vita, continues the story of the *Uncharted* series, which had three games on the PS3. The graphics resemble PS3 quality, and the orchestral score matches home console quality.

1979

INTERACTION WITH MUSIC THROUGH MUSIC COMPOSITION

Before 1979, the only way to compose music for computers was through

computer programming using either assembly language or, if very lucky, a programming language like BASIC or FORTRAN. The first computer software to allow users to compose music for computers (and use musical notation) was

Music Composer by Atari in 1979 for the Atari 400 and 800 (computer offerings by Atari). An 8 KB ROM cartridge stored the software. Unlike music creation in gameplay, interaction with music through music composition removes the gameplay aspect to allow players to create music on a game system. Although used on a game system, there is not necessarily a way to win nor a way to complete the game. The game is more about music creation than a game. Software like this is unique because users use the authentic sounds of early game systems in their compositions. Some games include user-friendly tools within the game to compose and create music on a game system. These games encourage musical exploration without an expected goal.

In *Mario Paint* for the Super NES in 1992, users can compose music on the music staff within Music Mode. There are some limitations to complete music composition. First, there are no accidentals. The range of notes is from B3 (the B below middle C) to G5 (the space above the top line of the treble staff). Each song can have a maximum of 96 beats. There is a maximum of three simultaneous sounds at a time. Most unfortunate, due to its release, there is no means to save the compositions within the game. The best option is to hook the Super NES to a video or audio recorder to preserve the songs. The sounds are represented by cute icons, some representing Nintendo characters and classic game sounds. For example, the Game Boy icon represents the square wave sound used all of the time in Game Boy games.

In *Music: Music Creation for the PlayStation*, released in Europe in 1998, users make music using 50 pre-recorded riffs and 300 sampled instruments. These are put into loops and mixed into a 16-track sequencer. The user can combine audio effects to each track. When the sequel reached North America in 1999, it received a new name, *MTV Music Generator*, to attract a younger audience influenced by the music videos of MTV. A Video Creator allows for syncing up some included videos and patterns. The software can also automatically preselect videos for the music. A multiplayer Jam mode allows for four-player turn-based fun in creating a complete song by adding beats, rhythms, and melodies.

Rhythm Tengoku is a GBA game released exclusively in Japan in 2006. In *Rhythm Tengoku*, the player takes control of a drummer on the drum kit. In Studio mode, the player decides to listen to each unlocked song or drum along to a selected song. Each button on the GBA corresponds to one of the parts of the drum kit. After the song concludes, the player can save the recording with all drum hits in the music. Then the recording is accessible from the song list. The player can pick from different drum sounds, including ordinary, techno, and sound effect. Later installments in the series were released worldwide under the title *Rhythm Heaven*.

Korg DS-10 is music-creation software for the DS released in 2008. Although released for a handheld game system, the sole purpose of the software is to create music. The software takes advantage of the dual screens and touchscreen capabilities of the DS. The software gives users access to all of the musical possibilities and features of the Korg MS range of synthesizers. Most of the software's understanding is left to the user to examine. Some of the Korg features emulated include VCOs (Voltage-Controlled Oscillator) capable of sawtooth, pulse, triangle, and noise waveforms. The user uses virtual knobs to edit the sounds by adjusting and patching parameters. The software also includes a drum machine with plenty of drum sounds. To create a composition, the user can either input the notes and sounds individually in the step sequencer or input them live in real-time. Korg

released later installments in the series on DSi and 3DS via the eShop and the iPhone.

1980

Wavetable Synthesis

Pac-Man, released to arcades by Namco in 1980, was the first game to generate sound via wavetable synthesis. Wavetable synthesis, also known as table-lookup synthesis, generates a unique waveform based on values selected from a stored table. An audio designer employs wavetable synthesis to create an original waveform. The waveform's unique shape depends on the bit depth and sample size for one single cycle of the waveform. For example, in 1989, the Game Boy, which uses wavetable synthesis, allows for a bit depth of 4 (16 values) and a sample size of 32 for each sound channel. If drawn out on a graph, the resulting waveform would have 32 points evenly spread out horizontally. At each point, there would be 16 possible locations on the vertical plane. The wavetable channel of the FDS (Famicom Disk System) allows for a bit depth of 6 (64 values) and a sample size of 64.

Wavetable synthesis is a form of sound generation used by the Nintendo Game Boy, Game Boy Color, Game Boy Advance, Nintendo FDS, Namco N163 chip for the Famicom, TurboGrafx-16, 3DO, Atari Jaguar, and the Namco arcade games *Pac-Man* (1980) and *Galaga* (1981). Wavetable synthesis is available on all six sound channels of the TurboGrafx-16. It is the primary means of sound generation in the FDS (1 sound channel) and Namco 163 chip (max of 8 sound channels). Games like *Pac-Man* (1980) used

the Namco WSG chip for wavetable synthesis (3 sound channels).

PCM (Pulse-Code Modulation)

Before 1980, the predominant types of sounds used in video games and computers were basic waveforms, generated by PSGs, and PWM, used by the PC speaker of a computer. When Namco released its arcade game *King & Balloon* in 1980, it contained a DAC that read PCM speech samples. PCM (Pulse-Code Modulation) is a digital audio representation of analog sound. PCM audio data can represent any sound. PCM is a lossless storage format for digital audio. A stream of 0s and 1s represents audio data. The quality of the PCM audio depends on the resolution and sampling rate. The bit resolution (or bit depth) represents the bits needed for a sample (a bit is a 0 or a 1). Some common bit resolutions are 8, 16, and 24 bits. The higher the bits and bit resolution, the better the audio quality. The sampling rate represents how many samples comprise one second. Some typical sampling rates are 22.05, 44.1, 48, and 96 kHz. The higher sampling rate, the better the audio quality. PCM supports anywhere from one channel (mono) to two channels (stereo) to six channels (5.1 surround sound). PCM is the final audio format sent to a DAC (digital-to-analog converter) for transmission to a speaker setup.

PCM is a means of sound generation on the Amiga 500, PlayStation, Sega CD,

Saturn, Dreamcast, Atari Jaguar, N64, and Game Boy Advance.

Audio quality improved over time in video games. When disc media was introduced, standards were defined that established the audio quality of an audio CD and DVD. CD-DA (Compact Disc Digital Audio, also known as Red Book Audio) is defined as audio data recorded for two channels at 16 bits per sample and 44,100 samples per second (16 bits, 44.1 kHz). Each second of audio data at this sampling rate takes up 176.4 KB (or 1,411,200 bits). The sample rate of 44.1 kHz is twice that of 22.05 kHz, the highest frequency that the human ear can hear (due to the Nyquist Sampling Theorem).

CD-quality audio is only a standard. Any audio sample can match the quality of CD-DA if its bit depth and sample rate match that of CD-DA. Game systems lacking a CD laser can generate CD-quality audio. For example, audio data on the Sega Saturn and Atari Jaguar is of CD-quality audio, even though the disc media for both systems is not of the CD-DA standard. A CD player or any device that reads audio CDs can play a disc with CD-DA audio.

Using the additional memory from CD media, video games achieved CD-quality audio. Games used CD-DA as early as 1991 in *Ys III: Wanderers of Ys*, one of the first games for the TurboGrafx-CD (TG-CD). The early CD-based games used CD-DA within the Mixed Mode CD. A Mixed-Mode CD has audio stored as CD-DA and game data stored in the same session on the same CD. A Mixed-Mode CD has many tracks. The first track of a Mixed Mode CD is the data track (game data). The remaining tracks are audio tracks stored as CD-DA. A CD player can read the audio tracks from game discs that are Mixed Mode CDs. In 1994, the PlayStation popularized CD-DA. CD-DA supports more memory for music and better-quality sounds at the expense of lengthy loading times. The delay is because the laser that reads a CD's data must track back and forth to load audio data into RAM. Soundchips never encountered this problem because they access audio data almost instantaneously. Some standard audio file formats that are forms of PCM are WAV and AIFF (any uncompressed audio data).

DVD-quality audio is defined as audio data stored at 16 bits, 48 kHz. DVD-Video uses this audio quality standard. Audio data on the N64 and Dreamcast are of DVD-quality audio without storing the audio data as CD-DA. CD-quality and DVD-quality audio are types of streaming audio, pre-recorded audio stored as CD-DA or other digital audio formats.

AUDIO SAMPLING

The first games that used speech synthesis in 1980 interpreted audio samples of words, stored as PCM. An audio sample is audio data that represents a sound. Sound captured by a microphone becomes an audio sample. The sound is stored as uncompressed audio data (PCM [Pulse-Code Modulation], PWM [Pulse-Width Modulation]) or lossy compressed audio data (DPCM [Differential Pulse-Code Modulation], ADPCM [Adaptive Differential Pulse-Code Modulation], MP3). After being recorded, the sound is now a digital audio file. The audio data becomes part of the game's programming. The game system can playback the audio sample in many ways. The simplest way is to send the audio sample directly to the DAC (digital-to-analog converter). The DAC works when the audio sample is in an uncompressed format. If the audio sample is compressed, it must be uncompressed to convert it to PCM or PWM data for the DAC. A PSG tone channel is capable of outputting uncompressed audio data. Even the PC speaker with one sound channel can output uncompressed audio data.

The best audio quality for audio samples comes from using the DAC. Audio samples capture sounds that PSG, FM, AM, or wavetable synthesis cannot generate. A common type of audio sample used in games is voice samples. Other audio samples include acoustic and electronic instruments like drums, guitar, and electronic keyboards. Audio samples take up significantly more memory than basic waveforms and other means of electronic sound synthesis.

1982

LICENSED MUSIC

Music is said to be licensed when the game developer and the copyright holder of the music agree on legal terms regarding the use of the music. All musical recordings are under copyright. The owner of the copyright can be one person, a group of people, or a company. It can be the composer of the music, the performers, and the studio that funded the recording. When video games use musical recordings, the game companies must pay the copyright holder to license the music for use. Without a license, there will be legal ramifications, especially if the game is a financial success. Games have used licensed music as early as 1982 with *Journey Escape* for the Atari 2600. The intro track is from "Don't Stop Believin'." The audio technology at the time could not reproduce the album recording of "Don't Stop Believin'." Nevertheless, Data Age, the developer, and the copyright holders for the composition made a legal agreement. "Don't Stop Believin'" is the only song from the Journey song collection to appear in the game.

In the late '70s and early '80s, most games had original music or borrowed music from the classical repertoire or public domain songs. These songs were covers arranged to work within sound-chip capabilities. Due to copyright laws, songs of these categories are not under copyright. Anyone is allowed to use them in derivative works without compensation to the copyright holder. There are, however, different copyright laws for audio recordings, which require a license agreement.

An example is the 1989 NES version of *Tetris*. One of the musical tracks in the game is Pyotr Tchaikovsky's "Dance of the Sugar Plum Fairy." The piece was originally from *The Nutcracker*, a two-act ballet that premiered in 1892. The NES was not capable of reproducing one of the many audio recordings of the piece available. Because the piece is in the public domain, Nintendo, the developer, did not need to pay the Estate of Tchaikovsky to license the work for use in a derivative work.

When CD-DA was available for video games, games were able to include covers of licensed music and the original master recordings. Both require arrangements with the copyright holders for use. Music and rhythm games use licensed songs and create covers with in-house bands for copyright reasons and programming efficiency. It is practical for these games to record the songs with cover bands so the new recordings can be programmed within the game to better match up with gameplay.

With exception to musical tracks from Nintendo properties, all of the songs in *Donkey Konga* are covers. For example, the game includes a cover of "We Will Rock You" by Queen. It is not the original 1977 audio recording. "Turkish March" by Wolfgang Amadeus Mozart is a cover version of the third movement from Piano Sonata No. 11. In contrast, the "Mario Bros. Theme" is the original version as heard in *Super Mario Bros.* for the NES.

In *Guitar Hero*, most of the songs are cover versions. The game makes clear which are cover versions by designating covers with "as made famous by" next to the musical performer or group that made the song famous. Another reason why a developer selects covers over the master recordings is that the copyright holder refuses permission of the original master track or the master track is not available for licensing. The copyright holder has the legal right to accept or deny any licensing terms by any outside party.

A game developer can consider it valuable to license the master recording for use in a video game. As long as the game developer and copyright holder prepare licensing agreements, players benefit from hearing the authentic recording, forming an association with the music as they complete a task within the game. The use of licensed music also helps indie and underground bands get wider exposure with other listeners. Lastly, the use of licensed music with master recordings adds authenticity to a game in which in-game characters would naturally hear those recordings in the game world.

In *Road Rash*, licensed music is used during full-motion video cutscenes, but not during motorcycle races. Released on the 3DO in 1994, the soundtrack includes 14 tracks of the master recordings. The bands featured on the soundtrack include Soundgarden, Paw, Hammerbox, Therapy?, Monster Magnet, and Swervedriver, all licensed under the

label of A&M Records. The audio director selected alternative rock and grunge music because of their rough instrument and vocal sounds that reflect the roughness of dangerous motorcycle riding and taking out opponents at top speeds. The soundtrack was also licensed for the Sega CD, PC, Saturn, and PlayStation versions. An example of unusual licensing is that of the five CD-based versions of the game that contain the licensed music. Only the Sega CD version plays the licensed music during the motorcycle races. There are different versions of *Road Rash* for other game systems like the Genesis, Game Boy, and SMS. However, they contain original music arranged to accommodate their soundchips.

The *Grand Theft Auto* series is known for supplying its in-game radio stations with licensed music from the master recordings and original talk shows and interviews. This trend began in *Grand Theft Auto: London 1969* for the PlayStation, released for PC and PlayStation in 1999. It is an expansion pack of *Grand Theft Auto*, the first game in the series. Besides a change in setting and new music, *Grand Theft Auto: London 1969* includes original songs and licensed music. Since the game was the second in the series for Rockstar, the game's developer, there were limited funds to license music when it already had contracted a composer to write music. Despite funds, Rockstar purchased the licenses for some early reggae songs and Italian film soundtracks. The soundtrack includes 21 original songs and nine licensed songs. The game's title track, which also plays during the credits and on the Westminster Wireless radio station, is "Le Malizie Di Venere—Seq. 3." The track is from the 1969 Italian film of the same name. Translated as "Devil in the Flesh," the track was composed by Piero Umiliani and Gian Franco Reverberi. The Bush Sounds radio station includes two reggae songs from The Upsetters. These songs were initially released on a double A-side single release in 1969. The songs are "Return of Django" and "Dollar in the Teeth."

Recent games in the series almost exclusively use licensed music in their soundtracks. When *Grand Theft Auto V* was first released in 2013 for PS3 and Xbox 360, the soundtrack included 242 licensed songs. When the enhanced version was released in 2014 for PS4 (PlayStation 4) and Xbox One, 162 new songs were licensed, bringing the total number of songs to 404. When the PC version was released in 2015, 13 new songs were added as a new radio station, bringing the total songs to 417.

In the internet age, developers can patch the game to remove music when licensing agreements have expired. This situation happened with *Grand Theft Auto IV* after the licensing agreements expired after 10 years. The April 2018 patch removed 54 songs and replaced 11 songs. Games that are played online or require an internet connection will add

and drop licensed music due to licensing agreements, especially when using the master recordings. Other games in the series to suffer a change in soundtrack include the PC version of *Grand Theft Auto: San Andreas* and the Steam version of *Grand Theft Auto: Vice City.*

The soundtrack of *Jet Set Radio Future* includes both original songs and licensed music from the original artists. Hideki Naganuma and Richard Jacques were the composers who had previously composed the music for *Jet Set Radio*, the previous game in the series. The licensed music includes Guitar Vader, BS 2000, Scapegoat Wax, the Latch Brothers, Cibo Matto, and the Prunes. Of the 30 songs included in the game's soundtrack, almost half of the songs are licensed music. The Latch Brothers contributed three remix tracks and five original tracks for the game. The Latch Brothers were a side project from Mike Diamond, known as one of the Beastie Boys. The game's official soundtrack did not include the Latch Brothers' contributions.

1983

RCA (Composite Video and Audio)

The Nintendo Famicom, released in Japan on July 15, 1983, was the first home console to support a connection to a TV set via an RCA cable. An RCA cable is an analog audio solution that transmits separate signals for composite video and one or two sound channels of audio. An RCA cable is identified by its colored tips. For audio, the white and red tips represent the left and right audio signals (in a stereo mix). For a monophonic mix, only the white tipped end transmits the mono audio signal. The first home console to

use RCA cables was the Nintendo Famicom and NES (video and monophonic audio). The Famicom and NES also had an RF-out port to be used for a connection with coaxial cables and an RF adapter. The last home console to support RCA cables was the Wii U (via AV Multi Out).

DPCM (Differential Pulse-Code Modulation)

Although PCM and PWM, as uncompressed audio sample formats, produced more realistic sounds than basic waveforms, audio programmers sought ways to compress the audio data so that it could be stored in the limited storage media of the time. In 1983, Nintendo released the Famicom in Japan, capable of producing sound from DPCM samples. DPCM is a lossy compressed variant of PCM. Instead of storing each sample at the bit depth, or resolution, of 8, 16, or 24 bits, DPCM instead stores the difference (differential) between consecutive samples in 4 bits. Less bits means a decrease in audio quality, but it also means a decrease in the amount of memory needed to store the audio data. DPCM results in a memory savings of 50 percent from 8-bit PCM or 75 percent from 16-bit PCM.

DPCM is a form of sound generation used in the Nintendo Famicom and NES (one of the system's five sound channels).

MICROPHONES

The first microphones used for video games were used simply to register blowing into the microphone as a button press. The Famicom was the first home console to include an internal microphone in the "II" controller. The Famicom did not support voice recognition. Other microphones used with video game systems include the microphone with the VRU (Voice Recognition Unit) of the N64 in 1998, the microphone with the Capture Cassette of the 64DD in 2000, the Dreamcast microphone in 2000, the PS2 Headset in 2002, and the Xbox Live Headset in 2002. The VRU was used with the N64 for voice recognition. The Capture Cassette imported recorded sound into video and audio projects on the 64DD. The headsets were used principally for online voice chat in online multiplayer games. The headsets included a headphone for listening and a microphone angled in front of the player's mouth for talking. The Nintendo DS in 2004 used its internal microphone for blowing or shouting, like the Famicom, speech recognition, like the VRU, and chatting with other players, via local LAN or online via the Nintendo Wi-Fi Connection.

RHYTHM GAMES

Melody Blaster was one of the first rhythm games, released in 1983. Music games are often described together with rhythm games. However, in rhythm games, the gameplay involves players interacting with music based on the timing of sounds and beats. Music is simply the means to hear the sounds and beats. Rhythm refers to the timing patterns of sounds in music. In games, players press buttons to match the rhythm of the music. This helps to hear the beat of the music to line up the rhythm properly. In rhythm games that use visual icons on the screen, a player could mute the audio and rely solely on the icons on screen to time each button press or movement.

Until CD-DA brought CD-like music to video games, the music of early rhythm games had to be compromised to work around the available soundchips in each game system. A game that is known for popularizing the rhythm game genre is *PaRappa the Rapper*. Released in 1997 for the PlayStation, the game was an early example of a successful game in the genre. It used the concept of watching a bar with the indicated button presses for the player to enter in time. Thanks to CD-DA, the musical tracks in the game use vocals for all of the characters. In addition, the game has a meter that indicates the player's accuracy when timing the button presses. Pressing each button on the PlayStation controller makes PaRappa, the main character, rap specific words to each song. There is some leniency in the timing, but players cannot veer off the indicated rhythms unless unlocking a special mode in the progress meter.

Another game for the PlayStation is *Vib-Ribbon*. Released in Japan in 1999 and Europe in 2000 (not released in North America), the player helps Vibri, the main character, dodge obstacles on a track by pressing the L, R, X, or Down buttons on the PlayStation controller. An interesting design choice for the PlayStation game is the minimalistic visuals. The game uses white vector lines for Vibri, the thin track, and the obstacles. The placement of the obstacles on the track indicates which button to press. The game consists of six songs that are used for the courses with bronze, silver, and gold status. Another unique design choice of *Vib-Ribbon*, especially for rhythm games, was allowing players to take out the game disc and put any audio CD into the PlayStation. The game would automatically generate a track with obstacles based on the sounds of each audio track. Players could decide how difficult a song to use based on how frenetic the music was. The game would generate more difficult courses based on the music. Track generation via audio data was possible because the entire game fits into the RAM of the PlayStation, leaving the lens of the CD drive available for reading audio data.

In the 2000s, other games in the rhythm genre used creative ways to interact with the music. In the *Donkey Konga* games, one or two players hit bongos and clap in rhythm to the music. In the middle of the screen, there is a bar with moving barrels that indicates the timing of each input. In the *Guitar Hero* games, the player uses one hand to press down colored fret buttons while the other hand toggles the strum bar. These motions are meant to imitate the motions of playing the guitar. The player still reacts to icons passing across the screen for the timing of the rhythm. In the *DJ Hero* games, the player presses and holds buttons in time with the icons moving on-screen. Colored icons represent the three stream buttons. Two of the three buttons correspond to two songs that are mixed together like a DJ would. The third button corresponds to additional samples with are adjusted with an effects dial.

Even rhythm games released on handheld gaming systems required players to interact with the rhythm of the music. *Elite Beat Agents* was a Nintendo DS game released in 2006. The player uses the DS stylus to tap to the music. Numbered circles appear on the lower DS screen. When a timed circle lands over each numbered circle, the player must tap the numbered circle in time. Other challenges include tapping and holding the stylus to trace a path and tapping and holding the stylus and then spinning it around the screen to move a disc. The top screen of the DS shows comic-book style characters in need of help and the bottom screen of the DS shows the Elite Beat Agents dancing to the music to assist the people in need. The success of the dance moves of the Elite Beat Agents is dependent on the player's rhythmic accuracy. *Superbeat: Xonic* was a PS Vita game released in 2015. It is a rhythm game in which the player matches the indicated rhythms using the face buttons and touchscreen of the PS Vita.

Musical Game Controllers

Before the release of the Intellivision Music Synthesizer that was included with *Melody Blaster* in 1983, the input devices for games were either the game controller or the computer keyboard and mouse. There are other controllers for PC gamers for precision movement, but these were the basic input devices. They have become the standard because players have become accustomed to the arrangement of buttons with relation to the hands and fingers. However, video gaming cannot be truly immersive when a player only interacts using an input device controlled by the hands. In an attempt to create realism, some games are designed for special controllers and these games are bundled with these controllers. Music and rhythm games, in particular, sometimes work with a controller that is shaped like a musical instrument. Without the game component, the controller may not work like a musical instrument it resembles. The game developer ultimately decides whether supporting a musical game controller is worth the time and effort. Developers continue to support a standard game controller so they do not shun players who simply want to play using the tried-and-true game controller.

The DK Bongos are an input device for the Nintendo GameCube, first bundled with *Donkey Konga* in 2003. The DK Bongos are shaped like a pair of bongos made from barrels. The barrels resemble the common items from the *Donkey Kong Country* series. The DK Bongos need to be plugged into the controller port of the GameCube, just like a standard controller. The player interacts with the bongos in three ways. The player may hit each of the two bongos with his or her hand. The third method of input is by clapping. The DK Bongos include a microphone to detect loud sounds. Compared to a standard game controller, the DK Bongos lack many buttons. However, it is still possible to navigate through games that use them.

The four games that support the DK Bongos are *Donkey Konga, Donkey Konga 2, Donkey Konga 3*, and *Donkey Kong Jungle Beat*. The three games in the *Donkey Konga* series are music games that use

the bongos as if the player were a bongo player performing the songs. Players are shown symbols to indicate when to hit the bongos, which bongo to hit, and when to clap. For one-player mode, Donkey Kong is seen on-screen with a pair of bongos as a representation of the player's inputs. For two-player mode, Diddy Kong is seen on the lower half of the screen hitting the bongos and clapping when the second player interacts with the DK Bongos.

Donkey Kong Jungle Beat is a GameCube game that uses the DK Bongos in a platformer setting. Rather than react to symbols that match the beat of songs, the player interacts with the DK Bongos to control Donkey Kong as he navigates each stage. In this way, the DK Bongos are acting more like a traditional game controller despite their musical appearance. By hitting the left bongo, Donkey Kong moves left. By hitting the right bongo, Donkey Kong moves right. Clapping makes Donkey Kong clap his hands, which can stun or kill enemies and collect nearby bananas for additional points. *Donkey Kong Jungle Beat* was later released on the Nintendo Wii in 2009. This version of the game does not support the DK Bongos. Instead the gameplay is modified to support the Wii Remote and Nunchuk. Instead of hitting each bongo from the DK Bongos, the player mimics the downward motion with either the Wii Remote or the Nunchuk.

Samba de Amigo is a music and rhythm game released in 2000 by Sega for the Dreamcast. The game was designed for the maraca controllers, which are shaped and held like a maraca. Amigo, the in-game monkey, shakes the maracas along with the music. The player holds a maraca in each hand. A sensor is placed on the floor to detect the placement of the maracas above. The songs in the game are taken from the genres of classic samba and samba pop. During each song, the player shakes the maracas based on blue and red balls that appear on screen that indicate beat hits. Sometimes a stick figure will appear on the screen, which indicates to strike a pose for extra points. The floor sensor can detect the pose based on where the maracas are above it. When the game was ported to the Wii in 2008, it supported the Wii Remote and Nunchuk, dropping support for the maraca controllers. The Wii Remote and Nunchuk can be placed in maraca cradle attachments to mimic the feel of maracas. However, the floor sensor with the Dreamcast version was able to detect the height of the controllers. The Wii Remote and Nunchuk, however, can detect angles that are used for high, mid, and low notes.

The *Dance Dance Revolution* series encourages full-body dancing through fun, upbeat songs. First appearing in arcades in 1998 and then on the Sony PlayStation, players move their feet to the music using a dance mat or board with marked arrows. The arrow arrangement is usually up, down, left, and right. Some mats offer the four diagonal directions. Other mats use the four corners for the standard four face buttons on a standard game controller. These are needed to navigate menus when not playing the game. The player knows when to tap the dance mat's arrow based on the timing of arrows that move upward on the screen. It does not matter how hard or which part of the body presses the dance mat's arrows. Nevertheless, players find create ways to dance with the music and even choose to move their upper bodies with the music.

The *Guitar Hero* series began in 2005 on the PS2. The game is a music and rhythm game based around the guitar. The game is designed around the guitar peripheral. The guitar controller is a ¾-scale model of the Gibson SG guitar. However, the guitar is designed for a video game. It lacks strings and cannot make sound on its own. Instead of frets, there are instead colored buttons that are used during gameplay as the notes. The guitar includes a strum bar where the player would strum and a whammy bar on the body of the guitar. The whammy bar is used to boost Star Power and to alter the pitch of sustained notes for additional points. The guitar peripheral is worn and held like a regular guitar. After the player selects a song, colored circles move toward the screen to indicate which fret button or buttons to press down. The player must press the fret buttons and wiggle the strum bar at the correct time with the music to receive points. Doing so successfully results in combos and a meter shows how well the player is doing. At the hardest difficulty, the player requires dexterous fingers to press down unusual combinations of fret buttons and to quickly switch from each combination.

Other games used electronic instruments. *The Miracle Piano Teaching System* was a piece of software for PC, Mac, NES, SNES, and the Genesis that used its own MIDI (Musical Instrument Digital Interface) keyboard to play music. It included minigames to teach the fundamentals of melodies and chords. At its essence, a 61-key piano keyboard is a glorified game controller with 61 buttons. Another game to use a real instrument is *Rocksmith*. The gameplay is similar to the *Guitar Hero* series, but the game uses a USB (Universal Serial Bus) cable to connect to the ¼-inch output jack of an electric guitar. The player could use any electric guitar or an acoustic guitar, provided the player owned a pickup for the acoustic guitar. If the player did not own an electric or acoustic guitar, the game was bundled with an Epiphone Les Paul Junior guitar, strap, and two picks.

BACKWARD COMPATIBILITY

Backward compatibility is the ability of a game system to play games from a previous game system. The Intellivision II, released in 1983, was a model revision of the Mattel Intellivision that supported the System Changer. This peripheral allowed the Intellivision to play Atari 2600 games. Game systems that support backward compatibility can play games from an older game system. Backward compatibility is beneficial to consumers because they can purchase newer gaming systems without losing access to their favorite games from the older systems. In designing gaming systems, console manufacturers consider backward compatibility and its effect on hardware design.

Game systems that support backward compatibility must maintain some consistency of audio hardware so that the older games play and sound as expected. To support older gaming systems, newer game systems needed to include more than one soundchip or a soundchip designed with all of the features of a previous one. These systems include soundchips from other systems in addition to their own, offering a variety of sound types and additional sound channels. The Atari 7800 was an improved version of the Atari 2600 and Atari 5200 in many respects. The graphics look significantly better than the Atari 2600. The Atari 7800 plays games from the Atari 2600 and 5200. The Atari 7800 uses the TIA (Television Interface Adapter) for audio, the same soundchip from the Atari 2600. When playing an Atari 2600 game on the Atari 7800, the game plays as if it were on an Atari 2600 console.

The reliance on older hardware, however, posed a problem for new Atari 7800 games. The Atari 7800, released in 1986, still relies on the soundchip used by the Atari 2600 since 1977. The TIA was never designed for musical purposes based on the tuning of its sounds. It also supports a maximum of two sound channels. The decision for backward compatibility over innovation stunted the Atari 7800, which was further challenged by the success of the Famicom from Nintendo in 1983.

The Sega Genesis, also known as the Mega Drive, is backward-compatible with the Sega Master System, Sega's previous home console system. Backward compatibility made the Genesis desirable. On the day of its release, the Genesis could play the entire game library of the SMS plus other Genesis games that attempted to simulate Sega's arcade success in the home market. The Genesis contains two soundchips. One is the Texas Instruments SN76489, the same soundchip used in the SMS. It is this chip that makes the audio possible for SMS games played on the Genesis. However, unlike the Atari 7800, which relied solely on an older soundchip, the Genesis also contains the YM2612 by Yamaha, supporting FM (frequency modulation) synthesis sound channels. The design of the Genesis looked back on Sega's previous offerings while looking ahead at adding new audio sounds to the more recent games. Using the two soundchips together was very common in Genesis games. The variety of sound generation from both soundchips allowed for more audio types than other game systems on the market.

The PS2 (PlayStation 2) from Sony is backward-compatible with the PlayStation. Backward compatibility was always part of the design for the PS2. Many gamers enjoyed the PlayStation games, and by supporting these games on the next iteration of the PlayStation, gamers had no reason not to upgrade. Even better, the DualShock controller from the

PlayStation worked perfectly on the PS2. Both systems read games on disc media. The PS2 reads CDs as well as DVDs. The PlayStation made use of CD-DA for the music. Sony, along with Philips, developed the storage standard for the CD and DVD in 1982 and 1997, respectively.

In the handheld market, the Game Boy Color is backward-compatible with the Game Boy. Backward compatibility made good business sense as the Game Boy Color was released nine years after the Game Boy. The Game Boy was a success for Nintendo, and they ported many of their NES and SNES games to the Game Boy. However, these games accommodated the monochromatic graphics and limited audio. When Nintendo released the Game Boy Color in 1998, it played original Game Boy games with some enhancements in color palettes.

Regarding audio, the Game Boy Color contains the Sharp LR35902, the same soundchip used by the Game Boy. That means that even in 1998, the audio and music could only sound as good as they sounded in 1989. Based on the technical specifications, that would seem to be true. However, developers were very familiar with working with the chip for eight years and could take advantage of its many quirks to produce exciting and impressive sonic possibilities.

When online gaming services and digital marketplaces emerged, backward compatibility was no longer a feature that manufacturers fully implemented upon a game system's release. Whereas the inclusion of a soundchip could resolve audio for an entire game system's game library, these systems instead relied on game developers to create software that could read the data from an older game. For example, the Xbox One supports backward compatibility on select titles from the Xbox 360. The PS4 supports backward compatibility on select titles from the PS3. Players on the Nintendo Wii and Wii U could purchase games from earlier game systems with additional features such as digital manuals and save points via the systems' "Virtual Console."

1984

FM SYNTHESIS (FREQUENCY MODULATION)

FM synthesis was first used by the arcade game *Marble Madness*, released in North America on December 15, 1984. FM synthesis is based on the principle of one frequency modulating another frequency to form a more complex frequency. FM was originally used for radio transmission as FM radio. John M. Chowning first explored FM synthesis for audio in his paper *The Synthesis of Complex Audio Spectra by Means of Frequency Modulation* (1973). Yamaha licensed the technology for their DX digital synthesizer series, of which the DX7 was its most successful model. Yamaha also produced soundchips with FM synthesis support that many arcade, PC, and home consoles used. The variety of possible waveforms using FM synthesis is more than those possible with a PSG.

There are two frequencies used to create a sound timbre. The starting frequency is called the carrier and the frequency that is used to modulate the carrier is called the modulator. The carrier frequency is the pitch that is audible. The modulator frequency must be in the range of human hearing (above 20 Hz) for FM synthesis to create sideband frequencies and timbres. If the modulator frequency is below 30 Hz, the effect of the modulator on the carrier will be a pitch vibrato (oscillating pitch bend much like a siren). Once the modulator frequency is above 20 Hz, the change in pitch is no longer audible and instead sideband frequencies are introduced. The additional sideband frequencies that are introduced to the carrier frequency are determined by the ratio between the carrier and modulator frequencies. Sideband frequencies change the tone and timbre of the carrier waveform.

An oscillator generates each carrier and modulator frequency. A combination of an oscillator, envelope, and amplifier is called an operator. Two or more operators can be arranged as carriers or modulators in algorithmic groupings. The more operators used in an algorithm, the more complex the resulting sound can be. The Yamaha DX7 digital synthesizer uses six operators for each voice. It also included 32 pre-configured algorithms involving arrangements of operators.

There are four types of FM-synthesis algorithms. In a stacked algorithm, one or more modulators are connected in series to one carrier. If there are two or more modulators, each modulator directly affects the next modulator and the result of all modulators directly affects the carrier. In a branch algorithm, two or more modulators directly affect one carrier. In a root algorithm, one modulator directly affects two or more carriers. Lastly, in a carrier-only algorithm, there are no modulators (no change in timbre without modulators). For any algorithm with more than one carrier, the resulting sound will be the additive synthesis of all carriers after having been modulated.

Each oscillator generates a sine wave. However, the ratio between carrier and modulator frequencies can create other waveforms. For example, a ratio of 1:1 results in a sawtooth wave. A ratio of 1:4 results in a square wave (50 percent duty cycle). If the ratio uses simple integers, the resulting sound will be harmonic (pleasant to the ear and with the carrier frequency). If the ratio uses decimals and fractions, then the resulting sound will be inharmonic (out of tune, dissonant to the ear, and with the carrier frequency). Some degree of inharmonic sidebands can add etheric depth to a sound.

The amplitude of the modulator frequency affects the timbre of the sound. The modulation index (the amplitude of the modulator) represents how prominent the sidebands will be in the resulting sound. The amplitude of the carrier frequency affects the volume of the sound. The envelope of an operator can alter the carrier or modulator frequency. If the operator is a carrier, the envelope alters the amplitude of the carrier frequency. If the operator is a modulator, the envelope alters the tone and timbre of the resulting waveform.

FM synthesis is a form of sound generation used by the Sega Mark III, Japanese SMS (Sega Master System), Sega Mega Drive/Genesis, Neo Geo AES (Advanced Entertainment System) and MVS (Multi Video System), Sega Saturn, Sega Dreamcast, Atari Jaguar, Konami's VRC7 (Virtual ROM Controller 7) chip for the Famicom, the AdLib and Sound Blaster PC sound cards, the Sound Board II for the PC-88, the arcade game *Marble Madness* (1984), the Sharp X68000 computer, the Yamaha DX keyboard series, and Williams pinball machines.

SALES IN THE MUSIC INDUSTRY

In 1984, video game music expanded into the music industry. The first commercially released album of video game music was *Video Game Music*, released on audio cassette by Alfa Records in Japan on April 25, 1984. The musical tracks were taken from three popular arcade games from Namco. It wasn't in 1994 that a video game composer released an album of video game music worldwide. Tommy Tallarico released *Tommy Tallarico Virgin Games Greatest Hits Volume One* on CD. Tallarico's album included his musical compositions from five video games developed by Virgin Games. His album also promoted the QSound surround sound format. Both video game audio and music albums embraced QSound in the 1990s. It was not uncommon for a developer to release an album of a game's soundtrack. Atari promoted the Atari Jaguar and the game *Tempest 2000* by selling the game's soundtrack on CD in 1994. Atari later included the audio CD with the Atari Jaguar CD to show off the peripheral's CD player. In 1995, Cyan, the developer of the 1993 Mac game *Myst*, released the game's soundtrack on CD. Soon, musicians from the audio industry became video game composers. The best-selling video game soundtrack of all-time is *Halo 2: Original Soundtrack Volume 1*, released on November 9, 2004, the same day as the North American release of *Halo 2* for the original Xbox. In 2005, two video game composers, Tommy Tallarico and Jack Wall, founded the Video Games Live concert tour, a live performance of video game music with an orchestra and guest artists.

Video game audio and music permeated in pop culture as well. In January 1982, Jerry Buckner and Gary Garcia released *Pac-Man Fever*, an album on LP, audio cassette, and 8-track tape of eight songs, each inspired by and using sound effects from a different arcade game. The first track, "Pac-Man Fever," was the standout hit in the United States, peaking at number nine on the Billboard Hot 100 in March 1982. On June 22, 1996, *Quake* was released for PC with a soundtrack and sound effects by the band Nine Inch Nails. A popular song still played at hockey games, "Kernkraft 400" by Zombie Nation in 1999 samples the musical track "Stardust" from the 1984 PC game *Lazy Jones*. On December 11, 1999, DJ Pretzel founded the Overclocked Remix website. In 2002, composer Jake Kaufman founded the VGRemix website. Both websites are repositories of user remixes of video game music, including content and albums from successful video game composers in the industry. Since the inception of hip-hop and rap music, and moreso to this day, artists have incorporated samples of video game sound effects and musical tracks in their derivative works (some artists were sued by the respective copyright owners).

1986

HARDWARE ADD-ONS

The previous year, 1985, introduced the Sega Mark III, Nintendo NES, and *Super Mario Bros.* Continuing to mark achievements in audio, the Famicom Disk System was released by Nintendo in 1986. It was the first hardware peripheral to add audio capabilities to a game system. Until 1986, it was customary for a console manufacturer to release a new game system when the technology of its current game system was obsolete or stagnant. However, each time this cycle happens, consumers are hesitant to lose value in the video game systems that they own. Console manufacturers need to offer new experiences in graphics, audio, and gameplay while honoring their loyal consumers. Console manufacturers offered a response in the early '90s when technology for CD media was available. At the time, all of the systems on the market from Sega, NEC, Atari, and SNK did not use CD media for their games. In the early '90s, console manufacturers did not include built-in CD drives with their game systems. Instead, Sega, NEC, Atari, and SNK released add-on devices for their system offerings from the early to mid–'90s. The add-ons worked in conjunction with the systems to improve graphics, audio, and memory resources. Additional sound channels, sound types, and CD-DA tracks improved audio capabilities.

The TurboGrafx-CD was a hardware add-on for the TurboGrafx-16. NEC designed the TG-CD so that new games could be stored on CD media. The TG-CD was the first CD-based system to market, being released in 1990. A CD has more memory than standard game cartridges at the time. The TG-CD supports CD-DA, which was used for the music of many of its games. However, being an add-on device, the TG-CD needed to be connected to the TG-16 to function. The soundchip of the TG-16 was still used in TG-CD games when CD-DA could not suffice. Rather than releasing a new CD-based system that could potentially flop, NEC took the safe route by extending the life of the TG-16 with the TG-CD.

The Sega Genesis is the greatest example of a core system overloaded with hardware add-ons. Sega had a runaway hit with the Genesis, the Genesis being the only true rival to Nintendo's dominance until Sony's PlayStation. For a future after the Genesis, Sega had two directions to take. One was the Sega Saturn, which wasn't released until 1994. The other was add-ons to the Sega Genesis. There were two add-ons for the Sega Genesis. The Sega 32X attaches to the cartridge slot of the Genesis. It requires its own power supply and A/V hookup to the Genesis. The 32X's main enhancement was in graphical power and in the number of colors available to use on-screen at any time. Regarding audio, it works in tandem with the Genesis. The 32X supports two channels of PWM audio, which was used for crude audio sampling. The soundchips of the 32X and the Genesis work together to offer numerous audio possibilities.

As if the 32X weren't enough, the Sega CD attaches to the side of the Genesis. Its main feature was CD media for game storage. The Sega CD was released in 1992, before the PlayStation popularized CD media for games. Regarding audio, the Sega CD supported CD-DA. The Genesis still had all of its own sound channels available for sound effects and music. It was indeed possible to hook up a 32X and a Sega CD to a Genesis. Sega designed both hardware add-ons to work together. There are six games that take advantage of all the graphical and audio features of these systems for some variety. The quality of gameplay is only as good as the development team and their ability to work with what they have. Developing a game with three different systems that need to communicate with each other to stay synchronized is not easy. Despite these challenges, each hardware add-on for the Genesis improved audio without leaving behind the entire hardware architecture of the Genesis.

The Jaguar CD is a hardware add-on for the Atari Jaguar. CD add-ons were the trend in the early to mid '90s. The Jaguar CD sat on the cartridge slot of the Jaguar. Unlike the other CD-based games, Jaguar CD games were encoded in Atari's own format based on the Red Book CD standard.

Although the Sony PlayStation is a standalone CD-based game system, it was originally designed as a hardware add-on for the SNES. When agreements between Nintendo and Sony fell through, possibly due to side talks with Nintendo and Philips, Sony released the PlayStation on its own. Suffice it to say, Sony understood well the hardware involved with CD media and created a system that appealed to developers. There is a working prototype of the original system, a collaboration between Nintendo and Sony, called the Nintendo Play Station.

In 2002, add-on technologies were not so necessary with the launch of Xbox Live, an online hub and marketplace for the Microsoft Xbox. Instead, internet-ready game systems received audio enhancements through downloadable system and game updates. In the present day, consumers can purchase extra external hard drives to add more storage memory to their video game systems. PC users have always had the option to add or remove hardware components to improve the computer specifications.

1987

INTERACTION WITH MUSIC THROUGH GAMEPLAY

The player can affect the music of a game through gameplay. Music in these games must be arranged so that the sounds a player makes fits within the pre-composed music. Games that allow the player to interact with music through gameplay first appeared with *Otocky*, released in 1987 on the Nintendo Famicom Disk System. The player creates musical notes and selects instrument sounds that become part of the background music. This gameplay mechanic is in contrast to music/rhythm games where the player hits buttons that correspond to a preconfigured musical track.

Rez is a musical rail shooter game for the Dreamcast released in 2001. The game is almost devoid of sound effects and dialogue. Instead, music is given priority. The player controls the position of an avatar on the screen. The avatar's path is predetermined, customary for a rail shooter. The player and enemy actions contribute to the music in the form of trills and drums. The timing when locking on to and shooting enemies aligns

with the beat of the music. In order to hear the full spectrum of each musical track, it is necessary to complete these actions. By missing the cues or by colliding with enemies, the player's life decreases and the music becomes sparse. The game was designed around synesthesia, the relationship of human senses and stimuli triggering one another.

In *Amplitude*, released for the PS2 in 2003, the player affects the music by traveling down different colored tracks representing different instruments of a musical track. Some of the instrument choices include drums, synth, bass guitar, lead guitar, and vocals. The player avatar reflects the instrument featured on the track. Some instrument choices are easier to play than others. By switching instruments on the fly, the player can add or detract from the music depending on how well the player is executing the indicated musical hits.

Sound Shapes was released for the PS3 and PS Vita in 2012. The player controls a small circular object that jumps and sticks onto surfaces. Each object in the game emanates a musical tone or sound that contributes to the music. Not only are these sounds pleasant to hear, but they also assist in the timing of the platformer elements. When the player touches these objects, the sounds that emanate from them align with the music. By collecting items scattered throughout each stage, additional layers of sounds and music add depth to the musical track. Like *Rez*, it is necessary for the player to interact with the items and the objects in each stage in order to evolve the music and complete the stage.

In *Fantasia: Music Evolved*, released for the Xbox 360 and Xbox One in 2014, the music is manipulated by the player's hand and arm movements. The game uses the Kinect sensor to detect body movements. Within the game are "compositional spells" in which gameplay stops for a moment while the player creates a unique melodic passage using his or her hands and arms. Once a player is satisfied with the resulting composition, the composition is locked into place by lowering the arms. Then the unique musical passage is inserted into the music that follows. During normal gameplay, the player reacts to visual markers that indicate when and how to move the hands and arms. Hitting the cues correctly results in the instrument hit. Missing the cue diminishes the volume of the music for that moment.

Music Games

Although not common, music creation can be an important gameplay element in music games. Besides featuring music in gameplay, music games allow players to create music through level design. This is different from composing music with musical notation. Instead, players use the various objects from a game to create new levels that create music when played. In 1986, *Otocky* for the Famicom Disk System was the earliest example of a game based entirely around music creation.

In *Otocky*, there is an unlockable Music Maker mode. In the Music Maker, the player can edit the music in the game. There are five sound channels to manipulate, corresponding to the five sound channels of the Famicom. A user interface allows the player to adjust the waveforms, volumes, tempo, and note placements within four measures of music. After previewing the musical selection, the player selects the Otocky icon in the lower-left corner to play the selected stage with the new musical composition.

The Remix mode of *Frequency* is not just for creating remixes. An additional purpose of Remix mode is to create new stages. Players place circles down on the sides of the octagonal tunnel. Their placement is in relation to eight measure phrases. After players are finished remixing and creating the new music, the stage can be saved and played just like any other stage in the game.

Sound Shapes offers the most robust level editor with tools for the placement of objects that directly affects the music and gameplay. The player can place down terrain, objects, and decorations as well as adjust the color palette and tempo of the music. The vertical placement of some objects affects the resulting sound. At any time, the player can test the level to see if the level is playable. In *Sound Shapes*, the music is an aural representation of the level design. The player can create and save the levels from the level editor and share them.

Musical Creativity

Otocky also introduced a mode to play with music freely. Players like to experiment with music and try out new things. They may not be musicians or have any musical background, but music games can promote fun gameplay in which players can improvise within the musical structure of the game. Some games encourage improvisation where the player can make music in a freestyle setting. This concept is the opposite of rhythm games. In rhythm games, players must react to pre-configured button presses that are timed with the rhythm of the music. Within musical creativity, players must maintain some form of musicianship, so they cannot press buttons at random and hope to achieve top scores. Games with musical creativity are programmed in such a way so that improvisation still exhibits musicality. In *Otocky*, there is a BGM mode that is unlocked. In BGM mode, there are no enemies and items in each stage. Instead, the player is free to be creative and travel within each stage in a safe manner conducive to musical creativity.

In *PaRappa the Rapper*, there is an improvisation mode that can only be accessed after a first successful playthrough of a stage. During each stage, there is a meter that indicates how accurately the button presses match with the music. If the player freestyles within the indicated button presses, that demonstrates mastery of the stage. Once the rating of "U Rappin Cool" is granted, the teacher for the given stage will congratulate PaRappa and float away, leaving PaRappa to rap on his own with no bar or icons to indicate what to do. To maintain the Cool rating, the player must continue to freestyle in rhythm with the music. The teacher's lyrics drop out and only PaRappa's raps comprise the vocals. As long as the player presses buttons with some rhythmic creativity, the player will maintain the Cool rating. This is the best way to achieve a high score in the game.

In *Rhythm Tengoku*, the player can jam out on the drums in studio mode. Released on the GBA in 2006, there is no scoring during studio mode. Instead, the player presses buttons to play the various

parts of the drum kit. It does not matter how well or poor the player plays the drums. It is a mode in which the player can experiment with the drum sounds and hear what sounds good.

In *Wii Music*, players arrange songs and improvise music. Released for the Wii in 2008, it has no scoring system based on accuracy. Instead, players can simply be creative for the love of music and the game will figure out the rest. Players use the Wii Remotes and Nunchuks to mimic the motions of playing various musical instruments. In Jam Mode, players can experiment with different instrument arrangements to create music videos. They select from the 50 songs available, which include classical, traditional, Nintendo, and licensed songs. After selecting an instrument to manipulate, players may select additional band members to play the other various parts of the music like the melody, harmony, bass, and drum parts. Players may be as creative as they want when playing in this mode. The game will do its best to compensate to make sure the music sounds somewhat decent. Adding to the creativity, patient players can overdub their sessions by performing up to six instruments for one music video. That means that one player can record an entire six-piece band. It is not likely that a player actually learns to perform on a musical instrument from this game, but the design of the game prioritizes musical creativity and fun.

Dance Games

One of the earliest games where dance was the primary gameplay mechanism was *Dance Aerobics*, released for the Famicom on February 26, 1987. Dance games are similar to rhythm games. However, dance games involve players physically moving to the music. Instead of pressing a button to match a rhythm, the player sends inputs to the game system using either a motion controller or their own bodies. Some games involve some or full body movement, reacting to dance moves in time with a music track. These games use either a dance mat or a motion input device to register player movements. *Dance Aerobics* requires the Nintendo Family Trainer (Family Fun Fitness in Europe and Power Pad in North America), a floor mat with colored circles that contained pressure sensors to recognize foot presses. The Power Pad connects to the Famicom and NES and interacts with the game like a controller. In dance games, there are dancing avatars on-screen that show players what they should be doing to earn points. The dance moves match up with music. For games that track the full body, an image appears on-screen to show what the game system sees with respect to the players' bodies.

The games in the *Dance Dance Revolution* series recognize foot presses in the same way as *Dance Aerobics*. In the *Dance Dance Revolution* games, players react to the music by pressing marked arrows on a dance mat or board using their feet. The game system only responds to presses on the dance mat or board. It may be possible to press the correct arrows with something other than feet, but the intended means of gameplay and the one that results in the best scores is to move with the feet. The music selection in these games is often fast-paced, and some of the songs at the higher difficulty require incredible footwork.

In the *Dance Central* games, the Microsoft Kinect, a sensor that identifies the full body of a player or players, tracks player movement. Unlike other dance games before 2010, *Dance Central* is much more accurate in determining whether players are matching the indicated dance moves. There are hundreds of dance moves and hundreds of dance routines to select from over the entire *Dance*

Central series. Unlike earlier dance games, the Kinect recognizes input in changes in shape throughout the entire body. *Dance Central* is also a rhythm game because players must follow and match the pre-arranged routines of dance moves.

ALGORITHMICALLY-GENERATED MUSIC

By 1987, the technology in video game system and consumer computers was powerful enough to create algorithmically-generated music. Instead of composing music that plays back within a game, programmers deconstruct music into musical fragments that are chosen at random in real-time during gameplay to create an original combination of pitches and rhythms. The programmer must consider lots of test cases so that the algorithmically-generated music is not a musical mess of dissonant tones and interrupted ideas. When music is algorithmically generated, the game is programmed to generate an original musical piece based on some criteria with an additional level of randomness. This is different from games that transition between prerecorded tracks using effects like fade ins and fade outs. This is also different from games where the player's actions create sounds that appear in the game. In algorithmically-generated music, once the parameters are defined, the music is generated solely by the computer based on the software programming.

The main theme of *Ballblazer*, "Song of the Grid," was the first algorithmically-generated musical piece in video games. Released for the Atari 7800 in 1987, the game's theme music is one of the first examples of music in video games that doesn't have an original form. This is possible because Peter Langston, one of the programmers, programmed an algorithm that monitors the speed and volume of music to assemble an original never-ending musical track. These parameters affect the melody, bass line, drum part, and chords. The algorithm assembles each instrument part from a musical "bank" of 32 different "riffs." Langston called the process of selecting riffs for the melody "riffology." The accompanying parts use a simplified version of the algorithm. They are assembled from a collection of four-bar segments. The melody contains the most variety while the accompanying parts vary slightly so that the music maintains musical cohesiveness. Some of the decisions made by the algorithm include how fast to play the riff, how loud to play it, when to omit or elide notes, and when to insert a rhythmic break. These choices are not completely random; there are weights assigned to each choice based on what has already occurred and what would make musical sense in the musical trajectory.

An expansion of algorithmically-generated music in video games exists within *C.P.U. Bach*. All of the program's music is algorithmically generated.

Released in 1994 for the 3DO, the software allows users to generate Baroque music in the style of the Baroque composer Johann Sebastian Bach. The software creates music after the user selects from a variety of parameters. The interface is user-friendly so there is no need to understand the music theory behind Bach's musical style. After selecting the venue for the performance (used for the visuals), the user can adjust the probability weights of 16 musical styles and 16 instruments. As the user adjusts each selection, the number of musical notes that appear in the selection give more weight to that style or instrument being represented in the resulting algorithmically-generated music. For example, the user can select a Bach Chorale performed on strings. The software takes a few seconds to generate the piece. Then an image of Bach and some instruments perform the piece. This software was designed by Sid Meier, who is recognized for the *Civilization* game series.

1989

ADPCM (ADAPTIVE DIFFERENTIAL PULSE-CODE MODULATION)

The Game Boy was the first video game system able to read ADPCM samples in 1989, using its wavetable channel. ADPCM is a lossy, compressed variant of PCM, similar to DPCM. Unlike DPCM, the number of bits used to store the difference between samples varies based on the audio signal (adaptive). An ADPCM sample begins as a PCM sample. Through some algorithms, a succession of samples is analyzed in the PCM and the value of the next sample is estimated. The value that is stored in the ADPCM sample is the difference (differential) between the estimated value and the actual value.

ADPCM is a form of sound generation used in the Nintendo SNES, TurboGrafx-CD, Neo Geo MVS and AES, Sony PlayStation, PS2, Sega Saturn, Dreamcast, Nintendo GameCube, the Wii Remote, and the Sound Blaster PC sound card. ADPCM is the primary means of sound generation for the SNES (all sound channels).

3.5 MM (⅛") CABLE

In 1989, the Sega Genesis and Game Boy systems had a 3.5mm audio-out port. A 3.5mm cable is an analog audio solution. It is the cable used most often by audio headphones. All handheld gaming systems and most mobile devices have a 3.5mm audio out port. The audio volume can be adjusted from the volume spinner on the side of the Game Boy and the volume slider on the top of the Genesis. A 3.5mm cable is thin and the plug on each cable's end has a diameter of 3.5mm. The number of black stripes on its tip determines audio functionality. One black stripe (TS) supports an unbalanced monophonic audio signal. Two black stripes (TRS) support a balanced monophonic or unbalanced stereo audio signal (used by the Genesis and Game Boy). Three black stripes (TRRS) add microphone support to the TRS features (used for headset communication with players during a multiplayer game). TRRS can also be used for an unbalanced stereo audio signal with video, used in plug-and-play game systems. The 2.5mm cable is identical to the 3.5mm cable in functionality. The only difference is the smaller tip size. The 2.5mm cable is used to connect small devices.

1990

SSG (SOFTWARE-CONTROLLED SOUND GENERATOR)

An SSG is a form of sound generation that generates square waves and LFSR (linear-feedback shift register) noise. Being that a PSG could do more, SSGs were rarely necessary for sound generation for video games. It is used in the Neo Geo MVS and AES. The Neo Geo systems contain the YM2610 soundchip, which supports three SSG channels (as well as FM, noise, and ADPCM channels).

ANALOG SURROUND AUDIO ENCODING

In 1990, the Super Famicom was the first gaming system to support analog surround sound. Game systems that support analog audio usually are hooked up with RCA cables (the yellow, red, and white cables). An analog signal varies based on variations in air pressure of the original sound. This is in contrast to digital audio, which came later, that converts the sound into a sequence of binary numbers. One of the early formats for surround sound was Dolby Pro Logic 1 (DPLI). This surround sound format first appeared video games in *King Arthur's World* (1994) for the SNES. The SNES mixes the game's audio into a surround sound configuration of four audio output signals intended for a left, right, center, and rear speaker. Beginning in 1992, Sega's disc-based systems from the Sega CD to the Dreamcast used QSound, another analog surround sound format. In 2001, the Nintendo GameCube was the first gaming system to support analog surround sound through DPLII (Dolby Pro Logic 2), an improved version of Dolby Pro Logic 1 supporting a five-speaker configuration. The five-speaker configuration included a rear left and rear right speaker. All analog surround sound formats require analog cables to be used to properly hook up devices.

DSP (DIGITAL SIGNAL PROCESSOR)

A DSP is a computer chip designed primarily to manipulate digital signals through mathematical calculations. DSPs are not limited to audio; in the realm of audio, they are used to change the digital audio data. A standard function of a DSP is to encode and decode audio data into a non–PCM format. A DSP is essential to encoding and decoding surround sound formats like Dolby Digital and DTS. Modern game systems capable of outputting LPCM contain a DSP that handles the decoding of audio data from Dolby Digital or DTS to PCM. A DSP can also compress and decompress a digital audio signal. For example, a DSP is used in a cell phone to compress and decompress voice signals for more accessible transport across phone networks. Besides audio conversion, the DSP can also alter the sound by amplitude, frequency, or other mathematically measured value. When recording audio, a DSP takes in a PCM signal and converts the signal into the desired audio format, like MP3 or M4A (lossy compression). A DSP consists of program memory, data memory, compute engine, and input/output. The program memory stores all of the functions needed to manipulate the data. The data memory stores the audio data to be managed. The compute engine runs the program memory on the data memory, thus performing the calculations. The input/output contains functions for the DSP to communicate with other chips. The DSP is, in essence, a computer chip specially designed to perform calculations on audio signals.

The Super Famicom and SNES contain the S-DSP, a digital signal processor used for audio. As a point of confusion, the DSP of the Sound Blaster 1.0 in 1989 stands for "Digital Sound Processor." It was not the same as a digital signal processor. The only resemblance of the Sound Blaster's DSP to a digital signal processor was its ability to decompress ADPCM samples.

1992

AMBIENCE

Up to this point in time, a game's sound effects were used more effectively than music to simulate the game world. Music rarely related to the game world. Ambience refers to the soundscape of a place. Ambient sounds are the real sounds that exist in the world. In the analog of attending a sporting event, the sounds of ambience are the cheering of the fans, the hard hits of the athletes, and the music playing over the loudspeakers. Ambient sounds appear in games to make the gaming experience more believable and compelling. Ambient sounds define a place and help people to identify where they are without seeing a place. The concept works the same when creating virtual worlds and experiences. Games in the horror genre rely on ambience to immerse players into the scary and unknown and later using musical cues and sounds to alert the player of danger.

Ambient music is a genre of music that emphasizes tone and atmosphere over traditional musical elements. One of the earliest games with ambient music was *Ecco the Dolphin*, released in 1992 for the Genesis. In ambient music, there is no persistent beat. It feels like there is no beginning or end to the music. There is not necessarily a catchy melody to remember. Like ambience in sound, ambient music exists to gives character or atmosphere to a scene. It feels a certain way without the structure of traditional music. Ambient music is instrumental, using lots of resonating sounds like synth pads, metallic tones, and bells. Sometimes ambient music may be emanating from the in-game world. Unlike video game music with catchy melodies, ambient soundtracks focus on atmosphere building. They often lack a sense of time and are more about the blending of sounds rather than using music theory for composition. They may include sound effects within the music to blend the music with the in-game world sounds.

The soundtrack of *Ecco the Dolphin* consists of ambient music. The musical tracks use long FM tones with repetitious melodic and rhythmic patterns. Water environments are good candidates for ambient music. Ambient music moves slowly, and this is reflected in movement through water. *Ecco the Dolphin* contains puzzle elements, so players will not be distracted by the ambient music when determining what to do next. The title track is a good example of ambience in music. Patterns and repetition set the mood for each stage rather than rousing melodies and pop-style rhythms.

The music of the *Metroid* and *Metroid Prime* series is primarily ambient music. *Super Metroid* is a great example of a game with ambient audio and music. Released on the SNES in 1994, ambience is used to set the mood and atmosphere of the two locations of the game. The first location featured in the game is the Ceres Space Colony. The setting is dark and lonely. There is no musical track. The player only hears the sounds of a siren in the distance and doors opening. This is designed to build suspense for the introduction of Ridley, the leader of the Space Pirates. He emerges out of nowhere and

the boss theme plays. The boss theme is a little over 30 seconds before looping. It repeats musical patterns at a quick tempo to represent urgency. Ambient sounds include more sirens. After escaping off the destroying space colony, the second location is Planet Zebes. Planet Zebes is a desolate world with lots of caverns and hidden surprises for the player to explore. The track "Crateria Theme (Exterior)" uses low-pitched, elongated tones. It includes the patter of rain and the crackling of thunder to set the scene. The combination of music with audio sounds adds depth to the overall sound of a game. Another example of ambience in the game is heard in an item room. The track consists of a low drone-like sound emanating from a machine with morse-code like high-pitched sounds as if coming from the dialing of a telephone. The lack of a beat or melodic content suggests to the player that something needs to be discovered.

The soundtrack of *Monument Valley* consists of ambient music. Released for iOS and Android devices in 2014, the 16 tracks use electronic sounds to slowly morph between musical patterns and ideas. Ambient music was a solid audio design choice for a game where the player is given ample time to consider the next action. Ambient music does not interfere with the player's ability to think. The music is relaxing and soothing, lacking a sense of time.

1993

AM (AMPLITUDE MODULATION)

AM synthesis is a form of sound generation based on the principle of one frequency modulating the amplitude of

another frequency to form a more complex sound. It works in a similar way to FM synthesis. AM synthesis was first used for video games by the Atari Jaguar in 1993. AM was originally used for radio transmission as AM radio. If the modulator frequency is below 20 Hz, it creates a tremolo effect in the carrier frequency. The tremolo effect is a fluctuation of volume (not pitch like in FM synthesis). When the modulator frequency is above 20 Hz, sideband frequencies are introduced into the carrier frequency. The principle of ratios and harmonic sound is the same as found in FM synthesis.

1994

CUSTOM SOUNDTRACKS

In 1994, it was possible for a player to replace a game's soundtrack with his or her own musical tracks.

A custom soundtrack is a playlist of songs selected by the player that are heard within a game. Prior to CD-DA, when games produced sound solely via soundchips, there was no method for players to convert their audio files for the soundchips. A game system that lacks CD support does not have programming to convert an audio track from a CD to a format usable by a soundchip. PCs were the first to include CD drives, and, therefore, custom soundtracks were possible. Some games and systems (the original Microsoft Xbox, for one) allow players to build a custom soundtrack of their own music files for a game's soundtrack. One method of sending audio tracks from a CD to a game was switching out a game disc with any music CD. The game system would then read the audio data from the CD and substitute it for the music of the game. On home consoles, the Sony PlayStation had some games that supported custom soundtracks through disc swapping. Disc swapping did not adversely affect the game because the game data remained in the system's RAM (read-access memory) even when the game disc was removed. *Ridge Racer* is an early example of a game that offers custom soundtracks. Released in 1994 for the PlayStation, the entire game is loaded in RAM, so the CD lens is available to read audio CDs. *Ridge Racer* was programmed with disc swapping in mind. When the game system reads the audio CD, the title of each audio track displays on the bottom of the screen in the game.

Unlike disc swapping, which only worked if games were developed to accommodate, the Xbox included an internal hard drive and software to rip music CDs onto the hard drive. Xbox games that supported custom soundtracks accessed the ripped audio files without the original audio CDs. *Grand Theft Auto III* and *Grand Theft Auto: Vice City* for the Xbox support custom soundtracks in a unique way. When entering a vehicle, the player could select a radio station to listen to or select to use a custom soundtrack from the Xbox's hard drive. For *Grand Theft Auto: Vice City*, the player selects the tape deck, which represents the player's music collection. For *Grand Theft Auto III*, the player selects the CD player, which represents the player's music collection. The choice of audio device within the game worlds reflects the time periods of the game worlds. Using audio devices within the game world is a unique way to integrate a user's musical collection into the game in a way that makes sense within the game world.

Custom soundtrack support is less common with modern game systems. This could be due to players recording gameplay and the risk of using copyrighted music in the recordings that are uploaded to online video websites. Also, popular streaming music services like Pandora and Spotify negotiate millions of music licenses for all of the music in each service's collection. There is greater control over music copyright than ever before. To protect the copyright holders, players are discouraged from using their own music as the soundtrack for their games.

1997

AUDIO GAMES

Since the beginning of video game audio history for consumers in 1972, video game audio enhanced the gaming experience, but it was rarely prioritized over graphics. Although rare, there are games that use audio as the primary gameplay element (with little to no visual indication to assist the player). In these games, players must listen carefully to the audio or else they will fail. There have not been too many games that have attempted to challenge the player to improve listening skills.

Real Sound: Kaze no Regret is a game released exclusively in Japan for the Sega Saturn in 1997. It is one of the only audio games ever released for a video game system. Its title translates to "Regret of the Wind." The game was designed to accommodate blind gamers who want to play adventure and action games. The audio is absolutely required to have any chance of completing the game. The game tells a story like an audio book. The player listens to the story, complete with voice acting. When the moment arises for the player to interact with the game, a set of chimes alert the player to choose what happens next by pressing a button on the game controller. The game design is like a "Choose Your Own Adventure" book. The game included a set of instructions in Braille. To this day, the game is still one of the only commercially released audio games designed for the blind population.

Handheld game systems were not known to have powerful internal speakers. Nevertheless, there was a game for the GBA in which the primary gameplay element was stereophonic audio. Unlike *Real Sound: Kaze no Regret*, *Soundvoyager*, released exclusively in Japan in 2006, had a visual component. The games are similar in that listening to the games' audio is essential to winning. For *Soundvoyager*, the only way to hear stereophonic sound from the GBA is to hook up a pair of headphones to the 3.5mm audio-out port of the GBA. It is not necessary to view the GBA's screen when playing "Sound Catcher," one of the game's minigames. In this minigame, instrument sounds fall from the top of the screen to the bottom. They are also panned within the audio mix to the left or right speaker. The player controls the movement of a dot to the left or right until the instrument sound is panned in the center of the mix. Then the player catches the falling sound, which is added to the music. As the game progresses, two instrument sounds fall, so the player must determine which sound is approaching first and line up that sound. For an additional audio challenge, the remix stage is a bonus stage for "Sound Catcher" that randomly selects from all of the individual sounds from the stages and makes an endless stage out of them.

1998

GAME AUDIO ACCOLADES

Before 1998, the only measure of success for a game was in its sales. While sales continue to be a measure of success, the video game industry gives out awards and accolades based on achievements in gameplay, graphics, audio, and other criteria. Games earning industry accomplishments receive a boost in sales and receive attention from people and organizations outside of the video game industry. The D.I.C.E. Awards, which began on May 28, 1998, are the video game industry's equivalent to the Academy Awards, with voting cast by its Academy's membership base. Receiving one of these awards acknowledges that the game is exceptional in one or more categories. There are games that, although not financially successful in the market, have critically-acclaimed soundtracks (*Shenmue* for the Dreamcast in 1999). With the rise of video game journalism in print and on the web, players can search for games that they like and discover an incredible backlog of games, many undiscovered hits that perhaps did not sell well because they were released near the end of a game system's life cycle or concurrently with the smash hit game of the year. Indeed, time is a valuable asset in evaluating games as some games age better than others with respect to graphics, audio, and gameplay. Other respected awards for video game audio are the G.A.N.G. Awards, first presented in 2003, and the Game Awards, first presented in 2014. Video game music crossed over in 2011 into the Grammy Awards, the annual award ceremony in the United States to recognize achievements in the music industry.

ORCHESTRAL SOUNDTRACKS

Nineteen ninety-eight was the year that a video game soundtrack used recordings from a live orchestra. Before CD media, the timbres of orchestral instruments could not be accurately generated on soundchips. Instead, developers had to manipulate the available waveforms to approximate orchestral sounds. For example, because white noise lacks a determinate pitch, composers treated it as if it were a drum or a percussive instrument. When game systems supported PCM channels, there was an opportunity to use audio samples of instruments. However, the cost of memory in the '90s hindered audio quality and sample duration. If games had access to larger storage memory, the audio quality could have been immensely better. Despite the limitations, sound designers and composers tried to emulate the sounds of an orchestra with short audio samples of orchestral instruments. *Chrono Trigger* is an example of a SNES game from 1995 that closely simulates an orchestra using instrument samples as PCM data.

When CD-based media supported larger memory for games, truly orchestral music was at last possible. The first game that featured true orchestral music was *The Lost World: Jurassic Park*. It was released in 1997 for the PlayStation, with an original soundtrack by Michael Giacchino. The orchestral soundtrack is made possible by the PlayStation's CD-DA support. With an emphasis on orchestral styles, video game music styles began to resemble film music styles. Michael Giacchino began his composing career in video games and expanded outward into television and film, composing the music for the hit television series *Lost* and the Disney/Pixar film *Up*. Nowadays, the means of composition for multimedia uses similar tools, so composers are not just limited to composing powerful orchestral scores for film. The creative skills for video game music composition, with exception to interactive elements, apply just as well for composing for television and film.

The sounds of the orchestra are a rich tradition of music history. Video game technology could not achieve an audio quality to support orchestral soundtracks until 1998. Game soundtracks that use orchestral instruments are hard to distinguish from movie soundtracks or film soundtracks. Despite access to orchestral musical works, the retro sounds of synthesized sounds and waveforms are still associated with video games, even as electronically-generated, artificial sounds.

1999

AUDIO-BASED LEVEL GENERATION

Audio data can be used for more than a custom soundtrack in a game. In some games, audio data is used to create level or stage content. In these games, the music is not treated as sound but rather like any other form of data. Within a game's programming, the game reads the sampling data of the audio and generates a new level based on some algorithm. These games offer the most variety when players can create content from their own musical collection. Although an algorithm for audio-based level generation could work with any digital file, audio files not only create the stages, but are also heard during the stages.

Vib-Ribbon was the first game to generate level content using audio data. Released for the PlayStation on December 12, 1999, *Vib-Ribbon* includes six original songs. Audio-based level generation takes place when the player inserts an audio CD into the PlayStation. Like *Ridge Racer*, the entire game fits on the PlayStation's internal RAM. Then, the disc drive is available to read the audio tracks on any inserted audio CD. When the player plays the game with an audio CD inserted, the game generates a stage based on the beat of the music. Obstacles will appear along the ribbon track to match the music using the algorithms in the game's programming. The generated content adds replayability, and players can try out different audio CDs and compare the generated stages.

Audiosurf is another game that uses audio data to generate new stages in the game. Released for PC in 2008, the player navigates a ship across a three-lane highway. Along the highway are blocks of various colors that the player must capture. Like *Vib-Ribbon*, *Audiosurf* contains algorithms to read from an audio file to generate new stages. Unlike *Vib-Ribbon*, *Audiosurf* reads digital audio files that are stored on a PC's hard drive. The game generates each stage by conducting a frequency analysis on the audio data. This determines whether the stage should be a downward slope for louder music or an uphill slope for softer music. The volumes of music fluctuate, resulting in hills and valleys for the stage's highway. For each sound spike in the music, a block appears on the highway. The color of the block determines how distinct the sound spike is. The distinct sounds are indicated as red blocks while the subtle sounds are purple. Each musical track affects the shape, speed, and mood of each stage.

2000

DIGITAL SURROUND SOUND ENCODING

Once digital surround formats developed, game systems supported analog surround formats as legacy formats and later dropped them completely. *The Bouncer*, released in 2000 for the PS2, was the first video game for home consoles to support digital audio. Digital surround sound formats began with a minimum speaker setup of 5.1 (5 speakers with one subwoofer). Dolby Digital 5.1 and DTS 5.1 were the two leading digital audio formats for surround sound. Dolby first introduced Dolby Digital 5.1 to the public with the American release of *Batman Returns* on June 19, 1992. *The Bouncer* supported Dolby Digital 5.1. DTS first introduced DTS 5.1 to the public with the American release of *Jurassic Park* on June 11, 1993. In 2000, the PS2 was the first game system to support Dolby Digital 5.1 and DTS 5.1.

In 2006, the PS3 was the first game system to support linear pulse-code modulation (LPCM). Dolby Digital 5.1 and DTS 5.1 require a proprietary decoder to decode the signal to send to the speakers. However, LPCM requires intensive processing power from the gaming system to internally decode surround sound channels. All current-generation systems are capable of this task. LPCM remains a popular digital audio format for players who don't have or want audio decoders supporting the other digital audio decodings. Another common speaker setup for digital surround sound is 7.1, especially for LPCM, Dolby TrueHD, and DTS-HD Master Audio.

BITSTREAM

As a continuation of digital surround sound encoding, Bitstream represents any digital audio format that encodes audio data as a stream of data bits for transmission. Bitstream includes lossy compressed formats (Dolby Digital, DTS) and lossless compressed formats (Dolby TrueHD, DTS-HD Master Audio). Although not yet termed Bitstream in 2000, *The Bouncer* supported Bitstream as Dolby Digital 5.1 audio. PCM and LPCM are not considered bitstream audio. Unlike PCM, Bitstream audio formats encode audio data, usually smaller in size than PCM data. When a device outputs bitstream audio, the device encodes the audio signal into a smaller signal for transmission (like a lossless zipped file), passed via cable to a decoding device. The decoder decodes the encoded audio signal into many sound channels of PCM audio, the intermediary digital audio format for audio speakers.

Bitstream was a popular audio output choice until game systems had the processing power to decode audio themselves. Dolby Digital and DTS support a maximum of 5.1 channels (six in total). Dolby TrueHD and DTS-HD Master Audio support a maximum of 7.1 channels (eight in all). Dolby Digital 5.1 is the standard for all worldwide DVD releases and all HD broadcasts in the United States. Additional audio channels require fast bitrates. DTS data has a bitrate of 1.5 Mb per second, and DTS-HD Master Audio has a bitrate of 3.5 Mb per second. Blu-Ray movie releases contain Dolby TrueHD and DTS-HD audio.

OPTICAL AUDIO (TOSLINK, S/PDIF)

The first cable to transmit digital audio was the optical audio cable (also known as TOSLINK). The connector end of an optical audio cable is called S/PDIF (Sony Phillips Digital Interface). When dealing specifically with audio (no video involved), the optical audio cable is the cable of choice. It can adequately transmit two channels of uncompressed audio (PCM) or compressed surround sound in 5.1 or 7.1 (Dolby Digital, DTS). The first home console to support an optical audio connection was the Sony PS2 in 2000.

Since the first HDMI cables were produced in 2003, HDMI has been the prominent single-cable solution for hooking up video game systems to televisions and audio systems. Latency or audio lag occurs during the decoding process of a digital signal to an analog signal before being output to analog speakers. At an audio latency of 16 ms, the audio lags behind the video in a distracting and even detrimental way. Analog audio solutions, like stereo PCM or Dolby Pro Logic II, are already in a readable format for audio speakers, so there is no additional time for decoding.

Multimedia Devices

Until the year 2000, video game systems had two functions. The primary function was to play video games and the secondary function was to play audio CDs. Beginning with the Microsoft Xbox in 2000 for home consoles and the Sony PSP in 2005 for handhelds, game systems began to incorporate multimedia functions into their design. Microsoft, known for the Windows operating system, added multimedia functions to the Xbox. The Xbox could play DVDs with the Xbox DVD Movie Playback Kit (a remote and infrared receiver). The Xbox could rip CDs to the internal hard drive that could be used in some games as custom soundtracks. The Xbox offered Xbox Live, an online subscription service where players could browse and download new games as well as play multiplayer games against players from around the world.

With these features, consumers could theoretically purchase one game system and use it for all of their multimedia needs: watching movies, listening to music, and playing games. The Xbox 360 and Xbox One continue this trend. The Xbox One in particular was originally designed with much more in mind. It originally was bundled with the Microsoft Kinect. When the Xbox One is hooked up to a user's cable box, the Kinect can operate the cable box using a user's voice commands. The Kinect was phased out, but game systems remained as multimedia machines.

Mobile devices had some multimedia functions in the 1990s and early 2000s (as a phone, calendar, game system, internet browser), but the release of the iPhone in 2007 sparked the smartphone movement. Multimedia devices are capable of reading various audio and video files and formats as well as running games, programs, applications, and online activity. It would be hard to imagine mobile devices today only making phone calls or only playing game apps.

Online Voice Chat

With the advent of the internet came the ability to play games online with many players. From this grew a greater need to communicate with other players to improve in strategy and to socialize in new social circles. The Dreamcast microphone was the first microphone used for online voice chat, used for *Alien Front: Online* for the Dreamcast in 2000. The PS2 headset was included with *SOCOM U.S. Navy SEALs* and supported voice recognition and online voice chat in 2002. Also in 2002, after the launch of Xbox Live, the Xbox Live Headset was released for the Microsoft Xbox to be used for online voice chat throughout all of the online multiplayer games supported by the Xbox Live online gaming service. The

Wii Speak, released in 2008 as the microphone for the Nintendo Wii, was situated by the video display and picked up sounds from an entire room. When used with the Wii Speak Channel, Wii users with Wii Speaks could talk with each other indefinitely (no game required).

2001

REMIX GAMES

A remix is a musical recording in which two or more musical tracks are mixed together by altering the volume balance of each track. Remixing is a common skill of deejays. A remix game is a video game where remixing is a primary gameplay element. In a remix game, the player takes parts of songs and remixes them into a new musical arrangement. This is usually done by pressing buttons to switch between songs. The gameplay may force changes that the player must make, or the adjustments are left up solely to the player. Remix games contrast from rhythm games in that the player has more control in changing the music, rather than reacting to a pre-arranged order of rhythms to achieve success.

Frequency, released for the PS2 on November 18, 2001, was the first remix game, allowing the player to create, save, and play remixes of the game's songs. The player controls an avatar called a "FreQ," navigating the avatar down a tunnel with eight sides, each side with a track representing a different musical phrase in the song. The player presses buttons that are indicated on each track to hit notes for that particular phrase. After completing two measures of music on a track, the music is captured and plays on its own until the next pre-arranged passage appears on the track. The player can navigate to any of the sides of the tunnel to interact with a different musical track. In Remix Mode, each song can be remixed by creating the timing and sounds of each song's instrument tracks. The tempo and instrument order remains intact for each song, but up to four players can set their own patterns using the sounds of each instrument. Players can either create a two-bar loop that is repeated three more times to form an eight-bar section or they can create an original right-bar section. Other settings in Remix mode like chorus, echo, stutter, guide, and volume are available so the players can hear what they have so far and line up all of their tracks without all of the after-effects on the tracks. For players who need assistance, the guide effect shows the song's original track with white gems on the track.

2006

LPCM (LINEAR PULSE-CODE MODULATION)

The PS3, released on November 11, 2006, was the first video game system to support audio output via LPCM. LPCM is a lossless audio format, storing audio data with a bit depth of 24 bits and a bit rate of 48 kHz. All current-generation systems can output LPCM and some support the other digital surround-sound formats. An LPCM audio stream is uncompressed and transmits via HDMI cables. LPCM is a variant of PCM with linear quantization. PCM and LPCM differ in their quantization levels. For PCM, the quantization levels change with amplitude. For LPCM, the quantization levels are linearly uniform. Some common digital audio formats that use LPCM are WAV, AIFF, and AC3 (Dolby Digital). LPCM settings on video game system support a speaker setup of 7.1. LPCM is the only digital audio output option that does not require an external audio decoder (necessary for encoded digital surround sound).

HDMI

An HDMI (High Definition Multimedia Interface) cable transmits digital video and audio in a single cable. The PS3 was the first home console with an HDMI port. HDMI supports the transmission of both video and audio streams on the same cable. It can transmit compressed (for example, Dolby TrueHD and Bitstream) or uncompressed audio data (for example, LPCM). A benefit of using HDMI cables with video game systems is called HDMI Pass-Through. By connecting the HDMI OUT of a home console to the HDMI IN of a home theater system (that connects to many audio speakers), the home theater system can receive the audio data effectively. HDMI also transmits the video stream with the audio stream, so the home theater system passes the video

data to its HDMI OUT, which is connected to the video display's HDMI IN. In effect, the video signal passes through the audio system without requiring additional cabling. All home consoles since the release of the PS3 in 2006 have an HDMI OUT port (except the Wii).

Although HDMI cables look the same, they vary in bandwidth and audio capabilities. HDMI 1.0 was released in December 2002 with a maximum bitrate of 4.9 Gbps and support for 8 channels of 7.1 PCM audio at 24-bit, 192 kHz. HDMI 1.1 was released in May 2004, adding support for the rare DVD-Audio format (a rival format to SACD). HDMI 1.1 was the first version actively supported for consumer devices at the time. HDMI 1.2 was released on August 8, 2005, adding support for DSD (the audio format used by SACDs). HDMI 1.2a was released on December 14, 2005, adding Consumer Electronic Control features and minor features not relating to audio. HDMI 1.3 was released on June 22, 2006, increasing the maximum bitrate to 10.2 Gbps. It also supported Dolby TrueHD and DTS-HD Master Audio, 7.1 lossless audio formats for surround sound and automatic audio syncing with video. The latest version of HDMI is 2.1, released on November 28, 2017, has a maximum bitrate of 48 Gbps and support for Dolby Atmos and DTS:X, object-based surround sound formats.

2007

DEVICE USAGE

Before 2007, there were two types of video game systems: home consoles and handheld gaming systems. These video game systems were devices designed primarily to play video games. The PC was a device used primarily for business,

with support for computer games as well. With the release of the Apple iPhone in North America on June 29, 2007, smartphones were mini computers with the processing and graphical power to play video games and interact with the world through the internet and mobile phone services. The audio needs of a device are dependent on the intended purpose of the device. An audiophile's dream would be to have a home theater with Dolby Atmos 7.1.4 with speakers around and overhead. However, that setup may be too extreme and costly for most players. For home consoles, the player remains in one general area for the most part. It is not ideal to carry home consoles around since they are a bit heavy and need a power supply to work. They offer the strongest video gaming experience. Home consoles are not the only way to play.

Handheld game systems are designed to be taken to play games on the go. They are lightweight and fit comfortably in the hands. They require batteries or a rechargeable battery unit to work. They are not as powerful as home consoles, but they have the advantage of traveling with players much easier. An ideal audio setup with a handheld game system is a decent pair of headphones with virtual surround sound support. The internal speakers cannot be loud and immersive in a small machine. Considering all of the real-world sounds around

players who take their games on the go, the game audio must compete with these sounds. It is not uncommon for players to turn down or mute the audio if it is not essential to gameplay.

Mobile devices like smartphones and tablets are even smaller and thinner than handheld game systems. Unlike handheld game systems, the manufacturers of these devices are not designing them specifically for gaming. They are designed as multimedia devices that are convenient for playing games, making phone calls, and updating social media. Mobile devices have become almost as essential part of many people's lives. The ease of having everything all in one device is the strongest feature of the mobile device. As for audio for games, headphones are again the best option. There are methods of transmitting the video and audio of a mobile device to a television, but the audio will not yet be as strong as a home console. Portability and accessibility are the primary design features. Audio and music are considered, but not prioritized.

2015

DOLBY ATMOS

Dolby Atmos is the next evolution of surround sound formats. Dolby Atmos was first introduced in theaters on June 22, 2012, with the Disney/Pixar CGI animated movie *Brave*. The first PC game to support Dolby Atmos was *Star Wars Battlefront* after a patch on December 10, 2015. The Xbox One gained Dolby Atmos support almost a year and a half after the first PC game supported Dolby Atmos. With Dolby Atmos, each sound recorded in a game or film is considered a sound object with a location in relation to the camera. So, when audio data is

transmitted to the Dolby-enabled audio receiver, the audio data contains all of the sound objects in the current frame and their placement from the camera. Then, the audio receiver distributes each sound object to the speaker or speakers that will best simulate the placement of the audio.

One principle of creating 3D audio is that sounds needs to be transmitted from all directions, even above the listener. So, Dolby Atmos sounds best with at least two overhead speakers (four is ideal) or two or more Dolby-enabled speakers that are facing upward to project sound. The Dolby website shows at least 39 configurations of surround speakers from as little as 2.1.0 Virtual (lacking true sound from above) to 11.1.8 Mounted or Overhead. In "11.1.8," the first number represents the number of traditional surround sound speakers. The second number represents the number of powered subwoofers, and the third number represents the number of overhead or Dolby Atmos-enabled speakers (these are the speakers that can project sound above the listener). The speaker setup is flexible, but the ideal setup should have at least two overhead speakers or two Dolby Atmos-enabled speakers so that the sounds intended above the listener can be heard above the listener. Alternatively, a Dolby Atmos-enabled soundbar simulates the height of sounds.

2020

DTS Headphone:X

DTS Headphone:X functioned similarly to Dolby Atmos for Headphones (and also Windows Sonic for Headphones). For all of the 3D audio systems, sound objects are placed in a virtual world and are distributed to the unique speaker setup by the audio system. In the case of DTS Headphone:X, headphones that support DTS Headphone:X contain enough speakers to simulate sound coming from all directions, even above the listener. Comparing DTS Headphone:X to Dolby Atmos, Dolby Atmos has a limit of 128 sound objects at any given time, while DTS Headphone:X (and DTS:X for home theaters) does not have an upper limit of sound objects. Both 3D audio formats from Dolby and DTS are comparable in their audio mixes. On July 8, 2020, Xbox One systems received support for DTS Headphone:X. Users need to download the DTS Sound Unbound app from the Xbox Store and pay the one-time fee of $20 for DTS Headphone:X functionality. DTS:X soundtracks are available on 4K Ultra Blu-ray discs, not so much in games at this time.

2022

Future Trends

Based on the current trends of the video game industry, audio fidelity and licensed music are here to stay. While surround sound setups continue to expand, especially with Dolby Atmos adding speakers above the listener, portability and pricing stunts any further growth. Users want their devices to travel with them, and ultra-immersion is not a priority when playing in environments with lots of people and external sounds. There are many more staff members on the development teams working on a game's audio and soundtrack needs. There are new opportunities for rising composers, musicians, bands, and DJs to license their music to reach a larger audience. Game patches distributed via the internet can add or remove tracks from a soundtrack for a variety of reasons. There will always be those designers who challenge the status quo by designing a game around music and sound. Even in the guise of a game, there are many software games available where users can create, save, and distribute music on their game system of choice. It would not be surprising if an upcoming game consulted with the top contributors in the community to provide a soundtrack by gamers for gamers. More control is given to players to compose music in level design without the years of study from a formal music education. The video game industry appears to prefer original content over players using their own music collection. Licensed music of the original recordings remains viable for the large-scale developers, but cover versions are more practical for programming and gameplay purposes. Audio is ever-changing in the video game industry, yet it remains an integral part of the video game experience along with the visuals and gameplay.

The video game industry is not what it was in its infancy. Once CD-DA and streaming audio were available, composers did not need to understand programming and how soundchips operated to create sounds and musical ideas. What was once specialized became much more accessible. Development teams expanded immensely, so much so that the ending credits from a major studio's game takes between 15 and 20 minutes to show all of the staff members from around the world who contributed in any small way. When it once seemed a dead-end job to compose for video games, now it is almost essential for making a name as a composer in not just the video game industry but the film, television, and music industries as well. Video games cross over into film and television and vice versa. Games receive sequels, sequels become franchises, franchises become movies and television series, and movies and television series become theme parks.

There are more opportunities for the recognition of achievements in video game audio nationally and internationally. Some of the international awards are the International Film Music Critics Association Award for "Best Original Score for a Video Game or Interactive Media" and the Global Industry Game Awards for "Music Composition," "Sound Design," and "Voice Acting." Video game soundtracks will be officially recognized by the Recording Academy at the 2023 Grammy Awards. The award for "Best Score Soundtrack for Video Games and Other Interactive Media" recognizes "excellence in score soundtrack albums comprised predominantly of original scores and created specifically for, or as a companion to, a current video game or other interactive media released within the qualification period." Unlike previous Grammy nominations and winners, composers no longer need to release their video game scores on their own or include their musical tracks in a compilation. Each eligible video game album collectively represents the musical score of its respective game. The award is a culmination of the journey of video game audio, recognizing the artistry and beauty of video game music in its purest form on the national stage of music.

Sources

Amenabar, Teddy. "A new trophy for video games: A Grammy." *The Washington Post*, 10 June 2022, www.washingtonpost.com/video-games/2022/06/10/grammys-award-video-games-score/. Accessed 13 July 2022.

Apple. "iPad Pro—Design." *Apple*, 2016, http://www.apple.com/ipad-pro/design/.

Apple. "IPad Pro—Technical Specifications." *Apple*, www.apple.com/ipad-pro/specs/. Accessed 3 Aug. 2018.

"A Beginner's Guide to Digital Signal Processing (DSP)." *Analog Devices*, www.analog.com/en/design-center/landing-pages/001/beginners-guide-to-dsp.html. Accessed 29 Nov. 2018.

Chowning, John M. "The Synthesis of Complex Audio Spectra by Means of Frequency Modulation." *Journal of the Audio Engineering Society*, vol. 21, no. 7, Sept. 1973, pp. 526–534, people.ece.cornell.edu/land/courses/ece4760/Math/GCC644/FM_synth/Chowning.pdf. Accessed 27 Nov. 2018.

DeBoer, Clint. "Understanding the Different HDMI Versions (1.0 to 2.0)." *Audioholics*, 11 Sept. 2013, www.audioholics.com/hdtv-formats/understanding-difference-hdmi-versions. Accessed 27 Apr. 2020.

"Difference Between a DSP & a DAC." *The Emotiva Lounge*, 3 Feb. 2013, emotivalounge.proboards.com/thread/28801.

"Difference Between PAM, PWM, and PPM—Comparison of PWM and PAM." *Electronic Projects for Engineering Students*, 23 Aug. 2017, www.elprocus.com/difference-between-pam-pwm-ppm/.

Dolby. "11.1.8 Mounted / Overhead Speaker Setup." *Dolby.com*, www.dolby.com/about/support/guide/speaker-setup-guides/11.1.8-mounted-overhead-speakers-setup-guide/. Accessed 21 Sept. 2020.

Dolby Laboratories. "Dolby TrueHD Audio Coding for Future Entertainment Formats." *Dolby Laboratories*, 2008, www.dolby.com/uploadedFiles/Assets/US/Doc/Professional/TrueHD_Tech_Paper_Final.pdf. Accessed 3 June 2020.

Fatnick. "IRQ: 7—The Complicated World of Early MS-DOS Sound Options." *Fatnick Industries*, 3 Sept. 2018, mechafatnick.co.uk/2018/09/03/irq-7-the-complicated-world-of-early-ms-dos-sound-options/. Accessed 29 Sept. 2020.

Fielder, Lauren. "MTV Music Generator Review." *GameSpot*, 10 Dec. 1999, www.gamespot.com/reviews/mtv-music-generator-review/1900-2548503/.

Fletcher, JC. "Rocksmith Also Available in $200 Epiphone Guitar Bundle." *Engadget*, 9 June 2011, www.engadget.com/2011/06/09/rocksmith-also-available-in-200-epiphone-guitar-bundle/.

Fries, Bruce, and Marty Fries. "Digital Audio Formats." *Digital Audio Essentials*, O'Reilly Media, Inc., 2005, pp. 155–166.

"Global Industry Game Awards—IGDA." IGDA—International Game Developers Association, 2022, igda.org/global-industry-game-awards/. Accessed 14 July 2022.

"Got Lag? Got Latency? READ THIS FIRST." *Ubisoft Forums*, 29 Oct. 2011, forums.ubi.com/showthread.php/282374-Got-Lag-Got-Latency-READ-THIS-FIRST?s=8c689cfb3d8ae47737537188776914dd.

Grammys. "New Categories for the 2023 GRAMMYs Announced: Songwriter of the Year, Best Video Game Soundtrack, Best Song for Social Change & More Changes." The Recording Academy, 9 June 2022, www.grammy.com/news/2023-grammys-new-categories-songwriter-year-best-video-game-soundtrack-social-impact-special-merit-award-65th-grammy-awards. Accessed 13 July 2022.

"GTA3 + VC Xbox—Custom Soundtracks?" *AVForums*, 16 Dec. 2003, www.avforums.com/threads/gta3-vc-xbox-custom-soundtracks.107903/.

"Jake Kaufman." *Video Game Music Preservation Foundation Wiki*, 13 Jan. 2016, www.vgmpf.com/Wiki/index.php?title=Jake_Kaufman. Accessed 6 Aug. 2018.

"The Journey of the 'PCjr./Tandy Sound Chip.'" *Nerdly Pleasures*, 10 Oct. 2015, nerdlyplea-sures.blogspot.com/2015/10/the-journey-of-pcjrtandy-sound-chip.html.

Kaufman, Jake. Interview. *Experimental Gamer Studios*, 16 Jan. 2014, www.experimentalgamer.com/interview-boot-hill-heroes-composer-jake-kaufman-download-3-tracks/.

Kaufman, Jake. Interview. *Gamasutra*, 27 Feb. 2015, www.gamasutra.com/view/news/237629/Road_to_the_IGF_Yacht_Club_Games_Shovel_Knight.php.

Kaufman, Jake. Interview. *Nintendo World Report*, 16 Oct. 2011, www.nintendoworldreport.com/interview/28011/nwr-interview-jake-kaufman.

Linneman, John. "DF Retro: Revisiting Sega's Nomad—the Original Switch?" *Eurogamer.net*, 13 May 2018, www.eurogamer.net/articles/digitalfoundry-2018-retro-revisiting-sega-nomad-the-original-switch.

Mantione, Philip. "The Fundamentals of AM Synthesis." *Pro Audio Files*, 5 Sept. 2018, theproaudiofiles.com/the-fundamentals-of-am-synthesis/.

Mantione, Philip. "Introduction to FM Synthesis." *Pro Audio Files*, 26 June 2017, theproaudiofiles.com/fm-synthesis/.

Mastrapa, Gus. "Elite Beat Agents." *The A.V. Club*, 11 Dec. 2006, games.avclub.com/elite-beat-agents-1798210323.

QSound Labs, Inc. "OEM Guide to QSound Q3D Positional 3D Audio." *QSound Labs, Inc*, Oct. 1998, www.qsound.com/2002/library/Q3d1_5.pdf. Accessed 11 Feb. 2020.

Ronspies, Wade. "REVIEW: 'Amplitude' Gifts Players with Simpler, Cheaper 'Rock Band.'" *The Daily Nebraskan*, 30 Jan. 2018, www.dailynebraskan.com/culture/review-amplitude-gifts-players-with-simpler-cheaper-rock-band/article_2092bf86-0568-11e8-9dfd-cf464005e2d6.html.

Saed, Sherif. "Rockstar Plans to Replace Music Removed from GTA 4 Due to Expired Licenses." *VG 24/7*, 11 Apr. 2018, www.vg247.com/2018/04/11/gta-4-soundtrack-songs-removed-expired-music-licenses/.

Stone, Dan. "What Is PCM Audio?" *Techwalla*, www.techwalla.com/articles/what-is-pcm-audio. Accessed 25 Nov. 2018.

Truax, Barry. "Tutorial for Frequency Modulation Synthesis." *Simon Fraser University*, www.sfu.ca/~truax/fmtut.html. Accessed 27 Nov. 2018.

"2020 IFMCA Awards." IFMCA: International Film Music Critics Association, 2 Apr. 2021, filmmusiccritics.org/awards-archive/2020-ifmca-awards/. Accessed 14 July 2022.

"What Is LPCM—Linear Pulse Code Modulated Audio." *AppGeeker*, www.appgeeker.com/audio/what-is-lpcm.html. Accessed 25 Nov. 2018.

Whitaker, Jed. "Review: Superbeat: Xonic." *Destructoid*, 30 Nov. 2015, www.destructoid.com/review-superbeat-xonic-323291.phtml.

"Yamaha DX7 FM Synthesis Tutorial: Algorithms Explained." *YouTube*, 3 May 2017, www.youtube.com/watch?v=Y1xPT5D7Oc0.

Chapter 2

The Timeline of Video Game Audio History (Hardware, Software, and Events)

Before Video Game Audio

Video game audio history begins with the convergence of gaming, video projected on a screen, and audio played through a speaker. Some developments leading up to video game audio are live musical, theatrical productions, operas and musicals, and silent film performances with live music played by an organist. Audio accompanied games in pinball machines, casino games, like slot machines, and arcade games like *Periscope*, released by Namco in 1966 in Japan, the first electromechanical game that accepted coins to operate. Video game audio is defined as audio transmitted via an audio speaker that accompanies a video display device, like a video screen or monitor. So, video game audio began with the convergence of purely electronic means for video and audio. Also, to be defined as a game, the video and audio served to accompany gameplay, a set of rules determining a win or lose condition. The inventions leading up to video game audio were the board game ("Go" sometime around 2356 BC), cathode ray tube electronic display (1897 by Ferdinand Braun, commercially released in 1922 by John B. Johnson and Harry Weiner Weinhart), an electrodynamic loudspeaker (1921 by C.W. Rice and E.W. Kellogg, commercially released in 1926), and lastly the programmable, digital computer (1941 by Konrad Zuse).

1951 in Review

Fall 1951—*Draughts*—Ferrante Mark 1

RELEASE DATE: Fall 1951 (UK). SOUND DESIGNERS: Christopher Strachey and Alan Turing. GENRE: Board. NOTABLE MUSICAL TRACK: "God Save the King."

The first song played in a video game was "God Save the King." In fall 1951, the University of Manchester in the United Kingdom was home to the Ferrante Mark 1 computer. The Ferrante Mark 1 was the first commercially available computer, although its components weighed five tons. Christopher Strachey, a mathematics teacher and a friend of Alan Turing, programmed draughts (checkers) for the computer. He also programmed the computer to play "God Save the King" at the game's conclusion. Alan Turing was responsible for adding support for musical tones on the Mark 1. At the time, the sounds of the Ferrante

Mark 1 were preserved in a recording. In 2016, researchers from the University of Canterbury in Christchurch, New Zealand, remastered the 12-inch acetate disc from 1951, removing all audio imperfections in software to create a recording that best represents the Mark 1's sounds. Other songs from the Mark 1 on the recording are "Baa, Baa Black Sheep" and "In the Mood." The tone of the computer is similar to that of a cello or a baritone saxophone. This example shows the first use of computer-generated sounds synchronized with a video game.

SOURCES

"Listening to the Music of Turing's Computer." BBC News, 1 Oct. 2016, www.bbc.com/news/magazine-37507707. Accessed 26 May 2021.

1971 in Review

November 1971—*Computer Space*— Arcade

PUBLISHER: Nutting Associates. RELEASE DATE: November 1971 (NA). Sound Designer: Ted Dabney. GENRE: Shooter.

Computer Space was the first commercially sold arcade game and video game. *Computer Space* was the work of Nolan Bushnell and Ted Dabney. Dabney was responsible for the game's audio. The game is housed within an arcade cabinet, a large unit with controls and a monitor. The cabinet includes a monaural audio speaker and audio hardware comprised of discrete audio circuits. The gameplay is similar to *Asteroids*, in which the player navigates a spaceship in a one-screen world, destroying incoming objects with bullets. *Computer Space* includes sounds for

- the rocket's engine and propulsion,
- the rocket's bullets, and
- the destruction of the rocket and enemy spaceships.

SOURCES

"Computer Space." *Media Fandom*, 13 Feb. 2017, media.fandom.com/wiki/Computer_Space. Accessed 22 Jan. 2021.

1972 in Review

November 29, 1972—*Pong*—Arcade

PUBLISHER: Atari. RELEASE DATE: November 29, 1972 (NA). Sound Designer: Allan Alcorn. GENRE: Sports.

Pong was the first commercial video game with sounds. *Pong* was designed to be simple and easy for two players to understand how to play. The game was also the first video game with commercial success. To generate the sound in the arcade cabinet, Atari engineer Al Alcorn used digital circuits to gate square wave tones from the sync generator. There are three brief sounds in the game when

- the ball hits a paddle.
- the ball hits the top or bottom wall.
- the ball moves out of play, awarding a point.

The inclusion of sound was a monumental moment in video games. The pitch frequencies between the wall and paddle sounds are just about one octave. A sound with a duration of almost three times the length of the paddle sound and a pitch frequency of a little more than a semitone higher than the paddle sound signifies a score. Also noteworthy was the synchronization of audio with graphics. In this way, players make an association between a sound and a change in the gameplay. For example, in *Pong*, a player recognizes a point based on the score sound and an increase in the displayed score number. Two players cannot play *Pong* solely through auditory cues. However, the sound cues convey the intensity of the action and the number of total points between the players.

SOURCES

"Al Alcorn Interview—Page 2." *IGN*, 10 Mar. 2008, www.ign.com/articles/2008/03/11/al-alcorn-interview?page=2.

Caprani, Ole. "The Pong Game." *Aarhus University*, 27 Sept. 2014, cs.au.dk/~dsound/DigitalAudio.dir/Greenfoot/Pong.dir/Pong.html.

1975 in Review

December 1975—*Tele-Games Pong*

PUBLISHER: Sears. RELEASE DATE: December 1975 (NA). LAUNCH PRICE: about $80. MODEL NUMBER: 25796. AUDIO: Mono.

Tele-Games Pong was the first home console with audio. Atari manufactured and sold the *Tele-Games Pong* as an exclusive for Sears for the Christmas 1975 season. The console includes two hard-wired controllers and a built-in speaker in the console

Sears Tele-Games Pong 1975. The audio output ports are coaxial (hardwired to the console's back) (Evan-Amos, "Tele-Games-Atari-Pong," CC-BY-SA 3.0).

center for analog mono audio, an audio stream representing sound emanating from one position. The console has a video out port that connects to an RF adapter that connects to the TV. The video-out port cannot send the audio signal to the television speakers. Unlike subsequent home consoles, the *Tele-Games Pong* console houses the audio speaker. *Tele-Games Pong* includes the built-in game *Pong* for one or two players. *Tele-Games Pong* was successful thanks to a proprietary *Pong* chip used for the digital score display and for the sounds of the ball hitting the paddle, the ball hitting the top and bottom walls, and the ball passing the paddle for a score. *Tele-Games Pong* is the first instance of a microprocessor chip's use for audio in place of discrete audio circuits. The benefit of the microprocessor chip is lower cost, fewer components, and reusability.

SOURCES

"Atari Pong History." *Atari Gaming Headquarters*, www.atarihq.com/dedicated/ponghistory3.php. Accessed 27 May 2021.

Manikas, Pantelis. "Atari Home Pong." *Game Medium*, gamemedium.com/console/pong. Accessed 26 May 2021.

1977 in Review

1977—*Auto Race*

MANUFACTURER: Mattel. RELEASE DATE: 1977 (NA). LAUNCH PRICE: $24.99. AUDIO: Mono.

Auto Race was the first handheld game with sound. *Auto Race* was the first completely digital handheld game. A handheld game, like *Auto Race*, fits comfortably between the player's two hands, with a digital screen for the visuals. Unlike home

consoles, which require power from a wall outlet, *Auto Race* runs on two AA batteries. In this early design, the handheld gaming system cannot connect to a TV. *Auto Race* only contains one game. It uses red LED lights for the visuals and an electronic beep from the internal speaker for mono audio. The game beeps at its conclusion, indicating either victory or defeat. Mark Lesser, the creator of *Auto Race*, also created *Football* (1977), another handheld

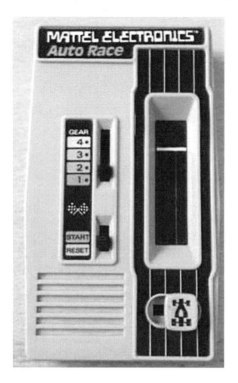

Mattel Auto Race 1977. The internal speaker is located on the device's bottom left corner (JMinter, "MAutoRace").

game. He later became a programmer for video games, working on *Frogger II* for the Atari 2600 and *NHL '94* for many gaming systems.

1977—Atari Video Music

MANUFACTURER: Atari. RELEASE DATE: 1977 (NA). PRODUCTION DATES: 1977–1978. LAUNCH PRICE: $169.95. MODEL NUMBER: C-240. AUDIO: Stereo.

Atari Video Music was the first commercial music visualizer for home use. Designed by Bob Brown at Atari, it was the first device to manipulate a television screen using audio and similar audio/visual technology to *Tele-Games Pong*. A music visualizer interprets musical data and produces a graphical display of colors and shapes based on the data. *Atari Video Music* is classified as a home console, although lacking rules or scores. The user adjusts settings on the home console, affecting what appears on the television screen. Any audio source with analog

stereo output can connect to the *Atari Video Music* with red and white analog RCA cables. *Atari Video Music* connects to the television using an RF switch box with a pass-through connector attached to the signal for TV channels. The pass-through connector allows both the *Atari Video Music* and the TV signal to reach the television without rearranging the cables. *Atari Video Music* was the first home device to support stereophonic audio. Stereophonic audio consists of two audio streams representing sounds emanating from two positions through two audio speakers.

The user manipulates the visualizations using one of five potentiometer knobs on the front of the home console. Two knobs control the size of the visual patterns for the left and right audio signals. One knob adjusts the color range from a solid color to an array of colors. The last two knobs adjust the scope of shapes generated by the left and right audio signals. The shapes vary between soft and geometric shapes. Below the knobs were 12 buttons. The buttons select between the solid, hole, and ring shapes and the number of duplicates of each shape in the horizontal and vertical directions, between one and eight. One button is an auto button used for a visualization that cycles through all button-based options. Despite the lack of rules or scores, the user can manipulate the images on the screen more so with the knobs of *Atari Video Music* than with controls of *Tele-Games Pong*. The Atari Video Music ceased manufacturing in 1978 as a financial failure.

June 10, 1977—Apple II

MANUFACTURER: Apple. RELEASE DATE: June 10, 1977 (NA). PRODUCTION DATES: June 10, 1977–1980. LAUNCH PRICE: $1,298. AUDIO: Mono.

The Apple II computer was the first personal computer with an internal audio speaker. Released by Apple, the Apple II was the first computer designed and marketed for home use. Unlike the Apple I, the price includes the Apple II computer with 4 kb of RAM, the keyboard, monochrome

Atari Video Music 1977. The audio output ports are stereo RCA (Martin Goldberg, "Atarivideomusic," CC-BY-SA 3.0).

the Atari 2600 was popular enough until 1992, even after Atari promoted its more powerful game systems. Before the Atari 2600, home consoles included dedicated audio circuits to produce sound. The Atari 2600 was the first home console to contain a PSG and to support monaural audio. The PSG is significant because programmers accessed the PSG chip to produce different types of audio. Unlike a PSG, programmers cannot write software for dedicated audio circuits, a complete hardware audio solution. The PSG makes different sounds via programming, not an entirely new set of hardware components. As a result, many games and game systems program PSGs in various ways to produce unique sounds and music.

Ron Milner was a game programmer at

monitor, two game paddles, and cassette deck (for memory storage). The Apple I, the predecessor, only included the computer unit minus the accessories. The CPU of the Apple II is the MOS 6502 microprocessor. The internal audio speaker, later known as the PC Speaker, outputs monophonic sound. In this setup, the internal speaker has two settings: "on" and "off." The computer creates musical pitches by altering the fluctuation rate between "on" and "off." The amount of time a sound is in the "on" position versus the "off" position affects the sound's timbre. For example, an audio signal 50 percent "on" and 50 percent "off" generates a square wave, a periodic waveform in which the amplitude fluctuates at a regular interval between the minimum and maximum. A monophonic audio stream is capable of a variety of timbres and pitches.

September 11, 1977—Atari 2600

MANUFACTURER: Atari. RELEASE DATE: September 11, 1977 (NA). PRODUCTION DATES: September 11, 1977–January 1, 1992. LAUNCH PRICE: $199.99 (with *Combat*). SOUNDCHIP: TIA. AUDIO: Mono.

The Atari 2600 was the first home console with a programmable sound generator (PSG) soundchip and audio output through the TV speakers. Released by Atari, Atari marketed the Atari 2600 as the Atari VCS (Video Computer System) upon initial release. It became known as the Atari 2600 after subsequent systems were called the Atari 5200 and Atari 7800. Production of

Apple II 1977. The main unit consists of the keyboard and base for the monitor and peripherals. Apple II contains a two-inch internal speaker that connects to the speaker port on the computer's back (Rama & Musée Bolo "Apple-II," CC-BY-SA 2.0 FR).

Atari in the mid–1970s responsible for the idea of Combat (1977, Atari 2600) and the programming of *Starship 1* (1977, Arcade). Regarding the decision of audio hardware for the Atari 2600, he felt that programmers could program "beyond beeps and buzzes" with the PSG, allowing the microprocessor to generate the sounds as "random noise for things like gunshots, regular sounds for motors." Although the PSG generates sounds electronically,

Atari 2600 back 1977. The audio output ports are coaxial (hardwired to the console's back) (Evan-Amos, "Atari-2600-Woody-BR").

players, through the experience of play, interpret the meaning of the sounds with whatever visual objects synchronize with the sounds. While the MOS 6502 microprocessor heralded the home computer revolution on September 16, 1975, the programmable sound generator heralded the age of video game audio.

The Atari 2600 contains a custom computer chip named the Television Interface Adaptor (TIA). The TIA controls the graphics, audio, and input for the Atari 2600, excluding the CPU. The TIA can have two sound channels of 1-bit monaural sound with 4-bit volume control (16 levels). Each sound channel from the TIA can select from 16 possible waveforms, including a square wave, sine wave, saw wave, and white noise. The Atari 2600 has at most two simultaneous sounds at any given time within the same audio signal. The TIA's mixes the two sound channels into one audio stream for the destination of one audio speaker.

Due to the TIA's design, prioritizing aural abilities over musical considerations, and the tuning accuracy of pitches, inconsistent for each of the 16 waveforms, programmers struggled to write compelling music. The out-of-tune pitches made music composition challenging for two sound channels. Most games on the Atari 2600 use the TIA for sound effects or monophonic music as a compromise. Games with more music use it as short jingles or longer loops. *Moon Patrol* (1983) and *Pengo*

(1984) allow a player to toggle the music using the left difficulty switch on the Atari 2600, but this was not common in Atari 2600 games. The Atari 7800, released in North America in May 1986, upgraded the graphical capabilities while retaining the TIA soundchip as the sole audio generator. The Atari 2600 and Atari 7800 ceased manufacturing on January 1, 1992.

SOURCES

Atari History Museum. "2600/7800 development kit." www.atarimuseum.com/ahs_archives/archives/pdf/videogames/7800/7800_devkit.pdf.

"Atari 2600 specifications." problemkaputt.de/2k6specs.htm. Accessed 3 Aug. 2018.

Boris, Dan. "The Atari 7800 ProSystem." 2013, www.atarihq.com/danb/a7800.shtml.

Boris, Dan. "Atari 7800 Tech Page." Atari Gaming Headquarters, www.atarihq.com/danb/a7800.shtml. Accessed 3 Aug. 2018.

Mattel. "Handheld Game Manual: Auto Race (Mattel)." *Internet Archive*, 1976, archive.org/details/manuals-handheld-games-Mattel-AutoRace/page/n1/mode/2up. Accessed 29 Jan. 2020.

McCrea, Nick. "Retired Developer Who Created 'NHL '94' Video Game in Maine Barn Reflects on Career." *Bangor Daily News*, 21 Feb. 2015, bangordailynews.com/2015/02/21/living/retired-developer-who-created-nhl-94-video-game-in-maine-barn-reflects-on-career/. Accessed 6 Apr. 2020.

"PC Speaker." *OSDev Wiki*, 27 June 2020, wiki.osdev.org/PC_Speaker. Accessed 26 May 2021.

"2600/7800 Development Kit." *The Atari Museum*, www.atarimuseum.com/ahs_archives/archives/pdf/videogames/7800/7800_devkit.pdf. Accessed 3 Aug. 2018.

1978 in Review

July 1978—*Space Invaders*—Arcade

MANUFACTURER: Midway. RELEASE DATE: June 19, 1978 (JP), July 1978 (NA). Designer: Tomohiro Nishikado. SERIES: *Space Invaders*. GENRE: Fixed shooter. SOUNDCHIP: SN76477. AUDIO: Mono.

Space Invaders was the first game with dynamic audio, audio that changes based on in-game actions. *Space Invaders* is the earliest example of dynamic audio that adapts to visual changes and player actions. The arcade cabinet contains the SN76477 soundchip by Texas Instruments. First released to the market in 1978, the soundchip supports one mono sound channel. That channel produces either a sine wave,

Space Invaders arcade cabinet 1978 (Coentor, "Tilt byte–11," CC-BY-SA 3.0).

pulse wave, or noise. Arcade games and home computers of the late 1970s and early 1980s preferred the SN76477. Besides *Space Invaders*, *Stratovox* (1980, also known as *Speak and Rescue*), *Vanguard* (1981), and the ABC 80 (Advanced BASIC Computer 80) contain the SN76477 soundchip.

The game's audio adjusts to gameplay changes. In *Space Invaders*, the audio's tempo, or speed, reflects how many aliens are still active on the screen. As the player destroys more and more aliens from the game area, the tempo and the audio speed reflect the intensity of the remaining aliens. Dynamic audio relays changes in gameplay to the player through sound. The player will improve in skill by listening to these audio cues. At the time of release, the CPU chip of the game was not fast enough to handle the numerous enemies on-screen, so the game lagged. *Space Invaders* exhibited dynamic audio due to the CPU processing the game more quickly as the player removes enemies from the game.

In *Space Invaders*, the player controls a laser cannon's horizontal position as rows of aliens descend toward the cannon. Four defense bunkers protect the cannon from a few shots and block the player from shooting the aliens. A short sound plays each time the aliens move horizontally or vertically. When the alien swarm reaches the side of the screen, they descend one row downward and move horizontally in the opposite direction. As the player shoots and eliminates aliens, the speed of the remaining aliens speeds up. The speed also affects the sound of the aliens' movement. The sound of the impending alien forces speeds up as fewer aliens are on-screen. When there is one remaining alien on-screen, the alien-movement sound repeatedly plays as quickly as the alien moves across the screen. If the player manages to shoot down the final alien, the movement sound ends. If the alien descends downward and reaches the player's cannon, a sound indicates destruction and loss. The flying "spaceship" sound takes precedence over the alien movement sound when a mystery spaceship travels across the top of the screen. The sounds leave much to the imagination, but their connection to gameplay activity set the standard for audio design, improving gameplay. Atari reproduced and remade the game countless times, some versions with music.

SOURCES

Kortink, J. "SN76489." 11 Dec. 2005, www.sms power.org/Development/SN76489.

"Player [1]—Space Invaders." *Discogs*, www.discogs. com/Player-1-Space-Invaders/release/944745. Accessed 23 Jan. 2021.

1979 in Review

December 3, 1979—Mattel Intellivision

MANUFACTURER: Mattel. RELEASE DATE: December 3, 1979 (NA). PRODUCTION DATES: December 3, 1979–1991. LAUNCH PRICE: $299.99 with *Las Vegas Poker & Blackjack* (1979). SOUNDCHIP: AY-3–8914. AUDIO: Mono.

The Intellivision was the first home console to support sound expansion. Released by Mattel, the Intellivision was the first home console with a CPU supporting a 16-bit instruction set. The Intellivision contains the AY-3–8914 microprocessor chip, a PSG manufactured by General Instrument supporting three sound channels, each with frequency and volume controls. A variant of the AY-3–8910, the chip includes a noise generator that sends white noise to one or more channels. A DAC mixes the three channels into a monaural audio output. Since the Intellivision, home consoles are upgraded through peripherals and add-ons, adding new capabilities and prolonging the profitability to remain relevant against modern technologies. There are two sound expansions for the Intellivision Master Component: the Intellivoice, released in 1982, and the ECS (Entertainment Computer System), released in 1983.

The Intellivoice, model 3330, released by Mattel as a peripheral for the Intellivision in North America in 1982 for about $100 with *B-17 Bomber*, added digitized voice samples to Intellivision games. The Intellivoice is a cartridge that plugs into the Intellivision to add digitized voices to Intellivision games. Although not the first peripheral supporting voice synthesis (Magnavox Odyssey 2 Voice), it was the first to send the audio output to the television speakers. The Intellivoice team was Ron Carlson, developer of the hardware; Ron Surratt, the software programmer; and Patrick Jost, analyst and editor of the voice data. The Intellivoice uses the General Instruments SP-0256 "Orator" speech-synthesis chip for audio. The chip's 16 KB of ROM (called Resident ROM internally) contains a standardized vocabulary of words and phrases available for all Intellivoice games, like "left," "right," and "Mattel Electronic Presents." The output of the Intellivoice is a 40 kHz Pulse Width Modulation (PWM) signal, which passes through a low pass filter, converted to analog audio, and directed to the Intellivision Master Component. Only five games supported its audio features.

Space Spartans was the first game for any home console to support synthesized speech. Along with *Space Spartans*, the other two games available at the launch of the Intellivoice were *Bomb Squad* (1982) and *B-17 Bomber* (1982). Of the five games, *World Series Major League Baseball* (1983) supports the ECS in conjunction with the Intellivoice, although it does not require the Intellivoice to operate. *World Series Major League Baseball, a*lso known as *Intellivision World Series Baseball*, was the first home console game with play-by-play audio commentary and stadium background music. The remaining Intellivoice game was *Tron: Solar Sailer* (1982). Mattel developed and published all five games for the Intellivision. *Magic Carousel*, a finished but unreleased Intellivoice game, is a children's educational game that asks players to play the piano and answer a telephone.

Mattel Intellivision 1979. The audio output ports are mono RCA (with RF adapter) (Evan-Amos, "Intellivision-Console-Set," CC-BY-SA 3.0).

Mattel Intellivision II 1983. The audio output ports are mono RCA (with RF adapter) (Evan-Amos, "Intellivision-II-Console-Set," CC-BY-SA 3.0).

Mattel Intellivoice 1982. The Intellivoice lacks audiovisual output ports. It communicates with the Intellivision through the cartridge port. The volume slider modulates the voice volume produced from the Intellivoice (Evan-Amos, "Intellivoice," CC-BY-SA 3.0).

The Intellivoice and all staff at Mattel Electronics assigned to the Intellivoice ceased manufacturing on April 4, 1983. Mattel never fulfilled an Intellivoice model for the Intellivision II and an integrated Intellivoice for an Intellivision III. The quality of voice data on game cartridges was restricted to 4 to 8 kB, forcing programmers to store voice samples at a lower sampling rate, even editing the rate mid-word between vowels and consonants. Due to the limited vocabulary and haphazard audio quality, demand for Intellivoice games waned quickly after the initial release.

The Intellivision II, released by Mattel in North America in the 2nd quarter of 1983 for $150, was the first revision of a home console. It was released in 1984 in Brazil under the name Digiplay Intellivision II. The main improvement was an external video input on the cartridge port for the System Changer, a peripheral for playing Atari 2600 games on the Intellivision. The EXEC (main game program), stored in the Intellivision II's ROM chip, causes minor audio problems in Intellivision games due to a slight timing error during the EXEC. In *Space Spartans*, the subroutine diminishes the audio quality of the explosions. In *Shark! Shark!*, the subroutine reduces the audio quality of the bubbles.

The Intellivision ceased manufacturing in 1991 after a 12-year run. The Intellivision was the first home console to embrace audio expansion through multiple peripherals: standard voice samples (Intellivoice), audio expansion (ECS), and a synthesizer controller (Music Synthesizer). The Intellivision is one of the only gaming systems to directly play the ROMs of another gaming system (similar functionality is associated with a single console manufacturer). Terrence Valeski, former vice president of Mattel Electronics, bought the rights to the Intellivision and its gaming library in 1984, forming INTV Corporation. The new company supported the Intellivision for seven more years, releasing two completed games by Mattel and publishing 21 games.

Sources

Blue Sky Rangers. "Intellivoice Speech Synthesis Module #3330." *Blue Sky Rangers Intellivision History*, history.blueskyrangers.com/hardware/intellivoice.html. Accessed 22 Apr. 2021.

"Intellivision Master Component #2609." *Intellivision Productions*, www.intellivisionlives.com/bluesky/hardware/intelli_tech.html. Accessed 3 Aug. 2018.

"Intellivoice." *Retro Consoles Wiki*, 28 May 2013, retroconsoles.fandom.com/wiki/Intellivoice. Accessed 31 Jan. 2020.

"Master Component #2609." *Blue Sky Rangers Intellivision History*, history.blueskyrangers.com/hardware/2609.html. Accessed 9 June 2021.

1980 in Review

May 1980—*Stratovox*—Arcade

Publisher: Taito. Release Date: May 1980 (JP), August 1980 (NA, EU). Soundchip: AY-3–8910, SN76477. Audio: Mono. Genre: Fixed shooter.

Stratovox was the first game to use speech audio samples. Released in arcades in Japan as *Speak and Rescue*, *Stratovox* plays audio samples of short phrases on two PSGs. The arcade hardware includes the AY-3-8910 and the SN76477. Programmers discovered how to synthesis speech on PSGs despite chip manufacturers never designing them to process speech samples. Despite the combined abilities of the two soundchips, the speech quality is inferior but adequate. In English, the short phrases include "help me," "very good," "we'll be back," and "lucky." In the Japanese release by Sun Electronics, the people in the game shout "Tasukete" instead of "Help me." With spoken audio in games, audio localization becomes vital to maintain comprehensibility across all world regions. Besides the voice samples, some of the other sounds in *Stratovox* are the enemy spaceships (the sounds change in pitch as they approach the player's ship), the player ship's bullets, the destruction of an enemy spaceship, a bonus jingle, and the destruction of the player ship.

May 22, 1980—*Pac-Man*—Arcade

Publisher: Midway Games. Release Date: May 22, 1980, as *Puck Man* (JP), October 1980 (NA), 1980 (EU). Series: *Pac-Man*. Soundchip: Namco WSG. Audio: Mono. Genre: Maze. Notable musical track: "Intermission."

Pac-Man was the first game to generate sound via wavetable synthesis. Released in the arcades, *Pac-Man* was a top-rated arcade game at the time. It was the first game to use the Namco WSG soundchip. *Pac-Man* was the first game to use the Namco Waveform Sound Generator (WSG) soundchip. The Namco WSG was released earlier in 1980, later used in *Galaga* (1981).

The Namco WSG was one of the earliest soundchips to generate sound via wavetable synthesis, also known as table-lookup synthesis, an evolution from programmable sound generation. Wavetable synthesis is a means to create sound using a data table of different waveforms. The Namco WSG supports three channels of single-cycle wavetable synthesis with 4 bits of waveform sampling. The Namco WSG uses 4 bits for each sample and one step. Each sound channel of the Namco WSG selects 16 unique waveforms (the number of samples multiplied by steps equals the number of possible unique waveforms). At the time, the lack of additional bits per sample and steps limited the possible sounds of the Namco WSG. Wavetable synthesis generates more convincing sounds using more bits per sample and many steps.

Pac-Man (1980) had a short jingle to introduce each level along with lots of sound effects. The jingle accompanies the words "Ready!" and lasts about four

Pac-Man arcade cabinet 1980 (BugWarp CC-BY-SA 4.0).

seconds with a melody and bass line. The famous "waka-waka" sound accompanies Pac-Man, the main character in yellow, as he swallows a pellet from the maze. A siren indicates the four ghosts actively searching for and moving toward Pac-Man throughout the maze. The siren switches to another wobbling sound to indicate the ghosts are in blue "defense" mode. A sound effect declares the moment in which Pac-Man eats the ghost and gains the points. Another high-pitched sound effect indicates an eaten ghost, represented only by a spooky pair of eyes, returning to the ghost home base. As Pac-Man consumes more and more of the maze pellets, the siren sound gets higher in pitch. A gulping sound indicates when Pac-Man consumes a piece of fruit or a key in the maze. There is no fanfare for completing a stage or

beginning the new one. The notable musical track, "Intermission," plays during the short, comical cutscenes.

July 1980—*Missile Command*— Arcade

Publisher: Atari. Release Date: July 1980 (NA), 1980 (EU). Soundchip: POKEY. Audio: Mono. Genre: Shmup.

Missile Command was the first video game to use the Potentiometer and Keyboard Integrated Circuit (POKEY) soundchip. *Missile Command* had the best audio of arcade games at its release due to the POKEY, an improved soundchip. The POKEY supports four sound channels with either square waves (and duty cycles very close to square) or white noise. When two or more sound channels are active at any given time, the soundchip's pitch accuracy worsens due to the control architecture of the chip. The soundchip mixes the four channels into a monaural audio signal. Some of the sounds in *Missile Command* include a siren, missile release, missile explosion, point tally, plane and flying objects, low missile warning, and bonus city award. The arcade games *Asteroids Deluxe* (1980), *Centipede* (1981), and *Gauntlet* (1985) also use the POKEY soundchip.

November 1980—*Rally-X*—Arcade

Publisher: Midway Games. Release Date: November 1980 (JP), February 1981 (NA). Composer: Nobuyuki Ohnogi. Series: *Rally-X*. Soundchip: Namco WSG. Genre: Maze. Audio: Mono. Notable musical track: "Rally-X Theme."

Rally-X was the first game with continuous background music. The game was released by Namco in Japan in 1980 and licensed to Midway Games for U.S. manufacture and distribution in 1981. Earlier games had music for brief moments in jingles or sound effects, nothing composed to continuously play over the main game and the game's sound effects. The gameplay involves driving a car around a maze to collect flags while avoiding chasing cars by shooting smoke screens. The arcade board includes the Namco WSG, which supports three channels of sound. The notable musical track, "Rally-X Theme," lasts about 12 seconds before looping. The game includes three jingles for game start, challenging stage start, and game over, and 10 sounds including car engine, checkpoint, and fuel added to score. Unlike the other game sounds, discrete audio circuitry generates the crash sound. *Rally-X* was the first game to feature a bonus round and a map view.

Sources

Midway Mfg. Co. "Midway's Rally-X Parts and Operating Manual." *Internet Archive*, Jan. 1981, archive.org/details/ArcadeGameManualRallyx/mode/2up. Accessed 26 May 2021.
"Rally-X Arcade Video Game by NAMCO (1980)." *Gaming History*, www.arcade-history.com/?n=-rally-x&page=detail&id=2171. Accessed 15 Aug. 2018.

1981 in Review

1981—*Snafu*—Intellivision

Publisher: Mattel. Release Date: 1981 (NA). Composer: Russ Lieblich. Genre: Snake game. Notable musical track: "Game Over."

Snafu was the first home console game with continuous theme music. The soundtrack contains two short melodic tracks. Unlike a musical jingle, a composer prepares music to play indefinitely for the duration of a game scene through looping and the repetition of musical sections. The first track indicates that the current round of play had reached the "showdown" stage, in which only two-player trails remain. When playing a two-player game, this track plays throughout the entire round. The notable musical track, "Game Over," signals the game's completion when only one player remains. Even in the absence of music, sound effects mark the movement and crashing of the serpents.

July 9, 1981–*Donkey Kong*—Arcade

Publisher: Nintendo. Release Date: July 9, 1981 (JP), July 31, 1981 (NA), 1981 (EU).

Series: *Donkey Kong*. Soundchip: i8035. Audio: Mono. Genre: Platformer. Notable musical track: "Radar (Stage Intro)."

Donkey Kong was one of the earliest arcade games to have background music throughout gameplay. The game introduced the world to Mario, the playable character used in most games by Nintendo. Hirokazu "Hip" Tanaka provided the sound effects for the game. A short jingle plays to begin each new stage. The jingle uses two sound channels in a minor key with a melodic trill. A thumping sound effect plays while Donkey Kong, the game's antagonist, bends the stage's platforms. Another sound effect represents Donkey Kong's laughter. The notable musical track, "Radar (Stage Intro)," is a more light-hearted jingle that accompanies the screen that displays the text "How High Can You Get?" There are no music or sound effects on the attract screen.

Sources

Red Bull Music Academy. "Hirokazu Tanaka on Nintendo Game Music, Reggae and Tetris." *YouTube*, 22 Nov. 2014, www.youtube.com/watch?v=F7J5GlE3YLQ. Accessed 9 Apr. 2020.

1982 in Review

1982—*Journey Escape*—Atari 2600

Publisher: Data Age. Release Date: 1982 (NA). Notable musical track: "Don't Stop Believin' (Intro)."

Journey Escape was one of the first games to use popular music in its soundtrack. The game was a collaborative work of the band Journey, the first tie-in of a video game with the release of a band's album (*Escape* in 1981). The music during the main gameplay is unrelated to Journey or the *Escape* album. The notable musical track "Don't Stop Believin' (Intro)" from the album *Escape* is heard on the title screen. Due to the audio limitations of the Atari 2600, the track was programmed as a chiptune, retaining only the melody and bass with basic waveforms.

August 1982—ColecoVision

MANUFACTURER: Coleco. RELEASE DATE: August 1982 (NA), July 1983 (EU). LAUNCH PRICE: $175 with *Donkey Kong*. SOUNDCHIP: SN76489A. AUDIO: Mono.

The *ColecoVision* offered the best graphics and audio for a home console at the time. Released by Coleco, the ColecoVision has the most advanced audio hardware of its competition, the Atari 2600 and the Intellivision. *Donkey Kong*, the pack-in game, looked and played much better than other ports on competing game systems. The ColecoVision contains the Texas Instruments SN76489A soundchip. The chip includes a PSG supporting a maximum of four sound channels. Three channels use tone generators to produce square waves only, and one channel operates a noise generator for white noise. The SN76489A mixes the four sound channels to a mono audio signal.

The ColecoVision ceased manufacturing in October 1985. The ColecoVision was the first home console of the 80s to conclude its manufacturing run. There were still games developed and released for the ColecoVision for another year. However, once a console is no longer manufactured, the release of new games will inevitably dry up as well. The video game industry crash hurt Coleco, and Coleco never released another console. Even though the ColecoVision had superior hardware, its advantages didn't translate to increased sales and business.

ColecoVision back 1982. The audio output ports are mono RCA (with RF adapter) (Evan-Amos, "ColecoVision-Console-BR").

ColecoVision RF adapter 1982. It connects to the ColecoVision's RF port and outputs audio in analog mono (Evan-Amos, "ColecoVision-RF-Adapter").

August 1982—Commodore 64

MANUFACTURER: Commodore. RELEASE DATE: August 1982 (NA). LAUNCH PRICE: $595. SOUNDCHIP: SID. AUDIO: Mono.

The Commodore 64 was one of the first personal computers with a soundchip. Released by Commodore, the C64 was a successful personal computer with many great computer games. The C64 contains the MOS Technology 6581, more commonly referred to as the SID (Sound Interface Device) soundchip. Bob Yannes, the developer of the SID chip, is the co-founder of the Ensoniq synthesizer company. The SID chip supports three sound channels, each with an ADSR envelope generator and filter capabilities. Ring modulation makes use of the third sound channel to work with the other two channels. Each of the SID's sound channels may use at least five different waveforms: pulse wave with variable duty cycle, triangle wave, sawtooth wave, white noise, and specific complex/combined waveforms when multiple waveforms are selected simultaneously. A sound channel using a triangle waveform can be ring-modulated with one of the other sound channels. Each sound channel can be routed into a standard, digitally controlled analog 12-dB/octave multimode filter. A programmer individually selects the filter's lowpass, bandpass, and highpass outputs for final output amplification via the master volume register. The filter's cut-off frequency and resonance are adjustable. External audio fed through the audio-in port can use the filter as well.

Commodore 64 back 1982. The audio output ports are mono RCA (with RF adapter) (Evan-Amos, "Commodore-64-Computer-BR").

Arpeggiation, the rapid cycling between two or more frequencies, is a technique used to simulate chords on the C64. Four-bit digitized audio playback is possible by continuously updating the master volume with sampled data. In 2008, a method was discovered to play four channels of 8-bit audio samples through one of the SID's sound channels. Some video game composers began experimenting with programming and music composition on a C64 computer.

The Magic Voice Speech Module, released by Commodore in 1984, plugs into the cartridge port of the C64. It allows any software to incorporate a female voice with a 235-word vocabulary. A game can adjust the quality of the voice to sound less feminine. A programmer sets the rate of speed between 0.65 and 1.4 times a "standard" speaking speed. Users could program the Magic Voice to talk in either BASIC or 6502 assembly language using a command like "SAY 'HI.'" The vocabulary includes all 26 letters, numbers from zero to one million (only 21-word fragments needed), 11 colors, and many other essential words for conversation. Two recreational games that use the Magic Voice are *Gorf* (1983) and *Wizard of Wor* (1983). Both games add additional vocabulary words for use with the Magic Voice that apply to their gameplay. One of the phrases in *Gorf* is "Prepare yourself for annihilation." One of the phrases of *Wizard of Wor* is "Garwor and Thorwor become invisible! Hahahaha!"

The voice used in both games is rather tinny and robotic. However, considering that speech technology was available and programmable in 1983, this was an advancement in audio. Atop the Magic Voice is a cartridge port. Almost all games, even those not optimized for the Magic Voice, work when plugged into the Magic Voice. A phono plug is required to connect the audio out port of the Magic Voice with the audio/video port of the C64.

The C64 ceased manufacturing in April 1994. Although still in demand despite obsolete hardware, the disk drive of the unit was more expensive than the entire computer. The C64 was most popular in the UK and Europe. Over 12 years of support, the C64 competed against the Amiga 500 (with PCM audio), disc-based machines (with CD-DA), and PC operating systems by Apple (Mac OS 7.1 and 7.5) and Microsoft (Windows NT 3.1 and 3.5). Developers targeted computer games to a specific OS rather than a particular computer model. Computer games could optionally support one or more soundcards (as supported by the OS).

October 1982—*Carnival*— ColecoVision

PUBLISHER: Coleco. RELEASE DATE: October 1982 (NA), 1982 (EU). NOTABLE MUSICAL TRACK: "Sobre Las Olas (Main Theme)."

Carnival was the first game for home consoles to use two or more sound channels for music. The game is based on

Carnival (1980, Arcade). The main action takes place in a shooting gallery. *Carnival* is the first game with a bonus round after regular gameplay. The bonus round takes place in the bear rack, in which targets with bear images move and switch direction. The music icon, located below the row scores on the right side of the screen, toggles the music. The notable musical track, "Sobre Las Obras (Main Theme)," is the 1888 waltz "Sobre Las Olas" ("Over the Waves") composed by Mexican composer Juventino Rosas. The track plays as background music throughout the game. This piece has a musical association with carnivals and fairs, used as one of the songs for the Wurlitzer fairground organs.

SOURCES

Boris, Dan. "ColecoVision Sound Generation Hardware." *Atari Gaming Headquarters*, www.atarihq.com/danb/files/CV-Sound.txt. Accessed 3 Aug. 2018.

Brannon, Charles. "Magic Voice Speech For The 64." *COMPUTE!*, Oct. 1984, p. 102, www.atarimagazines.com/compute/issue53/036_2_REVIEWS_Magic_Voice_Speech_For_The_64.php. Accessed 16 Nov. 2018.

"Carnival." *Blue Sky Rangers Intellivision History*, history.blueskyrangers.com/coleco/carnival.html. Accessed 18 Jan. 2021.

ColecoVision sound generation hardware. (n.d.). Retrieved from ftp://ftp.komkon.org/pub/EMUL8/Coleco/Docs/CV-Sound.txt.

"ColecoVision Technical." A Danish ColecoVision Site, 17 Sept. 2015, www.colecovision.dk/technical.htm.

Commodore. "Commodore Magic Voice Speech Module." *Cubic Team & $eeN and Other Demo Scene Related Stuff*, www.cubic.org/~doj/c64/magic.html. Accessed 16 Nov. 2018.

"Commodore 64–1872." *Obsolete Technology*, 21 July 2014, www.oldcomputers.net/c64.html.

Inns, Simon. "Commodore SID 6581 Datasheet." *Waiting for Friday*, 26 Mar. 2010, www.waitingforfriday.com/?p=661.

Jeepyurongfu. "The classics: Carnival." 2016, www.jeepyurongfu.com/86155946-the-classics-carnival/.

MSX Resource Center. "4 Channels of 8-bit Sound + 2 Original Sounds on Standard C64. Why Not MSX?" *MSX Resource Center*, 30 May 2010, www.msx.org/forum/development/msx-development/4-channels-8-bit-sound-2-original-sounds-standard-c64-why-not-msx.

1983 in Review

1983—*Melody Blaster*—Intellivision

PUBLISHER: Mattel. RELEASE DATE: 1983 (NA). COMPOSER: Hall Cannon. GENRE: Music/Rhythm. NOTABLE MUSICAL TRACK: "Blaster's Blues."

Melody Blaster was the first video game for home consoles to support a music keyboard. The game harnessed the full audio potential of the Intellivision. *Melody Blaster* was the only software ever released for the 49-key Music Synthesizer add-on for the Intellivision (*Melody Maker* and *Melody Conductor* were unreleased). The game requires both the Music Synthesizer and the Entertainment Computer System (ECS) Computer Module to properly play the game and hear the music as intended. *Melody Blaster* uses the combined audio hardware of the Intellivision Master Component, ECS, and music keyboard.

The screen displays a visualization of the musical keyboard, although lacking musical notation. The player presses the corresponding keys displayed on the on-screen representation to follow a song. Options include adjusting the song's speed and whether the player needs to play the right, left, or both hands or allow the computer to play everything. The player chooses from 11 songs. The notable musical track, "Blaster's Blues," is an original song for the game. Other musical tracks from the public domain include "Row, Row, Row Your Boat," "When the Saints Go Marching In," "Chopsticks," a Bach fugue, "Greensleeves," "Jingle Bells," "Beethoven's 5th," "The Entertainer," and "Twinkle, Twinkle, Little Star." The player can also record original songs. The game's instruction manual mentions additional song cassettes, but they were never produced. The skills from gameplay are transferrable to the musical study of the piano or organ. Other games that use musical keyboards connected to gaming systems or computers are *Doremiko* for the Famicom Disk System on December 4, 1987, and *The Miracle Piano Teaching System* for Mac, Windows, NES, SNES, and Genesis in 1990. *The Miracle Piano Teaching System* includes musical notation and lessons.

1983—*Journey*—Arcade

PUBLISHER: Bally Midway. RELEASE DATE: 1983 (NA). COMPOSERS: Elaine Ditton and Steve Meyer. GENRE: Action. NOTABLE MUSICAL TRACK: "Separate Ways (Worlds Apart)."

Journey was the first game to use the master recording of a popular song. The game was designed around the rock band Journey, projecting digitized graphics of the band's members in black and white. The game's plot revolves around each band member retrieving his musical instrument and then using it to return to the band's vehicle. Two AY-3–8910 soundchips produce the songs "Chain Reaction," "Don't Stop Believin'," "Lights," "Still They Ride," "Stone in Love," and "Wheel in the Sky." These songs come from the albums *Captured* (two songs), *Escape* (three songs), and *Frontiers* (one song). Unlike other Journey songs that play from the AY-3–8910 soundchips, the arcade unit houses a cassette player to play a looped excerpt of "Separate Ways (Worlds Apart)" from the master recording from *Escape* during the game's bonus round. Herbie Herbert, Journey's tour manager and bodyguard, prevents fans from stealing the musical instruments retrieved in the bonus round. The audio quality of the excerpt is as good as an audio cassette tape (acceptable quality over a PSG soundchip). Like laser-disc technology, cassette players have faults and audio degradation more regularly than soundchips.

June 19, 1983—*Dragon's Lair*— Arcade

PUBLISHER: Cinematronics. RELEASE DATE: June 19, 1983 (NA, EU). COMPOSER: Christopher Stone. AUDIO: Stereo. GENRE: Interactive movie. NOTABLE MUSICAL TRACK: "Opening Sequence."

Dragon's Lair was a game of many firsts: laserdisc technology, stereophonic audio, orchestral audio samples, and animated FMV (full-motion video). Released in the arcades, the game displays animated FMV cutscenes requiring critical actions to proceed. The player executes an action by moving the joystick or pressing the sword button at a specific moment to clear each QTE (quick-time event). FMV segments continue the scene for correct or incorrect input selections. The randomization of its limited scenes improves the game's replayability.

The game, released by Cinematronics, takes advantage of additional memory afforded by laserdisc technology, not marketed for consumer use until 1984. The Pioneer PR-7820 was the first mass-produced industrial LaserDisc player, included in *Dragon's Lair*. A laserdisc stores analog video and audio as PWM data represented on the disc's surface as pits and lands of varying widths, encoding FM video and audio. The 22 minutes of hand-drawn animation, drawn at $1.3 million, was by Don Bluth of Don Bluth Studios. The rest of the production team included Rick Dyer of Advanced Microcomputer Systems and Cinematronics. To save money, crew members provided the voices. The voice cast includes sound engineer Dan Molina as Dirk the Daring, head of assistant animators Vera Lanpher as Princess Daphne, and Michael Rye as the narrator. The game stores all sound as analog PWM samples, including water, monkey screams, bat shrieks, sword clangs, wind, human gasps and cries, explosions, lasers, bubbles, and fire. The soundtrack is stored as stereo analog FM audio. Unlike other games at the time, the arcade cabinet houses a left and right audio speaker. The soundtrack and audio samples contain panning data, information regarding which speaker to play from, and the intensity.

In addition to the stereo analog audio from the laserdisc, the arcade cabinet contains the AY-3–8910 soundchip for feedback sounds, acknowledging a coin drop to the arcade machine and joystick movement. The AY-3–8910, released by General Instrument in 1978, was a very popular soundchip since 1978 and through the 1980s in arcade games, home consoles, and personal computers. The AY-3–8910 is a PSG with support for three sound channels mixed to a mono audio output. The PSG contains a tone generator that produced square waves and a noise generator that converts one channel to white noise. It was common to take advantage of six sound channels by using two AY-3–8910 chips in tandem. Some popular arcade games that use the AY-3–8910 or its variants are the following: *Frogger* (1981), *Popeye* (1982), *Tron* (1982), *Dragon's Lair* (1983), *Spy Hunter* (1982), *Tapper* (1983), *1942* (1984), and *Solomon's Key* (1986). The variants of the AY-3–8910 are AY-3–8912, AY-3–8913, and AY-3–8914. Yamaha's modification of the AY-3–8910 was the YM2419. The AY8930P is an improved AY-3–8910 by Microchip Technology.

The notable musical track, "Opening Sequence," plays during the attract screen of the game, which highlights the game's characters, plot, and player role. The track, at 43 seconds, swells when the action is intense and ducks when the narration is prevalent. Some instruments heard alongside the narration and sound effects include trumpet, timpani, glockenspiel, and harp. A brass ensemble brings a heroic tone to the track, advancing the animated presentation toward a dangerous and courageous quest. At the time, these sounds were only possible through laserdisc technology (voice samples from a soundchip were still fair from the clarity of those on laserdisc).

July 15, 1983—Nintendo Family Computer

MANUFACTURER: Nintendo. RELEASE DATE: July 15, 1983 (JP). PRODUCTION DATE: July 15, 1983–September 25, 2003. LAUNCH PRICE: 14,800 yen. MODEL NUMBER: HVC-001. SOUNDCHIP: Ricoh 2A03. AUDIO: Mono.

The Famicom was the first home console to include an internal microphone in one of its controllers. Released exclusively in Japan, the Famicom was Nintendo's first home console. The Famicom paved the way for the Nintendo Entertainment System and great success for the Nintendo brand. The Famicom's audio output is monophonic through an RF adapter. The controller marked "II" contains the internal microphone. The two controllers of the Famicom are hardwired into the console. Only a few games use the microphone simply as an input recognizing activation (by blowing into it, whistling, or clapping). *Kid Icarus* and *The Legend of Zelda* (with the Famicom Disk System) are two Famicom games that cleverly interweave the microphone within gameplay.

The Famicom contains the Ricoh 2A03 soundchip, also included in the NES. It is a modified version of the MOS 6502, one of the most popular and least expensive microprocessors available since its introduction in 1975. The 2A03 supports five sound channels. Two of the sound channels support pulse waves with four selectable duty cycles. One sound channel supports triangle waves. One sound channel supports noise. The final sound channel uses rudimentary DMA (direct memory access) for the playback of audio samples encoded by Delta modulation. It also has channels for audio samples, especially DPCM, frequently used in Famicom and NES games.

The Famicom's hardware mixes audio from sound expansion chips embedded within Famicom cartridges. The transmission of audio moves from the Famicom through the cartridge and then back into the Famicom. The Famicom mixes the audio channel of its soundchip and the soundchips within Famicom cartridges into a mono audio signal. Only 26 Famicom games modify the Famicom's audio signal in this fashion with sound expansion chips. Game developers targeting the Famicom created custom soundchips, including them inside game cartridges to offer robust soundtracks. Sound expansion was a massive advantage for the Famicom, improving the quality of audio and music over the Famicom's lifespan. The NES design, almost identical to the Famicom, lacks the hardware necessary for this feature. NES ports of Famicom games had to be reprogrammed without the additional audio features to compensate for the lack of sound expansion support and to accommodate the five sound channels of the NES's soundchip. There were at least five sound-expansion chips used in Famicom games.

Each game developer designed its soundchip for the audio needs of its games. The sound-expansion chips add sound channels and sound types to the Famicom's exist-ing audio set. The Namco N163 (used in *Sangokushi: Chuu-gen no Hasha* [1988]) supports

Nintendo Family Computer 1983. The audio output ports are mono RCA (with RF adapter) (Evan-Amos, "Nintendo-Famicom-Console-Set-FL").

a configuration between one and eight sound channels capable of wavetable synthesis. The Konami Virtual ROM Controller 6 (used in *Akumajou Den-setsu* [1989]) adds two pulse wave channels with eight duty cycles and one sawtooth wave channel. The Konami Virtual ROM Controller 7 (used in *Lagrange Point* [1991]) supports six sound channels of two-operator FM synthesis. The Nintendo Multi Memory Controller 5 (used in *Shin 4 Nin Uchi Mahjong: Yakuman Tengoku* [1991]) adds two pulse wave channels and one PCM channel. The Sunsoft 5B (used in *Gimmick!* [1992]) adds three square wave channels.

The Famicom Disk System (HVC-022), released in Japan on February 21, 1986, for 15,000 yen, was the first peripheral for home consoles to read games from floppy disks. The Ricoh RP2C33 is the soundchip integrated into the hardware of the Famicom Disk System. The RAM adapter of the FDS contains the audio hardware. The RP2C33 supports one sound channel with primitive wavetable support. Using a wavetable, an audio programmer creates a unique sound wave. The precision of a wave sample is 64 steps of 8-bit samples, resulting in 4,096 possible waveforms. The FDS was capable of many more timbres than any other game system on the market at the time.

Most FDS disks used the wavetable chan-nel of the RP2C33. In the Famicom Disk Sys-tem version of *The Legend of Zelda* (1986), wavetable synthesis generates the bell-like

Nintendo Famicom with Famicom Disk System 1986. The Famicom Disk System lacks audiovisual output ports. It communicates with the Fami-com through the Famicom's cartridge port (Evan-Amos, "Nintendo-Famicom-Disk-System").

tones used in the music and sound effects. Other games with noticeable changes in music and audio between the FDS and NES/Famicom version include *Metroid* (1986) and *Kid Icarus* (1986). The Nintendo FDS ceased manufacturing in 1990. Since Nin-tendo sold the FDS exclusively in Japan, the FDS games were reprogrammed as ROM cartridges outside of Japan, lacking the sound expansion of the RP2C33 and using internal batteries within the cartridges to save data. Overall, there was more potential with inserting batteries and new chips in the cartridge than for the floppy disk of the FDS.

The Famicom ceased manufacturing on September 25, 2003. Nintendo fixed faulty Famicom units until 2007. The Famicom had a longer manufacturing run than the NES. However, they were similar gaming systems in terms of hardware specifications. Nintendo's first home console in Japan was widely popular even after the Super Famicom, N64, 64DD, and GameCube releases.

SOURCES

Blue Sky Rangers. "Melody Blaster." *Blue Sky Rangers Intellivision History*, history.bluesky-rangers.com/mattelelectronics/games/melody-blaster.html. Accessed 10 Apr. 2021.

"Entertainment Computer System." *Intellivision Productions*, www.intellivisionlives.com/bluesky/games/credits/ecs.shtml. Accessed 16 Nov. 2018.

"Famicom Disk System: The More You Play It, the More You'll Want to Play [Disk 2]." *Metroid Database*, Sept. 2004, wayback.archive.org/web/20160723015114/www.metroid-database.com:80/m1/fds-interview2-p0.php. Accessed 14 Aug. 2018.

"Famicom Expansion Audio Overview." *Nerdly Pleasures*, 4 Aug. 2017, nerdlypleasures.blogspot.com/2017/08/famicom-expansion-audio-overview.html. Accessed 30 Sept. 2020.

Famitracker Wiki. "Sound hardware." 28 Mar. 2015, famitracker.com/wiki/index.php?title=-Sound_hardware. Accessed 30 Jan. 2016.

"Four Player Games & Expansion Audio Games." *Analogue*, 25 June 2018, support.analogue.co/hc/en-us/articles/225770047-Four-Player-Games-Expansion-Audio-Games.

George, G.D. "Atari 7800 vs. Nintendo NES." 19 Mar. 2014, www.ataritimes.com/?Article IDX=632.

Hopkins, Christopher. *Chiptune music: An exploration of compositional techniques as found in Sunsoft games for the Nintendo Entertainment System and Famicom from 1988–1992.* Five Towns College, PhD Dissertation. *ProQuest Dissertations and Theses.* Accessed 25 Jan. 2020.

Iggy. "The Official Famicom Switch Controller's Microphone Actually Works." *NintendoSoup*, 24 Mar. 2019, nintendosoup.com/the-official-famicom-switch-controllers-microphone-actually-works/. Accessed 30 Sept. 2020.

"Journey (1983)/Walkthrough." *StrategyWiki*, 29 Oct. 2014, strategywiki.org/wiki/Journey_(1983)/Walkthrough. Accessed 15 Aug. 2018.

"Journey—Videogame by Bally Midway." *International Arcade Museum*, www.arcade-museum.com/game_detail.php?game_id=8242.

Kinder, Jeff, and Dave Hallock. "Dragon's Lair Cinematronics 1983." *The Dragon's Lair Project*, www.dragons-lair-project.com/games/pages/dl.asp. Accessed 6 Dec. 2018.

Kinder, Jeff, and Dave Hallock. "Dragon's Lair Manual." *The Dragon's Lair Project*, 9 Jan. 1984, www.dragons-lair-project.com/tech/manuals/lair/. Accessed 23 Apr. 2021.

Lakawicz, Steve. "Fidelity Concerns: The Lost Sound Expansion Chips of the NES." *Classical Gaming*, 27 Feb. 2011, classicalgaming.wordpress.com/2011/02/27/fidelity-concerns-the-lost-sound-expansion-chips-of-the-nes/.

"MOS Technology 6502." Gunkies.org, 28 Apr. 2016, gunkies.org/wiki/MOS_Technology_6502. Accessed 22 Jan. 2021.

Orth, Steven A. "Melody Blaster." *INTV Funhouse*, www.intvfunhouse.com/games/melo.php. Accessed 24 Jan. 2021.

"Sound Hardware." *Famitracker Wiki*, 28 Mar. 2015, famitracker.com/wiki/index.php?title=-Sound_hardware. Accessed 3 Aug. 2018.

Taylor, Brad. "2A03 Technical Reference." *NesDev*, 23 Apr. 2004, nesdev.com/2A03%20technical%20reference.txt.

1984 in Review

1984—*Gyruss*—Atari 2600

PUBLISHER: Parker Bros. RELEASE DATE: 1984 (NA). COMPOSER: Mashairo Inoue. NOTABLE MUSICAL TRACK: "Main Theme (Toccata and Fugue in D minor)."

The main musical track of *Gyruss*, "Main Theme (Toccata and Fugue in D minor)," is a chiptune arrangement of BWV 565, a famous work by the Baroque composer J.S. Bach. The game is a port of the 1983 arcade game. Considering the limitations of sound channels and tuning on the Atari 2600, the Atari 2600 port does a reasonable job playing the classical piece. The Atari 2600 port lacks sound effects, allowing the music to stand on its own. The track begins with a 13-second introduction. Then the main section lasts a minute and seven seconds before looping. The loop does not repeat the introductory section. The musical notes move quickly, masking the unusual tuning of the Atari 2600, which Atari never designed to produce music of this caliber. The piece also works well with two sound channels because the music achieves harmonies through chord arpeggiation within one sound channel. The classical structure has a straightforward melody and harmonic line, arranged well in the two sound channels, even when both channels have the same timbre.

1984—*Pitfall 2: Lost Caverns*— Atari 2600

PUBLISHER: Activision. RELEASE DATE: 1984 (NA). COMPOSER: David Crane. SERIES: *Pitfall!*. GENRE: Platformer. NOTABLE MUSICAL TRACK: "Main Theme."

Pitfall 2: Lost Caverns was the only game on the Atari 2600 to have music using four sound channels. *Pitfall 2: Lost Caverns* is one of the largest games on the Atari 2600. David Crane composed the music for the game. It includes the only use of the DPC (Display Processor Chip), a custom hardware chip designed by Crane. The DPC improves the power of the Atari 2600 by supporting smooth scrolling, detailed animation, and three additional sound channels plus drums, all of which *Pitfall 2: Lost Caverns* contains. Crane intended the DPC to be included in future Atari 2600 games to extend the life of the Atari 2600 (which lacked the video and audio capabilities of newer consoles).

Due to the DPC, the game exhibits a consistent four-part musical soundtrack, a first on the Atari 2600. The musical cues act as subtle rewards and punishments for performance. The central "heroic" theme plays for a short while before reaching a loop of atmospheric music. When Harry, the protagonist, collects a treasure, the central theme begins again. The notable musical track, "Main Theme," takes advantage of four-channel audio. One channel plays the bass, and two channels play the melody and harmony. The last channel plays the percussion sounds using a noise generator to simulate a hi-hat and tom. If Harry dies, a slower, minor-key version of the theme plays and then progresses into the atmospheric theme. The song "Sobre las Olas" plays when Harry ascends using the balloon.

April 25, 1984—*Video Game Music*—Music Album

PUBLISHER: Alfa Records. RELEASE DATE: April 25, 1984 (JP).

Video Game Music was the first commercially released album of video game music. Released exclusively in Japan by Alfa Records, *Video Game Music* was an audio cassette of musical tracks from 10 of Namco's arcade games, including *Pac-Man*, *Galaga*, and *Pole Position* (featured on the cassette's cover art). There was a demand and a market in Japan for commercially released video game music. Later in the year, Alfa Records released an album on 45 RPM vinyl called *Super Xevious: Video Game Music Dance Mix*. In 1984, Namco had an extensive library of popular arcade games to draw from for an album. As a result, video game soundtracks commercially released as albums became a viable and profitable market. Unlike *Video Game Music*, which includes the original music without alterations, *Super Xevious: Video Game Music Dance Mix* uses the musical tracks of three Namco games (*Super Xexious*, *Galaga 3*, and *The Tower of Druaga*) as a backdrop for a remix consisting of electronic drums and other sounds generating from the soundchips of the time. Video game music has a second life outside of the medium of the game.

June 1984—*Brain Strainers*— ColecoVision

PUBLISHER: Coleco Industries. RELEASE DATE: June 1984 (NA). GENRE: Music.

Brain Strainers was one of the earliest games designed around music education. The game contains two music games. Both games allow the player to hear the ColecoVision's SN76489A soundchip play musical pitches of the chromatic scale and visually see which notes they are on the music staff. The first game is "Follow the Leader," similar in gameplay to the electronic game Simon from 1978. The second game is Clef Climber, a music education activity of pitch identification by listening and viewing a musical note on the treble and bass staves.

In "Follow the Leader," the screen shows four colored triangles that collectively form a box. The computer plays a series of musical notes in each round. It points to the corresponding colored triangle with an arrow. After showing the pattern, the player must select the colored triangles to match the musical pattern heard. The game adds one note to the previous pattern until the player inputs an incorrect pattern. The game progresses up to 40 notes. In two-player mode, players work together. One player is responsible for the top and right colored triangles. The other player is accountable for the bottom and left colored triangles.

In "Clef Climber," the player can select whether to show notes on the staff when played, toggle between an electronic horn or piano key sounds, toggle a timer and its speed, and how to replay the musical note to match. So, the player can somewhat control the musical pitches of the ColecoVision's SN76489A soundchip. The player can also toggle between an electronic horn or piano sound. After the computer plays a note, the player must reposition the note on the screen up or down, seeking the staff position that matches the note played by the computer. In two-player mode, players alternate turns.

June 21, 1984—*Family BASIC*— Famicom

PUBLISHER: Nintendo. RELEASE DATE: June 21, 1984 (JP). GENRE: Creation.

Family BASIC included one of the first guides for creating sounds and music for video games. *Family BASIC* is a game exclusive to the Nintendo Famicom in Japan. The game allows users to use the BASIC computer language to operate the Famicom and create games. The game includes a manual with information and coding examples to use BASIC effectively. *Family BASIC* was Koji Kondo's second assignment after creating the sound effects for the arcade version of *Punch-Out!* Koji Kondo wrote the sections regarding sound effects and music. Using BASIC, a user calls the "BEEP" or "PLAY" function to represent

music as a series of musical data. The contained information describes tempo, duty effect (tone or timbre), envelope, octave (five octaves), interval (12 pitches from letter C to B), envelope's length or volume, rest, length (duration from a whole note to a 32nd note), and sound channel (a maximum of three simultaneous sounds). Using the sample code within the manual, the player can playback a sound after a specific action, like a character jump. Also, the manual includes the BASIC code for a three-part arrangement of *Mary Had a Little Lamb* and *Rock 'n' Rouge* (released on February 1, 1984, by composer Karuho Kureta for singer Seiko Matsuda) as well as the sheet music.

December 15, 1984—*Marble Madness*—Arcade

PUBLISHER: Atari Games. RELEASE DATE: December 15, 1984 (NA). COMPOSERS: Brad Fuller and Hal Canon. SOUNDCHIP: YM2151. NOTABLE MUSICAL TRACK: "Intermediate Race."

Marble Madness was the first game that produced sound via FM synthesis. Released in the arcades, it supports FM synthesis using the Yamaha YM2151 soundchip. *Marble Madness* is one of the first games in which the music dynamically changes with the in-game action. As the player advances, the music reflects the increase in difficulty through rhythm, tempo, and percussion. For example, "Intermediate Race" is a musical track with changes in percussion on each music loop. Another, "Silly Race," employs a gradual accelerando on each music loop.

The YM2151, released by Yamaha in 1983, was the most widely-used soundchip with FM-synthesis support found in arcade system boards in the early to mid–1980s. Released by Yamaha in North America in 1983, *Marble Madness* (1984) was the first game to use the Yamaha YM2151 soundchip. Atari, Konami, Capcom, Data East, and Namco used it in arcade games. The primary soundchip of the Sharp X68000 computer, the Yamaha DX keyboard series, and Williams pinball machines was the

YM2151. The YM2151 supports eight sound channels of FM synthesis (each FM sound requires two sound channels as operators) mixed to a stereo audio output.

SOURCES

"Koji Kondo." *Famous Composers*, www.famous composers.net/koji-kondo. Accessed 6 Aug. 2018.

Kondo, Koji. Interview. *Shmuplations.com*, 1990, shmuplations.com/supermarioworld. Accessed 6 Aug. 2018.

"Koji Kondo." *Video Game Music Preservation Foundation Wiki*, 21 Jan. 2018, www.vgmpf. com/Wiki/index.php?title=Koji_Kondo. Accessed 6 Aug. 2018.

"Marble Madness (ARC)." *Video Game Music Preservation Foundation Wiki*, 16 Jan. 2018, www.vgmpf.com/Wiki/index.php/Marble_Madness_(ARC). Accessed 15 Aug. 2018.

Nintendo. "Family BASIC Manual." *Famicom World*, 1984, famicomworld.com/Personal/uglyjoe/FamilyBasicManual.pdf. Accessed 17 Jan. 2021. English translation from Japanese.

"Rock'n Rouge." *Wikipedia*, Wikimedia Foundation, Inc., 20 Dec. 2020, ja.wikipedia.org/wiki/Rock%27n_Rouge. Accessed 22 Jan. 2021.

1985 in Review

July 1985—*Monty on the Run*—C64

PUBLISHER: Gremlin Graphics. RELEASE DATE: July 1985 (EU). COMPOSER: Rob Hubbard. SERIES: *Monty Mole*. GENRE: Platformer. NOTABLE MUSICAL TRACK: "Main Theme."

The soundtrack of *Monty on the Run* displays the soundchip techniques of the C64 masterfully. The music for the C64 version is admired as one of the best game scores for the computer. Composer Rob Hubbard created sketches of the game's three musical tracks on Casio MT30 and DX7 synths. He took two weeks manipulating the audio parameters of the C64 to simulate a Simmonds drum sound. The game's audio engine was programmed in assembly by Hubbard. The soundtrack includes tracks for the main theme, game over, and congratulations. The notable musical track, "Main Theme," is stylistically inspired by "Devil's Galop," composed by English composer Charles Williams and used as the theme song of the 1940s radio serial "Dick Barton: Special Agent." At five minutes and 47 seconds before looping, the musical track exhibits numerous soundchip techniques and effects at a brisk tempo.

September 13, 1985—*Super Mario Bros.*—Famicom/NES

PUBLISHER: Nintendo of America. RELEASE DATE: September 13, 1985 (JP), October 18, 1985 (NA), May 15, 1987 (EU). COMPOSER: Koji Kondo. SERIES: *Super Mario Bros.* GENRE: Platformer. NOTABLE MUSICAL TRACK: "Overworld Theme."

The soundtrack of *Super Mario Bros.* reflects the whimsical yet dangerous world of the Mushroom Kingdom. The game is refreshing for the quality of gameplay and graphics, with an equally impressive soundtrack. The game was a launch title for the NES in North America in 1985, even before the console was sold in large quantities to the public the following year. There are four musical tracks for the stages, each setting the mood for the four stage types: overworld, underworld, underwater, and castle stages. The notable musical track, "Overworld Theme," is one of the most recognizable video game music pieces. The track complements the gaming experience that defined many attributes of a platformer, and its melody and calypso rhythm are memorable without being irritating. The music of the underwater stages is set to a waltz to reflect the ebb and flow of water. The waltz would be used for underwater stages in subsequent games in the series. The remaining two musical tracks, shorter and used in particular instances, indicate the invincibility and game over state. When Mario, the main character, obtains a star invincibility power, the music abruptly switches to the brisk invincibility theme. The fast tempo indicates to the player that the invincibility effect is temporary. However, the player cannot simply ignore the invincibility music because as the music ends and segues into the stage music, so too does the invincibility effect on Mario.

October 18, 1985—Nintendo Entertainment System

MANUFACTURER: Nintendo. PRODUCTION DATES: October 18, 1985–August 14, 1995. LAUNCH PRICE: $179.99 (Deluxe). MODEL NUMBER: NES-001. SOUNDCHIP: Ricoh 2A03. AUDIO: Mono.

The Nintendo Entertainment System (NES) was the first home console capable of playing audio samples as DPCM or PCM. Released by Nintendo, the NES was the rebranding of the Famicom, released two years earlier. In August of 1983, a licensing deal between Nintendo and Atari fell through. Nintendo had approached Atari to license and sell its Famicom system under the Atari brand. Nintendo decided to sell the Famicom, rebranded as the Nintendo Entertainment System, in the United States without the Atari branding two years later. Nintendo, reacting to an industry recovering from the crash, marketed the NES as an "entertainment" device, similar to a VCR.

The NES contains the Ricoh 2A03 soundchip. The 2A03 is a modified version of the MOS Technology 6502 microprocessor. One of the modifications was the addition of an audio processing unit. Yukio Kaneoka was the designer of the APU (audio processing unit) for the 2A03 chip. He worked as a sound designer and composer for Nintendo on the arcade games *Donkey Kong* (1981), *Mario Bros.* (1983), and *Punch-Out!!* (1984) and the SNES games *F-Zero* (1990). The APU supports a maximum of five sound channels. These include two pulse wave channels of four variable duty cycles (25 percent and 75 percent are inverses of each other), 4-bit volume control (16 levels), and hardware pitch-bending supporting frequencies ranging from 54 Hz to 28 kHz. There is one triangle wave channel with fixed volume supporting frequencies from 27 Hz to 56 kHz. The white-noise channel selects from 16 preprogrammed frequencies with 4-bit volume control. Though

used the least, the differential pulse-code modulation (DPCM) channel supports 6-bit resolution and 1-bit delta encoding at 16 preprogrammed sample rates from 4.2 kHz to 33.5 kHz. The DPCM channel can also play standard pulse-code modulation (PCM) sound by writing individual 7-bit values at timed intervals. The APU mixes the five sound channels into an analog mono signal. The NES connects to a television using either RCA cables connected to the analog video and audio ports on the console's side or an RF adapter connected to the RF port on the console's back.

A distribution of sound channels for musical purposes places the melody and harmony in the pulse channels. The bass and occasional percussion reside in the triangle channel. Percussion and various sound effects reside in the white noise channel. Short, low-fidelity audio samples like voice clips or sampled instrument sounds that can be repitched are best suited for the DPCM channel. However, composers seldom used the DPCM channel due to memory constraints at the time. The NES was the first console capable of playing audio samples as DPCM or PCM. PCM (pulse-code modulation) and DPCM (differential pulse-code modulation) are ways to encode an audio sample (a DPCM sample is more compact than a PCM sample). PCM was a more straightforward method of playing audio samples than previous methods (dedicated audio circuits and PSGs). Unlike the Intellivision (which needed the Intellivoice for speech), the NES could play PCM or DPCM audio samples of speech or any recorded sound for that matter. The only limiting factor was the amount of memory to store the audio sample. For perspective, two launch games, *Ice Climbers* and *Super Mario Bros.*, are 24 and 40 kilobytes, respectively. DPCM was almost always favored for the sheer savings in memory. NES games used audio samples such as speech, guitars, and drums to enhance the remaining sounds produced by the PSG. Unlike the Famicom, the NES cartridge port lacks the pins necessary to transmit audio from a ROM cartridge's sound expansion chip.

Nintendo Entertainment System back 1985. The audio output ports are mono RCA (with RF adapter) and mono RCA (Evan-Amos, "Nintendo-Entertain-ment-System-NES-Console-BR").

Nintendo NES-101 back 1993. The audio output ports are mono RCA (with RF adapter) (Evan-Amos, "Nintendo-NES-TL-Console-BR").

The NES-101, released on October 15, 1993, for $49.99, replaced the toaster form factor with a rounded form factor similar to the SNES, a top-loading cartridge port, a bone-shaped controller, and the removal of analog video and audio ports. The NES ceased manufacturing on August 14, 1995. The company still manufactured the SNES as a home console and the Game Boy as a handheld gaming system. The NES Classic Edition, released in North America on November 11, 2016, for $59.99, is a dedicated console with 30 included NES games and a Linux operating system running an NES emulation engine with save state support. The success of the NES Classic Edition led to further retro consoles designed by the original console manufacturers, including the SNES Classic Edition, TurboGrafx-16 Mini, Sega Genesis Mini, and PlayStation Classic.

SOURCES

Greening, Chris. "Koji Kondo Profile." *Video Game Music Online*, 30 Dec. 2012, www.vgmonline.net/kojikondo/.

Hubbard, Rob. Interview. *C64.com*, www.c64.com/interviews/hubbard.html. Accessed 8 Aug. 2018.

Hubbard, Rob. "Interview with Rob Hubbard." Interview by Warren Pilkington. *SID*, www.sidmusic.org/sid/rhubbard.html. Accessed 6 Aug. 2018.

Lyon, Tony. "Monty on the Run." *Retro Video Game Systems*, 10 Oct. 2013, retrovideogamesystems.com/monty-on-the-run/.

Newsfield. "Monty on the Run." *ZZap!64*, Oct. 1985, pp. 16–17, archive.org/details/zzap64-magazine-006/page/n15/mode/2up. Accessed 28 May 2021.

"Rob Hubbard." *Video Game Music Preservation Foundation Wiki*, 5 Aug. 2017, www.vgmpf.com/Wiki/index.php/Rob_Hubbard. Accessed 6 Aug. 2018.

"7800 Compared to the NES." Atari 7800 Programming, *Google Sites*, sites.google.com/site/atari7800wiki/7800-compared-to-the-nes. Accessed 3 Aug. 2018.

"Yukio Kaneoka." *Video Game Music Preservation Foundation Wiki*, 4 May 2018, www.vgmpf.com/Wiki/index.php?title=Yukio_Kaneoka. Accessed 15 Nov. 2018.

1986 in Review

February 21, 1986—*The Legend of Zelda*—FDS

PUBLISHER: Nintendo. RELEASE DATE: February 21, 1986 (JP). COMPOSER: Koji Kondo. SERIES: The Legend of Zelda. GENRE: Action-adventure. NOTABLE MUSICAL TRACK: "Overworld Theme."

The soundtrack of *The Legend of Zelda* takes advantage of the additional sounds afforded by the Famicom Disk System. The soundtrack of the FDS version had richer sounds than the NES version of the same game. The game, originally designed for the FDS, supported save data by writing the player statistics on the floppy disk (similarly accomplished, though more costly, with a LR2032 battery stored within the NES ROM cartridge). Since the RP2C33 soundchip was included with the FDS, most FDS disks used the wavetable channel in some way. The bell-like tones used in the music and sound effects are made possible by wavetable synthesis. The second controller of the Nintendo Famicom contained an internal microphone. In the FDS version of the game, the player defeats Pols Voice by blowing into the microphone of the second controller. In the NES version, which lacks the microphone, arrows kill the Pols Voice.

Out Run arcade cabinet 1986 (Tiia Monto, "Out Run," CC-BY-SA 3.0).

Nintendo reused sounds for its object and character attacks. The sound of the Wizrobe's wand attack in *The Legend of Zelda* is the same as Birdo's egg attack in *Super Mario Bros. 2*. The recorder sound in *The Legend of Zelda* is reused as the warp whistle sound in *Super Mario Bros. 3*. Throughout the manufacturing lifespan of the NES, the NES never received a peripheral to restore the audio of NES games to match that of FDS games. The notable musical track "Overworld Theme" plays as Link explores the outside world of Hyrule. The song is very melodic with a melody and countermelody. The two parts become homophonic fairly quickly. When one melodic line is held out, the other part ascends with quick notes. The two parts play like trumpets.

GENRE: Racing. NOTABLE MUSICAL TRACK: "Magical Sound Shower."

Out Run was the first arcade game that allowed the player to choose the background music. Released in the arcades, the game's three musical tracks are "broadcast" through imaginary FM Radio stations, selected by the radio receiver in the Testarossa. Hiroshi Kawaguchi, the game's composer, previously composed soundtracks for other games designed by Yu Suzuki. He was a part of the S.S.T. Band, Sega's official band at the time. Before *Out Run*, the player could not select the music that plays. Before each race, the screen displays a radio knob that, when interacting with it, changes the audio, like a real car. The three tracks are titled "Passing Breeze," "Splash Wave" and "Magical Sound Shower." An additional track, "Last Wave," plays after completing the game when a player may insert his or her initials next to the score.

June 30, 1986—*Out Run*—Arcade

PUBLISHER: Sega. RELEASE DATE: June 30, 1986 (NA), September 20, 1986 (JP). COMPOSER: Hiroshi Kawaguchi. SERIES: *Out Run*.

September 1986—Sega Master System

MANUFACTURER: Sega. RELEASE DATE: September 1986 (NA), June 1987 (EU), October 1987 (JP). PRODUCTION DATES: September

1986–1992. LAUNCH PRICE: $199.99 with *Hang-On* and *Safari Hunt*. MODEL NUMBER: 3010. SOUNDCHIP: SN76489. AUDIO: Mono.

The Sega Master System was Sega's first home console released outside of Japan. Released by Sega, the SMS (Sega Master System) was a rebranded version of the Sega Mark III. The Sega Mark III, released by Sega in Japan on October 20, 1985, for 15,000 yen, was Sega's first home console. It was the first home console to support two types of game media. The SMS, like the Mark III, reads SMS games via the cartridge port or card port. The card port read Sega Game cards, SMS games that were smaller in size and cheaper to produce. Both the Mark III and SMS contained the Texas Instruments SN76489 soundchip, almost identical to the SN76489A found in the ColecoVision. The chip supports four sound channels. Three of the channels use square waves tone generators and the other sound channel uses a noise generator to generate either white noise or, at the expense of a pulse channel, periodic noise. Each channel has a four-octave range. The four channels mix to a monaural audio output, connected to a television using either an RF adapter or the A/V cable with RCA ends.

The FM Sound Unit, released by Sega exclusively in Japan in 1987 for 6,800 yen, was a peripheral that added FM-synthesis audio capabilities to the Mark III. Sega named the FM Sound Unit for the FM-synthesis properties of its Yamaha YM2413 soundchip. The YM2413 is a modified version of the YM3812, the soundchip used in the AdLib and Sound Blaster sound cards for PC. The modifications included the removal of many internal registers and the hard coding of 15 instrument settings. The YM2413 has two modes. FM mode adds nine monaural two-operator FM channels. Rhythm mode borrows three of the nine sound channels to use for percussion sounds. There are 16 different instrument sounds using FM synthesis and five different

percussion sounds using noise oscillation and white noise generation. Players only heard the FM sounds if the FM Sound Unit was connected to the Mark III. However, games still operated normally without the FM Sound Unit.

The SMS in Japan, released in October 1987 for 16,800 yen, differed from the SMS in other regions by the inclusion of the YM2413 chip. Coupled with the SN76489 soundchip, the Japanese SMS' audio capabilities are comparable to that of the Mark III with the FM Sound Unit. The Mark III and Japanese SMS were two of the earliest home consoles to produce sound through FM synthesis. Using both the YM2413 and the SN76489 soundchips, these home consoles support up to 13 sound channels. The U.S and European versions of the SMS lack the YM2413 soundchip. As a result, the Japanese soundtracks of SMS games have richer sounds than the U.S. and European soundtracks.

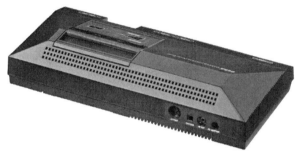

Sega Master System back 1986. The audio output ports are mono RCA (with RF adapter) and A/V (with composite video and mono audio adapter) (Evan-Amos, "Sega-Master-System-Console-BR").

Sega Master System II back 1990. The audio output ports are mono RCA (with RF adapter) (Evan-Amos, "Sega-Mastery-System-MkII-Console-BR").

Even though FM audio was only accessible via a Japanese SMS, there were some games with FM soundtracks released outside of Japan. *California Games* (1989) and *Ultima IV: Quest of the Avatar* (1990) are two games released outside of Japan for the SMS that include FM soundtracks. A player can hear each game's FM soundtrack by inserting the game into either a Mark III with FM Sound Unit or a Japanese SMS. At the time, it was uncommon and outright difficult to get a Japanese SMS outside of Japan for this purpose. U.S. and European gamers never realized that an enhanced soundtrack was available on SMS game cartridges, inaccessible due to the missing YM2413 soundchip.

The Sega Master System II, released in 1990, had a rounder and slimmer form factor, removed the Sega Card slot, expansion port, reset button, and A/V out port, and included *Alex Kidd in Miracle World* pre-installed in the system's BIOS (Basic Input/Output System). It retains the same soundchip as the standard SMS. The Sega Master System ceased manufacturing at the start of 1992. The SMS can be the longest-lasting gaming system still actively manufactured. Sega ceased manufacturing in 1992; however, TecToy, a gaming company with exclusive distribution rights in Brazil, has been manufacturing the SMS in Brazil since 1989 and still manufactures

the officially licensed SMS (as the Master System Evolution) in 2021. Although the SMS was not as globally successful as the NES, Sega established itself as a competitive company in the home console industry.

SOURCES

Bittencourt, Ricardo. "YM2413 FM Operator Type-LL (OPLL) Application Manual." *SMS Power!*, 2003, www.smspower.org/maxim/Documents/YM2413ApplicationManual. Accessed 16 Nov. 2018.

Copetti, Rodrigo. "Sega Master System Architecture." *Rodrigo's Stuff*, 28 Nov. 2020, www.copetti.org/writings/consoles/master-system/. Accessed 24 Apr. 2021.

DePapier. "SEGA: 'SEGA 3D Classics Collection Developer's Interview.'" *NintendObserver*, 2 May 2016, nintendobserver.com/2016/05/sega-sega-3d-classics-collection-developers-interview/. Accessed 30 Sept. 2020.

"OutRun (ARC)." *Video Game Music Preservation Foundation Wiki*, 31 Jan. 2017, www.vgmpf.com/Wiki/index.php?title=OutRun_(ARC). Accessed 15 Aug. 2018.

"Sega Saturn Tech Specs." *Dave's Sega Saturn Page*, 13 Apr. 2021, www.sega-saturn.com/saturn/other/satspecs.htm. Accessed 9 June 2021.

Talbot-Watkins, Richard. "Sega Master System Technical Information." *SMS Power!*, 10 June 1998, www.smspower.org/uploads/Development/richard.txt.

TecToy. "Master System Evolution Com 132 Jogos Na Memória." *Tec Toy*, www.tectoy.com.br/master-system-evolution-com-132-jogos-na-memoria-995020351822-p186. Accessed 24 Apr. 2021.

1987 in Review

1987—AdLib Music Synthesizer Card—Soundcard

MANUFACTURER: AdLib. RELEASE DATE: 1987 (NA). LAUNCH PRICE: $245 with *AdLib Visual Composer*, $195. SOUNDCHIP: YM3812. AUDIO: Stereo.

The AdLib Music Synthesizer Card was first widely supported soundcard for IBM-compatible PCs. The AdLib Music Synthesizer Card was the first widely supported soundcard for IBM-compatible PCs. Released by AdLib, the AdLib Music Synthesizer Card designer was Martin Prevel. He designed the soundcard to be

cost-effective, using surplus FM soundchips from Yamaha.

The Adlib Music Synthesizer Card connects to a PC via the ISA 8-bit port. It included a volume dial and a 1/4" audio-out port for stereo audio (later models switch this port with a 3.5mm audio-out port). Unlike the square waveform of the PC Speaker, the AdLib soundcard generated sound through FM synthesis. The AdLib sound card includes the Yamaha YM3812 chip, which supports 9 FM synthesis sound channels. The AdLib was the first soundcard for PCs with FM synthesis. FM synthesis was a popular means of sound generation popularized by Yamaha synthesizers, specifically the Yamaha DX7 synthesizer. Other features relating to frequency modulation include two operators per channel, a two-algorithm structure, and four waveforms, including a sine wave.

To sell their games to a large market, game developers supported multiple configurations of soundcards (or lack of). In maintaining support for other audio options, *King's Quest IV: The Perils of Rosella* offered options to use the PC Speaker, PCjr./Tandy, AdLib, and MT-32. The PC speaker was the option for a computer without a soundcard. The remaining options worked with computers with a soundcard. The purchase of a computer at the time did not necessarily include a soundcard. Computer users had to purchase a soundcard and install it in their computer for additional functionality.

The AdLib included *The AdLib Visual Composer* for DOS. It is a flexible, easy-to-use editor for creating music for the AdLib Music Synthesizer Card. The user composes music by adding instruments and musical pitches in a piano-roll interface. The user designates the musical data in either a configuration of nine sound channels of FM synthesis or a combination of six sound channels of FM synthesis and five sound channels for bass drum, snare, tom, hi-hat, and cymbal. The most difficult tasks in the software are changing the time signature and writing arpeggios and tuplets, pitch bends, and note slides. It also lacks an undo button. Using the Instrument Maker, the user can adjust each FM channel's carrier and modulator parameters to create new sounds. Some of the parameters are waveform, ADSR rates, output level, and frequency multiplier. The Jukebox is an area to playback finished creations from the Visual Composer. It also has sample songs in the styles of ballad, jazz, bossa nova, and ragtime.

The AdLib received a sales boost with the support of game company Sierra and the first soundtrack designed around the sound card in *King's Quest IV: The Perils of Rosella*. In maintaining support for other sound options, *King's Quest IV: The Perils of Rosella* offers options to use the PC Speaker

or soundcards: PCjr./Tandy, AdLib, and MT-32. The AdLib Music Synthesizer Card enjoyed only three years of market dominance until the Sound Blaster soundcard gained the market share.

1987—Roland MT-32—Soundcard

Manufacturer: Roland. Release Date: 1987 (NA). Launch price: $695. Audio: Stereo.

The MT-32 was a soundcard that used linear arithmetic synthesis, a combination of short, prerecorded samples with proprietary subtractive synthesis, for its sound library. Released by Roland, the MT-32 is a multi-timbre sound module that recognizes MIDI data. MIDI stands for Musical Instrument Digital Interface. Still in use today, MIDI is the means by which a device (an instrument) communicates with a computer. A Roland MT-32 can still be hooked up to a modern computer via a MIDI interface and work as advertised. One of the first games to support the Roland MT-32 was *Space Quest III: The Pirates of Pestulon* (1989).

The MT-32 used linear arithmetic synthesis, a type of sound generation similar to PCM and DPCM. This process of sound generation was an improvement over PSG and FM-synthesis options. The sound library included 128 preset synth sounds in 17 instrument groups and 30 preset rhythm sounds. The 30 rhythm parts have specific panning settings within the stereo audio mix, with conga drums panned to the left, bongos to the right, and hi hats in the center. The MT-32 supported eight instrument sound channels and one more reserved for rhythm. Each channel makes use of at most four partials to create a sound. In this way, the MT-32 can play at most 32 notes from the eight sound channels, each sound channel using four partials. The buttons on the front of the module allow the user to adjust the volume, tuning, reverb, and instrument patches. Beyond this, external MIDI messaging not accessible from the front panel can be adjusted in software when hooked up to a computer. Roland was instrumental in supporting and advocating for sound and music devices through their line of products. The MT-32 was designed before the General MIDI specification was approved, so the MIDI protocol used by the original version of the MT-32 is a unique implementation of MIDI. The DAC accepted 15-bit PCM, although with noise interference of the analog signal.

The MT-32 was updated with a better DAC that accepts 16-bit PCM, a ¼" stereo audio out port, and pre-installed demo songs. The MT-32 was never the dominant soundcard for a few reasons. The MT-32 lacked support for General MIDI, which standardized the alignment of instrument channels with instrument samples across all devices supporting General MIDI. The launch price was over three time more expensive than the AdLib soundcard. Nevertheless, both soundcards were successful in the market, supported in games and catering to different consumer bases.

General MIDI, established in September 1991, standardized the configuration of instrument sounds. It was a MIDI specification that all soundcard manufacturers would adhere to when preparing the audio specifications of their soundcards. With General MIDI, a game's audio could request a specific instrument sound. Any soundcard would find the corresponding instrument sound. Before General MIDI, each company implemented a unique MIDI configuration, as did the MT-32. Game developers adjusted the audio programming of their games to accommodate each MIDI setup. Music technology actively supports General MIDI today.

March 27, 1987—*Otocky*— Nintendo FDS

PUBLISHER: ASCII. RELEASE DATE: March 27, 1987 (JP). Designer: Toshio Iwai. GENRE: Music/Shooter.

Otocky is notable for being one of the first games with creative/procedural generative music. The game combines the music and third-person shooter genres. Designer Toshio Iwai also developed music and rhythm games such as *SimTunes* and *Electroplankton*. The player creates the music by interacting within the world of the game. The player does not trigger sound effects. Instead, the player triggers musical notes and sounds that are quantized in time with the beat of the musical track. The musical notes fit within the music as if they naturally belonged. Each action corresponds with a musical note and instrument sound that fits into the musical track.

The game plays as a musical shooter. Otocky, the controllable character, has a bubble beam for a weapon. Bubbles can be fired in eight directions. The direction of the bubble projectile corresponds to a different musical note. The note plays when the player presses the A button and a direction on the D-pad and is quantized in time so that it matches the beat playing in the background. The music plays at a tempo of 120 beats per minute and a meter of four beats per measure. The player improvises music within gameplay by using the weapon selectively. The ball catches various types of objects. Musical notes must be collected to finish the level. Wavetable synthesis from the FDS simulates instrument sounds that would not be possible from the Famicom soundchip. Letter "A"s change the musical instrument sound produced by the ball. Some of the instruments are organ, electric piano, viola, and clavichord. Letter "B"s provide a secondary weapon. The ball gets smaller when an enemy touches the player until the player loses a life. As the player gets stronger or weaker, the track shifts to acknowledge the attributes collected or lost.

Completing the game unlocks two additional modes. In the Music Maker, the player can edit the music in the game. There are five sound channels to manipulate (one channel for percussion). A user interface allows the player to adjust the waveforms, volumes, tempo, and note placements within four measures of music. After previewing the musical selection, the player selects the Otocky icon in the lower-left corner to play the selected stage with the new musical composition. Also unlocked is B.G.M. mode, which is a playable version of the Adventure mode, the only difference being that there are no enemies to harm the player. In this mode, the player can creatively move through any stage to generate music. Pressing the select button changes the instrument in this mode.

April 1987—Commodore Amiga

MANUFACTURER: Commodore. RELEASE DATE: April 1987 (NL), May 1987 (EU), October 1987 (NA). PRODUCTION DATES: April 1987–June 1992. LAUNCH PRICE: $595. MODEL NUMBER: 500. SOUNDCHIP: Paula. AUDIO: Stereo.

The Amiga 500 was a personal computer with PCM audio support. Released by Commodore, the Amiga 500 competed directly with the C64. It included a CPU at 7.15909 MHz (NTSC), 512 kB of RAM (expandable to a max of 9 MB), a 4,096-color palette, graphic modes (640 × 512 and 320 × 256), the Workbench 1.2 OS, and a 95-key built-in keyboard. Some of its I/O ports include a 3.5" floppy disk interface, cartridge slot, expansion interface, two joystick or mouse ports, an RS-32 serial port, a Centronics parallel port, and 2 RCA audio ports.

Regarding audio, audio samples, stored as PCM, were the source of all of the audio and music of the Amiga 500. Of all the options of sound generation available to personal computers and gaming systems at the time, PCM offered the most realistic sounds. It isn't surprising that computer companies wanted the most powerful audio hardware for the most realistic sounds. For the bottom line of business, companies hoped that improved audio meant improved sales.

The Amiga 500 contains the Paula chip. The chip controls audio playback, floppy disk drive control, serial port input/output, and mouse/joystick buttons 2 and 3. All Amiga models from Commodore share the same functionality. Amiga models like the Amiga 500 have a static "tone knob" type low-pass filter. This filter is a 6-dB/oct low-pass filter with a cutoff frequency at 4.5 or 5 kHz.

Paula supports four DMA-driven 8-bit PCM sound channels. Two sound channels are mixed into the left and right output as stereophonic audio at a sampling frequency of up to 28 kHz. Each sound channel has an independent frequency and 6-bit volume control (64 levels). An alternative function of a sound channel is to modulate the period or amplitude of another channel. However, music rarely applied this function due to better ways of controlling frequency and volume. Nevertheless, doing so can produce tremolo, vibrato, and FM synthesis effects. Disabling DMA, though seldom done, allows for playback of 14-bit 56 kHz audio by combining two channels set at different volumes.

The Amiga 500 ceased manufacturing in June of 1992. The Amiga 500 was succeeded by the Amiga 500 Plus and the Amiga 600. The Amiga was a good 16/32-bit computer (32-bit instruction set with a 16-bit arithmetic logic unit). The computer market is constantly evolving, even faster than the home console market.

Amiga 500 1987. The audio output ports are stereo RCA (Bill Bertram, "Amiga500 system," CC-BY-SA 2.0).

May 6, 1987—*The Great Giana Sisters*—C64

PUBLISHER: Rainbow Arts. RELEASE DATE: May 6, 1987 (EU). COMPOSER: Chris Hülsbeck. SERIES: *Giana Sisters*. GENRE: Platformer. NOTABLE MUSICAL TRACK: "Title Screen Theme."

The soundtrack of *The Great Giana Sisters* is one of the best for the C64. The soundtrack was composed by Chris Hülsbeck. The game sold well despite exhibiting gameplay influenced by *Super Mario Bros.* (1985) for the NES. Musically, *The Great Giana Sisters* is different from *Super Mario Bros.* There are two music tracks for the main game: one for overworld stages and one for boss stages. Composer Chris Hülsbeck explores the unique soundwaves and noise timbres of the C64 soundchip in the notable musical track, "Title Screen Theme." The music sets the tone of mystery, danger, and sci-fi. *Giana Sisters: Twisted Dreams*, the 2012 entry in the series, also has music by Chris Hülsbeck. He included new arrangements and extensions of his original soundtrack.

October 30, 1987—PC Engine/TurboGrafx-16

MANUFACTURER: NEC. RELEASE DATE: October 30, 1987 (JP), August 29, 1989 (NA), 1990 (EU). PRODUCTION DATES: October 30, 1987–1995. LAUNCH PRICE: $199.99. SOUNDCHIP: HuC6280A. AUDIO: mono (stereo with Turbo Booster).

The TurboGrafx-16 was the first home console capable of wavetable synthesis. Released by NEC in Japan as the PC Engine, NEC erroneously marketed the TurboGrafx-16 as the first 16-bit gaming system. Instead, it was the first home console with a 16-bit graphical processing unit. The TG-16 was the first video game console to have a portable counterpart with identical functionality in the Turbo Express. The TurboGrafx-16 plays games in TurboChip format (HuCard in Japan), a ROM cartridge with the size of a playing card, similar to the SMS' Sega Card. The TurboGrafx-16 supports an RF output of video and mono

audio. Though inaccessible without a peripheral, the expansion port on the back of the TurboGrafx-16 contains composite audio and stereo video signals.

Unlike its competitors, wavetable synthesis generates all of the audio of the TG-16. The TurboGrafx-16 contains the Hudson Soft HuC6280A soundchip. It supports six wavetable channels. Each channel creates sounds through wavetable synthesis, a means of sound production of various periodic waveforms. The waveforms are programmable, so the composers are not limited to basic waveforms. Despite the waveform choices, game audio used basic waveforms and semi-standard waveforms, such as a 25 percent pulse wave, relatively often. In addition, two of the channels support white noise generation. So, using the six sound channels, two combinations could be six channels of waveforms or four channels of waveforms and two channels of white noise. Any of the six channels can read a 5-bit PCM sample with 20 bytes of sample data. The soundchip can use the resources of two channels to playback as much as a 10-bit PCM sample. The soundchip also contains a Low-Frequency Oscillator, used to modify the sound with effects like vibrato or tremolo.

The TurboGrafx-16 was the first gaming system with upgradeable audio. Unlike the Genesis, the TG-16 does not support stereophonic audio. The Turbo Booster is an add-on unit for the TurboGrafx-16 that adds support for composite video and stereophonic sound output by accessing the TG-16's expansion port signals. The Turbo Booster Pro is an improvement over the Turbo Booster with included memory for saving high scores and game data.

The TurboGrafx-CD (TG-CD), released in North America in November 1989 for $399.99, was the first peripheral for a home console with the CD-ROM as a storage medium for video games. In addition to playing games, the TG-CD acts as a CD player, playing audio CDs. The TG-16 became the first home console with the TG-CD to have a CD-ROM peripheral and the first home console to use the CD-ROM as a storage medium for video games. Rather than releasing a new CD-based system that could potentially flop, NEC took the safe route by extending the life of the TG-16 with the TG-CD. Personal computers first supported CD-based games in the same year, beginning with *The Manhole* (1989).

The TurboGrafx-CD came with a TurboGrafx-CD System Card, a special Turbo-Chip that contains the BIOS. When inserted into the TurboGrafx-16, it can adequately access the TurboGrafx-CD hardware. Linking the TurboDuo with the TG-CD, the TG-CD could play Super CD-ROM² releases.

NEC TurboGrafx-16 with controller 1987. The audio output ports are mono RCA (with RF adapter) (Evan-Amos, "TurboGrafx16-Console-Set").

Owners of the TG-16 needed to purchase the Super System Card through mail order to play Super CD-ROM2 games.

The TurboGrafx-CD contains the Oki MSM5205 chip. The chip adds one ADPCM channel to the existing sound channels present in the TurboGrafx-16. The built-in CD player supports two sound channels of CD Digital Audio (CD-DA). When combining the TurboGrafx-16 and TurboGrafx-CD, there are a total of nine sound channels for musical purposes. The TurboGrafx-CD has a stereophonic audio output. The

NEC Turbo Booster back 1989. The audio output ports are stereo RCA (Evan-Amos, "NEC-TurboBooster-Back").

TurboGrafx-CD also plays standard audio CDs and CD+G (audio CD plus graphics) CDs. Commonly used for karaoke performances, CD+G consists of CD-DA with synchronized visuals, which could be anything like song lyrics or images.

The TurboDuo, released in Japan as the PC Engine Duo on September 21, 1991, for $299.99, combined the TG-16 and TG-CD into one unit. The system bundle included the TurboDuo console, a control pad, an AC adapter, RCA cables, a CD-ROM² of *Ys Book I & II*, a 3-in-1 Super CD-ROM² of *Bonk's Adventure*, *Bonk's Revenge*, and *Gate of Thunder*, and *Dungeon Hunter* on TurboChip. The TurboDuo included 256 MB of RAM. The TurboDuo outputs composite video

and analog stereo audio without the need for the Turbo Booster.

The TurboGrafx-16 and all subsequent models and peripherals ceased manufacturing in 1995. Although the TurboGrafx-16 was the first console marketed as 16-bit with a CD peripheral, its console sales were a quarter of those of the Super NES and Genesis. Despite its commercial failure, the TG-16 took game audio in another direction. The soundtracks for the games exhibit various waveforms, possible via the programmable aspect of wavetable synthesis. The TG-16 introduced wavetable synthesis to home consoles. In the early to mid–1990s, NEC was the number one manufacturer of personal computers in Japan. Its last home console, the

NEC TurboGrafx-CD back 1989. The audio output ports are 3.5mm. The volume slider modulates the 3.5mm volume. The TurboGrafx-CD communicates with the TurboGrafx-16 through the Interface Unit. The audio output ports of the Interface Unit are stereo RCA (Evan-Amos, "NEC-TurboGrafx-16-CD-Add-on-BR").

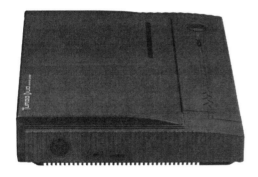

NEC TurboDuo left side 1991. The audio output ports are A/V (with composite video and stereo audio RCA adapter) (Evan-Amos, "NEC-TurboDuo-Console-Side-L").

PC-FX, resembled a computer in its form factor. So, NEC left the video game industry for a market with which it understood well.

December 1987—Ultimate Soundtracker—Amiga

PUBLISHER: EAS Computer Technik. RELEASE DATE: December 1987 (EU). GENRE: Music creation.

The Ultimate Soundtracker was the first tracker software. Released for the Amiga in September 1987 as version 1.21, the software creates MOD files containing musical data as numbers read in time vertically like a piano roll. The term tracker is itself derived from *The Ultimate Soundtracker*. The general concept of step-sequencing samples numerically, as used in trackers, is also found in the Fairlight CMI sampling workstation of the early 1980s. Some early tracker-like programs appeared for the Commodore 64, such as *Sound Monitor* by Chris Hülsbeck. However, these did not feature sample playback. Instead, they played notes on the computer's internal synthesizer.

The first trackers supported four-pitch and volume modulated channels of 8-bit PCM samples, a limitation derived from the Amiga's Paula audio chipset and the commonplace 8SVX format used to store sampled sound. However, since the notes were samples, the limitation was less critical than synthesizing music chips. A disk of instrument samples (ST-01) sourced from the Roland D-50, Yamaha DX21, and Casio CZ101 was distributed together with the program.

The Ultimate Soundtracker began as a tool for game sound development for the Amiga, coded by Karsten Obarski. The program allows for four-channel hardware mixing on all Amiga computers. Unlike subsequent versions, the program limited the number of samples/instruments in a song to 15. It strictly allocated the four channels: melody (lead), accompaniment, bass, and percussion. It exports the tracks as a sequence of assembly instructions. The original code of *The Ultimate Soundtracker* was disassembled. The modified versions of the program were spread across the Amiga demo scene. *The Ultimate Soundtracker* was a commercial product, but soon shareware clones such as *NoiseTracker* appeared.

December 1987—*Ballblazer*— Atari 7800

PUBLISHER: Atari. RELEASE DATE: December 1987 (NA). COMPOSER: Peter Langston. GENRE: Sports.

Ballblazer was the first video game to have algorithmically generated music. The game is one of only two games on the

7800 that use the POKEY chip. The game was first released for the Atari 5200 and Atari 800 in North America in March 1984. In the game, an algorithm generates the title music. The algorithm determines what will play next, affecting the tempo (speed), dynamics (volume), rhythm, pitches, and notes. The player cannot regulate the parameters of the algorithm. However, the result is the same. Algorithmically-generated music is never the same twice. Unique to the Atari 7800 port, the POKEY generates all music and sound effects. The TIA of the 7800 does not contribute to the audio.

The notable musical track, "Song of the Grid," is the game's title theme. It uses a fractal music system that algorithmically generates music; the music is never the same twice. *Ballblazer* is the first known application of such a musical technique in video games. Peter Langston, the game's composer, called his system "riffology," in which the "riff" is a small melodic fragment. Riffs are pieced together in real-time based on parameters including tempo, volume, when to omit or add notes, and when to insert a break. The melodic riffs are unified by the collection of eight pitches taken from the A blues scale. The musical content is different in every playthrough while remaining in tune and in time with the bass, drums, and chords. The use of music in new ways is not limited by the soundchips but rather by the imagination of the audio team.

December 20, 1987— *Phantasy Star*—SMS

PUBLISHER: Sega. RELEASE DATE: December 20, 1987 (JP), November 1988 (NA, EU). COMPOSER: Tokuhiko Uwabo. SERIES: *Phantasy Star*. GENRE: RPG. NOTABLE MUSICAL TRACK: "Title Theme."

The soundtrack of *Phantasy Star* exhibits audio differences between the Japanese and American/European versions. *Phantasy Star* was the original game that spawned a series that continues today. The game was one of the first home console JRPGs with a compelling storyline that features a female protagonist. The main overworld theme

is suitably stirring and heroic. The underground and battle themes are edgy, fitting with the RPG elements of entering dungeons and fighting monsters.

The SMS in Japan contains two soundchips, whereas the SMS outside of Japan contains one only. Consequently, the American and European versions of the game exclusively use the SN76489 soundchip, included in both versions of the SMS. The Japanese version of the game uses the four sound channels of the SN76489 and the nine channels of the YM2413. The combination of PSG and FM synthesis makes for a rich musical soundtrack.

SOURCES

"AdLib Visual Composer." *The Game Maker Archive*, 1 Feb. 2016, www.aderack.com/game-maker/index.php?title=AdLib_Visual_Composer. Accessed 29 Sept. 2020.

"AdLib Visual Composer." *Video Game Music Preservation Foundation Wiki*, 19 Feb. 2020, www.vgmpf.com/Wiki/index.php?title=AdLib_Visual_Composer. Accessed 29 Sept. 2020.

"Amiga Hardware Reference Manual." *The Evergreen State College*, ada.evergreen.edu/~tc_nik/files/AmigaHardRefManual.pdf. Accessed 3 Aug. 2018.

Bateman, Selby. "The Summer Consumer Electronics Show." *Compute*, Aug. 1984, p. 32, www.atarimagazines.com/compute/issue51/176_1_Software_Power.php. Accessed 10 Apr. 2020.

De Feo, Teresa. "Who Is Toshio Iwai?" *Digicult*, 9 Feb. 2016, digicult.it/design/who-is-toshio-iwai/.

Giant Bomb. "TurboGrafx-CD (Platform)." 13 June 2014, www.giantbomb.com/turbografx-cd/3045-53/. Accessed 28 Jan. 2016.

"The Great Giana Sisters (Rainbow Arts, 1987)." Finnish Retro Game Comparison Blog, 20 Sept. 2013, frgcb.blogspot.com/2013/09/the-great-giana-sisters-rainbow-arts.html. Accessed 24 Jan. 2021.

"History and Memories of the IBM PCjr and Tandy 1000." *The Oldskool Shrine to The IBM PCjr and Tandy 1000*, 10 Oct. 2015, www.oldskool.org/shrines/pcjr_tandy/.

Hüelsbeck, Chris. "Giana Sisters: Twisted Dreams—Original Soundtrack, by Chris Huelsbeck, Fabian Del Priore." *Chris Huelsbeck Productions*, 14 Nov. 2012, chrishuelsbeck.bandcamp.com/album/giana-sisters-twisted-dreams-original-soundtrack.

Langston, Peter S. "Six Techniques for Algorithmic Music Composition." 2 Nov. 1989, *International Computer Music Conference*. Columbus, OH. peterlangston.com/Papers/amc.pdf.

"MT-32." *SynthMania*, www.synthmania.com/mt-32.htm. Accessed 24 Jan. 2021.

NEC. "TurboGrafx-16 Unit Service Manual." *Console5*, Dec. 1989, console5.com/techwiki/images/b/bc/TurboGrafx-16_Unit_Service_Manual_-_SMTG16.pdf. Accessed 28 Sept. 2020.

"Otocky/Music Maker Mode." *StrategyWiki*, 12 June 2009, strategywiki.org/wiki/Otocky/Music_Maker_Mode. Accessed 12 Sept. 2018.

"PC Engine/Turbografx-16 Music for Beginners (Page 1)." *ChipMusic*, 21 Feb. 2010, chipmusic.org/forums/topic/790/pc-engineturbografx16-music-for-beginners/.

"The Price of PC Sound (and Some Other Stuff)." *Nerdly Pleasures*, 24 May 2013, nerdlypleasures.blogspot.com/2013/05/how-much-do-we-pay-for-sound-hardware.html. Accessed 29 Sept. 2020.

Roland Corporation. "Roland MT-32 Multi-Timbre Sound Module Owner's Manual." *Archive.org*, 1987, ia800709.us.archive.org/17/items/synthmanual-roland-mt-32-owners-manual/rolandmt-32ownersmanual.pdf. Accessed 29 Sept. 2020.

"Roland MT-32." *Vintage Synth Explorer*, www.vintagesynth.com/roland/mt32.php. Accessed 29 Sept. 2020.

Tiberio, David. "Famous Amiga Uses." *Amiga Report Magazine*, 1993, www.amigareport.com/ar134/p1-12.html.

"TurboGrafx-CD (Platform)." *Giant Bomb*, 13 June 2014, www.giantbomb.com/turbografx-cd/3045-53/.

"TurboGrafx-16 101: The Beginner's Guide." *Racketboy*, 12 Dec. 2014, www.racketboy.com/retro/turbografx-16/tubrografix-16-tg16-101-beginners-guide.

"Ultimate SoundTracker V1.21 (Amiga Soundeditor)." janeway.exotica.org.uk/release.php?id=17706. Accessed 18 Jan. 2021.

1988 in Review

1988—*Corruption*—Amiga

PUBLISHER: Rainbird Software. RELEASE DATE: 1988 (EU, NA). COMPOSER: John Molloy. GENRE: Text adventure.

Corruption uses speech samples and an audio cassette to enhance a text adventure. The Amiga version has unique audio compared to the other versions. The player controls a stockbroker who, after much success, must prove his innocence after being framed for a crime. Unlike other releases of the game, the Amiga version uses the Amiga Workbench speech synthesizer (part of the OS) to speak the commands selected by the player.

Corruption includes an audio cassette containing dialogue vital to the game. Collectively, a game consists of numerous pieces: the game media containing the code, the box (to hold the game and other contents), the manual (explaining the game's plot and control scheme), and additional materials (posters, strategy guide, registration card). The audio cassette didn't contain the game's soundtrack. A part of the game prompts the player to listen to the audio cassette for vital information pertinent to the frame-up. The audio cassette was physically marked as if someone had written on it (and given to the player as evidence). The audio cassette was a form of copy protection (using resources outside the game to verify that the player legally purchased a game). The experience combined the game's world (stored as a computer game) with the physical world (using an audio cassette and included diary pages).

September 1988—*King's Quest IV: The Perils of Rosella*—PC

PUBLISHER: Sierra. RELEASE DATE: September 1988 (NA). COMPOSER: William Goldstein. SERIES: *King's Quest*. GENRE: Graphic adventure. NOTABLE MUSICAL TRACK: "Introduction."

King's Quest IV: The Perils of Rosella was the first computer game to support a sound card. Released for MS-DOS, the game was responsible for boosting sales of the AdLib soundcard. The game was the first by game company Sierra with a complete musical soundtrack optimized for the Roland MT-32 sound card. Composer William Goldstein composed 75 tracks for the stereophonic, orchestral soundtrack. In 1985, he created the first completely computer-sequenced direct to digital musical score for the NBC TV documentary series *Oceanquest*. He was also the composer for the TV series *Fame* from 1982 to 1984.

The soundtrack includes stereophonic and orchestral sounds using audio samples from the soundcard. Sierra's Creative Interpreter (SCI) engine, used for the first time in the series, supports an orchestrated musical score in conjunction with sound effects. The game supports the Roland MT-32, AdLib, IBM Music Feature Card, Tandy 3 Voice, and PC Speaker. The notable musical track, "Introduction," accompanies the introductory animations setting up the game's exposition. It is approximately eight and a half minutes long.

October 29, 1988—Sega Mega Drive/Genesis

MANUFACTURER: Sega. PRODUCTION DATES: October 29, 1988–1999. LAUNCH PRICE: $189.99 with *Altered Beast*. SOUNDCHIPS: SN76489A and YM2612. AUDIO: Stereo.

The Genesis was the first home console capable of FM synthesis and stereophonic audio. Released as the Mega Drive by Sega in Japan, Sega leveraged its successful arcade games when designing an arcade experience for the home market in the Mega Drive. The console was renamed the Genesis in the United States (for all instances of "Mega" in later models and peripherals). On the Genesis Model 1, only the 3.5mm audio-out port on the front of the unit supports stereo audio. The A/V port supports composite video and monophonic analog audio.

The Sega Genesis contains two soundchips: the Texas Instruments SN76489A and the Yamaha YM2612. The YM2612 provides six monaural FM channels. One of the six channels can output 8-bit PCM sound samples via the Genesis' DAC. Drums, snares, and voice samples are typical on the DAC. The second soundchip, the SN76489A, has the same audio capabilities as the SN76489 found in the Sega Master System. The chip provides four sound channels: three square waves and one white noise. Using both soundchips, the Sega Genesis supports 10 sound channels

for music and sound effects. The Genesis contains the same soundchip as the SMS to provide backward compatibility for SMS games using the Power Base Converter. The Genesis is backward compatible with SMS games only via the Power Base Converter. Unlike other peripherals, the Power Base Converter exists solely as a slot that fits the cartridge size (and card size) of SMS games.

Some popular Japanese and American musical performers crossed over to compose Sega Genesis soundtracks. The J-Pop group Dreams Come True composed music for *Sonic the Hedgehog* (1991) and *Sonic the Hedgehog 2* (1992). *Michael Jackson's Moonwalker*, released by Sega for arcades and ports for the Genesis and SMS, used Michael Jackson's music and likeness. Michael Jackson also contributed to the Genesis soundtrack of *Sonic the Hedgehog 3* (1994).

GEMS (Genesis Editor for Music and Sound Effects) and SMPS (Sample Music Playback System) are two of the preferred sound engines used by Genesis developers. Recreational Brainwave developed GEMS in 1991 for Sega of America. The design team consisted of Jonathan Miller, Burt Sloane, Chris Grigg, and Mark Miller. Western Genesis developers mostly used GEMS. Approximately 186 games use GEMS or a modified form of GEMS. The GEMS application ran on MS-DOS. Its graphical interface was geared toward the musician or composer. It included many of the features that audio programmers could adjust but presented it in an accessible way even for those without a thorough programming background.

GEMS supported MIDI. As a result, a composer used a MIDI keyboard to communicate with GEMS on the computer, which then translated the MIDI into data compiled and stored on a Genesis game ROM. GEMS came with 104 pre-configured FM synth patches to be used as starting points for sound creation but was used unaltered in many games. Another valuable feature of GEMS was "mailboxes." The soundtrack could react dynamically based on conditional checks based on mailbox values within the game. A mailbox value could be something like

Sega Genesis Model 1 with controller 1988. The audio output ports are A/V (with RF adapter or composite video and mono audio RCA) and 3.5mm. The volume slider modulates the 3.5mm volume (Evan-Amos, "Sega-Genesis-Mod1-Set").

player health (is the player almost out of health?), stage timer (is the timer almost up?), player oxygen (is the player almost out of air?), enemies on-screen (is the player in great danger?), or any other value stored as a part of gameplay. Some games using the GEMS engine are *Kid Chameleon* (1992), *ToeJam and Earl in Panic on Funkotron* (1993), and *Earthworm Jim* (1994). At least nine Sega 32X games use GEMS.

SMPS was another sound engine used in many games for the Genesis and 32X. There were two versions of SMPS used: one for the 68K (the CPU of the Genesis) and one for Z80 (the CPU of the SMS) systems. Approximately 154 games use SMPS or a modified form of SMPS. The launch games for the Genesis by Japanese developers used an early version of SMPS. All of the Sonic games, except *Sonic Spinball*, used SMPS. Other games that used the SMPS were *Castle of Illusion starring Mickey Mouse* (1990), *Fatal Fury* (1993), *Dynamite Headdy* (1994), and all three games in the *Golden Axe* series. At least seven Sega 32X games use SMPS.

The Mega CD/Sega CD, released in Japan on December 12, 1991, for $299.99, was the first peripheral for a home console to support QSound and Roland Source, two analog surround sound formats. The Sega CD was sold with CDs: *Shinobi, Streets of Rage, Columns, Golden Axe, Sherlock Holmes, Sol Feace*, a music sampler and a karaoke CD+G sampler. When connected to the Genesis, the combined unit plays games on CD media, capable of low resolution, grainy

full-motion video (FMV) and CD digital audio (CD-DA). The Mega Drive II/Genesis Model 2, released in Europe in 1993, used a smaller form factor, added stereo audio support through the A/V port, and removed the 3.5mm audio-out port and volume knob. As a result of the different form factor, the Mega CD required another model to be compatible with the Mega Drive II.

The CDX, released in North America in 1994, for $359.99, combined a Sega Genesis and Sega CD within the form factor of a portable CD player. As the smallest and lightest home console at the time, the CDX took two AA batteries used only for audio CD functionality (audio CD functionality also worked when the CDX was plugged in). It has a small, backlit LED display used when operating the CDX as a CD player. The CDX has a 3.5mm audio-out port to output the audio CD's stereo audio. When used as a gaming system, the CDX requires power from the included power supply. The CDX had a front-loading disc tray. The CDX played both Genesis games and Sega CD games. Even better, it only needed one power supply to power both functionalities. The CDX

Sega Genesis Model 1 with Sega CD Model 1 1991. The audio output ports are A/V (with RF adapter or composite video and mono audio RCA) and stereo RCA (Evan-Amos, "Sega-CD-Model1-Set").

Sega Genesis Model 2 with Sega CD Model 2 back 1993. The audio output ports are A/V (with RF adapter or composite video and stereo audio RCA) and stereo RCA (Evan-Amos, "Sega-CD-Base-Mk2-wSystem-Back").

Sega 32X back 1994. The audio output ports are A/V (with RF or composite video and stereo audio RCA adapters). The Genesis outputs audio and video to the A/V-in port of the 32X (Evan-Amos, "Sega-Genesis-32X-02").

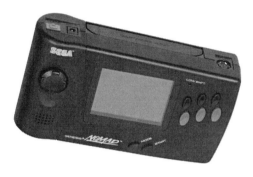

Sega Nomad back 1995. The internal speaker is located on the bottom-left corner of the device. The audio output ports are A/V (with RF or composite video and stereo audio RCA adapters) or 3.5mm. The volume slider modulates the internal speaker's volume (Evan-Amos, "Sega-Genesis-Nomad-Console-02").

Sega CDX 1994. The audio output ports are A/V (with RF or composite video and stereo audio RCA adapters) or 3.5mm. The volume slider modulates the 3.5mm output volume (Evan-Amos, "Sega-CDX-FL").

Sega Genesis 3 with controller 1998, licensed and manufactured by Majesco. The audio output ports are A/V (with RF adapter or composite video and stereo audio RCA) (Evan-Amos, "Sega-Genesis-Mod3-Set").

2

2

includes an A/V out port that supported composite video and analog stereo audio.

The 32X, released in North America on November 21, 1994, for $159.99, was a peripheral for the Genesis that upgraded the graphical and audio capabilities. In addition to playing 32X games, it acts as a passthrough for Genesis games. The 32X uses a crossover cable to send the A/V from the Genesis to the 32X. The A/V output of the 32X represents the systems' combined resources. The 32X contains a stereo PCM chip that adds two channels to the 10 on the Genesis, making 12 sound channels when paired together. The audio output of the 32X was 10- or 11-bit stereo PWM (Pulse Wave Modulation). A sample rate of 22 kHz is acceptable for audio samples in 32X games. The 32X supported QSound, just like the Sega CD. The 32X sound chipset proved to be poorly documented and difficult to program. As a result, most games ignored the QSound system. They used the Genesis' soundchip, leaving the 32X's audio capabilities vastly underutilized. Six games require the Genesis, Sega CD, and 32X to operate.

The Nomad, released in North America in October 1995, plays Genesis games as a hybrid home console/handheld gaming system. The unit can play audio through its monophonic internal speaker or stereophonic audio from either the 3.5mm audio-out port or the A/V port. The Genesis Model 3, released in North America and licensed by Majesco in 1998 for $49.95, had a smaller form factor and removed the expansion port. Like the CDX, the Genesis Model 3 includes a six-button controller. The first handheld system to play games from a home console was the TurboExpress, released by NEC in 1990, that used the same TurboChips as the TG-16. Unlike the TurboExpress, the Nomad functioned as both a handheld gaming system (using the Nomad's 3.25-inch backlit color screen and internal mono speaker) and a home console (using the Nomad's A/V port and the controller port for an additional Genesis controller).

The Sega CD and 32X ceased manufacturing in 1996, and the Genesis ceased manufacturing in 1999. During its manufacturing run, the Genesis received many peripheral upgrades to prolong its lifespan. There were even passthrough cartridges for the Genesis like *Sonic and Knuckles* that sat atop another Genesis cartridge inserted into the Genesis via the cartridge port. The Sega Genesis was the first truly 16-bit gaming system. For home consoles, the volume slider and headphone port on the Model 1 Genesis are unique. The Nomad is an example of the home console audio hardware expanded into a functional handheld gaming system. Its weakness was power consumption at six AA batteries between two to three hours of play.

December 1988—*Mega Man 2*—Famicom/NES

PUBLISHER: Capcom. RELEASE DATE: December 1988 (JP) as *Rock Man 2*, June 1989 (NA), December 14, 1990 (EU). COMPOSERS: Takashi Taeishi (credited as Ogeretsu Kun) and Manami Matsumae. SERIES: *Mega Man*. GENRE: Platformer. NOTABLE MUSICAL TRACK: "Dr. Wily Stage 1 and 2."

The soundtrack of *Mega Man 2* is well-regarded from the NES *Mega Man* games. Capcom credited its staff members by aliases in place of their full names. Takashi Taeishi, the primary composer, is credited as Ogeretsu Kun. Manami Matsumae composed a few tracks, including the title screen and Air Man's stage. Yoshihiro Sakaguchi, credited as Yuukichan's Papa, was the sound programmer for the game and *Mega Man* (1987). The notable musical track, "Dr. Wily Stage 1 and 2," accompanies the first two stages of Wily Castle. It is one of the most popular tracks of the series and one of the best on the NES. The track is in a minor key for a sense of danger and peril. The brisk tempo and melodic ideas, layered atop each other, add heightened tension and urgency.

SOURCES

Campbell, Keith. "Corruption: Adventure Reviews." *Computer and Video Games*, July 1988, pp. 92–93.
"Corruption: Hall of Light." *Hall of Light—The*

Database of Amiga Games, 13 May 2017, hol.abime.net/3094. Accessed 31 Jan. 2020.

Explained.Today. "Mega Man 2 Explained." 2016, everything.explained.today/Mega_Man_2/.

"How to Make Sega Genesis Music (in 1994)." *YouTube*, 16 Aug. 2017, www.youtube.com/watch?v=WEvnZRCW_qc.

"King's Quest IV: The Perils of Rosella: Making of." *The Sierra Chest*, www.sierrachest.com/index.php?a=games&id=4&fld=making. Accessed 16 Aug. 2018.

"Manami Matsumae." *Video Game Music Preservation Foundation Wiki*, 3 Oct. 2019, vgmpf.com/Wiki/index.php/Manami_Matsumae. Accessed 10 Apr. 2020.

"Master System." *Sega Corporation*, sega.jp/fb/segahard/master/data.html. Accessed 3 Aug. 2018.

Matsumae, Manami. Interview. *USgamer.net*, 20 Jan. 2016, *www.usgamer.net/articles/manami-matsumae*.

Matsumae, Manami. "Mega Man Theme Song Composer Still Jamming Over 20 Years Later." Interview by Mary-Ann Lee. *Tech in Asia*, 14 Dec. 2014, www.techinasia.com/manami-matsumae-video-game-music.

"Mega Drive/Genesis Sound Engine List." *Game Developer Research Institute*, 24 Dec. 2017, gdri.smspower.org/wiki/index.php/Mega_Drive/Genesis_Sound_Engine_List. Accessed 18 Nov. 2018.

"PC Speaker." *OSDev Wiki*, 27 June 2020, wiki.osdev.org/PC_Speaker. Accessed 22 Jan. 2021.

"Who Had a Trademark on 'Mega Drive' in 1989?" Sega-16, 13 May 2012, www.sega-16.com/forum/showthread.php?20946-Who-had-a-trademark-on-quot-Mega-Drive-quot-in-1989.

Sega Corporation. "Master System." sega.jp/fb/segahard/master/data.html.

"Sega Master System." *Sega Retro*, 29 Jan. 2016, segaretro.org/Sega_Master_System.

Sega Retro. "Sega Master System." 29 Jan. 2016, segaretro.org/Sega_Master_System. Accessed 30 Jan. 2016.

Wittel, Greg. "Sega Genesis: Specs." *Digital Extremes*, dextremes.com/genesis/gen-spec.html. Accessed 3 Aug. 2018.

1989 in Review

April 21, 1989—Nintendo Game Boy

MANUFACTURER: Nintendo. RELEASE DATE: April 21, 1989 (JP), July 31, 1989 (NA), September 28, 1990 (EU). PRODUCTION DATES: April 21, 1989–March 23, 2003. LAUNCH PRICE: $89.99 with *Tetris*. MODEL NUMBER: DMG-01. SOUNDCHIP: LR3502. AUDIO: Mono (stereo from the 3.5mm audio-out port).

The Game Boy was the first handheld gaming system with stereo audio. The Game Boy popularized portable gaming. The Game Boy was Nintendo's first handheld entry under the Game Boy brand. Handheld gaming systems supported stereophonic audio before home consoles. The Game Boy was the first handheld gaming system with stereophonic audio through the headphone port. The Game Boy has a built-in speaker capable of monaural sound. The headphone audio-out jack sends out a stereo signal. The Game Boy contains the Sharp LR35902 chip. The chip is the system's CPU, supporting four sound channels. The software can set each of the four sound channels toward the left audio channel, right, or both. However, the Game Boy

Nintendo Game Boy 1989. The internal speaker is located on the lower right corner of the device. The volume slider modulates the internal speaker's volume. The audio output ports are 3.5mm (Evan-Amos, "Game-Boy-FL").

does not support smooth stereo panning once the software assigns the channels in the stereophonic mix. Two sound channels support variable pulse waves through PSGs

Nintendo Game Boy Pocket 1996. The internal speaker is located on the lower right corner of the device. The volume slider modulates the internal speaker's volume. The audio output ports are 3.5mm (Evan-Amos, "Game-Boy-Pocket-FL").

Nintendo Game Boy Color 1998. The internal speaker is located on the lower right corner of the device. The volume slider modulates the internal speaker's volume. The audio output ports are 3.5mm (Evan-Amos, "Nintendo-Game-Boy-Color-FL").

with four duty cycle settings. One sound channel supports wavetable synthesis to create periodic waveforms or playback 4-bit PCM samples. The remaining sound channel supports white noise synthesis.

The Game Boy Pocket (MGB-001),

released in North America on July 21, 1996, used a smaller form factor, a true black and white screen (instead of a green monochromatic screen), and two AAA batteries (instead of four AA batteries). The Game Boy Light, released exclusively in Japan on April 14, 1998, added a backlight to the screen, making the screen much easier to see. The Game Boy Color, released in Japan on October 21, 1998, added a color screen, which enhanced Game Boy games and used more color palettes for Game Boy Color games. The original Game Boy ceased manufacturing in 1999, and the Game Boy Color ceased manufacturing on March 23, 2003. The audio capabilities offered more variety than the original Game Boy's monochromatic display. The Game Boy Color infused new life into the Game Boy and gave Nintendo time to develop the Game Boy Advance.

September 1989—Atari Lynx

MANUFACTURER: Atari. RELEASE DATE: September 1989 (NA), September 1990 (JP), 1990 (EU). PRODUCTION DATES: September 1989–1995. LAUNCH PRICE: $179.99 with *California Games* (1989). SOUNDCHIP: Mikey. AUDIO: Mono.

The Lynx was the first handheld gaming system with a color LCD screen, backlit display, and an ambidextrous button configuration. Released by Atari, the Lynx was Atari's first handheld system. The Lynx supports monaural audio from its internal speaker and 3.5mm audio-out port. The sound of the Lynx uses the custom "Mikey" chip. It supports four sound channels. Each channel has a waveform selector, including square, triangle, sine, and white noise. Each channel has an 8-bit DAC, which is ideal for digitized sound and voice synthesis. So, the Lynx could generate sounds from a waveform selector (a subset of waveforms) and PCM. The Lynx produces tones from 100 Hz to well above the range of human hearing. The Lynx sound processor understands MOD files, a music data format first used on the Commodore Amiga. When Atari released Lynx development documents, Christopher Grigg, music director

Atari Lynx back 1989. The internal speaker is on the right side of the device when held in its original position. The volume slider modulates the internal speaker's volume. The audio output ports are 3.5mm (Evan-Amos, "Atari-Lynx-Front-Top").

Atari Lynx II 1991. The internal speaker is on the right side of the device when held in its original position. The volume slider modulates the internal speaker's volume. The audio output ports are 3.5mm (Evan-Amos, "Atari-Lynx-II-Top-Laid").

at Epyx, developed SPL (Sound Programming Language).

The Lynx II, released in 1991, was a smaller, lighter model with longer battery life, improved hardware, and a clearer backlit color screen. Unlike the original Lynx model, which supports monaural audio from the 3.5mm audio-out port, the Lynx II supports stereo sound with panning from the 3.5mm audio-out port. The Lynx ceased manufacturing in 1995. All of the Lynx's innovations weren't enough to overcome the success of the Game Boy. No other handheld gaming system ever used the ambidextrous design of the Lynx. Atari's dominant years were in the early 1980s.

September 1989—*Xenon 2 Megablast*—Amiga

PUBLISHER: Image Works. RELEASE DATE: September 1989 (EU). COMPOSER: David Whittaker. SERIES: *Xenon*. GENRE: Shmup.

NOTABLE MUSICAL TRACK: "Megablast—Hip Hop on Precinct 13."

Xenon 2 Megablast was the first computer game to present a licensed song accurately. The game shows the Amiga's PCM capabilities, in contrast with other computers and gaming systems of the time. The Amiga version features the notable musical track, "Megablast—Hip Hop on Precinct 13," licensed by British musician Tim Simenon of "Bomb the Bass." The theme from the John Carpenter movie *Assault on Precinct 13* is the basis for the song. The song uses audio samples from the Sly and the Family Stone song "You Can Make It If You Try." There are two versions of the song in the game. The loading music is a nearly faithful rendition. The background music in the game is a simplified version. The Amiga version adds helicopter sound effects at the beginning and end of the track. David Whittaker, the game's composer, also wrote the track for the Commodore 64 game *Lazy Jones*, which was the basis for the dance hit "Kernkraft 400" by Zombie Nation, a number 1 song in many European countries.

September 14, 1989—*DuckTales*—Famicom/NES

PUBLISHER: Capcom. RELEASE DATE: September 14, 1989 (NA), January 26, 1990 (JP), December 14, 1990 (EU). COMPOSER: Hiroshige Tonomura. SERIES: *DuckTales*. GENRE: Platformer. NOTABLE MUSICAL TRACK: "The Moon."

The game is the first of two games for the NES based on the Disney afternoon cartoon of the same name. The title screen music uses the theme song from the Disney television series *DuckTales*. Each of the game's five locations has a unique upbeat track. The minor key of the music for the Transylvania stage fits the setting of ghosts, mummies, and tombstones. Other musical moments include invincibility music, boss music, defeat boss jingle, Gyro bonus stage music, and Stage Select music. The notable musical track, "The Moon," is praised as one of the best musical tracks by Capcom for the NES. The track reflects the space environment in its introduction, using an unusual 15/8 meter and a melody that rises and falls slowly, reflecting the stage's gravity and physics in a musical way. In 2013, Capcom released *DuckTales: Remastered*. Chiptune composer Jake Kaufman (composer of *Shantae* [2002], *Double Dragon Neon* [2012], and *Shovel Knight* [2014]) remastered the soundtrack, blending chiptune sounds with acoustic and electric instruments, extending musical content, and including chiptune versions of new content as a musical option.

November 1989—*Commando*— Atari 7800

PUBLISHER: Atari. RELEASE DATE: November 1989 (NA). GENRE: Run and gun. NOTABLE MUSICAL TRACK: "Title Theme."

Commando is the only Atari 7800 game to use the POKEY and TIA for audio. This game and *Ballblazer* are the only games ever to use the POKEY hardware for enhanced sound. Only *Commando* uses both the POKEY and the TIA for the music and sound effects. *Commando* exhibited the richest soundtrack and audio design for the very reason of having the most audio resources available. Specific to *Commando*, the POKEY generates in-game music, and the TIA generates the game's sound effects. The audio design harnesses six sound channels. Some of the game's sound effects include scrolling text, helicopter, bullets, an enemy death, an item pickup. The title theme uses four voices for bass, harmony, melody, and percussion. The stage music uses the same arrangement of voices, reserving the sound effects for the two sound channels of the TIA. There are also tracks for the final wave of soldiers at the end of each area and the area completion/briefing for the next area. The last area has unique stage music. The music is set in A minor

key using many triplet rhythms. For most of the game, the constant sounds of bullets overwhelm the audio design. However, these sounds never compromise the music.

1989—Sound Blaster—Soundcard

MANUFACTURER: Creative Labs. RELEASE DATE: late 1989 (NA). PRODUCTION DATES: late 1989—Still in production. LAUNCH PRICE: $239.95. MODEL NUMBER: 1.0. SOUND-CHIP: YM3821. AUDIO: Stereo.

The Sound Blaster was the top-selling sound card for the PC one year after its release. Released by Creative Labs, the Sound Blaster is compatible with all AdLib-supported games. It contains the Yamaha YM3821, the same soundchip as the AdLib Music Synthesizer Card, for FM synthesis. Unique to the Sound Blaster was the Digital Sound Processor (DSP). A feature of the DSP was the decompression of ADPCM samples, allowing for the Sound Blaster to playback monophonic audio samples of 8 bits. Also unique to the Sound Blaster was the inclusion of the game port. Before the acceptance of USB ports, the game port was the port used to connect joystick devices. For a price slightly more than the AdLib soundcard, the Sound Blaster supported all games with AdLib audio, with the bonuses of ADPCM support and the valuable game port. Within a year, the price of the Sound Blaster was already lower than its competitors. However, it lacked pre-installed sounds like the Roland MT-32.

The Sound Blaster Pro, released in May 1991, contained two YM3821 chips for

Sound Blaster 1989. The audio output ports are stereo RCA (Wdwd, "Soundblaster-1.0-ct1320," CC-BY-SA 3.0).

stereo audio with faster sampling rates for mono and stereo audio and a master volume control, and a built-in CD-ROM interface. The Sound Blaster 16, released in June 1992, supported CD-DA and included an expansion header for the Wave Blaster. This soundcard connects atop the Sound Blaster 16, adding General MIDI with wavetable synthesis support. The most recent soundcard in the series is the Sound Blaster AE-9, released on July 10, 2019.

SOURCES

"Architecture of the Atari Lynx." *Diary of an Atari Lynx Developer*, 20 Sept. 2010, atarilynxdeveloper.wordpress.com/2010/09/20/architecture-of-the-atari-lynx/.

"Chris Grigg." *Video Game Music Preservation Foundation Wiki*, 18 Jan. 2021, www.vgmpf.com/Wiki/index.php?title=Chris_Grigg. Accessed 30 May 2021.

Fayzullin, Marat. "GameBoy Technical Information." Home Page of Marat Fayzullin, fms.komkon.org/GameBoy/Tech/. Accessed 3 Aug. 2018.

"Gameboy Sound Hardware." *Gameboy Development*, 9 May 2008, gbdev.gg8.se/wiki/articles/Gameboy_sound_hardware. Accessed 24 Apr. 2021.

Horowitz, Ken. "GEMS Shine on the Genesis." *Playing at the Next Level: A History of American Sega Games*, McFarland, 2016, pp. 66–68.

"List of Every GBC Black Cart (dual Compatibility) Game." *RetroGaming with Racketboy*, www.racketboy.com/forum/viewtopic.php?f=6&t=48882. Accessed 11 Feb. 2020.

Nintendo. "Game Boy Programming Manual Version 1.1." 3 Dec. 1999, ia803208.us.archive.org/9/items/GameBoyProgManVer1.1/GameBoyProgManVer1.1.pdf. Accessed 21 Apr. 2021.

Vaskelis, Darius. "Atari Lynx FAQ." *AtariAge*, 3 Aug. 2003, atariage.com/Lynx/faq/index.html.

"Wavetable Archive." *GbdevWiki*, 16 Jan. 2017, gbdev.gg8.se/wiki/articles/Wavetable_Archive. Accessed 26 Nov. 2018.

1990 in Review

1990—*Klax*—Lynx

Publishers: Atari and Tengen. RELEASE DATE: 1990 (NA). COMPOSER: Lx Rudis. GENRE: Puzzle. NOTABLE MUSICAL TRACK: "Title Screen."

Klax is one of the only Lynx games to support stereophonic audio from the Lynx II. The music was composed on the Emu SP12, a drum machine with primitive sampling. The samples were manually transferred to the Amiga Cygnus line editor to make them playable. Then each song was composed again in Music-X, an Amiga program. *Klax* stands out within the Lynx game library because of the game's stereophonic audio. The original model of the Lynx supports monaural audio. The Lynx II supports stereophonic audio. Players never heard *Klax's* stereophonic audio until 1991, only when players owned a Lynx II and hooked up speakers or headphones into the system's headphone port. The notable musical track, "Title Screen," is the only musical track in the game. The track is comprised almost entirely of audio samples of a slap guitar, bass drum, distortion guitar, and other percussion and guitar samples. The title screen music exhibits stereo panning and the left and right placement of tiles during gameplay.

March 22, 1990—*After Burner II*— Mega Drive/Genesis

PUBLISHER: Sega of America. RELEASE DATE: March 22, 1990 (NA), March 23, 1990 (JP), 1990 (EU). SERIES: *After Burner*. GENRE: Combat flight simulator. NOTABLE MUSICAL TRACK: "After Burner."

After Burner II is the only known game on the Genesis to play 3 kHz 4-bit samples from the SN76489A soundchip. The game uses the Genesis's SN76489A for instrument samples and YM2612 for voice samples. The preferred method for playing 8-bit PCM samples was the Genesis's DAC. However, the YM2612 soundchip includes the DAC. PSGs are not designed to playback audio samples. However, audio designers and composers found innovative ways to generate new sounds with the audio hardware.

The instrument samples for the SN76489A are only at a bit depth of 4 bits. For the voice commands of the game, the game uses the YM2612 for PCM samples of better quality. Each sound channel is set as a specific volume before the sample can be played. Most Genesis games used the stereo DAC of the YM2612 to play 8-bit PCM. However, an FM channel is deactivated when using the DAC in this way. The music is not compromised, even though it too uses the YM2612. Some of the samples that play through the PSG are an orchestra hit, snare drum, toms, cymbal crash, triangle, and cowbell. At times, the sixth FM channel generates white noise to simulate brushes. In addition to the music, three PCM voice samples shout at the player continuously throughout the game. These voice commands are "Fire" to indicate the time to lock on to an enemy plane, "Be careful" to indicate an incoming missile from behind, and "The enemy" to indicate an enemy plane flies behind the player. During playback of one of the voice samples, the only compromise in audio is the loss of the Vulcan cannon sound. In a Sega Genesis launch title, *Altered Beast* (1989), the music would turn off during all voice samples. In *After Burner II*, voice commands are heard throughout the entire game without interfering with the music.

April 3, 1990—*Splatterhouse*— TG-16

PUBLISHER: NEC. RELEASE DATE: April 3, 1990 (JP), April 21, 1990 (NA). COMPOSERS: Katsuro Tajima and Yoshinori Kawamoto. SERIES: *Splatterhouse*. GENRE: Beat-em-up. NOTABLE MUSICAL TRACK: "Evil Cross and Nightmare (Stage 4)."

The dark and somber soundtrack of *Splatterhouse* complements the game's horror aspects. The game is a port of the 1989 arcade game of the same name. The composers for the game are Katsuro Tajima, credited as Chopin, and Yoshinori Kawamoto, credited as Kawagen. The soundtrack is sad, dark, and melancholy, almost etheric at times. All of the religious symbolism in the game, including the cross boss, the grave at the game's conclusion, and the altar in the church, were either replaced or removed in copies outside of Japan. Strangely, the organ music still plays, and the candles from the altar are visible floating in mid-air in a long hallway.

Music is an integral part of the exposition of Stage 4: The Forbidden Room. The boss fight of Stage 4 takes place in a church chapel. The notable musical track, "Evil Cross and Nightmare (Stage 4)," resembles the musical style of the Baroque period (1600–1750), particularly the composers Johann Sebastian Bach, composer of the Cantatas for the church, Johann Pachelbel, composer of the Pachelbel Canon, and George Frideric Handel, composer of the Messiah. After defeating the boss, organ music plays as the protagonist Rick approaches an altar. The music continues as Rick waits by the altar. When the organ music concludes, dissonant music plays as a fade-out leads into the next stage.

April 26, 1990—SNK Neo Geo Multi Video System

MANUFACTURER: SNK. RELEASE DATE: April 26, 1990 (JP), August 22, 1990 (NA), 1991 (EU). PRODUCTION DATES: April 26, 1990–December 1997. SOUNDCHIP: YM2610. AUDIO: Stereo.

The Multi Video System (MVS) was an arcade system that read at most six game cartridges at a time. Released by SNK, the games on the MVS looked and played like other contemporary arcade games of the time. The innovation of interchangeable game cartridges for the arcade market ensured that arcade owners could keep the machine stocked with the latest games without requiring an entirely new machine. Some arcade machines read from interchangeable cartridges, including the Nintendo PlayChoice-10 (1986–1992) and the Sega Mega-Tech (1988, released in Europe, Australia, and Asia but not in North America). Unlike the Neo Geo MVS, the purpose of these machines was to promote the games of the NES and Genesis, respectively. The MVS's audio capabilities include Software-Controlled Sound Generators (SSG), a limited subset of PSGs with only square waves and noise, FM synthesis, and ADPCM. The Neo Geo MVS ceased manufacturing in December 1997. It received games until July 2004 and technical support until August 2007.

SNK Neo Geo MVS 1990 (w:User:Beeble-brox, "Neo Geo full on," CC-BY-SA 3.0).

August 24, 1990—*Michael Jackson's Moonwalker*—Genesis

PUBLISHER: Sega of America. RELEASE DATE: August 24, 1990 (NA), September 29, 1990 (JP), January 25, 1991 (EU). GENRE: Platformer. NOTABLE MUSICAL TRACK: "Beat It."

Michael Jackson's Moonwalker is a collaboration between Sega of America and Michael Jackson. The game includes Jackson's likeness and music, arranged for the Genesis soundchips. The game was based on the 1988 movie *Moonwalker*, an anthology of music videos from Jackson's album *Bad* (1987). The soundtrack contains chiptune arrangements of Michael Jackson's hit songs from the albums *Bad* and *Thriller*. Some songs included in the Genesis version are "Smooth Criminal," "Beat It," "Another Part of Me," "Billie Jean," and "Bad." The game's levels and music are inspired by

the 1988 film of the same name. The player plays as Michael, whose move set is based on his dance moves. The player activates the "dance attack" by holding the Magic button until about half of the magic bar is depleted. Michael will break into a flash mob with the nearby enemies dancing to a short section of one of his songs.

The game is the first in only a few games with which Michael Jackson was involved. Some of the other games with his involvement include *Sonic the Hedgehog 3*, *Space Channel 5*, *Space Channel 5: Part 2*, and *Michael Jackson: The Experience*. The FM sounds lend themselves well in playing the notable musical track, "Beat It." The melody uses a synth trumpet sound. Light harmonies use square waves. The main repeating riff uses a grungy electric guitar-like sound. The sampled drum hits contribute to the 80s feel. There has been speculation as to the whereabouts of the song "Thriller" in the game. It does not appear in most versions of the game. However, a pre-production EP-ROM includes "Thriller" as Round 3 music during the appropriate graveyard scene in Stage 3–2. REV00 (the first revised version for release) plays "Thriller" during Jackson's dance attack in Stages 3–1, 3–2, 3–3, and 5–3.

October 6, 1990—Sega Game Gear

MANUFACTURER: Sega. RELEASE DATE: October 6, 1990 (JP), April 5, 1991 (NA), April 1991 (EU). PRODUCTION DATES: October 6, 1990–1997. LAUNCH PRICE: $149.99. MODEL NUMBER: 2110. SOUNDCHIP: SN76489. AUDIO: mono (stereo through 3.5mm audio-out port).

The Game Gear was Sega's first handheld game console released worldwide. Released by Sega in Japan on October 6, 1990, the Game Gear was heavily inspired in design and hardware by the SMS. The Game Gear could even play SMS games with a Master Gear Converter accessory. Many Game Gear games are conversions of SMS games. Unlike the SMS, the Game Gear supports stereo audio with panning through its 3.5mm audio-out port. The Game Gear contains the Texas Instruments SN76489 soundchip, the same soundchip as the

Sega Game Gear back 1990. The internal speaker is on the lower-left corner of the device. The audio output ports are 3.5mm (Evan-Amos, "Sega-Game-Gear-Handheld-02").

Sega Master System, almost identical to the ColecoVision, Tandy, and IBM PCjr. The SN76489 in the Game Gear supports four sound channels. Three of the channels generate square waves only, and the other sound channel generates white noise. Each channel has a four-octave range.

The Game Gear ceased manufacturing in 1997. Although the Game Gear has better graphics than the Game Boy, the Game Boy sold significantly better than the Game Gear due to issues with short battery life, lack of original titles, and weak support from Sega. Improvements and developments do not necessarily equate to profitability and success in the video game industry.

November 21, 1990—Super Famicom/Super NES

MANUFACTURER: Nintendo. RELEASE DATE: November 21, 1990 (JP), August 23, 1991 (NA), June 1992 (EU). PRODUCTION DATES: November 21, 1990–September 2003. LAUNCH PRICE: $199.99 with *Super Mario World*. MODEL NUMBER: SNS-001. SOUND-CHIP: Sony SPC700. AUDIO: Stereo (surround with Dolby Surround).

The Super Nintendo Entertainment System (Super NES, or SNES) was the first home console to support Dolby Surround. Released as the Super Famicom in Japan, the SNES was a "Super" version of the NES from 1985. Unlike the Famicom and NES, the Super Famicom and SNES are almost the same. The SNES has unique

audio capabilities, vastly different from the NES. There were many good video game soundtracks on the SNES, each game using its own set of ADPCM instruments and voice samples. The SNES was the first home console to support Dolby Surround. The audio options for games lacking the Dolby license are monaural or stereophonic via the A/V port.

The soundchip of the SNES is the S-SMP. Ken Kutaragi was the designer, and Sony was the manufacturer. The S-SMP contains two components: the Sony SPC700 and the S-DSP. The SPC700 is the CPU responsible for audio. It has eight ADPCM channels, and each channel plays a 16-bit audio sample for more realistic sounds. Each of the eight channels is mix via volume control to the left or right audio channel for a stereo mix. The channels can be played at different pitches and can have an Attack-Delay-Sustain-Release (ADSR) envelope applied to them. Instead of playing an audio sample, any of the channels can play white noise.

Additionally, the S-DSP can apply an echo to the audio. The S-DSP mixes the eight channels based on panning settings and outputs the audio signal. The S-SMP contains 64 kB of SRAM for loading audio samples and music data from a game cartridge. For each SNES game, the sound engine is sent to the SRAM of the S-SMP on game start when the SNES reads its boot ROM.

N-SPC is a sound engine found in many SNES games. Named after Nintendo and the SPC700 microprocessor, the SNES launch title *Super Mario World* (1990) and *Pilotwings* (1990) contain the earliest version of N-SPC. This version includes many features for manipulating audio, including Set Instrument, Notes, Rest, Volume, Tempo, Echo Parameters, and Tuning. *Super Mario World 2: Yoshi's Island* (1995) contains the basic version of N-SPC. This version adds such features as Per-Voice Transpose, Pitch Envelope Off, and Percussion Patch Base. N-SPC was limited in the memory size of samples. Other games that use the N-SPC sound engine or a variant include *F-Zero* (1990), *The Legend of Zelda: A Link to the Past* (1991), *Star Fox* (1993), and *Kirby Super Star* (1996).

Nintendo SNES back 1990. The audio output ports are mono RCA (with RF adapter) and A/V (with composite video and stereo audio RCA adapter) (Evan-Amos, "Nintendo-Super-NES-Console-BR").

SNES A/V composite cable 1990. It connects to the SNES, N64, and GameCube's A/V ports and outputs audio in analog stereo (Evan-Amos, "Nintendo-SNES-N64-Game-Cube-AV-Composite-Cable").

The New-Style Super NES, released in North America on October 20, 1997, for $99.95, removed the expansion port, cartridge eject button, power LED, and internal RF modulator and deactivated the pins for S-Video and SCART video outputs from the Multi A/V port. The SNES ceased manufacturing in 1999, the Super Game Boy ceased manufacturing in 2001, and the Super Famicom ended manufacturing in September 2003. The SNES soundtracks lack the Genesis' grungy and metallic sounds from FM synthesis. The SNES lacks backward compatibility with the NES. Subsequent Nintendo gaming systems could no longer rely on Sony for soundchips. The Super NES Classic Edition, released in North America on

September 29, 2017, for $79.99, is a dedicated console with 21 included SNES games, including the previously unreleased *Star Fox 2* and a Linux operating system running a SNES emulation engine with save state support.

Sources

Deleon, Nicholas. "Confirmed: Michael Jackson Composed the Music for Sonic the Hedgehog 3." *TechCrunch*, 3 Dec. 2009, techcrunch.com/2009/12/03/confirmed-michael-jackson-composed-the-music-for-sonic-the-hedgehog-3/.

"Gau of the Veldt." "SPC-700 Programming Information." *Emulator Review*, emureview.ztnet.com/developerscorner/SoundCPU/spc.htm. Accessed 3 Aug. 2018.

Loughrey, Clarisse. "Turns Out Michael Jackson Definitely Composed Music for Sonic the Hedgehog 3." *The Independent*, 26 Jan. 2016, www.independent.co.uk/arts-entertainment/music/news/michael-jackson-confirmed-to-have-composed-music-in-secret-for-sonic-the-hedgehog-3-a6835121.html.

"Nintendo Music Format (N-SPC)." *Super Famicom Development Wiki*, wiki.superfamicom.org/nintendo-music-format-(n-spc). Accessed 24 Nov. 2018.

"SPC Hacking Guide." *SMW Central*, 30 Aug. 2010, www.smwcentral.net/?p=viewthread&t=38116.

"SSG." *NeoGeo Development Wiki*, 11 Feb. 2017, wiki.neogeodev.org/index.php?title=SSG. Accessed 26 Nov. 2018.

"Unused/underused Solutions to Limitations of the Genesis/MD." *Sega-16*, 25 Oct. 2010, www.sega-16.com/forum/showthread.php?-14476-Unused-underused-solutions-to-limitations-of-the-Genesis-MD.

Nintendo New-Style SNES back 1997. The audio output ports are A/V (with composite video and stereo audio RCA adapter) (Evan-Amos, "Nintendo-Super-NES-Console-101-BR").

1991 in Review

1991—*Ys III: Wanderers from Ys*—TG-CD

PUBLISHER: NEC. RELEASE DATE: 1991 (NA). COMPOSER: Ryo Yonemitsu. SERIES: *Ys*. GENRE: Action RPG.

Ys III: Wanderers from Ys was one of the first home console games to use CD technology. The game's audio design uses the soundchips of the TG-16 and the CD-DA of the TG-CD at times. The CD-DA enhances the game's synth-rock soundtrack with sounds and audio quality that was impossible without CD technology's additional memory and audio capabilities. The musical tracks featuring electric guitar and the drum kit are stored as CD-DA. Voice acting and samples are made possible by the additional memory and audio capabilities of the TG-CD. The music enhances the game's characters and world. Some tracks generate sound from soundchips, while others use CD-DA exclusively.

An example of the interplay of soundchip-generated tracks and CD-DA tracks is the transition heard in Tigray Quarry's theme. The track slowly builds up, leading to a quick, powerful crescendo. The rock soundtrack is intensified in the notable musical track, "Beat of Destruction," heard after Adol exits the boat at Demanicus Island. The track is heard again after defeating Garland, the next-to-last boss in the game.

February 6, 1991—*Street Fighter II: the World Warrior*—Arcade

PUBLISHER: Capcom. RELEASE DATE: February 6, 1991 (JP), March 1991 (NA, EU). COMPOSERS: Yoko Shimomura and Isao Abe. SERIES: Street Fighter II. GENRE: Fighting. NOTABLE MUSICAL TRACK: "Guile's Theme."

Street Fighter II: The World Warrior was the best-selling arcade game during its time in arcades. Released in the arcades, the game established the fighting genre as a profitable genre in the industry. As a result of the game's success, many gaming companies designed fighting games with characters from their other games. It was one of the first games to encourage video game tournaments due to its two-player competitive fights. The game includes eight playable characters and four boss characters, each from a different country with an appropriate battle stage. Each fighting stage has a unique musical track that reflects the musical tradition of its country. For example, when the player's character fights Balrog (M. Bison for Japanese players), the fighter from Las Vegas, the musical track uses synthesized sounds and bell tones. These timbral choices are appropriate for a venue with lots of electronic sounds from slot machines at the casinos. For the stage music for matador Vega's (Balrog for Japanese players) stage set in Spain, the harmonic movement and rhythmic patterns are reminiscent of the paso doble, a musical dance style associated with bullfighting.

April 26, 1991—*Ninja Gaiden*—Lynx

PUBLISHER: Atari. RELEASE DATE: April 26, 1991 (NA). SERIES: *Ninja Gaiden*. GENRE: Beat-em-up. NOTABLE MUSICAL TRACK: "Level 1 Boss Theme."

Ninja Gaiden was one of the best-looking handheld games at the time of its release. It is the only home port of the arcade version of *Ninja Gaiden*. Unlike other handheld games at the time, each of the game's four stages and bosses has its unique musical track (eight unique tracks). With the end credits, there are nine music tracks in total. The tracks vary in tone based on the stage. The track that accompanies Level 3 uses the minor key to build up tension as the game progresses. In contrast, the track for Level 2 is slick and cool, using a jazzy bassline and a swing feel. The Level 3 Boss Theme is inspired by "Iron Man" by Black Sabbath.

July 1991—SNK Neo Geo Advanced Entertainment System

MANUFACTURER: SNK. RELEASE DATE: July 1991 (JP, NA), 1991 (EU). PRODUCTION DATES: July 1991–1997. LAUNCH PRICE: $649.99 with either *Baseball Stars Professional* or *NAM-1975*. SOUNDCHIP: YM2610. AUDIO: Stereo.

SNK Neo Geo AES back 1991. The audio output ports are A/V (with RF adapter or composite video and stereo audio RCA adapter) (Evan-Amos, "Neo-Geo-AES-BR").

The Neo Geo Advanced Entertainment System (AES) plays arcade-perfect games at home. Released by SNK first as a rental system in Japan on April 26, 1990, and then as a home console in Japan and North America in July 1991, the Neo Geo AES is the home console counterpart to the MVS, with matching hardware. MVS and AES games are identical in their ROM code but different when played on each device. The AES was a smaller device, like most home consoles, that could play one AES cartridge at a time. Games played on the AES may include additional in-game options for home play and different cartridge slot designs. The Neo Geo Advanced Entertainment System (AES) was the first home console capable of running arcade-perfect games. The AES plays MVS games with an adapter. So, while Sega promoted the Genesis as a home console with arcade-like graphics, the AES honestly brought the arcade experience to the home market. Also, the AES was the first home console to use external memory cards.

Neo Geo AES A/V composite cable 1991. It connects to the Neo Geo AES's A/V port and outputs audio in analog mono (Evan-Amos, "Neo-Geo-AES-Composite-Cable").

The AES contains the Yamaha YM2610 soundchip. The chip allows for 15 sound channels. Four channels use FM synthesis. Three channels generate square waves. One channel produces white noise. The remaining seven channels are ADPCM channels reserved specifically for digital sound samples. The majority of music on the Neo Geo uses the FM channels. The square wave channels have limited settings, best used for simple sound effects. The ADPCM channels are best for sounds that a PSG can't quickly synthesize, such as voices, percussions, and wind instruments.

The Neo Geo AES ceased manufacturing in 1997. The arcade and home console markets first merged with the MVS and AES and their audio options. Even in 1997, the AES was the only gaming system that faithfully played arcade games. Unfortunately, the cost of the system was the biggest obstacle to overcome. The Neo Geo Mini, released in Japan on July 24, 2018, is a dedicated console with 40 included AES games, in the form factor of an MVS arcade cabinet, with the ability to play games either on the arcade cabinet's mini screen or on television from the console's mini-HDMI port.

July 1991—Magician Lord— Neo Geo AES

PUBLISHER: SNK. RELEASE DATE: July 1991 (JP, NA). COMPOSERS: Yuka Watanabe, Hiroaki Shimizu, and Hideki Yamamoto. GENRE: Platformer. NOTABLE MUSICAL TRACK: "Surrender!! (Stage 2)."

The soundtrack of *Magician Lord* uses FM synthesis with speech samples. The game was a pack-in game for the system. Each of the game's five stages has a musical theme that sets the mood for the stage setting. Throughout the game are cutscenes with voice samples with subtitles whenever the dark wizard Gal Agiese speaks. The voice sample quality is good, although the voice acting is not very engaging. The notable musical track, "Surrender!! (Stage 2)," plays on Stage 2: To the Evil Mine. It is particularly intense with deep percussion, high bell tones, and FM synth sounds. The cymbal and drum hit samples drive the track even when the melody drops out to FM warbling effects.

August 30, 1991—*Wing Commander 2: Vengeance of the Kilrathi*—PC

PUBLISHER: Origin Systems. RELEASE DATE: August 30, 1991 (NA). COMPOSERS: Dana Karl Glover, George Sanger, and Nenad Vugrinec. SERIES: *Wing Commander.* NOTABLE MUSICAL TRACK: "Grim or Escort Mission."

Wing Commander 2: Vengeance of the Kilrathi was one of the first PC games to support the Sound Blaster sound card. Released for MS-DOS, the game's release merited the purchase of the Sound Blaster soundcard. The Sound Blaster was a soundcard a few years late into the PC audio competition that still managed to overcome all others in sales. The game supports many sound cards, including the Sound Blaster, Roland MT32, Microsoft GS, and FM Towns. The Speech Accessory pack was an upgrade to the game, stored on seven floppy disks that added voice acting to the game's characters, only for computers with the Sound Blaster. The disks contain pre-recorded ADPCM voice files by members of the development team. With the Sound Blaster card and game disks, characters in the game spoke with relatively decent vocal quality. The game's production quality elevated the game to that of a movie with improved visuals and voice acting.

December 1991—*Monkey Island 2: LeChuck's Revenge*—PC

PUBLISHER: Lucasfilm Games. RELEASE DATE: December 1991 (NA). COMPOSERS: Michael Land, Peter McConnell and Clint Bajakian. SERIES: *Monkey's Island.* GENRE: Point-and-click adventure. NOTABLE MUSICAL TRACK: "The Bone Song."

Monkey Island 2: LeChuck's Revenge was the first game by LucasArts to use iMUSE (Interactive Music Streaming Engine). Released for MS-DOS, Michael Land composed the music for the games in the *Monkey Island* series. iMuse was used in the adventure/point-and-click games by the LucasArts company from 1991 to 2000. The last game to use iMUSE at LucasArts was *Escape from Monkey Island* (2000, PC). iMUSE, the creation of Michael Land and Peter McConnell, is an audio system that adjusts the audio in real-time to match on-screen events through musical transitions. There are about 10 games, all developed and published by LucasArts, that use the iMUSE engine. Other games include *Sam and Max Hit the Road* (1993, PC), *Star Wars Dark Forces* (1995, PC), and *Grim Fandango* (1998, PC). iMUSE also worked for home console games. The development of iMUSE improved the soundtracks of games, allowing music to adapt more seamlessly to changes in real-time.

iMUSE adjusts the audio in real-time to match on-screen events through musical transitions. One dynamic musical example possible with iMUSE occurs when Guybrush, the protagonist, enters and leaves a building in the town of Woodtick. While inside the building, iMUSE selects the Woodtick theme with a different instrument. While outside the building, iMUSE picks a closing musical figure to transition smoothly to the original Woodtick theme. Unlike CD-DA or other linear music formats, iMUSE adapts to actions and events seamlessly and interactively. In an example of music influencing gameplay, Guybrush falls from a big tree and has a hallucination. He sees his parents as skeletons singing the notable musical track, "The Bone Song." He enjoys the song and dance routine and jots down the song's lyrics on a "spit-encrusted paper." The order of bones from the song is needed to navigate the corridors of LeChuck's Fortress.

Sources

Christensen, Ken. "Monkey Island 2 Walkthrough." *World of Monkey Island*, www.worldofmi.com/gamehelp/walk/monkey2.php. Accessed 16 Aug. 2018.

Giant Bomb. "Neo Geo (Platform)." 10 Mar. 2015, www.giantbomb.com/neo-geo/3045-25/. Accessed 30 Jan. 2016.

Goninon, Mark. "Where Are They Now?—Michael Z. Land." *Choicest Games*, 3 Dec. 2014, www.choicestgames.com/2014/12/where-are-they-now-michael-z-land.html.

Land, Michael. Interview. *GSoundtracks*, web.archive.org/web/20170815193359/www.gsoundtracks.com/interviews/land.htm. Accessed 6 Aug. 2018.

"List of AES and MVS Version Differences." *Neo-Geo.com*, 8 Dec. 2016, www.neo-geo.com/forums/showthread.php?269243-List-of-AES-and-MVS-Version-Differences.

Maher, Jimmy. "Wing Commander II." *The Digital Antiquarian*, 2 Mar. 2018, www.filfre.net/2018/03/wing-commander-ii/.

"Neo Geo (Platform)." *Giant Bomb*, 10 Mar. 2015, www.giantbomb.com/neo-geo/3045-25/.

Plasket, Michael. "Magician Lord." *Hardcore Gaming 101*, 13 Sept. 2017, www.hardcoregaming101.net/magician-lord/.

Ritz, Eric J. "An Introduction to Mode 7 on the SNES." *One More Game-Dev and Programming Blog*, 16 July 2013, ericjmritz.wordpress.com/2013/07/15/an-introduction-to-mode-7-on-the-snes/.

"SNK Neo-Geo 101: A Beginner's Guide." *Racketboy*, 20 May 2011, www.racketboy.com/retro/snk-neo-geo-101-a-beginners-guide.

1992 in Review

July 14, 1992—*Mario Paint*— Super Famicom/SNES

PUBLISHER: Nintendo. RELEASE DATE: July 14, 1992 (JP), August 1, 1992 (NA), December 10, 1992 (EU). COMPOSERS: Hirokazu Tanaka, Ryoji Yoshitomi, and Kazumi Totaka. GENRE: Graphics suite. NOTABLE MUSICAL TRACK: "Demo Song C (Mushroom Icon)."

The player composes chiptune music in *Mario Paint*. The game was one of the first with a music composition mode. There is a Paint mode (like the computer program *Kid Pix*), an animation mode (create a flipbook), a game mode (swatting flies in Knat Attack), and a Music mode. In Music Mode, the player places stamps on a musical staff (representing musical notes). Each stamp represents an instrument or sound (all ADPCM samples); the vertical position on the staff determines the musical pitch. There is no winning condition in Music Mode. Any music created can be used in the Animation Mode. The game has three default songs. The first is a remix of the main *Super Mario Bros.* theme by Koji Kondo. The second is a remix of "Twinkle, Twinkle, Little Star." The notable musical track, "Demo Song C (Mushroom Icon)," showcases the sound collection of the

SNES. The track includes basic waveforms and sampled instrument sounds interjected with dog barks, cat meows, pig snorts, and baby giggles. Music Mode is an accessible interface for anyone to compose music for the SNES soundchip without advanced programming skills.

Late 1992—*Power Factory Featuring C+C Music Factory*—Sega CD

PUBLISHER: Sony Imagesoft. RELEASE DATE: Late 1992 (NA). SERIES: *Make My Video*. GENRE: Music production. NOTABLE MUSICAL TRACK: "Gonna Make You Sweat (Everybody Dance Now) ft. Freedom Williams."

Power Factory Featuring C+C Music Factory is an instance of the music industry promoting itself through the video game industry. The game features full-motion video and CD audio in a game for a home console. Games more accurately show video and play back audio using CD technology (more memory and CD-DA). The player selects from one of three songs from *Gonna Make You Sweat*, the 1990 debut album of music group C+C Music Factory, and then edits many short video clips to create an original music video. The two members of C+C Music Factory recorded original FMV content for the game as part of the thin story. The songs are instantly recognizable as the original master recordings from the 1990s. The game was the first game designed around master recordings instead of covers. *Power Factory Featuring C+C Music Factory* was an example of a financial failure at the time. However, the game resides within video game audio history for its prominence in music and music culture.

December 20, 1992—*Streets of Rage 2*—Genesis

PUBLISHER: Sega. RELEASE DATE: December 20, 1992 (NA), January 14, 1993 (JP), January 1993 (EU). COMPOSERS: Yuzo Koshiro and Motohiro Kawashima. SERIES: *Streets of Rage*. GENRE: Beat-em-up. NOTABLE MUSICAL TRACK: "Go Straight (First Stage)."

The game's soundtrack reflects the maturity that Sega was evoking in their marketing of the Genesis. Composers Yuzo Koshiro and Motohiro Kawashima composed the music on an NEC PC-88 with the Sound Board II (FM synthesis support).

Koshiro modified MML (Music Macro Language), the audio programming language of the PC-88, to develop "Music Love," his own original audio programming language. Koshiro composed all but three tracks, with Motohiro Kawashima writing the remaining three tracks. In the place of catchy and repetitious melodies are musical tracks infused with techno beats, adding a rugged feel. The soundtrack displays nightclub influences in electronic funk, trance music, house synths, and dance rhythms. The notable musical track, "Go Straight (First Stage)," shows the Genesis' sound capabilities. It exhibits panning of the left and right speakers and melodic material that avoids feeling overly repetitious.

SOURCES

Auffret, Dominique. "Designing 2D Graphics in the Japanese Industry." *Video Game Densetsu*, 1 Nov. 2018, vgdensetsu.tumblr.com/post/179656817318/designing-2d-graphics-in-the-japanese-industry.

Hopkins, Christopher. "Mario Paint: An Accessible Environment of Musical Creativity and Sound Exploration." *Journal of Literature and Art Studies*, vol. 5, no. 10, Oct. 2015, pp. 847–858.

1993 in Review

1993—*Lords of Thunder*—TG-CD

PUBLISHER: Hudson Soft. RELEASE DATE: 1993 (NA). COMPOSER: Satoshi Miyazawa. GENRE: Shmup. NOTABLE MUSICAL TRACK: "Boss Theme 1."

Lords of Thunder is an enjoyable shmup game with a heavy metal soundtrack. The soundtrack relies on heavy metal instrumental music comprised of electric guitar distortions with occasional synths. The composer for the game is Satoshi Miyazawa, credited as Groove King. The game is regarded well in the shmup genre. The music sounds rather wild and untamed, reined in by the steady drum kit. The notable musical track, "Boss Theme 1," is heard for the first six boss battles. The track uses electric guitars that shriek as they slide in

pitch, downward and upward. A guitar rapidly plays upward and downward repeatedly in the background. The addition of the organ adds an ominous tone even with the frantic guitars engulfing its sound. The drum kit keeps the beat but does not get in the way of the guitar battle.

March 8, 1993—*The Terminator*—Sega CD

PUBLISHER: Virgin Games. RELEASE DATE: March 8, 1993 (NA). COMPOSERS: Tommy Tallarico, Bijan Shaheer, Joey Kuras, and TeknoMan. SERIES: *Terminator*. NOTABLE MUSICAL TRACK: "Taking to the Air."

The Terminator was the first game for home consoles with surround sound. The game is based on the 1984 movie of the same name, even though *Terminator 2: Judgment Day* was released in theaters in 1992. The game's audio uses QSound, an early form of surround sound. Tommy Tallarico, one of the game's composers, is the Video Games Live concert tour co-founder. The notable musical track, "Taking to the Air," accompanies the first stage of the game and showcases the audio quality of CD-DA. The track is upbeat with synths, electric guitars, and percussion. Audio effects allow the instrument sounds to morph and pan, in particular long, elongated sounds. The guitar riffs seem as if they were improvised. The game offers solid action and great graphics. The new medium on the Sega CD allows for actual clips from the movie and an excellent soundtrack.

May 23, 1993—*King Arthur's World*—Super Famicom/SNES

PUBLISHER: Jaleco. RELEASE DATE: May 23, 1993 (EU), September 4, 1994 (NA), October 10, 1994 (JP). COMPOSER: Martin Simpson and Justin Scharvona. GENRE: Real-time strategy. NOTABLE MUSICAL TRACK: "Funky Goblin (Goblin's Underworld Caverns 1 and 3)."

King Arthur's World was the first game for home consoles to license and support Dolby Surround. The short track that plays before the title screen is a surround sound test, adjusting the panning of each instrument and sound between the three speakers of Dolby Surround (left, right, and surround). The game announces in text: "Presented in Dolby Surround." Dolby Surround encodes and decodes multi-speaker audio signals to and from stereophonic audio signals. The game offers side-scrolling puzzles in the same vein as *Lemmings*, in which the characters move on their own while the player allocates resources and gives orders to ensure the characters move safely around obstacles. The addition of Dolby Surround encodings was completed near the release date by Jez San, the founder of the developer Argonaut. The game uses the SNES soundchip's volume registers to represent a sound's 3D

position in the speaker setup, mainly used in *King Arthur's World* for the sounds of the weather and the opening surround sound test. The track that plays after defeating the Demon Overlord, the game's final boss, is a canon resembling a Bach invention, especially with the harpsichord sounds, and "Canon in D" by Johann Pachebel.

The notable musical track, "Funky Goblin (Goblin's Underworld Caverns 1 and 3)," resembles a hip-hop track using drums, percussion, and primitive electronic instrument sounds. The track accompanies King Arthur's armies as they descend into the caverns of the Goblin Demons. The track begins with chords on an electronic organ and an unexpected tremolo that swells and diminishes in volume. Then a trumpet section repeats a chord seven times quickly as the drums and percussion enter. The melody is first played by the electronic organ and then passed to an electronic brass section. At the track's end is a brief improvised riff from the electronic keyboard.

September 24, 1993—*Myst*—Mac

PUBLISHER: Cyan. RELEASE DATE: September 24, 1993 (NA). COMPOSER: Robyn Miller. SERIES: *Myst*. GENRE: Graphic adventure. NOTABLE MUSICAL TRACK: "The Finale."

Myst is one of the best-selling computer games of all time. Released for the Mac, *Myst* was a phenomenon in the video game industry. It was the best-selling PC game of all time until *The Sims* surpassed it in 2002. Brothers Robyn and Rand Miller designed the game in their basement. The game is an adventure/point-and-click game that plays like an interactive storybook. The player navigates each world ("ages" in the game lore), comprised of pre-rendered 3D images. Much of the game's appeal is in the puzzles to solve. There are two men trapped within books who explain the game's lore through FMVs. The game originally had no music (the sounds were considered sufficient to create the worlds' soundscape). Cyan, the developer company of *Myst*, released the game's soundtrack on CD in 1995 (reprinted in 1998 by Virgin). There were few video game soundtracks released on CD by the parent company even in 1995.

The game's soundtrack, while light and subtle, complements the exploratory gameplay and stillness of time. The game immerses the player through storytelling and decision-making—music and ambient sounds fill the void as the player explores the desolate "ages," learning about its lore and navigating within it. One of the puzzles in the game involves inputting a musical pattern into a spaceship to activate it on Myst Island. Within the spaceship is an organ that the player can play to hear the pitches outlined in a journal entry. The pattern is C4->C5->Eb5->F4->Bb3. Inputting the correct musical sequence sends the player to the Selenitic Age. Once in this age, another puzzle involves a five-note melody of sounds heard from parabolic dishes to activate a door.

October 4, 1993—Panasonic 3DO

MANUFACTURERS: Panasonic, Matsushita Electric, GoldStar, Sanyo. RELEASE DATE: October 4, 1993 (NA), March 20, 1994 (JP), June 11, 1994 (EU). PRODUCTION DATES: October 4, 1993–1996. LAUNCH PRICE: $699.99 with *Crash 'n' Burn*. AUDIO: CD-DA.

The 3DO was the first gaming system to include a CD music visualizer. Released by Panasonic, the 3DO was unlike any other gaming system in that it is a set of specifications for the console. The 3DO Company received a royalty from each purchase. Panasonic released the first version of the 3DO, manufactured later by Matsushita Electric, GoldStar, Sanyo. The 3DO was the first home console with a 32-bit CPU, meaning that the 3DO's CPU had an instruction set with twice as many instructions as a 16-bit CPU. It has a front-loading CD tray (the 3DO reads CD-DA) and controllers with headphone ports and volume controls. The 3DO supports Dolby Surround sound.

The 3DO contains a customized digital signal processor (DSP) that processes and mixes audio data. The DSP works with high-quality digital audio stored as 16-bit samples, providing a running cycle that exactly matches the 44,100 sample

Panasonic 3DO back 1993. The audio output ports are mono RCA (with RF adapter) and stereo RCA (Evan-Amos, "3DO-FZ-1-Console-BR").

pairs per second needed for generating full-frequency digital audio. The DSP offers 13 channels to read standard audio samples through DMA input, each 16 bits wide, to read normal audio samples. The DSP can add reverb or filter effects to audio.

The 3DO was the first gaming system to include a CD music visualizer. A visualizer uses an algorithm to generate real-time animations of colors and images to match music or audio. The 3DO was marketed as a multimedia device rather than a gaming system. The 3DO was a gaming system and a CD player. When a CD is inserted, the 3DO plays the CD's music and shows the images of the music visualizer on-screen. The 3DO adds the music visualizer to music from CDs. The 3DO ceased manufacturing in January 1996. Surprisingly, the open standard model didn't catch on with the industry. The large console manufacturers liked receiving a cut from all game sales. Without the 3DO, all electronics manufacturers who sold the 3DO as their small start to the video game industry were eliminated. Ultimately, without a steady user base, a system can't sustain itself in the industry.

October 21, 1993—*Alone in the Dark*–3DO

PUBLISHER: Interplay. RELEASE DATE: October 21, 1993 (NA). COMPOSER: Philippe Vachey. GENRE: Survival horror. NOTABLE

MUSICAL TRACK: "In the Eye of the Storm (Title Theme)."

Alone in the Dark was a pioneering game for its 3D graphics, ambient sound design, and gameplay in the horror genre. The successful immersive quality of the game's tension and horror is due to the game's audio design. Philippe Vachey, responsible for the game's music and sound effects, was an in-house composer of developer Infogrames at the time. The 3DO version is unique for using 30 minutes of CD-DA music, contrasting with the PC version's MIDI soundtrack. The successful immersive quality of the game's tension and horror is due to the game's audio design. Despite being limited to synthesized instrument libraries, Vachey composed a haunting and organic soundtrack. The game's music shares orchestral traits with horror movie soundtracks like slow piano hits and pizzicato strings. Considering that the game was released in 1992, film score elements were impressive within the medium of a video game. The 3DO soundtrack is much more realistic than the MIDI soundtrack of the PC and stands out more within gameplay. Even without the gameplay, the game's soundtrack is good enough on its own and resembles a horror movie soundtrack.

September 23, 1993—*Sonic CD*—Mega CD/Sega CD

PUBLISHER: Sega. RELEASE DATE: September 23, 1993 (JP), October 1993 (EU), November 19, 1993 (NA). COMPOSER: Naofumi Hataya and Masafumi Ogata (JP), Spencer Nilsen (NA, EU). SERIES: *Sonic the Hedgehog*. NOTABLE MUSICAL TRACK: "Sonic Boom (Intro and Title Theme)."

The North American and Japanese soundtracks of *Sonic CD* differ in audio generation and mood. Both soundtracks are recognizable amongst the Sega CD soundtracks. For its American release, Sega of America replaced some musical tracks to differentiate the music from other games with similar electronic dance music. The "Present" and "Future" songs are recorded as CD-DA, while the "Past"

songs are played via PCM. The American soundtrack only replaces the CD-DA tracks, so the PCM tracks are identical in all regions. The PCM tracks were written with the Japanese soundtrack in mind. The Japanese soundtrack is upbeat and lively. The American soundtrack is more reflective with a harder rock edge at times. The intro song in each reflects the musical style of the soundtracks. Both versions make use of CD-DA for a song with vocals. The Japanese version is "You Can Do Anything." The notable musical track, "Sonic Boom," the theme of the American version, is sung by San Francisco jazz trio Pastiche. Despite the differences, players favor both soundtracks.

November 23, 1993—Atari Jaguar

MANUFACTURER: Atari. RELEASE DATE: November 23, 1993 (NA), June 27, 1994 (EU), December 8, 1994 (JP). PRODUCTION DATES: November 23, 1993–1996. LAUNCH PRICE: $249.99 with *Cybermorph*. SOUNDCHIP: Jerry. AUDIO: Stereo.

The Jaguar was the sixth and last programmable console developed under the Atari brand. Released by Atari, the maximum number of sound channels in the Jaguar is limited only by the software. The Jaguar contains "Jerry," the nickname for Atari's proprietary chip with sound control. Some sound types available for any sound channel include wavetable synthesis, FM synthesis, PCM, and Amplitude Modulation (AM) synthesis. Unlike the previous gaming systems, the Jaguar's proprietary chip has no limit to the number of simultaneous sound channels. Instead, the games themselves determine the number of concurrent sound channels. The Jaguar's limited amount of internal RAM computes only so much audio at a time (the "Jerry" chip does more than just audio processing). Four channels for music and four channels for sound effects are reasonable considering the limited amount of internal RAM. Other audio hardware includes a DSP with eight kB of storage for audio data and code and a stereo DAC with a bit depth of 16 bits.

The Jaguar CD, released by Atari in

Atari Jaguar and Jaguar CD back 1995. The audio output ports are A/V (with composite video and stereo audio RCA adapter) (Evan-Amos, "Atari-Jaguar-CD-Back").

North America for $149.95 on September 21, 1995, was a peripheral for the Jaguar that supported CD media, adding CD-DA capabilities and an interactive music visualizer for audio CDs. The peripheral was shipped with *Vid Grid* (1995) and *Blue Lightning* (1995) as pack-in games, the *Tempest 2000* soundtrack, and a demo disc of *Myst* (1995). The Jaguar CD was the last peripheral for an Atari gaming system. The Jaguar CD adds two CD-DA channels as audio tracks from the game disc. The Jaguar CD games can also use the sound capabilities of the Jaguar. Unlike sounds generated from soundchips, a laser within a CD player needs to position itself to scan the part of a disc with the audio information. Audio from a disc is often referred to as streaming audio due to scanning a disc. CD-DA works best for musical tracks, not short audio clips (the laser needs time to search for each clip and reposition itself).

The peripheral has a built-in music visualizer called the "Virtual Light Machine." Designed and programmed by Jeff Minter with Ian Bennett, the VLM converts a CD's audio data into colorful video displays that react in time with the music. Although the 3DO was the first gaming system with a music visualizer, Virtual Light Machine is unique in that it responds to user input. The player can adjust the effects using the Jaguar's game controller. By keying the number pad on the Jaguar controller, users can implement 81 unique effects in real-time. Tapping on the "B" button causes the screen image to flash in a strobe-light effect. Also, although the 3DO's music

visualizer was released first, the VLM first appeared in the early 1990s as an independent device, accompanying live concerts and parties.

The Jaguar and Jaguar CD ceased manufacturing in 1996, barely a year after its release. Atari was still in a financial mess, even with the new owner. In mid–1996, Atari merged with JTS, but this didn't lead to anything for the Atari brand. The Jaguar CD had one of the shortest manufacturing runs in the entire timeline. The Jaguar will be remembered as the first home console without a dedicated soundchip and software-driven sound channels. Only 11 games were released for the Jaguar CD during its production run. Jaguar CD games had access to the combined audio hardware of 2 CD-DA channels and a variable number of sound channels using wavetable synthesis, FM synthesis, PCM, and AM synthesis, all mixed into a stereo audio signal. Almost every home console used CD-based media (except the Nintendo 64). Atari no longer has a gaming system on the market.

SOURCES

"Atari Jaguar System Info." *The Video Game Museum*, www.vgmuseum.com/systems/jaguar/. Accessed 3 Aug. 2018.

"Audio Hardware–3DO." altmer.arts-union.ru/3DO/docs/DevDocs/ppgfldr/mgsfldr/mpgfldr/02mpg002.html. Accessed 28 Sept. 2020.

Brennan, Martin, et al. "Technical Reference Manual: Tom & Jerry." *Emu-Docs*, 28 Feb. 2001, emu-docs.org/Jaguar/General/jag_v8.pdf.

Campbell, J. "Audio Hardware." 2010, hackipedia.org/Platform/3D0/html,%203DO%20SDK%20Documentation/Type%20A/ppgfldr/mgsfldr/mpgfldr/02mpg002.html.

Coleman, J. "Atari Jaguar CD." 8 June 2004, www.gamefaqs.com/jaguarcd/916378-jaguar-cd/reviews/74108.

"King Arthur's World (Europe) SNES ROM." *CDRomance*, 23 May 1993, cdromance.com/snes-rom/king-arthurs-world-europe/. Accessed 18 Jan. 2021.

Krotz, Scott A. "Michel Buffa's 3DO FAQ WWW Page." *Polytech Nice Sophia*, users.polytech.unice.fr/~buffa/videogames/3do_faq2.4.html. Accessed 3 Aug. 2018.

"Macintosh User." "Jaguar CD Review for Jaguar CD." *GameFAQs*, 8 June 2004, www.gamefaqs. com/jaguarcd/916378-jaguar-cd/reviews/74108.

Reese, Emily, and Nora Huxtable. "Top Score: Robyn Miller and the Story of Myst." *Classical MPR*, 25 Aug. 2014, www.classicalmpr.org/story/2014/07/31/robyn-miller-myst-top-score.

Simpson, Martin P. "The First King Arthur, and Dolby Surround." *Martin P Simpson*, 17 Sept. 2011, www.martinpsimpson.com/2011/09/first-king-arthur-and-dolby-surround.html. Accessed 21 Apr. 2021.

Tallarico, Tommy. "Interview: Tommy Tallarico (Composer)." Interview by Ken Horowitz. *Sega-16*, 1 June 2005, www.sega-16.com/2005/06/interview-tommy-tallarico/.

The Video Game Museum. "Technical Specs." www.vgmuseum.com/systems/jaguar/.

1994 in Review

1994—*C.P.U. Bach*–3DO

PUBLISHER: MicroProse. RELEASE DATE: 1994 (NA). DESIGNER: Sid Meier. GENRE: Music creation.

C.P.U. Bach was one of the first games for home consoles with algorithmically generated music based on user parameters. The game results from at least a year of work by Sid Meier and Jeffrey L. Briggs on a computer algorithm that creates original compositions imitating the musical style of Baroque composer Johann Sebastian Bach. The gaming software displays its original composition as sheet music on the screen. It generates the matching audio through wavetable MIDI. There are seven primary settings from the "Change Concert" menu: Concert, Sunrise, Sandman, Party, Soiree, Literary, and Reverie. There are 16 different styles of composition, including Prelude and Concerto. Unlike earlier instances of algorithmically generated music (without influence by the player), the player influenced the musical output by adjusting sliders that skewed the probabilities of different musical elements. The user alters the sliders (displayed as music staves, with increasing numbers of notes acting as a makeshift bar graph) to adjust how frequently the program will choose to generate that type of music. The user can change how often a given instrument will appear in the composition. Twelve instruments are available from pianos, woodwinds, brass, and even a chorus and a synthesized square wave.

The four visual presets range from a basic kaleidoscope-style visualizer to a gallery of scrolling nature photographs and even a Musical Analyzer. The Musical Analyzer displays the currently-playing piece in musical notation, along with a textual description of what each instrument is doing and some definitions of the musical terminology used by the program. Bach appears for the "In Concert" setting, playing the lead instrument of the current piece while typically accompanied by floating instruments representing the rest of the orchestra. Meier expressed concern that his project would not be received well in the world of music composition due to any claim that a computer could write music as well as a human. The game represents an overlap of technology and art that is more acceptable today than at the time of the game's release.

1994—*Tommy Tallarico Virgin Games Greatest Hits Volume One*—Music Album

PUBLISHER: Tommy Tallarico. RELEASE DATE: 1994.

Tommy Tallarico Virgin Games Greatest Hits Volume One was the first commercial album released worldwide by a video game composer. Released by Tommy Tallarico, the album is a 1-disc CD set featuring music from five games published by Virgin Games. Before this release, Japan was the primary market of audio sales of video game soundtracks, boosted overall with the introduction of the CD (originally released in 1983 in the U.S.). Seven of the 13 tracks from *Tommy Tallarico Virgin Games Greatest Hits Volume One* are original video game compositions by Tallarico. Nevertheless, he produced, arranged, performed, and recorded the album. Tallarico encoded the album in QSound, the surround sound format supported by the Sega CD. One year prior, Tallarico composed the soundtrack to *The Terminator*, the first video game to use QSound. After *Tommy Tallarico Virgin Games Greatest Hits Volume One*, video game composers realized that they possess the prestige and name recognition necessary for promoting their work to a worldwide audience. The quality of the soundtracks on the albums remained faithful to the audio fidelity of the soundtracks from the games themselves due to CD-DA, the audio standard for audio CDs, and early CD-based video games.

March 19, 1994—*Super Metroid*— Super Famicom/SNES

PUBLISHER: Nintendo. RELEASE DATE: March 19, 1994 (JP), April 18, 1994 (NA), July 28, 1994 (EU). COMPOSERS: Kenji Yamamoto and Minako Yamano. SERIES: *Metroid*. GENRE: Action-adventure. NOTABLE MUSICAL TRACK: "Lower Maridia."

The soundtrack of *Super Metroid* is eerie and ambient, evoking isolation and the unknown. The soundtrack, the collaboration of composers Kenji Yamamoto and Minako Hamano, is highly regarded. The soundtrack is eerie and atmospheric, fitting the setting of an unknown planet with secrets to uncover. The game opens with a powerful, foreboding arrangement of the central theme to the original NES game, bridging the previous *Metroid* games musically. Next, the pounding drums announce an intergalactic gladiatorial fanfare in "Theme of Super Metroid." The melody references the "Samus Aran Appearance Jingle." Some ambient tracks accompany Upper Maridia and Lower Maridia, the rocky underwater zones. The ambient tracks use a bell and flute tones, moving at a slow pace reflective of the calmness of the water.

The game combines textual, audio, and visual cues to set up pivotal moments. In the opening sequence, the first cinematic moment, Samus Aran, the protagonist, recognizes her inevitable defeat by Ridley in the first boss encounter. The player cannot prevent this outcome. During the countdown escape that follows, the music sets the game's overall tone, supporting the story and gameplay in just the first 10 minutes. The soundtrack exploits the audio capacity of the SNES to promote an intimate connection between the zones of Planet Zebes.

April 2, 1994—*Final Fantasy VI*— Super Famicom/SNES

PUBLISHER: Square Soft. RELEASE DATE: April 2, 1994 (JP), October 11, 1994, as *Final Fantasy III* (NA). COMPOSER: Nobuo Uematsu. SERIES: *Final Fantasy*. GENRE: RPG. NOTABLE MUSICAL TRACK: "Aria di Mezzo Carattere (Opera Scene)."

An original opera, comprised of an aria and three instrumental pieces, ties into the plot of *Final Fantasy VI*. The scenes and music at the opera house allow Celes, the protagonist, to embark mistakenly onto the Blackjack, the airship of Setzer. The musical instrumentation of the opera is simpler, most noticeably in the vocals, on the SNES when compared to the PlayStation. The PlayStation port (as *Final Fantasy VI*) includes FMV cutscenes. The audio for the PlayStation port copies that of the SNES version.

The notable musical track "Aria di Mezzo Carattere (Opera Scene)" is the vocal aria from the opera *Maria and Draco*. *Final Fantasy VI* director Yoshinori Kitase wrote the lyrics for the song, and Nobuo Uematsu composed the music. The player actively participates in the aria by selecting the correct lyrics for Celes to sing three times. If the player hesitates or chooses incorrectly, the opera concludes abruptly, and the player begins a new attempt. Ted Woolsey, the English translator for the U.S. release, found the opera scene unique and exciting and consequently spent time translating the scene's dialogue in battle texts, the opera text displayed during the different cinematics, and the standard screen text.

April 13, 1994—*Tempest 2000*— Jaguar

PUBLISHER: Atari. Release Dates: April 13, 1994 (NA), June 27, 1994 (EU), December 15, 1994 (JP). COMPOSERS: Alastair Lindsay and Kevin Saville. GENRE: Tube shooter. NOTABLE MUSICAL TRACK: "Mind's Eye (Stage 1)."

Tempest 2000 was the first game to have its soundtrack included separately on a gaming system. The game takes its inspiration from *Tempest* (1981, Arcade). At the time of its release, the soundtrack could also be purchased on CD directly from Atari. The CD includes remixes of the tracks with more variety in instrumentation. The CD was later bundled with the Atari Jaguar CD system to demonstrate the system's music playing abilities. The soundtrack CD is the source for the audio for later ports of the game. The music was composed in the chip-based MOD music file format, first used on the Commodore Amiga. The tracks loop without an audible gap while maintaining great audio clarity due to the MOD format. A quick programmed fade seamlessly switches between musical tracks. The game was exclusive to the Jaguar for two years. The techno soundtrack is a highlight of the game, benefiting from the Jaguar's CD-quality audio despite the ROM cartridge media. The notable musical track, "Mind's Eye (Stage 1)," is an outstanding techno-rave track that complements the psychedelic visuals and frantic gameplay.

June 1994—Nintendo Super Game Boy

MANUFACTURER: Nintendo. RELEASE DATE: June 14, 1994 (JP), June 1994 (NA, EU). LAUNCH PRICE: $59.99. SOUNDCHIP: LR3502. AUDIO: same as SNES.

The Super Game Boy, released by Nintendo, allows Game Boy games to be fully playable on a home console. The Super Game Boy inserts into the SNES cartridge port. The Super Game Boy contains a cartridge port for Game Boy games (it doesn't support Game Boy Color nor Game Boy

Nintendo Super Game Boy 1994. The Super Game Boy lacks audiovisual output ports. It communicates with the SNES through the cartridge port (Evan-Amos, "Nintendo-Super-Game-Boy").

Advance games). The Super Game Boy has almost all of the hardware components of the Game Boy within. However, it lacks an A/V out port, so its signals pass through the SNES. It lacks an internal oscillator, instead of using the clock speed of the SNES, which causes between a 1.5 percent and 2.4 percent difference in gameplay and audio rate between games played on the Game Boy compared to the Super Game Boy (The Super Game Boy divides the CPU Clock Speed of the SNES by 5 to calculate roughly the Game Boy CPU Clock Speed). Games on the Super Game Boy use the audio hardware of the Super Game Boy (the same as the Game Boy) and the audio hardware of the SNES.

Game Boy games published after the release of the Super Game Boy took advantage of the additional capabilities of the Super Game Boy and SNES. For example, *Donkey Kong*, the Super Game Boy enhanced game, was released in Japan on June 14, 1994. The cartridge contains game data for the Game Boy (normal) and additional data for the enhancements of the SNES, two versions of the same game. The audio of *Donkey Kong* is improved on the Super Game Boy because the game uses DPCM samples on the SNES. In particular, a voice sample vastly improved the sound of Pauline, the damsel in distress, crying for help. Also, the ending credits theme uses additional sounds not available on the Game Boy.

In July 1995, *Animaniacs* was released in North America as a Super Game Boy enhanced game. Not only does the game have its color palette and border, but it has a soundtrack that is almost entirely different from the Game Boy soundtrack. The title screen music is unique to the Super Game Boy version. The Genesis port of the game is the source of the other musical tracks. These soundtrack decisions explain why the Super Game Boy version has an enhanced soundtrack because there already was a 16-bit soundtrack from which to take inspiration. So, the development staff did not need to hire a new composer to compose new music tracks for the Super Game Boy component of the cartridge.

The Super Game Boy was the first device to allow players to turn on and off the audio without a menu nor physical switch. The mute feature was a button combination: R, L, L, R, R, L. Hori, a Japanese company, made the Super Game Boy Commander, a licensed controller specifically for the Super Game Boy in Japan with additional support for the Super Famicom

Nintendo Super Game Boy 2 1998. The Super Game Boy 2 lacks audiovisual output ports. It communicates with the Super Famicom through the cartridge port (Evan-Amos, "Nintendo-Super-Game-Boy-JP-2").

(the controller also works with the SNES). It has the button layout of the Game Boy, except for a switch for Super Game Boy and Super Famicom and the L and R buttons of the SNES placed on the face of the controller. Of particular interest to us is the L button, labeled on the controller as "Mute-L." When the player sets the mode switch to Super Game Boy while playing a Super Game Boy game, this button will toggle the Super Game Boy and SNES audio on and off (using a macro to submit the button combination from a single press of the Mute-L button).

The Super Game Boy 2, released exclusively in Japan on January 30, 1998, improved the Super Game Boy by using its internal oscillator, configured to the exact clock speed of the Game Boy, thus avoiding the speed differences in gameplay and audio. The Super Game Boy 2 adds additional themed borders and includes a game link port used to connect two Game Boys, two Super Game Boy 2s, or a combination of both. The Super Game Boy ceased manufacturing in 1994, shortly after its release. The Super Game Boy succeeded as the first peripheral to ever play handheld games on a home console, considering that it contained almost all of the hardware of a Game Boy. Nintendo continued to design peripherals to play their handheld games on their home consoles (Game Boy Player for the GameCube).

July 1994—*Road Rash*—3DO

PUBLISHER: Electronic Arts. RELEASE DATE: July 1994 (NA). COMPOSER: Don Veca. SERIES: *Road Rash*. GENRE: Racing. NOTABLE MUSICAL TRACK: "Rusty Cage" by Soundgarden.

Road Rash was one of the first video games to license master recordings from mainstream rock bands. The game includes FMV cutscenes and a soundtrack of musical tracks by Soundgarden, Monster Magnet, Paw, Therapy?, Hammerbox, and Swerve Driver. Of all the ports of *Road Rash*, the 3DO version is the only version with additional music. Soundgarden is the band most represented in the soundtrack, with their tracks "Outshined," "SuperUnknown," "Kick Stand," and "Rusty Cage." The soundtrack of *Road Rash* includes original music during the races and the licensed musical tracks during cutscenes. At the menu screen, referred to in-game as the "Restroom," the player can listen to the songs through the virtual jukebox. The notable musical track, "Rusty Cage," plays during the game's attract screen. The musical track in the 3DO version lasts for a little over a minute and 15 seconds. The master recording by Soundgarden and the full-motion video add realism to the 3DO version, differentiated from the cartoony style of the other versions of *Road Rash*. The electric guitar, drums, and vocals are of good quality. The FMV shows motorcycles weaving through traffic with a police car trailing. The FMV scenes contrast with the static attract screens of the other versions of *Road Rash*, which are brief with pixelated art and chiptunes.

November 11, 1994—*Sonic Triple Trouble*—Game Gear

PUBLISHER: Sega. RELEASE DATE: November 11, 1994 (JP), November 15, 1994 (NA), November 1994 (EU). COMPOSER: Yayoi Fujimori. SERIES: *Sonic the Hedgehog*. GENRE: Platformer. NOTABLE MUSICAL TRACK: "Sunset Park Act 3."

Sonic Triple Trouble has an original soundtrack, with visuals and gameplay closely resembling the *Sonic the Hedgehog* games on the Genesis. It was the first of the five *Sonic* games for the Game Gear to be a Game Gear exclusive. The game had Sonic and Tails as playable characters with Knuckles as an adversary, much like *Sonic the Hedgehog 3* for the Genesis. Unlike the Genesis games, *Sonic Triple Trouble* added the Jet Board and Propeller Shoes items for Sonic and the Hyper Heli-Tails and the Sea Fox for Tails. The game's sound

test included 29 songs. The notable musical track, "Sunset Park Act 3," is the game's only Act 3 with a unique musical track. During the Act, Sonic runs atop a moving train toward a cannon at the train's front. At times, harmony joins the melody. In the middle of the track, there is a melody with a countermelody. The rhythmic pulse of the bass line and percussion propel the track. Due to the limited number of sound channels for both music and sound effects, it is difficult to appreciate both themes at once when attacking enemies and jumping. The gameplay and visuals more closely match the 16-bit visuals and gameplay from the Genesis.

November 22, 1994—Sega Saturn

MANUFACTURER: Sega. RELEASE DATE: November 22, 1994 (JP), May 11, 1995 (NA), July 8, 1995 (EU). PRODUCTION DATES: November 22, 1994–April 3, 1999. LAUNCH PRICE: $399.99 (with *Virtua Fighter*). SOUNDCHIP: YMF292. AUDIO: Stereo with QSound.

The Saturn was Sega's first CD-based home console, with 34 sound channels from its soundchip and disc sensor. The Saturn's audio output options were either analog stereo or QSound over stereo (for games that supported surround sound). The Saturn's audio hardware includes the Yamaha YMF292 microprocessor with FH-1 DSP and the CD laser. The YMF292 microprocessor, also known as the SCSP (Saturn Custom Sound Processor), supports 32 sound channels, each generated

Sega Saturn Back 1994. The audio output ports are A/V (with composite video and stereo audio RCA adapter) (Evan-Amos, "Sega-Saturn-Mk-II-NA-BR").

as FM synthesis or PCM. As PCM or ADPCM, the channels use 16-bit bit depth and a sample rate of up to 44.1 kHz. Each of the 32 sound channels passes through the FH-1 Digital Signal Processor. The DSP provides 16 sound effect presets: Reverb, Early Reflection, Delay, Pitch Shift, Chorus, Flanger, Symphonic, Surround, Voice Canceler, Auto Pan, Phaser, Distortion, Filter (high-pass, low-pass, BP), Dynamic Filter, Parametric EQ, and Mixer. The CD sensor reads two CD-DA sound channels (stereo). The Saturn's DAC mixes the sound channels from all sources to an analog stereo signal, with or without QSound encodings.

On April 3, 1999, the Sega Saturn ceased manufacturing. In the case of Sega, there were internal conflicts within Sega of America and Sega of Japan. Sega of Japan researched and developed the Saturn, while Sega of America researched and developed the 32X. The Saturn was not compatible with the 32X nor the Sega CD. This dilemma confused consumers who expected a manufacturer to readily support a new gaming system or peripheral for many years.

December 3, 1994—Sony PlayStation

MANUFACTURER: Sony. RELEASE DATE: December 3, 1994 (JP), September 9, 1995 (NA), September 29, 1995 (EU). PRODUCTION DATES: December 3, 1994–March 26, 2006. LAUNCH PRICE: $299.99 with PlayStation Picks demo disc. MODEL NUMBER: SCPH-1001. SOUNDCHIP: Sony SPU. AUDIO: Stereo with Dolby Surround.

The PlayStation was the first successful CD-based gaming system. Video game soundtracks on the PlayStation were further expanded from their cartridge counterparts with the additional memory of CD. Before the PS1 (PlayStation), Sony was responsible for designing and producing the soundchip of the SNES and the Sony Walkman, the first portable audio device to read audio cassettes. It co-produced the compact disc with Phillips. Later, Sony co-developed the Blu-Ray disc with Philips. Philips co-produced the

S/PDIF cable end used by optical audio cables. At its launch, the Sony PlayStation was a powerful game console, friendly for game developers. It popularized polygonal 3D graphics and playback of games and music on CD. The PlayStation first began as the SNES CD-ROM, a planned CD drive for the SNES, similar to the Sega CD. Nintendo developed it together with Sony, who had designed the Sony SPC700 soundchip for the SNES. Eventually, the SNES-CD became the standalone Play Station, which took both SNES cartridges and CD-ROMs. However, Sony decided later to create a competing console based on the Play Station. These actions eventually led to the Sony PlayStation.

Sony promoted the system well. The games show off the benefits of CD-based media in visuals and audio. The PlayStation contains the Sony SPU (Sound Processing Unit) soundchip. The chip delivers 24 ADPCM channels and a stereo audio mix. Each ADPCM channel has 16-bit audio and a 44.1 kHz sampling rate. The SPU's DSP supports digital effects such as Pitch Modulation, Envelope, Looping, and Digital Reverb. The SPU interprets musical data in the MIDI and PlayStation Sequenced formats.

The built-in CD player provides two CD-DA sound channels. The CD-DA channels were used for most, if not all, of the musical tracks, leaving more than enough sound channels available for sounds. The 26 sound channels are mixed by the system's DAC to analog stereo audio, with or without Dolby Surround encodings (on a per-game basis). Although the PlayStation didn't offer the most advanced audio options at the time, it nevertheless dominated the home console market during its years of manufacture. The video game industry observed Sony's success in its first home console, and gaming manufacturers and developers adjusted their designs to accommodate the PlayStation.

The PS One, released on July 7, 2000, is a smaller model of the PlayStation. The LCD Screen for PS One, released on January 8, 2001, is a portable screen with audio speakers that converts the PS One into a portable gaming system. On Sunday, March 26,

2006, the Sony PlayStation ceased manufacturing. The Sony PlayStation was so popular that its lifespan almost overlapped with the PS3, released in November

Sony PlayStation back 1994. The audio output ports are A/V (with composite video and stereo audio RCA adapter) (Evan-Amos, "Sony-PlayStation-5501-Console-BR").

Sony PS One 2000. The audio output ports are A/V (with composite video and stereo audio RCA adapter) (Evan-Amos, "Sony-PSone-Console-FL").

PlayStation A/V composite cable 1994. It connects to the PlayStation's A/V port and outputs audio in analog stereo (Evan-Amos, "Playstation-composite-cables").

2006. Due to CD-DA, one can listen to the soundtracks of PlayStation discs on a CD player, beginning at track 2. When gaming systems no longer used CDs for game discs, disc swapping for custom soundtracks was no longer functional. Sony released a dedicated console called the PlayStation Classic on Monday, December 3, 2018. The PlayStation Classic plays PlayStation games through emulation pre-installed on the console (lacking online capability).

December 3, 1994—*Ridge Racer*—PlayStation

PUBLISHER: Namco. RELEASE DATE: December 3, 1994 (JP), September 9, 1995 (NA), September 29, 1995 (EU). COMPOSERS: Shinji Hosoe, Nobuyoshi Sano, and Ayaka Saso. SERIES: *Ridge Racer*. GENRE: Racing. NOTABLE MUSICAL TRACK: "Ridge Racer (Sound Select 01)."

Ridge Racer was the first game on a home console to support custom soundtracks via disc swapping. *Ridge Racer's* soundtrack is techno music. The game is a home port of *Ridge Racer* (1993, Arcade). The player can select six techno musical tracks to use on the race options screen during each race. As the race begins, the number and title of the musical track scroll at the bottom of the screen. The entirety of the game programming of the PlayStation port of *Ridge Racer*, at 4 MBs, loads into the system's RAM. Once the system reads the game disc upon system power-up, the system no longer reads the game disc for game content. The disc sensor is then exclusively used to read CD-DA tracks from the inserted disc. The player can open the disc tray and swap the game disc for any disc with CD-DA tracks. Whenever the system searches for the game's musical tracks, it selects the audio tracks from the enclosed disc.

The procedure of swapping a game disc for another disc for an intended effect is called disc swapping. The player, via disc swapping, can create an original musical playlist with his or her audio collection for games programmed in this way. Consequently, game soundtracks, specially composed to reflect gameplay elements, lost some authority with gamers, who could easily replace the musical tracks with unrelated audio. The notable musical track, "Ridge Racer (Sound Select 01)," uses electronic sounds, despite the CD-DA format. The track is fast as a reflection of the game's fast-paced action. The track is over five minutes long. Although prerecorded, melodic passages seem improvised and original as if a musician were performing live.

SOURCES

Brence, C. "Sid Meier's C.P.U. Bach–3DO (1994)." 20 Sept. 2015, www.hardcoregaming101.net/cpubach/cpubach.htm.

Chilly Willy. "Tell me about the 32X sound chip." 12 June 2012, forums.sonicretro.org/index.php?showtopic=29056.

Frey, Angelica. "Video Game Music: Focus on Nobuo Uematsu." *CMUSE*, 21 Mar. 2015, www.cmuse.org/video-game-music-focus-on-nobuo-uematsu/.

Greening, Chris. "Nobuo Uematsu Profile." *Video Game Music Online*, 18 Mar. 2013, www.vgmonline.net/nobuouematsu/.

"Guide To: The Super Game Boy." *Ancientelectronics*, 16 May 2015, ancientelectronics.wordpress.com/2015/05/16/guide-to-the-super-game-boy/. Accessed 1 June 2020.

Harley, Trevor. "The Different Iterations of the Super Game Boy." *Snail Tooth Gaming*, 5 Feb. 2017, www.snailtoothgaming.com/articles/the-different-iterations-of-the-super-game-boy/. Accessed 1 June 2020.

"Kenji Yamamoto." *Kyoto Report*, 16 Sept. 2017, kyoto-report.wikidot.com/kenji-yamamoto. Accessed 14 Aug. 2018.

"Kenji Yamamoto." *Video Game Music Preservation Foundation Wiki*, 25 June 2016, www.vgmpf.com/Wiki/index.php?title=Kenji_Yamamoto. Accessed 14 Aug. 2018.

Lee. "Best Super Game Boy Games." *Pug Hoof Gaming*, 28 Sept. 2018, www.pughoofgaming.com/videos/best-super-game-boy-games/. Accessed 1 June 2020.

Lee. "Super Game Boy Commander—The Definitive Guide." *Pug Hoof Gaming*, 15 Dec. 2016, www.pughoofgaming.com/videos/super-game-boy-commander/. Accessed 1 June 2020.

"Nobuo Uematsu." *Video Game Music Preservation Foundation Wiki*, 24 June 2016, www.vgmpf.com/Wiki/index.php?title=Nobuo_Uematsu. Accessed 6 Aug. 2018.

"PS1 Ridge Racer Insert Music CD While Playing?" *Digital Press*, 8 Dec. 2008, forum.digitpress.com/forum/showthread.php?125450-PS1-Ridge-Racer-insert-music-CD-while-playing.

"PSX Specifications." *NO$FUN*, problemkaputt.de/psx-spx.htm. Accessed 3 Aug. 2018.

ReyVGM. "Super Game Boy Borders." *The Video Game Museum*, www.vgmuseum.com/features/sgb/. Accessed 1 June 2020.

"Sega Saturn System Info." *The Video Game Museum*, www.vgmuseum.com/systems/saturn/. Accessed 3 Aug. 2018.

"SEGA Tunes: Sonic Triple Trouble's Sunset Park Act 3." *Sega Bits*, 13 Mar. 2012, segabits.com/blog/2012/03/13/tuesday-tunes-sonic-triple-troubles-sunset-park-act-3/.

"Sid Meier's C.P.U. Bach." *Hardcore Gaming 101*, 4 May 2017, www.hardcoregaming101.net/sid-meiers-c-p-u-bach-3do-1994/.

Snail Tooth Gaming. "Super Game Boy 1 and 2 Comparison." *YouTube*, 5 Feb. 2017, youtu.be/7YVw1-3QRfU. Accessed 1 June 2020.

"Super Game Boy Enhancement." *Giant Bomb*, www.giantbomb.com/super-game-boy-enhancement/3015-4804/. Accessed 1 June 2020.

"Super Game Boy 2." *Nintendo Fandom*, 4 Dec. 2020, nintendo.fandom.com/wiki/Super_Game_Boy_2. Accessed 18 Jan. 2021.

"32X." *Sega Wiki*, 13 Oct. 2020, sega.wikia.com/wiki/Sega_32X. Accessed 9 June 2021.

"Tommy Tallarico." *Video Game Music Preservation Foundation Wiki*, 28 May 2018, www.vgmpf.com/Wiki/index.php?title=Tommy_Tallarico. Accessed 6 Aug. 2018.

Zdyrko, Dave. "LCD Screen (for PS One) Review." *IGN*, 13 Dec. 2001, www.ign.com/articles/2001/12/13/lcd-screen-for-ps-one-review.

1995 in Review

March 11, 1995—*Chrono Trigger*— Super Famicom/SNES

PUBLISHER: Square Soft. RELEASE DATE: March 11, 1995 (JP), August 11, 1995 (NA). COMPOSERS: Yasunori Mitsuda and Nobuo Uematsu. GENRE: RPG. NOTABLE MUSICAL TRACK: "Corridors of Time (Zeal)."

The soundtrack of *Chrono Trigger* is vast, with orchestral samples and musical tracks reflecting the characters' personalities. The game popularized the New Game Plus mode. In this mode, the player begins the game again, retaining the experience and items from the previous playthrough. The soundtrack at the time was one of the largest based on the number of tracks and sound effects. Composer Yasunori Mitsuda composed most tracks. Square Soft composer Nobuo Uematsu wrote the remaining tracks after Mitsuda contracted stomach ulcers.

From the very first screen of the game, the sound of a clock ticking matches with the large clock pendulum on the screen. When visuals cannot fully capture the severity of situations, the player's imagination fills in the scene through audio. The screen goes black, allowing the sounds of an impending tsunami or the destruction of the planet and the scream of the alien destroyer to suffice in the player's imagination.

There are many musical genres to give unique identities to each character, place, and era. "Robo's Theme," the track that accompanies the fixing of Robo the robot in 2300 A.D., bears a similarity to Rick Astley's "Never Gonna Give You Up." Musical motifs connect characters appearing in different eras (Melchoir, Lavos). The notable musical track, "Corridors of Time," accompanies the Kingdom of Zeal in the Antiquity era. The instrumentation of Indian classical instruments like the sitar, table, gamelan, and tambourine adds a mystical element to exploring the fate of civilization. The game reuses the musical track when Melchoir repairs the Masamune sword with the Dreamstone, linking him to the Kingdom of Zeal.

April 1995—*Knuckles Chaotix*— 32X

PUBLISHER: Sega. RELEASE DATE: April 1995 (NA). COMPOSER: Junko Shiratsu and Mariko Nanba. SERIES: *Sonic the Hedgehog.* GENRE: Platformer. NOTABLE MUSICAL TRACK: "Door Into Summer (Isolated Island)."

The soundtrack of *Knuckles Chaotix*, the only 32X game from the *Sonic the Hedgehog* series, uses the combined 13 sound channels of the audio hardware of the Genesis and 32X. The game's sound test shows the current activity of all of the available sound channels for each selected track. Eight-octave piano keyboards represent FM sound channels 1 to 6 and PSG sound

channels 1 to 3. The game lights the piano keys of the active pitches in the FM channels red and the PSG channels green. Two rows of 11 hexagons represent PWM samples 1 to 4 (a maximum of four PWM samples mixed in two stereo channels). Each hexagon represents a different PWM sample used in the game. The game lights the hexagons of the active samples in different colors. The bottom right corner of the sound test shows the volume bars of the FM and PSG sound channels. The notable musical track, "Doors Into Summer (Isolated Island)," accompanies the tutorial stage. The drums and percussion play in the PWM channels of the 32X, the melody in the PSG channels, and the harmonies and bass in the FM channels.

May 16, 1995—*The Adventures of Batman and Robin*—Genesis

PUBLISHER: Sega. RELEASE DATE: May 16, 1995 (NA), June 1995 (EU). COMPOSER: Jesper Kyd. GENRE: Run and gun. NOTABLE MUSICAL TRACK: "Space Boss."

The techno soundtrack of *The Adventures of Batman and Robin*, with lengthy musical tracks, exclusively uses the Genesis' YM2612 soundchip, ignoring the SN76489 microprocessor completely. The soundtrack exhibits traits of techno music through electronic sounds and addictive beats. The Genesis soundtrack exclusively uses the FM synthesis properties of the Genesis. Composer Jesper Kyd used the Zyrink sound driver to program the game's sound effects and music. The title theme is nine minutes long before looping. A highlight of the soundtrack is the notable musical track, "Space Boss," accompanying the Mad Hatter boss fight of Level 3.

September 1995—*Blackthorne*–32X

PUBLISHER: Interplay. RELEASE DATE: September 1995 (NA). COMPOSER: Glenn Stafford. GENRE: Platformer. NOTABLE MUSICAL TRACK: "Mountains Sand."

The sound effects and music of *Blackthorne* are generated entirely by the 32X.

The gameplay and visual style of *Black-thorne* resembles *Prince of Persia* and *Flashback: A Quest for Identity*. The 32X version contains additional content from the SNES and DOS versions. The soundtrack resembles the SNES version rather than the MIDI soundtrack of the DOS version. After 20 years on Earth, Kyle, the protagonist, realizes his mission to save his planet's people and defeat the evil shaman Sarlac. The notable musical track, "Mountains Sand," through an exotic scale and sampled percussion sounds, evokes an Eastern music vibe. The sampled percussion dominates the track, with samples of bongos, hand drums, and rattles. Unlike other 32X games, *Blackthorne* does not use the Genesis' soundchips in the game's audio production.

September 21, 1995—*Vid Grid*— Jaguar CD

PUBLISHER: Atari. RELEASE DATE: September 21, 1995 (NA). COMPOSER: Eric Nofsinger. GENRE: Interactive movie.

Vid Grid was a game to show off the CD capabilities of the Jaguar CD, in which players listen and watch popular music videos. Released as a pack-in game for the Jaguar CD, the gameplay involves arranging jigsaw puzzle pieces to view a completed music video. There are 10 music videos to unlock; some songs are "Cryin" by Aerosmith, "No More Tears" by Ozzy Osbourne, and "Right Now" by Van Halen. The game was an early example of intertwining real music and video with gameplay. The development team of *Vid Grid* licensed the master recordings and music videos of the musical artists.

December 1995—*Battlemorph*— Jaguar CD

PUBLISHER: Atari. RELEASE DATE: December 1995 (NA). COMPOSER: Will Davis. GENRE: Shooter. NOTABLE MUSICAL TRACK: "Battle 1."

Battlemorph has a great CD-DA soundtrack, FMV cinematics, and improved voice acting. The game is a sequel to *Cybermorph* (1993), a game without music. Fortunately,

the music takes advantage of CD-DA, and switching between tracks does not slow down the game. An example is the smooth musical transition when the player flies from the air into the water or from the air into a first-person perspective. Improved CD capabilities support FMV cinematics. The Welsh actor Rob Brydon, known for his role as Bryn West in the British sitcom *Gavin and Stacey*, provided the Scottish male voice that narrates the introductory sequence, menu screen, and mission briefings. A female voice from the ship, recorded by Vicky Lowe, shares the ship's status and any items acquired.

December 1995—*Defender 2000*— Jaguar

PUBLISHER: Atari. RELEASE DATE: December 1995 (NA). COMPOSER: Alastair Lindsay. GENRE: Shmup. NOTABLE MUSICAL TRACK: "Level Set 1."

Defender 2000 has a techno soundtrack with dance and rave influences and sound effects from the arcade game. The game reimagines *Defender* (1980, Arcade). The techno soundtrack infuses the sound effects from the *Defender* arcade game. Collecting four Warp powerups in the Defender 2000 mode unlocks the Warp Level, a bonus stage in which the player's ship travels toward the screen in a tunnel, accompanied by a rave remix of the first movement of Beethoven's 5th Symphony (Allegro con Brio). The track uses short excerpts of vocal phrases and FM-synthesized sounds. The game's three modes are Classic Defender (the unaltered arcade game), Defender Plus (original gameplay with updates to the visuals and sound effects), and Defender 2000. Defender 2000 is the only mode with music.

The soundtrack is inspired by dance and rave music, which were popular at the game's release. The music is characterized by its rapid tempo, short, repeated melodic and rhythm patterns, pulsating drums, and heavy use of synthesized sounds and audio effects. Other instruments are the electronic organ, used for light harmonies, low strings, and metal guitar. The soundtrack was initially prepared as CD-DA because the game was to be one of the first games on the Atari Jaguar CD. Atari decided at the last minute to release the game for the Jaguar on a ROM cartridge. The tracks were converted to tracker format in due haste.

November 21, 1995—*Donkey Kong Country 2: Diddy's Kong Quest*—Super Famicom/SNES

PUBLISHER: Nintendo. RELEASE DATE: November 21, 1995 (JP), December 1995 (NA), December 14, 1995 (EU). COMPOSER: David Wise. SERIES: *Donkey Kong Country* series. GENRE: Platformer. NOTABLE MUSICAL TRACK: "Stickerbush Symphony."

The soundtrack of *Donkey Kong Country 2: Diddy's Kong Quest* is captivating, with various styles like hip hop, disco, and big band. The soundtrack maintains a tribal feel through increased percussion. Like the first game in the series, the game uses pre-rendered 3D images for the sprites and backgrounds. The player controls Diddy Kong or Dixie Kong to rescue Donkey Kong from the evil crocodile King K. Rool. The title theme "K. Rool Returns" features seductive strings, heroic horns, and deep timpani, with similarities to the musical style of the *Monkey Island* series. The notable musical track, "Stickerbush Symphony," heard in the stages "Bramble Blast" and "Bramble Scramble," is a highlight of the soundtrack. It is a peaceful and dignified ambient track, simulating sounds in the distance or through water using synth pads, crescendos, and sound filters. Various web sources erroneously cite the track as "Stickerbrush Symphony."

SOURCES

Charnock, Tom. "Jag Star." *Do the Math*, Apr. 2014, www.atarijaguar.co.uk/2014/04/jag-star.html.
"Jesper Kyd: Music Transcends All Platforms." *Plarium*, plarium.com/en/blog/jesper-kyd/. Accessed 14 Aug. 2018.
Kyd, Jesper. "Home." *The Official Website of Jesper Kyd*, www.jesperkyd.com. Accessed 14 Aug. 2018
Kyd, Jesper. "Interview with Jesper Kyd: Award Winning Games Composer." Interview by Steven Wiliamson. *Hexus*, 13 Apr. 2006, hexus.net/gaming/features/industry/5268-jesper-kyd-unreal-tournament-2007/.
Kyd, Jesper. "Sound Byte: Meet the Composer—Assassin's Creed's Jesper Kyd." Interview by Sophia Tong. *GameSpot*, 19 Nov. 2010, www.gamespot.com/articles/sound-byte-meet-the-composer-assassins-creeds-jesper-kyd/1100-6284304/.
Mitsuda, Yasunori. Interview. *The Official Homepage of Yasunori Mitsuda*, Nov. 1999, www.procyon-studio.com/profile/biog.html.
Mitsuda, Yasunori. "Music (Chrono Trigger)." *Chrono Compendium*, 21 Jan. 1995, www.chronocompendium.com/Term/Music_(Chrono_Trigger).html#Chrono_Trigger_Arranged_Version:_The_Brink_of_Time.
Redifer, Joe. "Did Any 32X Games Take Advantage of the Enchanced Sound?" *Sega-16*, 24 Feb. 2013, www.sega-16.com/forum/showthread.php?23425-Did-any-32X-games-take-advantage-of-the-enchanced-sound.
Redifer, Joe. "32X PWM Sound." *Sega-16*, 7 Oct. 2007, www.sega-16.com/forum/showthread.php?3317-32X-PWM-sound.
"Sega 32X." *Sega Retro*, 29 Jan. 2016, segaretro.org/Sega_32X.
"Yasunori Mitsuda." *Square Enix Music Online*, www.squareenixmusic.com/composers/mitsuda.html. Accessed 10 Aug. 2018.
"Yasunori Mitsuda." *Video Game Music Preservation Foundation Wiki*, 4 Dec. 2017, www.vgmpf.com/Wiki/index.php?title=Yasunori_Mitsuda. Accessed 14 Aug. 2018.

1996 in Review

April 6, 1996—*SimTunes*—PC

PUBLISHER: Maxis. RELEASE DATE: April 6, 1996 (NA). COMPOSERS: Jerry Martin, Toshio Iwai, Benimaru Itoh, UrumaDelvi. SERIES: *Sim*. GENRE: Simulation.

SimTunes is a fun way to create music in a visual representation of colors and crawling bugs. Released for Windows 3.1 and Windows 95, the game began as *Music Insects*, a 1992 exhibit designed by Toshio Iwai for the San Francisco Exploratorium. Maxis, the company that released the original *SimCity* games, saw the exhibit and published it as *SimTunes*. The gameplay involves painting a picture in which each color represents a musical note. The player then places up to four different-colored "Bugz" on the picture. Each bug represents a musical instrument or vocal syllable. The player can adjust each bug's starting directions and relative speeds. When ready, the bugs crawl over the picture, playing notes corresponding with the colors; and they turn, move randomly, or jump in response to function symbols added to the dots. The game's options include audio output as wave or internal MIDI.

June 22, 1996—*Quake*—PC

Publisher: id Software. Release Date: June 22, 1996 (NA). Composers: Trent Reznor and Nine Inch Nails. Series: *Quake*. Genre: 1st person shooter. Notable musical track: "Main Theme (Track 2)."

Quake is a 1st person shooter game with audio design and a soundtrack by Nine Inch Nails, the industrial band led by Trent Reznor. Released for MS-DOS and Windows 95 as shareware version 0.91 in North America on June 22, 1996, Reznor composed the ambient soundtrack and sound effects. He is also the voice of Ranger, the game's protagonist. Chris Vrenna, a former member of Nine Inch Nails, composed the game's theme song. Trent Reznor recently was awarded his second Oscar in 2021 as a co-composer for the score of Disney's *Soul*. Industrial rock music blends ambient machine noises with synthesized drone tones. The game retrieves game data exclusively from the hard drive, leaving the disc drive accessible for a personalized soundtrack via disc swapping. The game disc contains CD-DA tracks on tracks 2 to 11 when inserted in a CD player (track 1 contains game data). The notable musical track, "Main Theme (Track 2)," exhibits an industrial feel with sounds that resemble machinery revving. The music then transitions into buzzes, rumbles, and synthesized tones. The tones sound off in the distance as if sucked out of existence. At the track's end, the music gives way to the ambiance of low-pitched vibrations with reverberation.

June 23, 1996—Nintendo 64

Manufacturer: Nintendo. Release Date: June 23, 1996 (JP), September 26, 1996 (NA), March 1, 1997 (EU). Production Dates: June 23, 1996–April 30, 2002. Launch price: $199.99. Model number: NUS-001. Soundchip: RCP (graphics and audio). Audio: Stereo.

The Nintendo 64 (N64) was the last home console to use ROM-based game cartridges. Released by Nintendo, the N64 lacks a discrete soundchip nor a laser sensor to read disc-based media. At the time, Nintendo's decision to use cartridges over CDs as the storage media was contrary to the success of the Sony PlayStation from the previous year. One potential reason for this hardware decision was to curb piracy (the illegal duplication of video games by burning game discs).

The N64 computes audio requests, along with graphics, with the RCP (Reality Coprocessor), a 64-bit SGI coprocessor. The RCP chip is split internally into two major components, the RDP (Reality Display Processor) and the RSP (Reality Signal Processor). The RSP manages the graphics and audio, much like a DSP. The Reality Display Processor is a pixel rasterizer and handler of Z-buffer computations. Collectively, the RSP and the N64's CPU perform audio functions. The N64's coprocessor understands the music-data formats of PCM, MP3, MIDI, and tracker music. MP3 is a compressed audio data format (a similar concept to ADPCM). MIDI data contains musical information without the actual sounds corresponding to each instrument (each N64 ROM cartridge separately includes all required audio samples). Unlike CD-based gaming systems, there were no loading times connected to audio production or playback. The N64 supports Dolby Surround audio, four audio channels encoded to an analog stereo signal.

Since the N64's coprocessor handled a game's graphics and audio, the N64's audio capabilities vary. Due to the N64 using a microprocessor with multiple duties, the number of sound channels was no longer based on the design specifications of a soundchip but rather on the game's programming and memory. On average, a musical track on the N64 uses between 16

Nintendo N64 with controller 1996. The audio output ports are A/V (with RF adapter or composite video and stereo audio RCA adapter) (Evan-Amos, "N64-Console-Set").

and 32 sound channels. If the coprocessor were entirely devoted to audio without graphical concerns, the N64 could produce an audio output of 16-bit, 48 kHz audio fidelity. However, the limited storage memory of the N64 cartridge and graphical calculations hindered such audio quality. Some N64 developers understood the audio strengths of the gaming system and produced soundtracks with creative audio capabilities.

The N64 ceased manufacturing on April 30, 2002. The N64 was Nintendo's first gaming system with audio generation through software instead of hardware. Since the N64, almost all gaming systems process audio in software with the CPU or another processor with multiple functions. This approach to audio generation surpassed CD-DA, limited by the Redbook standard, and no longer supported on other physical disc sizes (GameCube disc, GD-ROM disc) and disc formats (Blu-ray disc).

June 26, 1996—*Super Mario 64*— N64

PUBLISHER: Nintendo. RELEASE DATE: June 26, 1996 (JP), September 29, 1996 (NA), March 1, 1997 (EU). COMPOSER: Koji Kondo. SERIES: *Super Mario Bros.* GENRE: Platformer. NOTABLE MUSICAL TRACK: "Dire Dire Docks (Water Theme)."

Super Mario 64 was the first game in the series with 3D graphics and a MIDI

soundtrack. The game is considered one of the greatest games of all time, particularly for its use of a dynamic camera system, the implementation of its 360-degree analog control, and open-world design. The soundtrack retains the charm of the series while using MIDI instrument sounds. The music is adaptive to the game's activities within a level. For example, the music is calmer while Mario is swimming underwater, while the game emphasizes the musical beat while Mario is on land in the second area. The notable musical track, "Dire Dire Docks (Water Theme)," creates a mood of flowing atmosphere through its use of bell-like synths with an extended sound release, reverberation, broken chords spanning over an octave, and elongated harmonies. The countermelody, played on synths, moves more slowly than the melody. When on land, the drum track adds rhythmic action to the otherwise tranquil track.

July 30, 1996—*The King of Fighters '96*—Neo Geo MVS/AES

PUBLISHER: SNK. RELEASE DATE: July 30, 1996 (WW, MVS), September 27, 1996 (WW, AES). COMPOSER: Shinsekai Gakkyoku Zatsugidan. SERIES: *The King of Fighters.* GENRE: Fighting. NOTABLE MUSICAL TRACK: "Esaka Hero Team Theme."

The soundtrack of *The King of Fighters '96* is exciting, with synth and instrument samples to delineate the game's fighters and teams. The game, the third annual installment in the series, is a fighting game like *Street Fighter 2: The World Warrior.* The game was the second of three games in the story arc called the Orochi Saga. There were, however, changes in the character roster and the teams. The Boss Team consists of the three villains from the *Fatal Fury* and *Art of Fighting* series: Geese Howard, Wolfgang Krauser, and Mr. Big. Unlike the other teams, each member of the Boss

Team had a unique musical track. For example, the theme music for Wolfgang Krauser von Stroheim's stage is "Dies Irae," composed by Wolfgang Amadeus Mozart. This song choice is fitting for the character's namesake and story. The notable musical track, "Esaka Hero Team Theme," is associated with the fighter Kyo Kusanagi. The track prominently features synth brass in octaves, distorted guitars, and drum set samples. Its tone is reflective of Kusanagi's personality in the game. Later iterations of the series use the track, including *The King of Fighters '98* and *The King of Fighters 2003*.

December 6, 1996—*PaRappa the Rapper*—PlayStation

PUBLISHER: Sony. RELEASE DATE: December 6, 1996 (JP), September 26, 1997 (EU), November 17, 1997 (NA). COMPOSER: Masaya Matsuura. SERIES: *PaRappa the Rapper*. GENRE: Music/Rhythm. NOTABLE MUSICAL TRACK: "PaRappa's Live Rap with MC King Kong Mushi (Final Stage)." AWARDS: D.I.C.E. 1998 Sound Design.

PaRappa the Rapper was one of the first games to popularize the music/rhythm genre. The game links button presses to the words of the songs, infused with witty rhythms and comical rapping. The game rewards those players who create original freestyle button patterns within the musical beat. PaRappa, the protagonist, must rap well with attention to rhythm through the game's six stages. In each stage, PaRappa trades rap back and forth with a teacher. The song's lyrics appear on the bottom of the screen. The teacher's instructional raps reinforce the rhythmic pattern that the player must input, represented visually by a bar at the top of the screen with icons of PlayStation controller buttons. Immediately after the teacher's rap phrase, the player must press the buttons with the correct timing as indicated by the bar to make PaRappa match the teacher's line. The game awards points for correctness and style.

By simply replacing the given sequence, the best a player can attain is the "U rappin' GOOD" rating. After completing a level, the player can return to the stage to obtain a "U rappin' COOL" rating. The player must freestyle original button patterns that keep time with the beat to achieve the highest rating. The notable musical track, "PaRappa's Live Rap with MC King Kong Mushi (Final Stage)," occurs in an auditorium. MC King Kong Mushi encourages PaRappa to direct the audience in a live rap concert. It is the first and only time PaRappa performs in front of an audience. The song's lyrics summarize the journey of PaRappa in his training from the four trainers, incorporating the raps from the previous stages and the game's motto, "I gotta believe." The song concludes with PaRappa rapping toward the crowd without further instruction.

SOURCES

Byrne, Brian C., and Console G. Magazine. *History of The Nintendo 64: Ultimate Guide to the N64's Games & Hardware. Console Gamer Magazine*, 2017.

Eggebrecht, Julian. "What's Wrong with Music on the N64?" *IGN*, 24 Feb. 1998, www.ign.com/articles/1998/02/25/whats-wrong-with-music-on-the-n64.

Ford, Brody. "Trent Reznor Soundtrack for Video Game Quake to Be Released on Vinyl." *Mxdwn Music*, 12 June 2017, music.mxdwn.com/2017/06/12/news/trent-reznor-soundtrack-for-video-game-quake-to-be-released-on-vinyl/.

Manes, Stephen. "Lights! Cameras! Music! Insects!" *The New York Times*, 29 Apr. 1997, www.nytimes.com/1997/04/29/science/lights-cameras-music-insects.html.

"MMCA Chairman's Award—Toshio Iwai (Media Artist)." *Multimedia Grand Prix '97*, wayback.archive.org/web/20090609223028/www.dcaj.org:80/oldgp/97awards/english/person/person01.htm. Accessed 6 Aug. 2018.

"Nintendo 64 Technical Specifications." *Video Game Review*, videogamereview.tripod.com/n64/specs.html. Accessed 3 Aug. 2018.

"N64 Hardware Specifications." *Angelfire*, digitalfantasy.angelfire.com/n64-hardware-specifications.html. Accessed 3 Aug. 2018.

"Quake." *Quake Fandom*, 2 Jan. 2021, quake.fandom.com/wiki/Quake. Accessed 18 Jan. 2021.

Regel, Julian. "Inside Nintendo 64." *Nintendo 64 Tech*, 21 June 1999, n64.icequake.net/mirror/www.white-tower.demon.co.uk/n64.

"SimTunes." *PC Gaming Wiki*, 12 Jan. 2020, www.pcgamingwiki.com/wiki/SimTunes. Accessed 27 May 2021.

"Toshio Iwai 'From Flipbooks to Media Art.'" *MIT Media Lab*, www.media.mit.edu/events/talk-iwai.html. Accessed 7 Aug. 2018.

1997 in Review

January 31, 1997—*Final Fantasy VII*—PlayStation

PUBLISHER: Sony. RELEASE DATE: January 31, 1997 (JP), September 7, 1997 (NA), November 17, 1997 (EU). COMPOSER: Nobuo Uematsu. SERIES: *Final Fantasy*. NOTABLE MUSICAL TRACK: "One-Winged Angel."

Final Fantasy VII was one of the first PlayStation games to use sequenced PlayStation format audio instead of CD-DA. Nobuo Uematsu, who composed, arranged, and produced the soundtrack, used the PlayStation's soundchip so that the soundtrack would not become excessive and crazy. As PlayStation Sequenced Format (PSF), the entire soundtrack is less than one megabyte of memory. Music as PSFs are similar to MOD files or MIDI files in that instrument samples are used in a program to be interpreted by the soundchip, thus producing a musical track with much less memory than a CD-DA track. Uematsu was very knowledgeable of the capabilities of the PS1's soundchip, and he used it to his musical strengths in his compositions. The notable musical track, "One-Winged Angel," is considered one of the best in the *Final Fantasy* series. It accompanies the final confrontation with Sephiroth, the main villain of the game. The song contains lyrics in Latin, taken from Carl Orff's *Carmina Burana*.

July 18, 1997—*Real Sound: Kaze no Regret*—Saturn

PUBLISHER: Warp. RELEASE DATE: July 18, 1997 (JP). COMPOSER: Keiichi Suzuki. GENRE: Audio game. NOTABLE MUSICAL TRACK: "A New Nostalgia."

Real Sound: Kaze no Regret is one of the only audio-only games ever released on a home console. Released exclusively in Japan, the game, which lacks visuals of any kind, was designed to accommodate blind and visually impaired players. Japanese studio WARP, Inc. released the game for the Sega Saturn, and the company's founder Kenji Eno directed and produced the game. "Kaze no Regret" translates in English to "The Wind's Regret." The soundtrack to Kaze no Regret was composed by Keiichi Suzuki, who is most known for his work on the *Mother* series.

The game idea arose from contact that Eno had with blind and visually impaired fans of WARP games. Eno was fascinated that the visually impaired would-be fans of his games. He thought his games were very visually rich. He even went so far as to contact visually impaired fans to determine how they played his games without sight. As a result, Eno decided to make a game that would be audio-only, with no graphics at all. The gameplay resembles an audio "choose your own adventure" game. The player listens to the game's story, similar to a radio play, and makes decisions in the branching storyline when prompted by an audible chime. The notable musical track, "A New Nostalgia," has a simple melody, first played on the acoustic guitar and then matched with human whistling.

August 27, 1997—*The Lost World: Jurassic Park*—PlayStation

PUBLISHER: Electronic Arts. U.S. RELEASE DATE: August 27, 1997 (NA), September 5, 1997 (EU). COMPOSER: Michael Giacchino. SERIES: *Jurassic Park*. GENRE: Action. NOTABLE MUSICAL TRACK: "Primordial Forest."

The soundtrack of *The Lost World: Jurassic Park* was the first to be recorded by a full orchestra. The soundtracks of the PlayStation and Saturn versions of *The Lost World: Jurassic Park* were recorded with real musicians and real instruments. In May 1997, *The Lost World: Jurassic Park* was released in U.S. theaters. The game's soundtrack was composed by Michael Giacchino, who, when hired by Dreamworks Interactive, composed a synth score to show to the game's producer, Steven

Spielberg. Spielberg was impressed by his music and assumed he would expand the synthesized instrumentation to a live orchestra. The notable musical track, "Primordial Forest," is entirely orchestral and could easily accompany a scene in a film with exploration and unexpected turns. Its composition borrows from classical composition and film scoring. The live orchestral soundtrack was so well-received that Dreamworks offered Giacchino an orchestra for his musical scores for the *Medal of Honor* games. Live orchestration proved to be a viable option in place of synth instruments or brief instrument samples due to the acceptance of disc-based media, particularly the 700 MB capacity of the compact disc and the suitable audio quality of audio tracks at 16-bit, 44.1 kHz resolution (CD-DA).

December 12, 1997—*Grand Theft Auto*—PlayStation

PUBLISHER: Take-Two. RELEASE DATE: December 12, 1997 (EU), June 30, 1998 (NA). COMPOSERS: Craig Conner, Colin Anderson, and Grant Middleton. SERIES: *Grand Theft Auto*. NOTABLE MUSICAL TRACK: "Benzoate."

Grand Theft Auto's soundtrack exists diegetically in the game world as seven radio stations plus a police band track. The soundtrack contains 19 original songs. The radio stations cover various music genres, including techno, hip-hop, country, and pop. Once the player enters a vehicle, the player selects from two of the eight radio stations. The radio station names and their musical genres are N-CT FM (east-coast hip hop and gangsta rap), Radio '76 FM (funk), Head Radio (mainstream pop, rock, and techno), The Fix FM (house and dance), It's Unleashed FM (hard rock, alternative rock, and big beat), The Fergus Buckner Show FM (one country song on repeat), Brooklyn Underground FM (drum and bass, techno, and trance), and the police band. Each radio station is its own CD-DA track on the game disc. The police

band uses a stock audio sample from the 20th Century–Fox sound library called "5 George K.," often heard in movies and television shows.

The developers could not convince music publishers to license their music for the game, so the game's 19 musical tracks are original, designed to resemble professional tracks. As Robert DeNegro, Johnny Wilson was the vocal rapper for the three tracks on N-CT FM. The track "Joyride" is heard on the N-CT FM radio station, with music by Craig Conner and lyrics by Johnny Wilson, although credited collectively in-game as Da Shootaz, a fictitious music group. The notable musical track, "Benzoate," written by Craig Conner and performed by Retrograde, is one of three tracks on the Brooklyn Underground FM radio station. The track repeats the vocal phrase "and unity" at the track's beginning, later relying upon swirling electronic sounds to generate the trance feel. The vocal phrase returns, accompanied by the drum kit. The vocal phrase fades out, leaving only a horn-like synth. Other vocal distortions include a gasp and the track's ending phrase "You know, just go for it" by a female voice.

SOURCES

Giacchino, Michael. "An Interview with Michael Giacchino." Interview by Peter Van der Lugt. *ScreenAnarchy*, 11 Aug. 2009, screenanarchy.com/2009/08/an-interview-with-michael-giacchino.html.

Giacchino, Michael. "Exclusive: Interview … Film Composer Michael Giacchino." Interview by Mark Ciafardini. *GoSeeTalk.com*, 14 May 2012, goseetalk.com/interview-film-composer-michael-giacchino/.

"N-CT FM." *GTA Wiki*, Fandom, 19 Mar. 2021, gta.fandom.com/wiki/N-CT_FM. Accessed 10 Apr. 2021.

"Script for Real Sound: Regret of the Wind." *OneSwitch.org.uk Blog*, 17 Oct. 2018, switch-gaming.blogspot.com/2018/10/script-for-real-sound-regret-of-wind.html. Accessed 2 June 2020.

"That Police Dispatch Noise. You Know. That One." *Giant Bomb*, 5 July 2010, www.giantbomb.com/forums/off-topic-31/that-police-dispatch-noise-you-know-that-one-429586/. Accessed 9 Apr. 2021.

1998 in Review

1998—Nokia 6110

MANUFACTURER: Nokia. RELEASE DATE: 1998 (WW). LAUNCH PRICE: $899.99, $199.99 (with cell phone service contract). MODEL NUMBER: 6110. AUDIO: Mono.

The Nokia 6110 was the first mobile phone that included a game with sound. Released by Nokia, the mobile phone was the first with an ARM processor. The phone's screen was monochromatic like the original model Game Boy. Like the earliest personal computers (before sound-cards), the phone only supports one sound channel with beeps of different pitches. The phone allowed users to program original ringtones as a series of pitches and rhythms. The phone only has an ear speaker as the mono audio output. The Nokia 6110 comes preinstalled with three games: *Memory*, *Snake*, and *Logic*. The mobile phone market began to grow in 1998, along with the demand for games on cell phones.

May 28, 1998—D.I.C.E. Awards—Event

The D.I.C.E. Awards were the first awards show to recognize achievements in audio. The D.I.C.E. Awards, named for "Design Innovate Communicate Entertain," was first held on May 28, 1998, at the E3 Expo in Atlanta, Georgia. Each year since, the Academy of Interactive Arts and Sciences, an organization of video game industry professionals, hosts the D.I.C.E. Summit. From 1998 to 2012, the awards were called the Interactive Achievement Awards (still awarded during the annual D.I.C.E Summit). Before the D.I.C.E. Awards, audio designers and composers received recognition for their work only from game reviews and internet postings. The D.I.C.E. Awards have merit because the Academy of Interactive Arts and Sciences members vote on the winners in each category.

The audio categories are "Outstanding

Sound Design" (since 1998) and "Outstanding Original Music Composition" (since 2000). The Academy of Interactive Arts and Sciences awarded the "Outstanding Licensed Soundtrack" category in 2004 and 2011. At the 1st D.I.C.E. Awards, the award for Outstanding Sound Design went to *PaRappa the Rapper*. A few composers on the panel for the 2020 D.I.C.E. Awards are Tommy Tallarico, Marty O'Donnell, Austin Wintory (composer of *Journey* [2012, PS3]), and Winifred Phillips (composer of *Assassin's Creed III: Liberation* [2012, PS Vita]). The D.I.C.E. Awards, voted on by video game industry professionals as members of the Academy of Interactive Arts and Sciences in video game development, distribution, and reporting, reflect the industry's distinguished games of the year.

July 23, 1998—*Radiant Silvergun*—Saturn

PUBLISHER: Entertainment Software. RELEASE DATE: July 23, 1998 (JP). COMPOSER: Hitoshi Sakimoto. GENRE: Shmup. NOTABLE MUSICAL TRACK: "Penta (Stage 4D)."

The soundtrack of *Radiant Silvergun* uses synth orchestrations with musical motifs. Released exclusively in Japan, the game's soundtrack is a continuation of composer Hitoshi Sakimoto's musical development from *Final Fantasy Tactics* (1997). Like *Final Fantasy Tactics*, *Radiant Silvergun* employs synth orchestrations, trumpets, violins, drums, and bells. Despite the similarities, these musical timbres are revitalizing in the shoot-em-up genre. One of Sakimoto's signature styles is a strong, recognizable musical motif, prominently identifiable in the soundtrack, especially the musical tracks "Feel Invisible Matter" and "The Stone-Like." The notable musical track, "Penta (Stage 4D)," accompanies an intense pseudo-3D air battle with the Penta, an Earth Defense Alliance (EDA) space cruiser revived by the Stone-Like, the main antagonist. The melody moves between synth strings and trumpets, while percussion, particularly timpani and tubular bells, add rhythmic intensity within the musical beats. In the middle of the track, the two instrument groups have a call and response interaction which eventually overlaps, with increased percussion bringing the track to its peak.

September 3, 1998—*Metal Gear Solid*—PlayStation

PUBLISHER: Konami. RELEASE DATE: September 3, 1998 (JP), October 21, 1998 (NA), February 22, 1999 (EU). COMPOSER: Tappi Iwase. SERIES: *Metal Gear*. GENRE: Action-adventure/Stealth. NOTABLE MUSICAL TRACK: "Main Theme."

Metal Gear Solid is a cinematic experience with an orchestral soundtrack, cutscenes rendered in-engine, and believable voice acting. The game received critical acclaim for its involved storyline, believable voice acting, and cinematic presentation. The player controls Solid Snake, a soldier who must free hostages and stop FOXHOUND, a renegade special forces unit and terrorist organization, from launching a nuclear strike. The cutscene music is cinematic with substantial orchestral and choral elements. The music reacts to gameplay tension, synthetically growing with increased pace and the introduction of strings during tense moments. The notable musical track, "Main Theme," begins with a robust percussive presence with a broad string section. A solo trumpet plays the melody with the strings as a countermelody. Then the lower strings play while cymbals crash, followed by a short drum break and a synth section. The lower brass plays elongated melodic lines, accompanied by vocal aahs. The melody emanates from the lower brass expanding to the upper brass in a triumphant finale. The track ends with the sound of wind sucking all of the sounds. Although CD-DA tracks with finite endings, the game's musical tracks work well within the audio design for repeated play.

September 12, 1998—*Pokémon Yellow Version: Special Pikachu Edition*—Game Boy

PUBLISHER: Nintendo. RELEASE DATE: September 12, 1998 (JP), October 19, 1999 (NA), June 16, 2000 (EU). COMPOSER: Junichi Masuda. SERIES: *Pokémon*. GENRE: RPG. NOTABLE MUSICAL TRACK: "Wild Pokémon Battle."

Pokémon Yellow Version: Special Pikachu Edition has a beautiful soundtrack that complements the towns and battles of the Kanto region of the Pokémon world. It was the last commercial game sold for the Game Boy in North America and Europe. The game differed from *Pokemon Red and Pokemon Blue*, the previous games in the series, with character designs and plots based on the *Pokémon* anime series. All three Game Boy games share the same sound effects and musical tracks. The game was released late in the Game Boy's life cycle to be compatible with Game Boy and Game Boy Color. *Pokemon Yellow Version: Special Pikachu Edition* is one of many Game Boy games that includes additional colors or features when played on a Game Boy Color. The player hears the notable musical track "Wild Pokémon Battle" countless times in a playthrough during the turn-based scenes when the player encounters a Pokémon in the wild and battles it. Characteristics of the musical track include a descending pitch cascade at the start, a bass pattern of alternating fifths moving up a half step, and a harmonic line that mimics a bee's erratic flight, traveling chromatically up and down in pitch around the melody line.

September 26, 1998—*Dance Dance Revolution*—Arcade

PUBLISHER: Konami. RELEASE DATE: September 26, 1998 (JP), March 1999 (NA), March 9, 1999 (EU). GENRE: Music/Rhythm. SERIES: *Dance Dance Revolution*. NOTABLE MUSICAL TRACK: "Butterfly" by Smile.dk.

Dance Dance Revolution popularized the music/dance genre in video games. Released in the arcades, the game is one of many music games released in arcades by Bemani, Konami's music video game division. The arcade machine includes a dance floor with large arrows representing places on which to step. As the music played, arrow icons scrolled downward on the screen to indicate on which markings on the dance floor to step. When an arrow reaches the action bar near the bottom of the screen, it is time for the player to step on the corresponding arrow on the dance pad. The game evaluates the player by the accuracy of steps with the timing of the arrows. The game's soundtrack consisted of original upbeat, electronic songs. The Japanese release of *Dance Dance Revolution* features 11 songs licensed from the *Dancemania* series, the most of all the international releases. Master players at the highest skill level, maneuvering their bodies to accurately hit the correct floor marking at record speed, move their feet at insane speeds. Due to the success of the series, there are still national and international tournaments of players playing and dancing to the latest entries in the series. Other Bemani games include *Guitar Freaks* (play the guitar to music), *Drum Mania* (play the drum kit peripheral), and *Beatmania* (scratch turntables to music).

November 1998—*Music: Music Creation for the PlayStation*—PlayStation

PUBLISHER: Codemasters. RELEASE DATE: November 1998 (EU). GENRE: Music creation.

Music: Music Creation for the PlayStation lets players create music on a home console. Released exclusively in Europe, the game contains 850 pre-recorded riffs and other sound samples to create a song. In addition, users can create original riffs, composing using a piano roll interface, similar to Garageband and Logic Pro. The game supplies hundreds of sampled instruments, with several melody and vocal samples and many ready-made demo tunes and beats. Supported effects include panning, volume, phase, reverb, and vibrato. The game also supplies a video effect editor

with controls for text, particle effects, and cameras. The user can save all compositions to a memory card.

November 3, 1998— *Wipeout 64*—N64

PUBLISHER: Midway. RELEASE DATES: November 3, 1998 (U.S.), January 1999 (EU). COMPOSERS: Rob Lord and Mark Bandola. SERIES: *Wipeout*. NOTABLE MUSICAL TRACK: "Bang On! (Track 7)."

The soundtrack of *Wipeout 64* fits nine musical tracks on an N64 ROM cartridge, three licensed from master recordings. The game is one of a few N64 games requiring load times for sound decompression. The game displays "Please Wait" while decompressing the sounds. The load times between levels are approximately three to four seconds. At the start of each musical track, the game displays the track number, title, and performer on the bottom of the screen. The licensed songs are programmed as fragments to load the licensed songs faster and create a loopable musical track. Rob Lord and Mark Bandola (listed as "PC MUSIC" in the game) wrote six of the game's nine tracks. The remaining three are licensed tracks by British music groups Fluke and Propellerheads. The notable musical track, "Bang On!," was approved for the game, written by Alex Gifford and performed by the Propellerheads. The track abounds with audio manipulation, utilizing echoes of voice samples, electronic guitar distortion, and unusual electronic sounds. Throughout the track, the drum kit is the only instrument unaffected by the audio effects.

November 21, 1998—*The Legend of Zelda: Ocarina of Time*—N64

PUBLISHER: Nintendo. RELEASE DATES: November 21, 1998 (JP), November 23, 1998 (NA), December 11, 1998 (EU). COMPOSER: Koji Kondo. SERIES: *The Legend of Zelda*. GENRE: Action-adventure. NOTABLE MUSICAL TRACK: "Gerudo Valley."

In *The Legend of Zelda: Ocarina of Time*,

the player acquires and performs songs for the ocarina using the N64 controller's buttons as ocarina holes. The game's soundtrack was the last entirely composed by Nintendo veteran composer Koji Kondo. The game's music swaps instruments and melodic layers depending on the state of calm, horseback riding, or danger. The game features 12 songs that Link learns to play on the ocarina. The ocarina is a musical instrument in the shape of a sweet potato with holes on top for the fingers to cover and a mouthpiece into which to blow. The player must remember the button presses for each to "perform" the song. These significant melodies are full of power and mystery. They are required throughout the game to effect specific changes and allow Link to progress further in the story. The pitches of the melodies are re, fa, la, ti, and the upper re. There are six songs that Young Link learns and six that Adult Link learns. Link can use either the Fairy Ocarina instrument or the Ocarina of Time instrument to play the songs. There is a hidden 13th song to acquire, which is not visible on the screen showing the songs learned.

November 27, 1998—Sega Dreamcast

MANUFACTURER: Sega. Release Dates: November 27, 1998 (JP), September 9, 1999 (NA), October 14, 1999 (EU). LAUNCH PRICE: $199.99. MODEL NUMBER: HKT-3020. SOUND-CHIP: Yamaha AICA Super Intelligent Sound Processor. AUDIO: Stereo (surround with QSound).

The Sega Dreamcast was the first home console to include an audio speaker on its memory card and the first with a hand-held gaming component. Released by Sega, the Dreamcast was Sega's final home console before leaving the hardware business to focus on software. The Dreamcast was the first internet-ready console to receive a worldwide release. The console shipped with a 56 Kbps modem and a copy of the latest Planetweb browser. Sega launched a network service called SegaNet, and online support for several Dreamcast titles

followed. The platform provided DLC (downloadable content) for games such as *Skies of Arcadia* and *Jet Set Radio*. At the same time, the launch of Sonic Team's *Phantasy Star Online* represented a giant leap for online console gaming.

The Dreamcast contains the Yamaha AICA Super Intelligent Sound Processor with a 32-bit CPU core built-in. It can produce 64 sound channels that output PCM or ADPCM at 16-bit depth and 48 kHz sampling rate. This rate is of better quality than CD-DA and equal to the audio standard for DVD-quality audio. Although the Dreamcast game discs resemble CDs and DVDs, game discs were a proprietary GD-ROM with 1 gigabyte of storage. The maximum audio quality of the Dreamcast was that of DVD quality. Other audio features include a DSP for reverb, chorus, and other musical effects and XG MIDI support. Like the Sega CD and Sega Saturn, the Dreamcast supports QSound for analog surround sound audio.

In contrast to the Sega CD and Sega Saturn, which included internal backup memory, the Dreamcast uses a 128 kB memory card called the VMU (Visual Memory Unit) for data storage. It was the first home console to include an audio speaker on its memory card. The VMU features a small LCD screen, audio output from a one-channel PWM sound source (like the beeps of the Nokia 6110

Sega Dreamcast back 1998. The audio output ports are A/V (with RF adapter or composite video and stereo audio RCA adapter) (Evan-Amos, "Sega-Dreamcast-Console-BR").

Sega Dreamcast VMU 1998. The VMU contains an internal speaker (Evan-Amos, "Sega-Dreamcast-VMU").

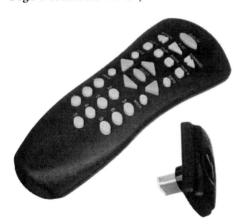

Microsoft Xbox remote 2001. The remote reeceiver connects to the Xbox controller's memory card port. The remote communicates wirelessly with the remote receiver (Evan-Amos, "Xbox-Remote-wReceiver").

and Mattel's *Auto Race*), non-volatile memory, a directional pad, and four buttons. While its most basic function is as a removable storage device, the VMU has other purposes. It serves as an auxiliary display during normal gameplay. Through the use of additional software, it functions as a micro console, independent of the Dreamcast. Detached from the console,

Dreamcast A/V composite cable 1997. It connects to the Dreamcast's A/V port and outputs audio in analog stereo (Evan-Amos, "Sega-Dreamcast-AV-Cable-Composite").

the VMU plays games independently from the Dreamcast.

On March 31, 2001, the Dreamcast ceased manufacturing after less than two years. Since then, Sega has made video games, arcade games, gambling machines, and retro systems. Since then, there aren't any memory cards with screens that a player can use independently of the gaming system.

December 12, 1998—*Hey You, Pikachu!*—N64

PUBLISHER: Nintendo of America. RELEASE DATES: December 12, 1998 (JP), November 6, 2000 (NA). COMPOSER: Miki Obata. GENRE: Digital Pet/Life Simulation.

Hey You, Pikachu! is one of only two games to use the VRU and microphone for the N64 (the other game being the Japan-exclusive *Densha De Go! 64*). The game uses an early form of voice recognition that foreshadows voice-enabled smart devices. It is unique as the only N64 game to use both the VRU (Voice Recognition Unit) and a microphone as an essential input method. The player converses with Pikachu by holding down the Z button and speaking into the microphone. The microphone hooks onto the back of the N64 controller and into the VRU unit. The VRU unit plugs into controller port 4 of the N64. The VRU interprets the vowel and consonant sounds to send the correct words to the N64. The accuracy of voice recognition is limited.

N64 VRU 2000. The microphone connects to the microphone port. The VRU communicates with the N64 through the controller port (WikiY at English Wikipedia, "N64 VRU," CC-BY-SA 3.0).

Using the VRU, Pikachu in *Hey You, Pikachu!* reacts to approximately 459 unique words and phrases (640 when including alternate pronunciations). Some common phrases are "what are you doing," "listen to me," and "let's go." The game highlights in red any text that the player can say for a reaction throughout the game.

SOURCES

AIAS. "23rd Annual D.I.C.E. Awards Panelists." *The Academy of Interactive Arts & Sciences*, 6 Feb. 2020, www.interactive.org/awards/23rd_diceawards_panelists.asp. Accessed 6 Feb. 2020.

Base Media. "Sega Dreamcast." *Console Database*, www.consoledatabase.com/consoleinfo/segadreamcast/. Accessed 3 Aug. 2018.

"Dance Dance Revolution—Videogame by Konami." *International Arcade Museum*, www.arcade-museum.com/game_detail.php?game_id=7489. Accessed 16 Aug. 2018.

"D.I.C.E. Awards (Concept)." *Giant Bomb*, www.giantbomb.com/dice-awards/3015-4604/. Accessed 6 Feb. 2020.

Dreamcast Technical Pages. "Nintendo's Gamecube technical overview." 2004, www.segatech.com/gamecube/overview/.

Dreamcast Technical Pages. "Saturn Overview." 2004, segatech.com/technical/saturnspecs/index.html.

Eckster. "Hey You, Pikachu! Voice Command List." *Pastebin*, 6 Apr. 2015, pastebin.com/ZRkdZQgy. Accessed 31 Mar. 2020.

Eckster. "Hey You, Pikachu! Voice Command List (Duplicates Merged)." *Pastebin*, 6 Apr. 2015, pastebin.com/NaPmSBuR. Accessed 31 Mar. 2020.

Giant Bomb. "Last game released on a console." 5 Oct. 2015, www.giantbomb.com/last-game-released-on-a-console/3015-3262/. Accessed 29 Jan. 2016.

"Metal Gear Solid 2: Making of The Hollywood Game." *YouTube*, 20 Aug. 2012, www.youtube.com/watch?v=2B7yLQV70e0.

Phillips, Yoh. "How a PlayStation Music-Making Game Inspired a Generation of Producers." *DJBooth*, 19 May 2017, djbooth.net/features/2017-05-19-mtv-music-generator-history.

Saucedo, Kaylyn. "Dance Dance Revolution Retrospective: Arcade Machines." *YouTube*, 5 Apr. 2016, www.youtube.com/watch?v=Neca_EddxQ.

Tyson, Jeff. "How Dreamcast Works." *HowStuffWorks*, 19 Oct. 2000, electronics.howstuffworks.com/dreamcast.htm.

Wenz, John. "End of An Era: The Last Games for 12 Iconic Consoles." *Popular Mechanics*, 17 June 2015, www.popularmechanics.com/culture/gaming/g2071/last-video-games-for-12-consoles/.

1999 in Review

April 10, 1999—*Dance Dance Revolution*—PlayStation

PUBLISHER: Konami. RELEASE DATES: April 10, 1999 (JP), March 6, 2001 (NA). SOUND PROGRAMMER: Tomokazu Koizumi. SERIES: *Dance Dance Revolution*. GENRE: Music/Rhythm. NOTABLE MUSICAL TRACK: "Paranoia."

Dance Dance Revolution for the PlayStation was the first version of the arcade series for home consoles. It helped popularize the music/dance genre, much like its arcade counterpart. The player uses either the standard PS1 controller or the included soft plastic dance pad to play the game. Similar to the arcade game, the player steps on the colored arrows marked on the dance pad in time with the icons on the screen that match with the music. This game is an example of a craze first popularized in Japan and later came to North America. A muffled voice acts as a narrator throughout the menus and main game. Some phrases include "You have good taste in music" and "Show me your hottest moves." The audience cheers and encouraging words from the narrator indicate good progress. During each song, a player-selected avatar moves and dances around the screen with color-changing backgrounds.

The game contains a soundtrack of 27 songs and eight courses consisting primarily of music featured in previous DDR (Dance Dance Revolution) arcade games. Unlike the arcade version, the PS1 version included nine covers with songs by Olivia Newton-John, Dan Hartman, and Deep Purple. One track, "Paranoia Kcet clean mix" by 2MB, is original to the game. The remaining tracks were from previous DDR arcade games. "Paranoia," the musical track performed by 180, was originally from *Dance Dance Revolution* (1999, Arcade). It is the only track in the game with two other mixes ("Paranoia Kcet clean mix" and "Paranoia Max Dirty Mix").

May 27, 1999—*Metal Slug X*— Neo Geo AES

PUBLISHER: SNK. RELEASE DATES: May 27, 1999 (WW). COMPOSERS: Takushi Hiyamuta and Yoshihiko Wada. GENRE: Run and gun. SERIES: *Metal Slug*. NOTABLE MUSICAL TRACK: "Livin' on the Deck (Mission 3–1)."

The soundtrack of *Metal Slug X* exhibits its sound generation from PSG, FM synthesis, and PCM. The game remixes the soundtrack of *Metal Slug 2*. The game was also released on the Neo Geo MVS in North America on March 18, 1999, and in Japan on March 19, 1999. The soundtrack was remixed in *Metal Slug X* to be more intense than *Metal Slug 2*. Some of the PCM instrument samples heard throughout the soundtrack are vocal aahs, piano guitar, saxophone, tambourine, timpani, sleigh bells, chimes, snare drum, and drum kit. The music reflects the Egyptian pyramid setting in Mission 2–3 with the sounds of tubular bells, hand drums, and vocal aahs. The notable musical track, "Livin' on the Deck," accompanies Mission 3–1, during which the player's soldier battles his or her way through enemies on a moving train. The bass line is continuously moving, and the drum hits are quick. Even the melody played by the guitar and the saxophone

is very active over a wide range of pitches, further creating the mood of movement from the train.

December 1, 1999—Nintendo 64DD—Peripheral for the N64

MANUFACTURER: Nintendo. RELEASE DATE: December 1, 1999 (JP). PRODUCTION DATES: December 1, 1999–February 28, 2001. LAUNCH PRICE: 2,500 yen per month for 12 months. MODEL NUMBER: NUS-010. SOUND-CHIP: 36-megabit ROM chip.

The 64DD was the Japan-exclusive peripheral for the N64 with a universal soundfont and audio library. The peripheral for the N64 was sold in Japan first as a mail-order subscription called the Randnet Starter Kit on December 1, 1999. For a subscription rate of 2,500 yen per month for 12 months, the consumer received the 64DD unit, online access to the Randnet online service, the Modem cartridge with cable and software, and the Expansion Pak. In addition, the consumer received a 64DD disk in the mail every two months with a new game (six games in total over the year). The 64DD connects to the expansion port on the bottom of the N64. The 64DD includes a slot to play 64DD disks, each with a memory size of 64.45 megabytes. Unlike ROM cartridges (not writeable), 64DD disks are writeable (players could share and save content). The 64DD also supported an optional internet service packaged as the Randnet Starter Kit.

The 64DD includes a 36-megabit chip that stores a soundfont and an audio library of sounds. The pre-installed audio library helps free up space when previously, N64 games would have used much memory for PCM samples. Any 64DD game had access to the 64DD's soundfont and sounds. There were nine games released in Japan over two years on 64DD disks, four from the *Mario Artist* series. The 64DD also worked alongside the N64 to modify or enhance N64 games (with a 64DD disk and N64 cartridge). The Randnet Browser Disk had an E-commerce mode where users could buy audio CDs.

On February 28, 2001, the 64DD ceased

Nintendo 64 with 64DD 1999. The 64DD lacks audiovisual output ports. It communicates with the N64 through the expansion port (Evan-Amos, "64DD-Attached," CC-BY-SA 3.0).

manufacturing. The 64DD lasted a little over a year, having never gained traction. When Nintendo announced the Game Boy Advance and GameCube in 2000, it didn't mention the 64DD. Randnet, the 64DD's online service, was discontinued in October 2000. All of the games in development for the 64DD were either unreleased or ported to the N64. The 64DD was Nintendo's best internet-enabled system at the time, working as promised. In total, there were nine game disks and one browser disk released for the 64DD.

December 12, 1999—*Vib-Ribbon*—PlayStation

PUBLISHER: Sony. RELEASE DATE: December 12, 1999 (JP), September 1, 2000 (EU). COMPOSERS: Laughs and Beats, Toshiyuki Kageyama, Kouichi Hirota, Yoko Fujita, and Masaya Matsuura. SERIES: *Vib-Ribbon*. GENRE: Music/Rhythm.

Vib-Ribbon was the first home console game to generate new level content based on audio data from an audio CD. The game automatically generated appropriate gameplay to match with the audio tracks of any audio CD placed into the PS1. *Vib-Ribbon* had original musical tracks as well. Unlike previous rhythm games, *Vib-Ribbon* did not use icons to indicate button presses.

Instead, the player avatar walked along a track and stopped at each obstacle. The player pressed a corresponding button on the PS1 controller to move past the obstacle without penalty. The entire game of *Vib-Ribbon* loads into the RAM of the PS1, freeing the CD drive for disc swapping, the switching of discs in the CD drive in order to read audio data from an audio disc. The audio track that generated the in-game track also was heard during the track. In addition, the placement of obstacles in the in-game track reflected the tempo and sounds of the audio track. Not only does the game use the disc-swapping technique as a form of custom soundtracks, but it also generates content within the game that reflects musical elements heard in the audio tracks.

December 29, 1999—*Shenmue*—Dreamcast

PUBLISHER: Sega. RELEASE DATE: December 29, 1999 (JP), November 8, 2000 (NA), December 1, 2000 (EU). COMPOSERS: Takenobu Mitsuyoshi, Yuzo Koshiro, Takeshi Yanagawa, Osamu Murata, and Ryuji Iuchi. SERIES: *Shenmue*. GENRE: Action-adventure. NOTABLE MUSICAL TRACK: "Sedge Tree."

Shenmue is an open world action-adventure game known for its film-like cut scenes and soundtrack and its massive $45 million budget. The game is vast, including such things as NPCs (non-playable characters) who have their own voice acting (in Japanese and in English for their respective regions) and places to be as well as QTEs (Quick Time Events), moments in the game when the player must press a button quickly to be successful. In the game, Ryo Hazuki seeks revenge after witnessing his father's murder by a Chinese man. He first explores in Yokosuka, Japan and later in Hong Kong, China. The game's soundtrack uses orchestral sounds as well as the piano and erhu, a traditional Chinese two-stringed instrument. Throughout the game, Ryo collects audio cassette tapes that contain musical tracks and arrangements of songs from the game. Also, after placing third (specifically) in the Lucky Dip prize draw (accessible at Tomato Convenience stores), he is rewarded with one of four tapes with a musical track from the Sega games *After Burner, Hang-On, Out Run,* and *Space Harrier.* The remaining 23 cassette tapes are located in Ryo's desk and at the many Tomato Convenience stores (for purchase). Ryo is only able to listen to the tracks when he finds either a cassette player or a boom box (both devices have a slot for cassette tapes). There was another way to listen to the game's music. One of the game's discs is a "Passport disc." Although the online features have been deactivated since April 2002, the disc, when inserted in the Dreamcast and even when offline, allows a player to view cutscenes and listen to 32 musical tracks from areas unlocked and saved on the Dreamcast VMU.

SOURCES

B., Michelle. "Vib Ribbon." *Pioneer Project,* www.pioneerproject.net/games/vib-ribbon/. Accessed 12 Sept. 2018.
"The 64DD: Nintendo's Disk Drive." *IGN,* 29 Jan. 1998, www.ign.com/articles/1998/01/29/the-64dd-nintendos-disk-drive. Accessed 31 Mar. 2020.

2000 in Review

February 23, 2000—*Mario Artist: Talent Studio*—64DD

PUBLISHER: Nintendo. RELEASE DATE: February 23, 2000 (JP). COMPOSERS: Kazumi Totaka, Kenta Nagata, and Toru Minegishi. SERIES: *Mario Artist.* GENRE: Graphics suite. NOTABLE MUSICAL TRACK: "The Catwalk (Act 1)."

Mario Artist: Talent Studio was the first game for home consoles to let users record and use sound sources in-game. Released exclusively in Japan, the graphics suite is a fully-featured character creator and movie production application. *Mario Artist: Talent Studio* is an evolution of ideas from the SNES game *Mario Paint.* The gaming software lets users create simple movies with animations and sound. The game included the Capture Cassette for the 64DD. The Capture Cassette was an N64 cartridge with ports on the back for analog video, analog left and right audio, and a microphone. The purpose of the Capture Cassette was to take the video and audio from any analog source and insert it into the gaming software. With it, the N64 could interface with multimedia from a VCR, old camcorder, or another gaming system with RCA cables.

In the "Make a Talent" mode, the player creates and customizes 3D characters. The Capture Cassette can capture a still image from a video later used as a texture on a 3D character. The Capture Cassette also contains an attached microphone for the user to record a voice for the character. In the "Make a Movie" mode, the user creates a movie using the Talents. Each movie can have at most 3 Talents, with only one Talent on-screen at a time and at most four background images. The Capture Cassette can capture a still image from a video as a background image.

Each movie can use up to three short sounds recorded from either the microphone or analog stereo inputs on the Capture Cassette. The sound vault can store up to eight sounds. The game also has its own set of background images, sound samples, and Talents from which to choose. Combining the gaming software's assets and imported content from the Capture Cassette and microphone, one could create scenes, animate the Talents, and include sounds. The game does not export the movies as digital files for viewing outside of the game. However, a player can export the video and audio from the Cassette Cassette when connected to a VCR or other device able to record from a feed of composite video and stereo audio.

March 4, 2000—Sony PlayStation 2

MANUFACTURER: Sony. RELEASE DATE: March 4, 2000 (JP), October 26, 2000

Sony PS2 "Phat" back 2000. The audio output ports are A/V (with RF adapter and composite video and stereo audio RCA adapter) or S/PDIF (Evan-Amos, "Sony-PlayStation-2–30001-Console-BR").

Sony PS2 Slim back 2004. The audio output ports are A/V (with RF adapter and composite video and stereo audio RCA adapter) or S/PDIF (Evan-Amos, "Sony-PlayStation-2–70001-Console-BR").

(NA), November 24, 2000 (EU). PRODUCTION DATES: March 4, 2000–January 4, 2013. MODEL NUMBER: SCPH-30001 (USA). AUDIO: Dolby Digital 5.1 and DTS 5.1.

The PS2 (PlayStation 2) is, to this day, the best-selling gaming system of all time, with sales of over 155 million units (this includes the PS2 Slimline redesign) over an almost 13-year manufacturing run. Released by Sony, the PS2 was the first home console to support Dolby Digital and DTS digital surround sound formats. The PS2's audio hardware consists of two CXD2922 SPU chips, previously used in the PS1, with a RAM upgrade and a selectable audio output quality of either 44.1 or 48 kHz. The PS2

supports 48 ADPCM sound channels, and software can mix additional sound channels. Since PS2 discs do not adhere to the data format of audio CDs, PS2 discs do not contain CD-DA tracks. However, the PS2 was backward-compatible with most PS1 games (the few problems were graphical glitches, memory card errors, bugs). As a multimedia device, the PS2 played CDs and DVDs. The PS2 was cheaper to buy than a dedicated DVD player.

The popular digital audio outputs, available for the first time in a home console, were Dolby Digital 5.1 and DTS. Dolby Digital 5.1 is a multi-channel surround system designed by Dolby Labs (also responsible for Dolby Surround and Dolby Pro Logic II). A 5.1 audio signal contains six discrete channels of audio (left front, right front, center, left rear, right rear, and low-frequency effects subwoofer). DTS is a digital surround sound format designed by DTS (Digital Theater Sound) that delivers six discrete channels (5.1) of high-quality 20-bit audio. Although the bit depth of DTS audio data is greater than that of Dolby Digital (16-bit depth), DTS audio data is not as compressed as Dolby Digital audio data. Therefore, the same amount of audio information encoded in Dolby Digital will use less space than encoded in DTS. Digital audio outputs include Dolby Digital 5.1 surround sound and DTS for full-motion video only. Games released later in the PS2's lifespan achieved analog 5.1 surround audio during gameplay via Dolby Pro Logic II.

April 21, 2000—*F-Zero X Expansion Kit*–64DD

PUBLISHER: RandnetDD Co. RELEASE DATE: April 21, 2000 (JP). COMPOSERS: Taro Bando and Hajime Wakai. SERIES: *F-Zero*. GENRE: Racing.

F-Zero X Expansion Kit added new musical tracks and enhanced musical tracks when used in conjunction with *F-Zero X* for the N64. Released exclusively in Japan, the game was the first expansion disk released for the 64DD. The expansion disk functions only when the player inserts the disk into the 64DD and the *F-Zero X* cartridge into the N64. All of the eight new musical tracks from the expansion disk were stereophonic, in contrast with the entirely monaural musical tracks from *F-Zero X*. This was due to the increased memory size of the 64DD disk compared to the N64 cartridge. In total, the expansion disk added about 20 minutes of new music. Also, the music took advantage of the 64DD's internal audio library, so the musical tracks used a wider variety of sounds than the *F-Zero X* musical tracks alone. Also, since the two games worked together, the 64DD disk could enhance the musical tracks from the N64 cartridge. Some of the alterations included extending the musical track, panning the guitars, and adding drums.

Regarding memory size, the *F-Zero X* N64 cartridge is a size of 16 MB. In contrast, the *F-Zero X Expansion Kit* disk is 64MB, which contains 10 new racetracks, two editors for "Course Edit" and "Create Machine," and eight new musical tracks. As memory storage became larger and cheaper, more space was available for more audio of higher quality.

April 27, 2000—*Samba de Amigo*— Dreamcast

PUBLISHER: Sega. RELEASE DATE: April 27, 2000 (JP), October 16, 2000 (NA), December 8, 2000 (EU). SERIES: *Samba de Amigo*. GENRE: Music/Rhythm.

Samba de Amigo was a music and rhythm game using unique maraca controllers with a Latin-infused soundtrack of popular covers. The game continues the rhythm game trends of *PaRappa the Rapper* and *Dance Dance Revolution*. The game was also released in arcades in Japan on December 21, 1999, and arcades in North America on March 29, 2000. The game includes maraca-shaped controllers to use instead of the standard Dreamcast controller. The Dreamcast recognizes the shakes from the left and right maraca based on a floor sensor underneath each maraca. The bar has sensors at each end to detect the placement of each maraca above it. Each maraca also contains an ultrasonic transmitter to assist in the triangulation of the maracas' positions. The player shakes either the left, right, or both maracas at a high, middle, or low height in time with the blue and red balls on the screen. The game's soundtrack mainly included covers of popular Latin songs. Some of the covers are from Ricky Martin, Quincy Jones, and Ritchie Valens. Sega's in-house musicians at Wave Master, the audio production team for video game series such as *Sonic the Hedgehog*, *Phantasy Star*, and *Super Monkey Ball*, produced the song covers.

December 14, 2000—*Little Nicky*— Game Boy Color

PUBLISHER: Ubisoft Entertainment. RELEASE DATE: December 14, 2000 (NA). COMPOSER: Robert Baffy. GENRE: Platformer. NOTABLE MUSICAL TRACK: "Zany Bus."

Little Nicky is one of the only GBC games to use all of the system's sound channels for music, specifically the PCM channel. The game is a licensed game based on the movie of the same name starring Adam Sandler. The Game Boy's PCM channel was rarely ever used within the music of neither Game Boy nor Game Boy Color games because PCM audio samples used up too much memory on the game cartridge. Game developers did not reserve much space for audio, let alone music within the ROM cartridge. PCM, then, was the choice for brief sound effects.

Little Nicky uses the PCM channel for an electric guitar sound, heard in the tracks "Zany Bus" and "Metal Head." The game also has full-sentence voice samples, although at the poor audio quality of the Game Boy Color. The title theme, "Zany Bus," is similar to Ozzy Osbourne's 1980 song "Crazy Train." "Zany Bus" uses PCM samples of a guitar. Game Boy Advance soundtracks used audio samples much more frequently.

Nevertheless, the GBC soundtrack of

Little Nicky resembles the soundtracks of Game Boy Advance games. Video games designed for systems with limited audio capabilities struggled to use the PCM channel for anything more than sound effects. Other games that use the PCM channel for music for the GBC are *101 Dalmatians: Puppies to the Rescue* and *Project S-11*.

December 23, 2000— *The Bouncer*—PS2

PUBLISHER: Square Electronic Arts. RELEASE DATE: December 23, 2000 (JP), March 6, 2001 (NA), June 22, 2001 (EU). COMPOSERS: Noriko Matsueda and Takahito Eguchi. GENRE: Beat-em-up. NOTABLE MUSICAL TRACK: "Love Is the Gift (Ending Credits)."

The Bouncer was the first video game on a home console to support Dolby Digital 5.1. Only the audio of the game's cutscenes supports Dolby Digital 5.1. The game's story progresses primarily through the cutscenes, which end with the player selecting one of three characters for gameplay mode. The PS2 supported digital surround sound options. To set up the PS2 properly for the digital audio formats, the player must connect the PS2 to an audio decoder via an optical audio cable. The PS2 first encodes the audio signal based on the desired digital audio format, then passes it to the audio decoder. From there, the audio decoder passes the decoded signal as analog audio to the speaker setup. *The Bouncer* supports Dolby Digital 5.1, a speaker setup

of 5 speakers and a subwoofer. Dolby Digital 5.1, a digital surround sound format, is a noticeable improvement from Dolby Pro Logic II, the popular analog surround sound format. The notable musical track, "Love Is the Gift (Ending Credits)," is missing from the official soundtrack. Only appearing in the English version of the game, Shanice Wilson sings the song that resembles a 90s R&B song.

SOURCES

Foss, Christopher. "F-Zero X: EXpansion Kit—Red Canyon." *YouTube*, 24 Aug. 2007, www.youtube.com/watch?v=EfxO7lht5-Y. Accessed 1 Apr. 2020.

"(Incomplete) List of GB/GBC Games to Use PCM Samples (Page 1)." *ChipMusic.org*, 7 July 2015, chipmusic.org/forums/topic/16824/incomplete-list-of-gbgbc-games-to-use-pcm-samples/.

Retropete. "Sony PlayStation 2 (PS2)." 2016, www.8-bitcentral.com/sony/playStation2.html.

"Sega Dreamcast's Samba De Amigo." *The Game Goldies*, 15 July 2009, wayback.archive.org/web/20130625002520/www.gamegoldies.org/samba-de-amigo-sega-dreamcast/.

Sony. "SPU2 Overview." *Dropbox*, Apr. 2002, www.dropbox.com/s/87xwmydprwubmyh/SPU2_Overview_Manual.pdf.

"Sony PlayStation 2 (PS2)." *8-Bit Central*, www.8-bitcentral.com/sony/playStation2.html. Accessed 3 Aug. 2018.

Sorrel, Charlie. "PS2 Still Outselling PS3 by Four to One." *WIRED*, 24 Aug. 2007, www.wired.com/2007/08/ps2-still-outse/. Accessed 21 Sept. 2020.

Turboboy215. "(Incomplete) List of GB/GBC Games to Use PCM Samples." *ChipMusic.org*, 7 July 2015, chipmusic.org/forums/topic/16824/incomplete-list-of-gbgbc-games-to-use-pcm-samples/. Accessed 21 Sept. 2020.

2001 in Review

January 8, 2001—LCD Screen for PSone—Peripheral for PlayStation

MANUFACTURER: Sony. RELEASE DATE: January 8, 2001 (NA). PRODUCTION DATES: January 8, 2001–March 26, 2006. LAUNCH PRICE: $149.99 with PSone, $99.99 sold individually in November 2001. MODEL NUMBER: SCPH-131. AUDIO: Stereo.

The LCD Screen for PSone was the first peripheral to convert a home console into a portable gaming system (though bigger than could fit in the hands). Released by Sony, the LCD screen is a 5-inch thin-film transistor liquid crystal screen with a left and right audio speaker hooked on to the back of the PSone. Released in North America on July 7, 2000, the PSone (model number SCPH-101) was a smaller model

Sony LCD screen for PS One 2001. The audio output ports are A/V (with RF adapter and composite video and stereo audio RCA adapter) or 3.5mm. The volume slider modulates the 3.5mm audio (Evan-Amos, "Sony-PSone-Console-wScreen-Closed-BR").

of the Sony PlayStation, maintaining the exact audio specifications. Until the LCD Screen for PSone, home consoles needed to be hooked up to a television to operate. When a player connects the LCD screen to the PSone, a player could play PS1 games using the small screen and speakers. With the LCD Screen and PSone, a player could take the console gaming experience on the go. Both units were not that heavy nor oversized.

The combination of the PSone with the LCD Screen made the PSone the first home console designed for portability and travel. At its release, Sony sold the LCD Screen as a bundle with the PSone for $149.99. When it was available as an individual item in November 2001, it sold for $99.99. Other features include

- hooking the PSone to a television.
- sending the stereo audio output to headphones.
- hooking up external devices such as VCRs and camcorders to the LCD screen via the screen's A/V input port.

The sale and promotion of a portable screen and speakers allowed gamers to break away from playing video games in a fixed location with a large television.

February 20, 2001—*Rez*— Dreamcast

PUBLISHER: Sega. RELEASE DATE: November 22, 2001 (JP), February 20, 2002 (EU). COMPOSERS: Keiichi Sugiyama, Ken Ishii, Adam Freeland, Coldcut. GENRE: Rail shooter/Music. NOTABLE MUSICAL TRACK: "Fear (Area 5)."

Rez is a unique mashup of the rail shooter and music genres, one of many music games by producer Tetsuya Mizuguchi. The game is a rail shooter in which the player creates the sounds and melodies of the game. Synesthesia is integral to the game's design, in which the stimulation of one sense provokes another sense. Electronic sounds replace typical sound effects, seamlessly blending into a musical soundscape while the player targets and destroys the game's enemies. Mizuguchi controlled the player's mood through quantization, the synchronization of rhythm with emotion. The special package in the Japanese release included the Trance Vibrator, a device plugged into the Dreamcast's USB port to provoke the tactile sense along with the game's audio and video. Each area on the sub-system lists the track title and artist. The notable musical track, "Fear (Area 5)," is an excellent example of how the player's actions create the sounds that naturally fit into the track. Dialogue boxes describing a location change appear as moments of repose in the musical track, marking a place within the track. The sounds made from destroying enemies include synthesized sounds, drum hits, and short vocal phrases. The track intensifies with additional enemies and targets. A loose bass line and drum beat remain constant as a foundation to the track.

March 21, 2001—Game Boy Advance

MANUFACTURER: Nintendo. RELEASE DATE: March 21, 2001 (JP), June 11, 2001 (NA), June 22, 2001 (EU). PRODUCTION DATES: March 21, 2001–December 9, 2009. LAUNCH PRICE: $99.99. MODEL NUMBER: AGB-001. SOUNDCHIPS: LR35902, ARM7TDMI. AUDIO: Mono (stereo from the headphone port).

Nintendo Game Boy Advance 2001. The internal speaker is located on the bottom-right corner of the device. The audio output ports are 3.5mm. The volume slider modulates the internal speaker's volume (Evan-Amos, "Nintendo-Game-Boy-Advance-Purple-FL").

The Game Boy Advance was the last handheld gaming system in the Game Boy series of handheld gaming systems. It was the successor to the Game Boy Color. Although the GBA had backward compatibility with GB and GBC games, it displayed the games on its widescreen 2.9-inch color LCD screen. The audio of the GBA was comparable in many ways with the Game Boy and Game Boy Color. All of the handheld gaming systems have a built-in speaker capable of monaural audio. The headphone audio-out jack sends out a stereo audio signal. The GBA includes two soundchips. One of the soundchips is the Sharp LR35902, the same soundchip used in the GB and GBC. The inclusion of this chip maintains compatibility with the games of the GB and GBC. The LR25902 has four sound channels. Two of the channels use PSGs to produce pulse waves

with four duty cycle settings for different sounds. One sound channel was used either for periodic waveforms through wavetable synthesis or 4-bit PCM playback. The last channel produced white noise through white noise synthesis.

The second chip used for audio was the ARM7TDMI, the GBA's CPU, licensed by ARM. Created by Nintendo specifically for the GBA, the chip includes two 8-bit PWM DACs for stereophonic audio, collectively called "Direct Sound" by Nintendo. The GBA uses Direct Sound to play 8-bit signed PCM samples. Direct Sound operates either as DMA (Direct Memory Access) or Interrupt. In DMA mode, the DMA controller automatically retrieves samples when the loaded samples are empty. Most developers chose not to play samples directly using either mode because it was easier to mix audio and sound effects through the CPU. However, the audio quality varied from game to game. The sampling rate and number of instruments and sound effects at one time vary depending on CPU usage. Although games stored samples at a sample rate of 44 kHz or higher, the GBA mixes all audio down to 32.768 kHz for output. The

Nintendo Game Boy Advance SP 2003. The internal speaker is located in the middle of the device's lower panel. The volume slider modulates the internal speaker's volume. The GBA SP lacks audiovisual output ports (Evan-Amos, "Game-Boy-Advance-SP-Mk1-Blue," CC-BY-SA 3.0).

Nintendo Game Boy Advance headphone adapter 2003. The adapter connects to the extension port of the GBA SP, adding a 3.5mm audio output port (Evan-Amos, "Nintendo-Game-Boy-Advance-Headphone-Adapter").

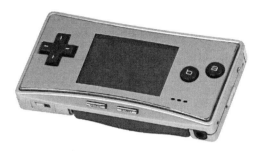

Nintendo Game Boy Micro 2005. The internal speaker is located on the bottom-right corner of the device. The audio output ports are 3.5mm. The volume up and down buttons modulate the internal speaker's volume (Evan-Amos, "Game-Boy-Micro," CC-BY-SA 3.0).

DACs support mono or stereophonic audio output. Although rare, it is possible to produce music using both chips (like *Kuru Kuru Kururin* [2001]).

The GBA SP, released in Japan on February 14, 2003, was a model with a clamshell form factor, a frontlight for the screen, and the lack of a 3.5mm audio-out port (an adapter is needed to connect an audio cable to the GBA SP's AC port). The Game Boy Micro, released in Japan on September 13, 2005, has a tiny form factor with a two-inch screen, a backlight for the screen, removable faceplates, restoration of the 3.5mm audio-out port, and the removal of a cartridge port for Game Boy and Game Boy Color games. On December 9, 2009, the Game Boy Advance ceased manufacturing. The Game Boy Advance was the handheld system with the most extensive library of backward-compatible games.

June 21, 2001—*Gitaroo Man*—PS2

PUBLISHER: KOEI. RELEASE DATES: June 21, 2001 (JP), February 18, 2002 (NA), June 21, 2002 (EU). COMPOSER: COIL. GENRE: Music. NOTABLE MUSICAL TRACK: "The Legendary Theme (Acoustic Version)."

Gitaroo Man is a music game that naturally combines various genres into the game's storyline. Released for the PS2 in Japan on June 21, 2001, the game includes many musical genres, including slow rock,

synth pop, blues, reggae, Latin, and metal. The protagonist of the game holds a guitar when entering battle. Unlike earlier music games, in *Gitaroo Man*, the player hits the right notes by tracing a line with the controller's analog stick and pressing the X button in time with the riffs. There are no discernible patterns and no natural structure to the button inputs. *Gitaroo Man* is different than other music games that used visual icons that moved in time with the music to indicate button presses. Some musical segments in *Gitaroo Man* involve pressing other controller face buttons (X, O, triangle, square) in rhythm with the song. After completing Story Mode, the player unlocks Master's Play, which adds a few remixes and more difficult input patterns to the game. Remixing gives the player a creative musical outlet within the confines of the game.

The acoustic version of "The Legendary Theme" accompanies Stage 6. U-1 plays the musical track when he first meets Kirah under a tree on Planet Gitaroo. The piece is reflective and sad, matching the visual storytelling. The musical track brings U-1 and Kirah closer together. Ultimately, Kirah rests her head on U-1's shoulder, and he blushes. The song's album version returns in Stage 9 when Kirah battles U-1, who refuses to fight. After trading solos, U-1 plays an electric version of the melody, stunning Kirah. He convinces Kirah to fight for good as they perform a remixed duet of "The Legendary Theme."

August 1, 2001—*Golden Sun*—GBA

PUBLISHER: Nintendo. RELEASE DATE: August 1, 2001 (JP), November 12, 2001 (NA), February 22, 2002 (EU). COMPOSER: Motoi Sakuraba. SERIES: *Golden Sun*. GENRE: RPG. NOTABLE MUSICAL TRACK: "Venus Lighthouse (Final Dungeon)."

Golden Sun's soundtrack makes use of MIDI instrument samples. MIDI and samples of strings, brass pan flute, woodwinds, voices, bass guitar, synth pads, and percussion vastly improved the soundtrack of *Golden Sun*. Despite the use of MIDI samples in a handheld gaming system, the audio hardware of the GBA locks the audio output at a sample rate of 32 kHz. Nevertheless, due to the GBA's Direct Sound, handheld games could use samples more liberally than before.

The soundtrack makes use of instrument groups to differentiate between peaceful and battle moments. When with the local townsfolk, the mood is calm with MIDI strings and pan flute. When in a battle, MIDI bass guitar, synth pads, and percussion samples convey intensity and urgency. The drum hit samples add some realism to the soundtrack despite being limited by the soundchips of the GBA. The notable musical track, "Venus Lighthouse," accompanies the final dungeon. The track fits the epic tone near the game's conclusion. The track makes use of MIDI instruments, including synthesized brass, strings, woodwinds, and voices.

August 9, 2001—*Alien Front Online*—Dreamcast

PUBLISHER: Sega. RELEASE DATE: August 9, 2001 (NA). COMPOSERS: Howard Drossin and Makito Nomiya. GENRE: Action.

Alien Front Online was the first video game on a home console with online voice chat. Released exclusively in North America, the game includes the Dreamcast microphone, a simple microphone that connects to the Dreamcast controller via the VMU port. The game is a port of *Alien Front: Team Based Combat*, an arcade game released exclusively in Japan on January 23, 2001. Before this game, online voice chat was limited to PC gaming. The Dreamcast had a built-in modem and a web browser. Therefore, it was designed with online connectivity in mind. Using the Dreamcast microphone, players could communicate verbally with either all of the players within the match or just those on the same team. In this first instance of online voice chat on a home console, there was no subscription for online services and no system of censoring inappropriate language or blocking players for inappropriate behavior.

The online modes of *Alien Front Online* only worked using the Dreamcast

Sega Dreamcast microphone 2001. The microphone connects to the microphone port. The Dreamcast Microphone communicates with the Dreamcast through the controller's VMU port (Evan-Amos, "Dreamcast-Microphone").

Modem; the modes would not function with the Broadband Adapter. Although the game was released months after the Dreamcast ceased manufacturing, there were still innovations in audio. To this day, most online games support voice chat or, at the very least, an online messaging system. Players are accustomed to verbal communication with other players, sometimes for strategic purposes and other times for fun.

September 14, 2001—Nintendo GameCube

MANUFACTURER: Nintendo. RELEASE DATE: September 14, 2001 (JP), November 18, 2001 (NA), May 3, 2002 (EU). MANUFACTURING DATES: September 14, 2001–February 2007. LAUNCH PRICE: $199.99. MODEL NUMBER: DOL-001. SOUNDCHIP: Custom Macronix 16-bit DSP. AUDIO: Dolby Pro Logic II.

The GameCube was the first home console to support Dolby Pro Logic II. Released

Nintendo GameCube with controller 2001. The audio output ports are analog A/V (with RF adapter or composite video and stereo audio RCA adapter) (Evan-Amos, "GameCube-Console-Set").

by Nintendo, the GameCube was the first Nintendo home console to use disc-based media instead of cartridges for game storage. Instead of standard-sized CDs (4.7 inches), Nintendo used a proprietary disc size that resembled a MiniDVD (3.1 inches). During this time, there was a concern of piracy of video games on disc. Especially for Nintendo, it did not want to lose sales due to piracy on its first disc-based gaming system. Due to the proprietary format, GameCube discs were much more difficult for consumers to duplicate. The maximum memory of a GameCube disc was 1.5 GB. The GameCube disc is larger than the 700 MB for a CD but smaller than the 4.7 GB for a single-layer DVD. Considering that the largest N64 game cartridge was 64MB (the same memory size as

a 64DD disk), the GameCube discs stored much more memory.

The GameCube contains a custom Macronix 16-bit DSP (digital signal processor) as its integrated audio processor. The DSP has a sampling frequency of 48 kHz, capable of a maximum of 64 simultaneous ADPCM channels. Unlike the original Xbox and PS2, the GameCube only has analog audio outputs. Therefore, digital surround sound formats like Dolby Digital and DTS are not available from the GameCube. However, the GameCube was the first home console to support Dolby Pro Logic II. Dolby Pro Logic II is the improved analog surround sound format of Dolby Surround. Like the digital formats, it too supports a 5.1 speaker setup. Despite the lack of digital sound offerings, the GameCube has stereo output, with some games containing 5.1-channel analog surround sound via Dolby Pro Logic II.

September 24, 2001—*NHL 2002*— PS2

PUBLISHER: EA Canada. RELEASE DATE: September 24, 2001 (NA), October 19, 2001 (EU), February 7, 2002 (JP). SERIES: *NHL*. GENRE: Sports.

NHL 2002 was the first game on a home console to support real-time DTS. The game's programming generated the proper 5.1 audio while the player changed the activities in the game. During cutscenes, the audio is fixed, so the software doesn't have to generate the audio in real-time. During gameplay, the action on the ice is unpredictable, much like a hockey game. In the game, the player interacts with the game through button presses on the controller. DTS 5.1 reflects the sound of the puck and players on different sides of the ice from five separate locations. So, *NHL 2002* was the first game with real-time 5.1 digital audio. Despite this achievement in audio, most games on the PS2 that supported DTS only worked in a 4.0 speaker setup (this arrangement excludes the center speaker and subwoofer signals). Both Dolby Digital and DTS are still available today, and both work well in real-time,

Nintendo GameCube microphone. The microphone communicates with the GameCube through the memory card port (Evan-Amos, "GameCube-Microphone").

with their origins in *NHL 2002* for the PS2.

November 15, 2001—Microsoft Xbox

MANUFACTURER: Microsoft. RELEASE DATE: November 15, 2001 (NA), February 22, 2002 (JP), March 14, 2002 (EU). PRODUCTION DATES: November 15, 2001–March 2, 2009. LAUNCH PRICE: $299.99 (with 8GB internal hard drive). MODEL NUMBER: Revision 1.0. SOUNDCHIP: MCPX. AUDIO: Dolby Surround (Dolby Digital 5.1 for DVD playback).

The Microsoft Xbox was the first home console capable of ripping audio tracks from a CD and storing them in its internal hard drive. Released by Microsoft, the Xbox was the first gaming system developed and manufactured by Microsoft. Nowadays, the Xbox from 2001 is the "original Xbox" to differentiate from later gaming systems by Microsoft. The Xbox was the first home console to include an internal 8 GB hard drive. The internal hard drive was crucial for a particular audio feature of the original Xbox. The Xbox was the first home console capable of ripping audio tracks from a CD and storing them in its internal hard drive. The hard drive was used with the Xbox's Custom Soundtrack

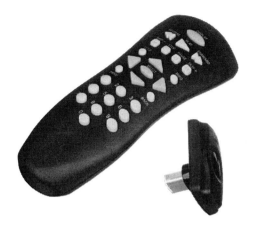

Microsoft Xbox remote 2001. The remote reeceiver connects to the Xbox controller's memory card port. The remote communicates wirelessly with the remote receiver (Evan-Amos, "Xbox-Remote-wReceiver").

feature, which allowed gamers to use stored music seamlessly throughout gameplay. Each game required programming to support a custom soundtrack. Racing and driving games lent themselves well to custom soundtracks. While custom soundtracks were easy to configure, future gaming systems phased out the feature.

The original Xbox is designed much like a computer, complete with multimedia functionality. Microsoft, as the company behind the Windows operating system, understood the computer industry very well. The original Xbox can connect to a PC. *Xbox Music Maker* (2003) allows a user to transfer certain types of music and pictures directly from a PC to the Xbox. The transfer requires the installation of special software on the PC. Using *Xbox Music Mixer*, a user views photos on a TV screen and creates customized soundtracks to accompany a photo slideshow. The Xbox borrowed the idea of combining multimedia functionality into a gaming device from the 3DO.

Microsoft Xbox back 2001. The audio output ports are A/V (with composite video and stereo audio RCA adapter, component video and stereo audio RCA adapter, or component video and stereo audio and S/PDIF adapter). The Xbox headset communicates with the Xbox through the controller's memory card port (Evan-Amos, "Xbox-Console-BR").

The Xbox could also read DVDs with the remote and infrared receiver from the *Xbox Movie DVD Playback Kit*. Unlike the PS2, which read DVDs natively, the original Xbox required the DVD remote and infrared receiver hooked up to the console to activate the DVD features. The Xbox began a trend of home consoles designed

Xbox advanced AV adapter 2001. It connects to the Xbox's A/V port and outputs audio in analog stereo or optical audio (Evan-Amos, "Xbox-Advanced-AV-Adapter").

as PCs with gaming functionality. A movie DVD could include a playable demo for the Xbox alongside the movie. When an Xbox recognized a DVD with both types of content, the player could navigate the movie menu to find the option to play the game demo. Then the game content seamlessly loaded up. This practice helped to boost DVD sales and to promote movies and games based on them. The first DVD release of the Star Wars Trilogy (Episodes

Xbox A/V composite cable 2001. It connects to the Xbox's A/V port and outputs audio in analog stereo (Evan-Amos, "Xbox-Composite-Cable").

4, 5, and 6) in 2004 included dual content. The set contained four DVDs. The fourth DVD had the special features and demo of *Star Wars: Battlefront*. The demo consists of a single-player and two-player split-screen round on the Battle of Endor. Each player can select a fighter class from either the Imperial or Rebel teams. The Star Wars Trilogy DVD set and *Star Wars: Battlefront* for Xbox were released on September 21, 2004.

The Xbox contains the NVIDIA Media Communications Processor for the Xbox, also known as MCPX, also known as the Sound-Storm "NVAPU." The MCPX is dedicated to 3D audio and network processing. The MCPX also performs the processing for broadband networking functions and high-speed peripherals. It is capable of 64 positional-3D sound channels supporting surround sound or up to 256 stereo sound channels. It also has support for MIDI.

The original Xbox supported analog and digital audio outputs. The Xbox had a SCART (Syndicat des Constructeurs d'Appareils Radiorécepteurs et Téléviseurs, "Radio and Television Receiver Manufacturers' Association") port on the back of the unit. The Xbox came with the Xbox Standard A/V Cable that the Xbox used for analog composite video and audio (monaural, stereo, and Dolby Surround). The Xbox Advanced A/V Pack, sold separately, was used for S-video and digital audio via an optical audio cable. Also sold separately was the Xbox High Definition A/V Pack; this was used for component video and digital audio. In Europe, the Xbox Advanced SCART cable was used for SCART high-definition video and digital audio. All digital audio configurations supported Dolby Digital 5.1 and DTS (DTS was only available for DVD movie playback).

November 18, 2001—*Rogue Squadron 2: Rogue Leader—GameCube*

PUBLISHER: LucasArts. RELEASE DATE: November 18, 2001 (NA), May 3, 2002 (EU). COMPOSER: Chris Hülsbeck. SERIES: *Star Wars: Rogue Squadron*. GENRE: Action.

Rogue Squadron 2: Rogue Leader was the first game for a home console to support Dolby Pro Logic II throughout the game. The game was a launch title for the GameCube in North America and Europe. There was already a game supporting the most advanced analog surround sound format from the GameCube's launch. Although Dolby Pro Logic II is an analog format, it still produces authentic surround sound, just through different encoding/decoding algorithms and cabling.

DPLII (Dolby Pro Logic II) is an encoding and decoding algorithm that encodes six sound channels into two. The sound channels originate from a game's programming. Using *Rogue Squadron 2: Rogue Leader* as an example, the game's programming contains audio and music that is already separated into the six sound channels for the 5.1 speaker setup. Then, the goal is to transmit these six sound channels as a two-channel analog signal through the RCA cable. The RCA cable, containing a left and a right audio cable usually marked in red and white, has a maximum threshold of two analog signals. DPLII uses mathematical formulas to encode the 5.1 audio of the game to a stereo audio signal.

As a stereo audio signal, a TV would play stereo audio as is. However, when the gaming system encodes the audio, another device, called the decoder, reverses the process. An audio receiver is necessary to decode audio that has been encoded to proprietary surround sound formats, like DPLII, Dolby Digital 5.1, and DTS. The gaming system first sends the encoded signal to the audio receiver. The audio receiver decodes the signal. Once again, the audio receiver uses mathematical formulas to recognize the DPLII-encoded signal and extract the six individual channels. There is indeed a way to detect six sound channels from a stereo signal accurately. DPLII,

therefore, is the algorithms for encoding and decoding. Although *Rogue Squadron 2: Rogue Leader* wasn't the first game with 5.1 audio, it was the first game using DPLII for this process. *Rogue Squadron 2: Rogue Leader* was the first video game to use 5.1 audio throughout the game for sound and music.

November 19, 2001—*Frequency—PS2*

PUBLISHER: Sony. RELEASE DATE: November 19, 2001 (NA), June 28, 2002 (EU). COMPOSER: Kasson Crooker. GENRE: Music. NOTABLE MUSICAL TRACK: "The Winner" by The Crystal Method.

Frequency is a music game that allows players to remix music by altering a song's instrumentation. The game lets players create, save, and play remixes of the game's songs. The player controls a virtual avatar called a "FreQ" traveling down an octagonal tunnel. Each wall of the tunnel corresponds to a musical track, a sequence of musical notes. The player presses buttons on the game controller that match the placement of notes on the selected track. Doing so unlocks "sonic energy," and the musical notes play in their intended arrangement. After the player accurately presses buttons for two measures of music on the track, the track is "captured," and the music plays automatically until the avatar reaches a new section of the song. This gameplay mechanic is a unique way of interaction in a music game.

In *Frequency*, the player could create remixes of any song in the game. While the player was limited to the instruments and structure of the music, the remix could include

- different melodies or beat lines.
- changes in tempo.
- modulation of an instrument sound.

To do this, the player shifted the avatar from one of eight tracks on the octagonal tunnel. These shifts, collectively, reflected the remix. Remixes could then be saved on the PS2 memory card and played as regular songs within the game, although the game didn't keep high score records for the remixes. The notable musical track, "The Winner" by The Crystal Method, plays on Stage 1–1. Because of the remix feature, the player hears the track in many different instrument arrangements throughout the game.

SOURCES

Benfield, Lee. "Gitaroo Man." *Hardcore Gaming 101*, 23 Aug. 2017, www.hardcoregaming101. net/gitaroo-man/.

Bramwell, Tom. "Golden Sun." *Eurogamer.net*, 21 Feb. 2002, www.eurogamer.net/articles/r_goldensun_gba.

"Console wars system specifications." 2006, wars. locopuyo.com/cwsystemspecsold.php.

Cvxfreak. "PSone LCD Screen FAQ." *Game-FAQs*, 8 Apr. 2007, gamefaqs.gamespot.com/ps/916392-playstation/faqs/15131. Accessed 31 Mar. 2020.

Deku. "Sound on the Gameboy Advance." deku. gbadev.org/program/sound1.html.

"Gameboy Advance Direct Sound." *BeLogic Software*, belogic.com/gba/directsound.shtml. Accessed 29 Nov. 2018.

"GameCube Spec Sheet." *GameCubicle.com*, 2001, www.gamecubicle.com/system-gamecube-specs.htm. Accessed 3 Aug. 2018.

"Golden Sun / Awesome Music." *TV Tropes*, 26 July 2018, tvtropes.org/pmwiki/pmwiki.php/AwesomeMusic/GoldenSun.

Govoni, Jim. "Frequency FAQ/Walkthrough for PlayStation 2." *GameFAQs*, 28 Jan. 2003, game-faqs.gamespot.com/ps2/516506-frequency/faqs/21435.

Kuchera, Ben. "Remembering One of the Best Songs in Gaming History." *Polygon*, 29 Mar. 2017, www.polygon.com/2017/3/29/15106794/gitaroo-man-legendary-theme-acoustic.

Mathurin, Jeff. "Welcome to the Xbox FAQ." *Biline.ca*, www.biline.ca/xbox-faq.htm. Accessed 3 Aug. 2018.

Parish, Jeremy. "Last of the Line: Game Boy Advance Ended One Legacy as It Began Another." *USgamer.net*, 25 Mar. 2016, www.usgamer.net/articles/last-of-the-line-game-boy-advance-ended-one-legacy-while-beginning-another/page-2.

Schilling, Chris. "Gitaroo Man Retrospective." *Eurogamer.net*, 8 Apr. 2013, www.eurogamer.net/articles/2013-08-04-gitaroo-man-retrospective.

"Sound on the Gameboy Advance—Day 1." *Deku's Tree of Art*, deku.gbadev.org/program/sound1.html. Accessed 3 Aug. 2018.

Stridsberg, Douglas. "XBOX Hardware Specifications." *Thy Old XBOX—Tips, Tweaks and Guides*, xbox.douglasstridsberg.com/xbox-hardware-specifications/. Accessed 3 Aug. 2018.

"Xbox 101: A Beginner's Guide to Microsoft's Original Console." *Racketboy*, 2 Mar. 2014, www.racketboy.com/retro/microsoft/xbox/xbox-101-a-beginners-guide-to-microsofts-original-console.

2002 in Review

2002—G.A.N.G. (Game Audio Network Guild)—Event

In 2002, the Game Audio Network Guild was founded. G.A.N.G. is a non-profit organization founded by game audio specialists to support all aspects of interactive audio, especially game audio and sound design. It is the largest group of people who specialize in audio, including composers, sound designers, voice actors, and audio engineers. Composer Tommy Tallarico is one of its founding members. G.A.N.G. acknowledges the value, work, and growth of the people who work in interactive audio. Since 2003, G.A.N.G. members vote for and give out awards annually dedicated to game audio.

February 22, 2002—*Jet Set Radio Future*—Xbox

PUBLISHER: Rare. RELEASE DATE: February 22, 2002 (JP), February 25, 2002 (NA), March 14, 2002 (EU). COMPOSER: Hideki Naganuma. SERIES: *Jet Grind Radio*. GENRE: Action/Extreme sports. NOTABLE MUSICAL TRACK: "The Concept of Love (Intro/Main Theme)."

The soundtrack of *Jet Set Radio Future* is a creative blend of J-pop and funk music by foreign and underground artists. The soundtrack creates a futuristic world with music from musical groups without much mainstream recognition. The player controls a protagonist who rides around on inline skates spraying over graffiti tags from rival gangs in a futuristic Tokyo. The game world feels foreign to the player, partly by the unfamiliarity of the musical artists and musical tracks. The soundtrack introduces artists that are either foreign, not found mainstream, or work under gaming licenses such as Hideki Naganuma, Guitar Vader, BS 2000, Scapegoat Wax, The Latch Brothers, Cibo Matto, and The Prunes. The game includes 31 tracks, including the credits medley. Each level has a playlist of songs. The music plays like a radio in the background; the player's actions seldom change the music. There is an exclusive song within the game's jukebox. The song "Like It Like This Like That" uses a small instrumental sample from Nas's song "H to the Omo."

November 15, 2002—Xbox Network—Online Service for Microsoft Game Systems

Xbox Network began as a system-wide online service for the original Xbox, required for online features and gaming. Microsoft introduced Xbox Network as Xbox Live on November 15, 2002. Xbox Network supports a standard protocol for voice chat across all games on Xbox Network with a headset, significantly streamlining the programming for game developers. There were no other voice systems for online play for home consoles at the time. The voice chat in Xbox Network began as a way for people to communicate during a game and evolved to meet the strategic needs of serious gamers. Another great feature of Xbox Network is its system of downloading content. Internet-ready game systems received audio enhancements through downloadable system and game updates. Before online services, a game developer released an updated version of a game with improvements on physical media. The implementation of voice chat and the Xbox Network online service brought the features of computer gaming to home console gaming. Xbox Network is the oldest online service for home consoles that is still active, used in the Windows OS since Vista on May 29, 2007,

with *Shadowrun* (as "Games for Windows Live") and in all of Microsoft's Xbox home consoles.

December 13, 2002—*The Legend of Zelda: The Wind Waker*—GameCube

PUBLISHER: Nintendo. RELEASE DATE: December 13, 2002 (JP), March 24, 2003 (NA), May 2, 2003 (EU). COMPOSERS: Kenta Nagata, Hajime Wakai, Toru Minegishi, Koji Kondo. SERIES: *The Legend of Zelda*. GENRE: Action-adventure. NOTABLE MUSICAL TRACK: "The Great Sea (Ocean Theme)."

The Legend of Zelda: The Wind Waker is the first entry in the series with live orchestral tracks, with a unique representation of musical conducting to summon powers via the left and right thumbsticks. The Wind Waker, referred to in the game's title, is a magical conductor's baton that can change the direction of the wind and manipulate the world around him. This shift in instrumentation elevated the epic tone of the game, despite a 3D art style that resembles cel shading and cartoons. Link summons each power, conducting with the Wind Waker to one of six songs discovered throughout the game.

The six songs are divided into three groups of two in 3/4, 4/4, and 6/4 meters. The player activates each spell by moving the left thumb Control Stick in one direction while moving the right thumb C-Stick in a 3, 4, or 6-move pattern. Each song has a distinct timbre and tempo. For example, "Wind's Requiem" is learned at the Wind Shrine on Dragon Roost Island. Performing the song allows Link to change the direction of the wind, which enables him to navigate the Great Sea much more quickly. The notable musical track, "The Great Sea," plays whenever Link sails the ocean. The music is lighthearted, much like the game. The song reflects adventure by its swelling orchestration and triumphant trumpet. The music makes what would otherwise be a mundane but necessary task a pleasant ocean voyage. Link's mastery of music through the Wind Waker fits the magical themes of the game.

SOURCES

Barry. "SEGA Retrospective: Jet Set Radio Future and The Latch Brothers." *Sega Bits*, 21 Apr. 2015, segabits.com/blog/2015/04/21/

sega-tunes-jet-set-radio-future-and-the-latch-brothers/.

"Wind Waker (Item)." *Zelda Wiki*, 9 Aug. 2017, zelda.gamepedia.com/Wind_Waker_(Item). Accessed 7 Aug. 2018.

2003 in Review

March 2003—G.A.N.G. Awards—Event

The G.A.N.G. Awards, named for the Game Audio Network Guild, are the only awards that exclusively acknowledge achievements in video game audio, voted on by members of G.A.N.G., people who work on or study video game audio. The Game Developers Conference hosted the 1st Annual G.A.N.G. Awards in San Jose, California, in March 2003. Some of the nominees from the first year were games released in 2002: *Hitman 2: Silent Assassin*, *Splinter Cell*, *Kingdom Hearts*, and *James Bond 007: Nightfire*. Some of the categories were "Best Use of Multi-Channel Surround in a Game" and "Best Interactive Score." The awards also acknowledge handheld games and educational games, including the audio of baby products (not video games) and interactive books. The awards were all-inclusive, acknowledging audio in games in a broader sense beyond video games. The G.A.N.G. Award recipients form a history of video game audio that reflects the views and opinions of those who worked in video game audio at the time as game audio specialists. The further exploration of video game audio builds upon the G.A.N.G. Awards' framework with additional perspective and significance from the years following each game's release. The G.A.N.G. Awards still take place annually.

October 7, 2003—Nokia N-Gage

MANUFACTURER: Nokia. RELEASE DATE: October 7, 2003 (NA, EU). PRODUCTION DATES: October 7, 2003–November 26, 2005. LAUNCH PRICE: $299.99. MODEL NUMBER: NEM-4. AUDIO: Mono.

The N-Gage was the first cell phone designed for handheld gaming. Released by Nokia, the N-Gage received ports of *Sonic the Hedgehog* and *Call of Duty*, with sound effects and music. The release of the N-Gage marked the start of the mobile gaming market. Commercially, the N-Gage could not compete with the Game Boy Advance. Nevertheless, the system received games from the *Sonic the Hedgehog* and *Call of Duty* series. Although the N-Gage was a hybrid cell phone and gaming system, it was still first and foremost a cell phone and PDA. The right-hand button layout on the original model N-Gage resembles the Mattel Intellivision with its phone number button layout. Unlike other cell phones at the time, the N-Gage contained a cartridge slot to read the games. However, to insert a game, the player must remove the phone's plastic cover and battery compartment to access the cartridge slot.

Regarding audio, the internal mono speaker and microphone are located on the side edge of the phone. The phone's form factor, described as a taco, is awkward, especially when listening to a game's audio with the speaker angled away from the screen. The N-Gage did not have dedicated sound hardware (no soundchips). Instead, the software handles the audio mixing of PCM samples. One of the N-Gage's PDA functions is as an audio recorder of FM radio. The Nokia Audio Manager is an application for the N-Gage and Windows OS to facilitate the transfer of MP3 and AAC audio files between the systems and extract audio tracks from CDs and create playlists in the M3U format. By 2003, cell phone technology had enough processing power for good stereo music and sound effects for video games.

The N-Gage QD, released in 2004,

Nokia N-Gage 2003. The audio output ports are 3.5mm. The internal speaker and internal microphone are located on the top edge of the device (Evan-Amos, "Nokia-NGage-LL").

improved the N-Gage with the placement of the cartridge slot to the bottom of the system, the internal speaker to the front of the system, and the separation of the OK button from the D-Pad. However, the N-Gage QD lost support for native MP3 playback, FM radio, and USB connectivity. There are two attachments: an MMC expander for the N-Gage QD to read two games at a time and a Snap-on Speaker for louder sound (although in mono instead of in stereo without the attachment). The N-Gage QD was sold as a bundle with a 128 MB MMC (MultiMediaCard) of the movie *Million Dollar Baby* or *Sky Captain and the World of Tomorrow* and the games *Pool Friction* and *N-Gage Freestyle*.

On November 26, 2005, the N-Gage

Nokia N-Gage QD 2004. The audio output ports are 3.5mm. The internal speaker and internal microphone are located on the upper-right corner of the device (Evan-Amos, "Nokia-NGage-QD").

ceased manufacturing. The N-Gage attempted innovation like the GBA and PSP, but the N-Gage did not find support from game developers nor consumers. The experiment in mobile gaming failed for the time being.

December 12, 2003—*Donkey Konga*—GameCube

PUBLISHER: Nintendo of America. RELEASE DATE: December 12, 2003 (JP), September 27, 2004 (NA), October 15, 2004 (EU). COMPOSER: Junko Ozawa. SERIES: *Donkey Konga*. NOTABLE MUSICAL TRACK: "Donkey Konga Theme." AWARDS: G.A.N.G. 2005 Most Innovative Use of Audio.

Donkey Konga is a music/rhythm game with an original bongos controller with an internal microphone. The game includes 29 musical tracks from rock, pop, children's songs, and Nintendo games. The game works with the DK Bongos, a unique controller designed as a pair of bongos. The player interacts with the game by hitting either the left drum, the right drum, both drums, or clapping. The DK Bongos has an internal microphone between the bongos, next to the Start/Pause button. The microphone only detects loud sounds in the game (not for speech recognition or voice chat).

Donkey Konga displays an icon system to designate which bongo to hit with the music. Musical notes are represented in each song by different colored barrels that roll across the screen. The player must hit the right note as the barrel reaches the target ring. The four types of notes are as follows: yellow for the left bongo, red for the right bongo, pink for both bongos, and white for a clap. Other games that use the DK Bongos are *Donkey Konga 2*, *Donkey Konga 3* (a Japan-exclusive), and *Donkey Konga: Jungle Beat* (a platformer game). The notable musical track, "Donkey Konga Theme," is the only one of the 29 selectable tracks original to the game. Some of the covers included

"We Will Rock You" popularized by Queen, "99 Red Balloons" popularized by Nena, "Oye Como Va" popularized by Santana, and "September" popularized by Earth, Wind & Fire.

SOURCES

Langshaw, Mark. "Feature: The History of Mobile Gaming." *Digital Spy*, 10 Apr. 2011, www.digitalspy.com/gaming/news/a313439/feature-the-history-of-mobile-gaming/.

Nokia. "Nokia N-Gage Extended User's Guide." *Archive.org*, 2003, ia800402.us.archive.org/20/items/nokia-n-gage/nokia-n-gage.pdf. Accessed 5 Apr. 2021.

Reed, Kristan. "E3 2003: Nokia N-Gage." *Eurogamer.net*, 14 May 2003, www.eurogamer.net/articles/news140503nokiae3. Accessed 17 Jan. 2021.

2004 in Review

May 2004—GBA Video Paks—GBA

GBA Video Paks are GBA cartridges containing television episodes and movies playable on a GBA. First released by Majesco, the GBA Video Paks converts the GBA into a mobile multimedia device. Some of the first 12 paks released in May 2004 were *Nicktoons Collection Vol. 1* and *Cartoon Network Collection Vol. 1*, both cartridges, including cartoon episodes from Nickelodeon and Cartoon Network. Majesco used a proprietary compression algorithm to play color video and audio on a GBA. With heavy video compression (the video resolution was usually 240 by 160, matching the dimensions of the GBA screen), a cartridge contains between 45 and 183 minutes of video and audio. The GBA Video Movie paks are stored on a 64 MB GBA cartridge, the largest size made for the GBA. A two-in-one Video Movie Pak released in 2005, *Shrek/Shark Tale*, has a runtime of 183 minutes. People bought the GBA video paks to take their favorite shows and movies on the go.

November 21, 2004—Nintendo DS

MANUFACTURER: Nintendo. PRODUCTION DATES: November 21, 2004 (NA), December 2, 2004 (JP), March 11, 2005 (EU). LAUNCH PRICE: $149.99. MODEL NUMBER: NTR-001. SOUNDCHIP: ARM7TDMI. AUDIO: Stereo (with virtual surround).

The Nintendo DS was the first handheld gaming system with internal stereo speakers and virtual surround sound. Released by Nintendo, the DS includes an internal microphone, used as an input button by blowing into it, for speech recognition or an audio chat with other DS players. The DS is backward-compatible with GBA games (the DSi and DSi XL models lack a GBA port). Unlike the Game Boy series of handheld gaming systems, the DS contains two screens. The bottom screen is a resistive touchscreen capable of touch recognition from either the DS's included stylus or human fingers. The DS's speakers are located on each side of the top screen. The DS also sends stereo audio through the 3.5mm audio-out port. The soundchip of the DS is the ARM7TDMI, capable of at most either 16 ADPCM or PCM sound channels or 8 PSG sound channels. Despite stereo audio output, the DS was the first handheld gaming system to support virtual surround sound. The DS encoded a 5.1 speaker setup within a stereo signal. This signal used varying sound pressures from both speakers to simulate the ear's ability to detect direction.

For the first time since the Famicom, Nintendo released a gaming system with a built-in microphone. Like the Famicom, some games on the DS require the player to blow or shout into the microphone (for example, blowing the microphone in *Mario & Luigi: Bowser's Inside Story* increases Giant Bowser's fire breath on the train battle). The DS microphone also supported speech recognition (for example, giving commands to the dogs in *Nintendogs*). Like the original Xbox, the DS microphone is used for chatting with other players between and during game sessions

Nintendo DS 2004. The audio output ports are 3.5mm. The internal speakers are located on the lower-left and lower-right of the device's top panel. The internal microphone is located on the lower-left corner of the lower panel. The volume slider modulates the internal speakers' volume (Evan-Amos, "Nintendo-DS-Fat-Blue").

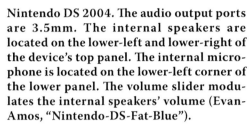

Nintendo DS Lite 2006. The audio output ports are 3.5mm. The internal speakers are located on the left and right of the device's top panel. The internal microphone is located in the middle of the hinge between the top and bottom panels. The volume slider modulates the internal speakers' volume (Evan-Amos, "Nintendo-DS-Lite-Black-Open").

(for example, players can talk with friends during local or online matches in *Metroid Prime Hunters* by holding the X button). The DS supported wireless LAN communication for local multiplayer against nearby DS players. Nintendo introduced the Nintendo Wi-Fi Connection, its free online service for multiplayer gaming, on the DS on November 24, 2005.

The DS Lite, released on June 11, 2006, was a thinner model with a brighter screen, larger stylus, and a rechargeable battery with longer life. The DSi, released on April 5, 2009, added a front and back-facing camera, SD card slot (supporting up to 2GB of external storage), and the Nintendo DSi Shop, an online marketplace to buy and download games and other content from Nintendo. The DSi contains an improved microchip that amplified audio and converted it from digital to analog. The DSi also includes the Nintendo DSi Sound app, allowing users to listen to music files stored on the SD card and record and edit up to eighteen 10-second voice clips using the DSi's microphone (stored on internal memory). The DSi XL, released on March 28, 2010, was a larger DSi with an expanded viewing

angle of the screens and larger internal speakers, diminishing audio distortion at high volumes. On September 30, 2014, the DS ceased manufacturing. The DS was the first handheld gaming system with dual screens and the first with a touchscreen. It brought back the internal microphone of the Famicom and introduced virtual surround audio within a stereo signal (prepared in real-time in hardware).

With the Nintendo DSi Sound app, installed on all DSi models, users can record and save up to 18 10-second clips using the DSi's microphone. Each voice clip is stored within a speech bubble icon filled with different-colored liquid. The player can adjust the playback speed and pitch of each voice clip and apply goofy effects. The player can set voice clips to repeat or play randomly. Unfortunately, these voice clips cannot be exported to the SD card or shared beyond the app. In a first for a Nintendo handheld gaming system, the DSi can play audio files stored on the SD card. The audio files must be AAC audio in the MP4, M4A, or 3GP formats with a bitrate between 16 and 320 bits per second and a sample rate of between 32 and 48 kHz (these ranges are more than sufficient for simple listening). The app includes a visualizer. Using audio filters, the user can transform the song into a chiptune version reminiscent of the NES. The recorded voice clips can play over the music.

Nintendo DSi 2009. The audio output ports are 3.5mm. The internal speakers are located on the lower-left and lower-right of the device's top panel. The internal microphone is located in the middle of the hinge between the top and bottom panels. The volume slider modulates the internal speakers' volume (Evan-Amos, "Nintendo-DSi-Bl-Open," CC-BY-SA 3.0).

Nintendo DSi XL 2010. The audio output ports are 3.5mm. The internal speakers are located on the left and right of the device's top panel. The internal microphone is located in the middle of the hinge between the top and bottom panels. The volume slider modulates the internal speakers' volume (Evan-Amos, "Nintendo-DSi-XL-Burg," CC-BY-SA 3.0).

November 24, 2004—*Pathway to Glory*—N-Gage

PUBLISHER: Nokia. RELEASE DATE: November 24, 2004 (NA), November 26, 2004 (EU). COMPOSER: Jarno Sarkula. SERIES: *Pathway to Glory*. GENRE: Turn-based tactical. NOTABLE MUSICAL TRACK: "Soldiers of the Mission (Mission End)."

Pathway to Glory was the first mobile game with voice acting and voice communication between players. The musical tracks are prominent during the mission briefing and mission award screens. *Pathway to Glory* was the first published game by Nokia. The game is a turn-based strategy game based on World War II from the summer of 1943 to the winter of 1944. The game's soundtrack was well-received at the time. There are short musical moments during the enemy's turn. During the player's turn, the player hears only the sounds of gunfire and verbal acknowledgments of the player's troops. The soundtrack uses instrument sounds reminiscent of a war movie, emphasizing percussion and brass instruments (instruments used on the battlefield). The notable musical track, "Soldiers of the Mission (Mission End)," plays after completing each mission, when the soldiers are either promoted or awarded the purple heart (died in battle).

A positive feature of the game was the Field Radio feature. When two to six players play with each other in local multiplayer mode via Bluetooth, the players can record and send voice messages to each other. Furthermore, within the game's world, the voice messages are played back on the N-Gage like a field radio on the battleground, adding diegetic meaning to mobile voice communication and effectively leveraging the quality of the N-Gage's internal speaker. As an impressive game for the N-Gage, *Pathway to Glory* is an example of how good audio design and music worked around the strengths and weaknesses of a mobile gaming device.

December 12, 2004—Sony PSP

MANUFACTURER: Sony. RELEASE DATE: December 12, 2004 (JP), March 24, 2005

Sony PSP-1000 2004. The audio output ports are 3.5mm. The internal speakers are located on the lower-left and lower-right corners of the device. The volume up and down buttons modulate the internal speakers' volume (Evan-Amos, "Sony-PSP-1000-Body").

(NA), September 1, 2005 (EU). PRODUCTION DATES: December 12, 2004–January 2014. LAUNCH PRICE: $249.99. MODEL NUMBER: PSP-1000. AUDIO: Stereo (with virtual surround).

The PSP (PlayStation Portable), Sony's first handheld gaming system, plays games and full-length movies on UMD media. Released by Sony, Sony designed the PSP as a multimedia device and a handheld gaming system. The PSP was Sony's attempt to break into another gaming market. The PSP was pre-installed with software to play audio and video files stored on Sony's proprietary Memory Stick Pro and Pro Duo. The maximum memory size of a Memory Stick Pro was 128 MB, and the Memory Stick Pro Duo was 32 GB. The PSP reads audio files as ATRAC3plus, AAC, WMA, and MP3 and video files as MP4 and AVI. The PSP contains two internal speakers for stereo audio and a 3.5mm audio-out port for stereo audio. The PSP supports virtual surround in real-time to the stereo audio output sources.

An innovative feature of the PSP was the Remote Play feature. When Sony released the PS3 in 2006, the PSP could connect wirelessly to the PS3 via WLAN or internet hotspot. Using Remote Play, the PSP could stream media files stored on the PS3, like audio and video files. After firmware update 2.10 and 3.80 for the PS3 and PSP, respectively, in December of 2007, the PSP could also play PS1 games stored on the PS3 and a few PlayStation Network games and PS3 games stored on Blu-ray disc (*Lair, Rayman Legends*). When the player enables Remote Play, the PSP displays the system screen of the PS3 and grants access to its installed software. However, Remote Play did not support Blu-ray discs, DVDs, and video files with copyright protection from the PS3. The PSP lacked buttons for Remote Play of PS2 games. Remote Play wasn't possible for many PS3 games that did not target the hardware specs of the PSP, including its CPU, controller configuration, and wireless connection speed. Unique to the PSP, it connected wirelessly to both the PS3 and PS4. Through Remote Play, a handheld

Sony PSP-2000 2007. The audio output ports are 3.5mm. The internal speakers are located on the upper-left and upper-right corners of the device. The volume up and down buttons modulate the internal speakers' volume (Evan-Amos, "PSP-2000-trans").

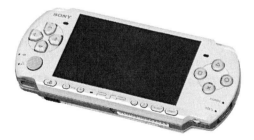

Sony PSP-3000 2008. The audio output ports are 3.5mm. The internal speakers are located on the upper-left and upper-right corners of the device. The volume up and down buttons modulate the internal speakers' volume. The internal microphone is located on the bottom of the device (Evan-Amos, "PSP-3000-Silver," CC-BY-SA 3.0).

gaming system could recreate the home console experience for the first time.

The PSP-2000, released in North America on September 6, 2007, for $200, was the first handheld gaming system since the Sega Nomad to have a video-out port to play games on a television screen. The system included *Daxter* (2006) for PSP, *Family Guy: The Freakin' Sheet Collection* UMD video, and a 1GB Memory Stick Duo. The video output resolution of the PSP-2000 was 480 by 272 pixels, the exact resolution as the system's screen.

The PSP-3000, released in North America on October 14, 2008, added an internal microphone, used for phone calls with the pre-installed Skype over the internet and audio communication in online games. Some of the games and applications that use the PSP's microphone are as follows: *Skype, Beaterator, Resistance: Retribution, Talkman Travel,* and *Syphon Filter: Logan's Shadow.* Additional improvements are in the screen, colors, and video-out options.

The PSP Go, released in North America and Europe on October 1, 2009, for $249.99, was the first handheld gaming system with support for Bluetooth wireless audio and controllers. The PSP Go contains a Bluetooth chip (supporting the Bluetooth 2.0 and EDR [Enhanced Data Rate] protocol), used for Bluetooth headphones and headsets (microphone input and stereo output), for internet access through cell phone tethering, and for connecting Sixaxis and Dualshock 3 controllers. The PSP Go was one of the first gaming systems to only play downloaded digital games, with 16GB of internal storage and without a UMD drive to play PSP UMD games. The PSP Go included *Patapon 2* as a pre-installed demo game (a music game). The PlayStation Store is the only way to purchase and download games. With the Cradle for PSP Go (PSP-N340) and video-out cables, the PSP Go was the first handheld gaming system to function as a home console in a dock. UMD media faded out when PSP models could no longer read UMDs.

The PSP Street, released in Europe on October 26, 2011, stripped Wi-Fi, the internal microphone, and the video-out port. It swapped the internal stereo speakers for a monaural speaker (the headphone port still supported stereophonic sound) and the Memory Stick Micro port for the Memory Stock PRO port. The PSP Street was the last Sony device to read UMDs.

The PSP ceased manufacturing in January 2014. Without the PSP, there are no other means to play the content from the UMD. Sony addressed this with the PS Vita by offering PSP UMD games as digital downloads on the PlayStation Store (with additional purchase). Sony did very

Sony PSP Go 2009. The audio output ports are 3.5mm. The internal speakers are located on the upper-left and upper-right corners of the front panel. The volume up and down buttons modulate the internal speakers' volume. The internal microphone is located on the bottom of the lower panel (Evan-Amos, "PSP-Go-FL-Open").

PSP A/V component cable 2004. It connects to the PSP's A/V port and outputs audio in analog stereo (Evan-Amos, "PSP-Component-Cables").

well to sell around 80 million units, considering that Nintendo had decades of experience designing and marketing handheld gaming systems (154 million units of the Nintendo DS). The PSP still has functionality as a multimedia player and still plays multiplayer games via ad-hoc connections with other PSP units. The PSP was the first device to support Remote Play with the PS3 before the Wii U offered Off-TV Play. Movie distributors supported movies on UMD (today, there are very few legal methods to watch movies and TV shows on a handheld device without an internet connection).

Sources

Gantayat, Anoop. "PSP-2000 Tops 100,000 in Japan." *IGN*, 22 Sept. 2007, www.ign.com/articles/2007/09/22/psp-2000-tops-100000-in-japan. Accessed 19 Jan. 2021.

IGN. "PSP Specs revealed." 29 July 2003, www.ign.com/articles/2003/07/29/psp-specs-revealed.

Nintendo. "Majesco Ships first 'Game Boy Advance Video' Titles." *Game Boy Advance Video*, 5 May 2004, web.archive.org/web/20040623124828/www.gba-video.com/pressrelease2.html. Accessed 31 Mar. 2020.

"Nintendo DS NTR-001." *TechInsights*, www.techinsights.com/DeviceProfileSF_AustinParts.aspx?TeardownId=222. Accessed 3 Aug. 2018.

"Nintendo DSi Sound." *Nintendo Fandom*, 29 Apr. 2020, nintendo.fandom.com/wiki/Nintendo_DSi_Sound. Accessed 23 Sept. 2020.

North, Dale. "Play Your PS1 Discs on Your PSP Via PS3's Remote Play." *Destructoid*, 18 Dec. 2007, www.destructoid.com/stories/play-your-ps1-discs-on-your-psp-via-ps3-s-remote-play-60261.phtml. Accessed 22 Sept. 2020.

"Pathway to Glory—NG—Review." *GameZone*, 4 May 2012, www.gamezone.com/reviews/pathway_to_glory_ng_review/.

"PSP Specs Revealed." *IGN*, 29 July 2003, www.ign.com/articles/2003/07/29/psp-specs-revealed.

Rick. "Nintendo DS Specs." *GameCubicle.com*, Aug. 2004, www.gamecubicle.com/hardware-nintendo_ds_spec_sheet.htm.

Score, Avery. "Pathway to Glory Review." *GameSpot*, 8 Dec. 2004, www.gamespot.com/reviews/pathway-to-glory-review/1900-6114566/.

2005 in Review

March 24, 2005—*Spider-Man 2* Movie on UMD

Spider-Man 2 was the first movie released on UMD (Universal Media Disc), playable on the early PSP models. Released for the PSP in North America, Sony initially sold the PSP as a bundle with the *Spider-Man 2* movie UMD (not in the Japanese release). The UMD is the storage media for the early PSP models, embraced by game publishers and film studios. It is an exclusive optical disc format for the PSP with the shape of a minidisc. PSP games and movies were sold as UMDs for playback on the PSP. As a multimedia device, the PSP can watch movies from all of the major movie studios, especially Sony Pictures. A UMD holds 900 MB for a single-layer disc or 1.8 GB for a dual-layer disc. Movies on UMD are encoded as H.264 MP4 video with ATRAC3plus audio. UMDs contain enough memory for full-length films.

In a rare instance, one UMD combines both the movie *Stealth* (which did poorly in theaters) and *Wipeout Pure: Stealth Edition*, an exclusive demo version of *Wipeout Pure* not playable anywhere else. The UMD format lost support beginning with the PSP Go in 2009, a redesigned model of the PSP without a UMD drive, and the PS Vita, the 2012 successor to the PSP, also lacking an optical drive. Sony then shifted from disc-based media for handheld gaming systems to digital downloads. The last UMD released was *Harry Potter and the Deathly Hallows—Part 2*, released on December 16, 2011.

April 7, 2005—*Electroplankton*—DS

Publisher: Nintendo of America. Release Date: April 7, 2005 (JP), January 9, 2006 (NA), July 7, 2006 (EU). Developer: Toshio Iwai. Composers: Koichi Kyuma and Yuichi Ozaki. Genre: Music.

Electroplankton is a music game in which the player creates music by interacting with animated plankton in 10 different interfaces. The player interacts with the plankton, moving objects through the DS's buttons and touchscreen and affecting the resulting sounds. *Electroplankton* doesn't have a goal or a way to complete the game. The game's designer by Toshio Iwai, who also developed *Otocky* and *SimTunes*. The game's two modes are Performance and Audience. In Performance mode, the user creates music by interacting with plankton using the DS stylus, touchscreen, and microphone (buttons not necessary). In Audience mode, the plankton moves about on their own, creating a musical demo that the user can watch and listen to (although the user can interact at any time). Two of the 10 interfaces are Hanenbow and Nanocorp. In Hanenbow, the user maneuvers plant leaves to bounce leaping tadpoles around. In Nanocorp, the user moves musical sprites into new formations by clapping or whistling.

October 18, 2005—*Shadow of the Colossus*—PS2

PUBLISHER: Sony. RELEASE DATE: October 18, 2005 (NA), October 27, 2005 (JP), February 17, 2006 (EU). COMPOSER: Kow Otani. GENRE: Action-adventure. NOTABLE MUSICAL TRACK: "The End of the Battle."

The soundtrack of *Shadow of the Colossus* is rich in emotion, reflecting the heavy burden of responsibility. The game's soundtrack conveys the emotional weight of each victory of the colossus. The game has a beautiful soundtrack rich in emotion, achieved with orchestral scoring that emphasizes vocal chant and classical strings, which are very expressive, encompassing a range of intensities. Some of the darker emotions include moodiness and fierceness. *Shadow of the Colossus* lingers in the moment of victory, reflecting on the gravitas and aftermath of the triumph of the colossus. Each colossus is massive in size compared to the protagonist. When the player expects a heroic brass fanfare after a long-fought battle, the expected musical catharsis is instead somber and elongated. The notable musical track, "The

End of the Battle," exemplifies the balance of emotions, even in victory. After Wander defeats each colossus, the resulting musical passage expresses sadness in the haunting strings. Even when expecting a more heroic brass fanfare, the severity of the tasks weighs on the player. The music reminds the player of the emotional toll of battle, emotions that the player must not ignore in the game.

October 25, 2005—*Sid Meier's Civilization IV*—PC

PUBLISHER: 2K Games. RELEASE DATE: October 25, 2005 (NA), November 4, 2005 (EU). COMPOSER: Jeffrey L. Briggs, Mark Cromer, Michael Curran, and Christopher Tin. SERIES: *Sid Meier's Civilization*. GENRE: Turn-based strategy. NOTABLE MUSICAL TRACK: "Baba Yetu (Main Menu)." AWARDS: G.A.N.G. 2007 Best Original Vocal Song—Choral.

The soundtrack of *Sid Meier's Civilization IV* reflects international styles and many historical periods, with Grammy award-winning song. Released for Windows 2000 and XP, the game's soundtrack uses established pieces from each musical period, adding authenticity to the game. Each period in the game has a unique musical track that reflects the culture. The soundtrack consists of music from over 30 composers, including Mozart, Brahms, and John Adams. *Civilization IV* was the first game to have a song win a Grammy award.

The notable musical track, "Baba Yetu," heard on the main menu, won the Grammy for "Best Instrumental Arrangement Accompanying Vocalist(s)" at the 53rd Annual Grammy Awards on February 13, 2011. The song was eligible for the Grammy not because of its video game origins but because of its inclusion on composer Christopher Tin's 2009 classical crossover album *Calling All Dawns*. The song lyrics are the Lord's Prayer in Swahili. The musical track uses African rhythms and instruments, similar in sound and style to the Disney movie *The Lion King*. Tin, previously an intern for *The Lion King* score composer Hans Zimmer, helped create the main menu song with Talisman, an a cappella group from Stanford University. A Grammy Award for a video game song demonstrated the equal merit of musical tracks written for video games with those composed for music albums.

November 8, 2005—*Guitar Hero*— PS2

PUBLISHER: Red Octane. RELEASE DATE: November 8, 2005 (NA), April 7, 2006 (EU). DEVELOPER: Harmonix. SERIES: *Guitar Hero*. GENRE: Music/Rhythm. NOTABLE MUSICAL TRACK: "Cowboys from Hell." AWARDS: G.A.N.G. 2006 Best Use of Licensed Music, Most Innovative Use of Audio.

Guitar Hero popularized plastic music controllers in the music genre, spawning a craze of music and rhythm games. The game earned the D.I.C.E. Award for Best Soundtrack (Collection of Songs). Harmonix, the game's developer, was and is recognized for its music games. It previously worked on *Frequency* and *Amplitude* and, later in the timeline, will also work on *Dance Central* and *Fantasia: Music Evolved*. Harmonix is the most recognized developer for music games. The growth of Harmonix was remarkable, considering how far it had come since its first game, *Frequency*, in 2001. RedOctane, the publisher of *Guitar Hero*, was already familiar with unique controllers for games. Before *Guitar Hero*, RedOctane manufactured its dance pads for *Dance Dance Revolution* games for PlayStation and PS2 consoles.

Guitar Hero was the first game in the *Guitar Hero* series. This series of games are known for their plastic instrument-shaped controllers. The controller included with the game was a 3/4-scale reproduction of a Gibson SG guitar. Unlike a real guitar, five brightly colored buttons replace the top five frets closest to the nut of the plastic guitar. These are the buttons to be pressed during gameplay to mimic the changing of notes in the music. A strum bar replaces the soundhole. For each note in a song, the player needs to press the correct fret button and flick the strum bar. Lower on the guitar's body is a whammy bar, a bar

sticking off the front of the guitar used to bend the pitch or boost Star Power. Lastly, the controller includes buttons for Start, Select, and Back so the player could navigate the game's menus. Although a player can play *Guitar Hero* with a standard controller, the game's popularity was partly due to its integration of the guitar controller. Visually, the game shows a fretboard on the screen with colored boxes that represent the colored buttons on the guitar controller's fret moving toward the player. The player presses the fret button and toggles the strum bar when the corresponding color reaches the front area of the visual fretboard. The game's soundtrack includes 47 songs, 30 being covers of popular songs and 17 being master recordings from indie musical groups. The notable musical track "Cowboys from Hell" by Pantera is the second to last song in career mode and is part of the sixth tier. The song is challenging to get more than three stars on.

The video game industry still feels the impact of *Guitar Hero* today. *Guitar Hero* was the game that became an international success and attracted the most players to music games. Also, thanks to *Guitar Hero*, music games included alternative ways to interact with the game, whether through controllers shaped as drums, a microphone, and a D.J. turntable or through total body movement.

November 22, 2005—Microsoft Xbox 360

MANUFACTURER: Microsoft. RELEASE DATE: November 22, 2005 (NA), December 2, 2005 (EU), December 10, 2005 (JP). PRODUCTION DATES: November 22, 2005–April 20, 2016. LAUNCH PRICE: $299.99 (Core), $399.99. AUDIO: Dolby Digital 5.1.

The Xbox 360 was the first home console with system-wide Dolby Digital 5.1 surround sound and cross-game audio communication between remote consoles. Released by Microsoft, the Xbox 360 was the first home console to approach backward compatibility through emulation instead of hardware. The Xbox 360 contained a 4 GB internal hard drive and a

Microsoft Xbox 360 back 2005. The audio output ports are A/V (VGA with stereo audio RCA adapter, composite video and stereo audio RCA adapter, and component video and stereo audio RCA adapter) (Evan-Amos, "Microsoft-Xbox-360-Pro-Console-BR").

20 GB detachable hard drive (the original model Xbox 360 had a maximum hard drive size of 320 GB). The total memory of updates for a game with online capabilities could be larger in memory than the game itself. The Xbox 360 used Xbox Live as its online service.

The Xbox 360 was the first home console to support backward compatibility through downloadable emulation software. The Xbox 360 was unable to read the original Xbox discs. The Xbox 360 supports about 460 original Xbox games through download. However, players didn't need to repurchase the game on Xbox Live. When the Xbox 360 detected an original Xbox disc in its disc tray, it prompted the user to download the emulated version for free. Microsoft added support for more original Xbox games through system updates (Microsoft supported each game on a case-by-case basis).

The console supports over 256 sound channels and 320 independent decompression channels with 32-bit processing. The channels support 16-bit, 48 kHz audio. The sound files of games use the XMA (Xbox Media Audio) encoding format by Microsoft, an extension of WMA (Windows Media Audio). The Xbox 360 console provides voice communication protocols for all games. Since voice communication was not handled individually by each game developer, voice communication could

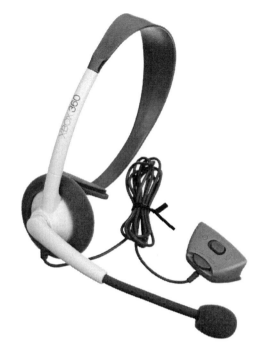

Microsoft Xbox 360 headset 2005. The headset communicates with the Xbox 360 through the controller's 2.5mm port (Evan-Amos, "Xbox-360-Headset-White").

Microsoft Xbox 360 S headset 2010. The headset communicates with the Xbox 360 S through the controller's 2.5mm port (Evan-Amos, "Microsoft-Xbox-360-S-Headset").

Microsoft Kinect for Xbox 360 2010. The Kinect communicates with the Xbox 360 through the USB port. The internal microphone is located between the front-facing cameras (Evan-Amos, "Xbox-360-Kinect-Standalone").

continue outside of the game environment and even between two different games. Using Xbox Live's online services, friends could talk with each other.

All games developed for the Xbox 360 were required to support at least Dolby Digital 5.1 surround sound. At the system's launch, the Xbox 360 Pro included a Component HD A/V cable with a S/PDIF port to connect to an audio decoder for optical audio (unlike the PS2, the Xbox 360 did not have a separate port for optical audio). In 2007, a redesigned model of the Xbox 360 would be the first home console to support digital audio via HDMI. And in 2010, another redesigned model of the Xbox 360 would include an optical audio port on the console.

The Xbox 360 was the first home console to have at least four models with minor adjustments to the hardware. The Xbox 360 Elite, released on April 29, 2007, was the first home console with an HDMI port. HDMI 1.2a supports uncompressed stereo audio, Dolby Digital 5.1, DTS 5.1 at 1.5 Mbps, and WMA-Pro 5.1 (the system can decode the surround sound encoded formats to uncompressed stereo). The Xbox 360 S, released on June 19, 2010, had a smaller form factor than the earlier models and an exclusive port for the Kinect sensor. The Xbox 360 E, released on June 10, 2013, had a smaller form factor than the

Xbox 360 S, an HDMI port, a new 3.5mm port for composite video and stereo audio, but removed the S/PDIF port, one USB port, and the A/V connector.

The Microsoft Kinect (1414), released in North America on November 4, 2010, for $149.99, was a peripheral with camera sensors and microphones that was used by Microsoft systems as an alternative user input device through natural body gestures and voice commands. Released for the Xbox 360 in North America on November 4, 2010, the Kinect was successfully used in great effect for dance games and squad-based games. The Kinect was also released in Europe on November 10, 2010, and in Japan on November 20, 2010. The Kinect looks like a computer webcam. The sensors within the Kinect track the physical movements of one to four players. The players control the Xbox and its games

Xbox 360 S back 2010. The audio output ports are A/V, S/PDIF, HDMI, and USB (Evan-Amos, "Xbox-360-S-Console-Back").

Xbox 360 E back 2013. The audio output ports are 3.5mm (with composite video and stereo audio RCA adapter or component video and stereo audio RCA adapter) and HDMI (Evan-Amos, "Xbox-360-E-Inputs-&-Outputs").

using full-body motion without a controller in their hands. Relating to audio, the Kinect contains four internal microphones, so users can navigate menu screens and interact with Kinect-based games with verbal commands. The Kinect would later gain compatibility for PCs running Windows and the Xbox One.

The most common use of the Kinect's four microphones was for voice commands. Some games for the Xbox 360 that use the Kinect microphones within gameplay are *Kinectimals*, *Kinect Sports: Season Two*

Xbox 360 A/V composite cable 2005. It connects to the Xbox 360's A/V port and outputs audio in analog stereo (Evan-Amos, "Microsoft-Xbox-360-AV-Cables-Composite").

(similar in gameplay to *Wii Sports Resort*), *Binary Domain*, *Kinect Star Wars*, *Kinect Party*, *Tom Clancy's Splinter Cell: Blacklist*, and *Plants vs. Zombies: Garden Warfare*. In *Tom Clancy's EndWar* and *Mass Effect 3*, voice commands are used to select from a dialogue tree of possible responses to in-game situations. Each game includes programming that accesses the Kinect's speech recognition functions for a limited number of words and phrases. Unlike the microphone peripherals for the N64 and Dreamcast, the Kinect worked across all Xbox 360, Windows, and Xbox One games. When the Xbox 360 E was released on June 20, 2013, the Kinect was no longer required nor universally supported on the Xbox systems.

On April 20, 2016, the Xbox 360 ceased manufacturing. The Xbox 360's manufacturing run overlapped the run of the Xbox One by two and a half years. The Xbox 360 was the best-selling gaming system from a North American company. Microsoft's Xbox Live online service was a boom for online multiplayer games on the Xbox 360. The Xbox 360 was the first gaming system to support full-body movement controls with the Microsoft Kinect. Unlike later gaming systems, the Xbox 360 still reads games via disc without downloading large portions of the disc data to the internal hard drive. Microsoft ended support

Xbox 360 A/V component cable 2005. It connects to the Xbox 360's A/V port and outputs audio in analog stereo (Evan-Amos, "Microsoft-Xbox-360-AV-Cables-Component").

Xbox 360 audio adapter 2013. It connects to the Xbox 360 E's A/V port and outputs audio in analog stereo. It provides analog audio with HD video via the Xbox 360 E's HDMI port (Evan-Amos, "Xbox-360-Audio-Adapter").

for the Kinect for the Xbox 360, Windows, and Xbox One on October 25, 2017. Voice systems like Alexa by Amazon or Bixby by Samsung are evolutions of the voice recognition technology of the Kinect.

SOURCES

"Electroplankton." *IGN*, 10 Jan. 2006, www.ign.com/articles/2006/01/11/electroplankton.

"Electroplankton—Press Kit." *IGDB.com*, www.igdb.com/games/electroplankton/presskit. Accessed 20 Aug. 2018.

Gardner, Matt. "The End of the Battle (Shadow of the Colossus) Review." *GameTripper*, 5 Feb. 2018, www.gametripper.co.uk/games/music/shadow-of-the-colossus-end-battle/.

Harris, C. "Electroplankton." 10 Jan. 2006, www.ign.com/articles/2006/01/11/electroplankton.

Microsoft. "Connect and Configure Digital Audio on Xbox 360." *Xbox Support*, support.xbox.com/en-US/xbox-360/console/configure-audio-settings. Accessed 3 Aug. 2018.

Microsoft. "Video and Audio Playback on Xbox 360 FAQ." *Xbox Support*, support.xbox.com/en-US/xbox-360/console/audio-video-playback-faq. Accessed 3 Aug. 2018.

Morton, Philip. "Xbox 360 Tech Specs." *Thunderbolt*, 20 Apr. 2005, www.thunderboltgames.com/feature/xbox-360-tech-specs.

Plunkett, Luke. "So THAT'S What They're Saying in Civ IV's Intro." *Kotaku*, 19 Aug. 2014, kotaku.com/so-thats-what-theyre-saying-in-civ-ivs-intro-1624242582.

"Soundtrack (Civ4)." *Civilization Wiki*, 17 Mar. 2018, civilization.wikia.com/wiki/Soundtrack_(Civ4). Accessed 16 Aug. 2018.

2006 in Review

June 23, 2006—*LocoRoco*—PSP

PUBLISHER: Sony Computer Entertainment America. RELEASE DATE: June 23, 2006 (EU), July 13, 2006 (JP), September 5, 2006 (NA). COMPOSERS: Nobuyuki Shimizu and Kemmei Adachi. SERIES: *LocoRoco*. GENRE: Puzzle/Platformer. NOTABLE MUSICAL TRACK: "LocoRoco No Uta (Main Theme)." AWARDS: D.I.C.E. 2007 Original Music Composition.

LocoRoco features a whimsical soundtrack that changes in instrumentation based on the number of characters moving on-screen. The game's song lyrics use a fictional LocoRoco language. The game's tone is lighthearted, supplemented with children's voices and singing in solo or group arrangements. Each LocoRoco character, a gel-like blob with a face, has a unique voice. The fluid mechanics of the LocoRoco affects the number of voices in the audio mix. The LocoRoco merge to become a soloist or split apart to become a choir. The player interacts with the LocoRoco by rotating the game world clockwise or counterclockwise. By doing so, the LocoRoco reacts to the physics of momentum and gravity. The game's soundtrack includes vocals in the fictional LocoRoco language. The game's designer, Tsutomu Kouno, requesting live sounds over electronic, combined Japanese sounds from katakana so that the made-up language was somewhat familiar to Japanese gamers. The melodies are jolly and straightforward, reflective of the energetic and child-like LocoRocos. The notable musical track, "LocoRoco No Uta (Main Theme)," resembles a children's song through the solo child's voice and children's choir. The instrumentation includes a solo trumpet, flute, clarinet, tuba, and snare drum. The instruments perform independent parts, much like a New Orleans jazz band. The lyrics, despite familiar sounds, lack meaning. The interplay between the solo voice and choir reflects the interplay of the LocoRoco.

July 27, 2006—*Soundvoyager*—GBA

PUBLISHER: Nintendo. RELEASE DATE: July 27, 2006 (JP). SOUND DESIGNERS: Hirotoh Morikawa, Shinichiro Hirata, Kazuomi Suzuki, Hiromichi Fujiwara. SERIES: *bit Generations*. GENRE: Audio game.

Soundvoyager is a collection of minigames that involve careful listening, one designed for stereo audio through the GBA's headphone port. Released exclusively in Japan, it is one of the only games in which stereophonic audio is the primary gameplay element. In the main minigame,

"Sound Catcher," dots of light representing instrument sounds descend from the top of the GBA's screen. Each dot has an associated panning value between the left and right audio channels. The objective is to use the left and right buttons on the GBA to align the falling dots so that each dot's sound pans to the center of the audio mix. To achieve this, the player shifts the viewport left or right, shifting the panning of each dot on-screen. When the player catches a falling sound, the music integrates the sound. When more than one dot fall, the player must also listen for which sound is approaching the player first based on volume. As the minigame progresses, the dots are invisible, forcing the player to rely solely on hearing to catch the falling sounds. There is also a remix stage for Sound Catcher that creates an endless stage of all individual sounds from all of the game's stages. Of all of the games on the timeline, this is the only game that requires stereo audio to win.

There are other modes in *Soundvoyager* that aren't reliant on stereo audio. In Sound Drive, the player avoids crashing into other cars based on the sound of the car engines and horn honking. In Sound Chase, the player must dodge cars to catch a runaway sound. In Sound Cock, the player catches roosters by listening to their clucking to pinpoint their position. All of the minigames require critical listening to succeed.

August 3, 2006—*Rhythm Tengoku*—GBA

PUBLISHER: Nintendo. RELEASE DATE: August 3, 2006 (JP). COMPOSERS: Tsunki and Masami Yone. SERIES: *Rhythm Heaven*. GENRE: Rhythm.

Rhythm Tengoku was the first handheld game to allow the player to record a track and combine it with another. Released exclusively in Japan, the player can create, save, and playback original drum tracks to the game's music. *Rhythm Tengoku* was the last commercial game sold for the GBA. In the game's studio mode, the player can either listen to the unlocked songs or play the drums along with these songs. The

game allowed players to play the drums using the GBA buttons and then save the recording for future listening. Each button on the GBA corresponds to one of the parts of the drum kit. Some of the different drum kits to choose from are ordinary, techno, and sound effect. After creating a drum track alongside the selected song, the player can save the recording to the song list.

November 11, 2006—Sony PlayStation 3

MANUFACTURER: Sony. RELEASE DATE: November 11, 2006 (JP), November 17, 2006 (NA), March 23, 2007 (EU). MANUFACTURING DATES: November 11, 2006–October 2016. LAUNCH PRICE: $499.99 (20GB), $599.99 (60GB). MODEL NUMBER: CECHA01. AUDIO: LPCM 7.1.

The PlayStation 3 brought many innovations in audio, including a native HDMI-out port, support for LPCM 5.1 and 7.1, support for Super Audio CD format, and including a Blu-ray disc drive. Released by Sony, the PS3 supports the most analog and digital audio options of any home console. The inclusion of an HDMI-out port allows the PS3 to transmit lossless digital audio without the need for an audio decoder box (necessary for encoded surround sound formats like Dolby Digital and DTS). The PS3 also supports Dolby Digital 5.1 and DTS 5.1 via the optical audio port and analog stereo via the AV Multi Out port. The PS3 was the first home console to support Blu-ray discs for movies and games.

In the same way that the PS2 helped DVD sales, the PS3 helped Blu-ray disc sales (Sony created the Blu-ray standard). Sony first released movies on Blu-ray discs on Tuesday, June 20, 2006, months before the release of the PS3. The PS3 contains disc lasers for CD and DVD support as well. For perspective, a CD holds 700 MB, a GD-ROM (Dreamcast) holds 1.2 GB, a GameCube disc holds 1.5 GB, a single-layer DVD holds 4.7 GB, a double-layer DVD holds 8.5 GB, and a Blu-ray disc holds 25 GB.

Sony PS3 back 2006. The audio output ports are A/V (composite video and stereo audio RCA adapter, component video and stereo audio RCA adapter), S/PDIF, and HDMI (Evan-Amos, "Sony-PlayStation-3-CECHA01-Console-BR").

Sony PS3 Slim back 2009. The audio output ports are A/V (composite video and stereo audio RCA adapter, component video and stereo audio RCA adapter), S/PDIF, and HDMI (Evan-Amos, "Sony-PlayStation-PS3-Slim-Console-BR").

PS3 A/V component cable 2006. It connects to the PS3's A/V port and outputs audio in analog stereo (Evan-Amos, "Ps3-component-cables").

The PS3 was the only gaming system to support the Super Audio CD (SACD), specifically the 20GB, 60 GB, and 80GB early PS3 models (CECHBxx, CECHAxx, CECHCxx, CHCHExx). The SACD is the successor to the Audio CD. A Super Audio CD looks like a CD, but it has the same storage capacity as a DVD (4.7 GB). Unlike an audio CD, a SACD supports copy protection, a 5.1 surround sound signal with lossless compression by Direct Stream Transfer, a 1-bit depth with a bit rate of 2.8224 Mhz (64 times larger than 44.1 kHz), and a maximum frequency of 50 kHz. Although record labels barely supported SACD, Sony heavily marketed the PS3 as a multimedia system supporting the best video and audio options. Unlike the audio output of a dedicated SACD player, the PS3 converts the SACD's DSD audio signal to PCM for output via the PS3's HDMI port. Via optical audio, the PS3 supported SACD output as multichannel DTS with PS3 Firmware Update 2.00 but subsequently removed it in PS3 Firmware Update 2.01. Configuring the PS3 for the optimal audio for SACD was complicated with minimal benefits.

The PS3 Slim (CECH-2001A), released in North America and Europe on September 1, 2009, was the first home console with support for 7.1 audio bitstreams of Dolby TrueHD and DTS-HD Master Audio. It no longer had memory card slots for CompactFlash, Memory Stick Pro, and SD/miniSD. Instead of four, it only had two USB slots, compensated with the additional feature of storing save data and downloadable games and content. In October of 2016, the PS3 ceased manufacturing. The PS3 was an audio innovation in the video game industry. It was the first home console to support HDMI video and audio and 7.1 LPCM. And, like the PS2's DVD player, the PS3's sales boomed due to its Blu-ray player. The PS3 was the last gaming system to support Super Audio CDs and other operating systems. The PS4 lacks the hardware to play PS3 games natively, so the PS4 achieves backward compatibility through the PlayStation Now streaming service or game downloads through the PlayStation Network.

November 19, 2006—Nintendo Wii

MANUFACTURER: Nintendo. RELEASE DATE: November 19, 2006 (NA), December 2, 2006 (JP), December 8, 2006 (EU). MANUFACTURING DATES: November 19, 2006–2017. LAUNCH PRICE: $249.99 with *Wii Sports*. MODEL NUMBER: RVL-001. AUDIO: Dolby Pro Logic II.

The Wii was the first home console with standard motion-based controllers and an internal speaker in its controllers. Released by Nintendo, games used the internal speaker of the Wii Remote to play different audio than the audio directed to the television or audio speakers. The storage capacity of Wii optical discs is similar to single-layer and double-layer DVDs (4.7GB and 8.54 GB, respectively). The Wii is backward-compatible with GameCube

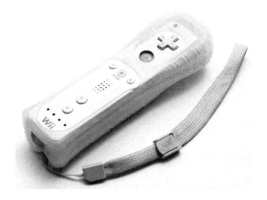

Nintendo Wii remote, released in 2006. The internal speaker is located in the middle of the device (Evan-Amos, "Wiimote-Safety-First").

games, memory cards, and controllers (not the Wii Mini redesign).

The Wii was the first home console to include an internal speaker in its controllers. The Wii Remote's speaker can play audio samples using 4-bit ADPCM or 8-bit signed PCM. However, when in 8-bit mode, the sampling frequency and audio quality are much lower. The mono audio travels from the Wii console to the Wii Remote via a wireless Bluetooth signal. The Wii Remote moves freely without a tether to the console so that the player can move the Wii Remote in any direction. As a result, the player can hear audio from any side, depending on the Wii Remote's placement (the Wii Remote is used as a phone in *No More Heroes*).

Nintendo Wii back 2006. The audio output ports are A/V (composite video and stereo audio RCA adapter) (Evan-Amos, "Wii-Console-Back").

Nintendo Wii Mini back 2013. The audio output ports are A/V (composite video and stereo audio RCA adapter) (Evan-Amos, "Nintendo-Wii-Mini-Console-BR").

The Wii Mini (RVL-201), released in Europe on March 15, 2013, was a budget model that removed hardware for online functionality, external memory storage, and GameCube backward compatibility but maintained the Wii Remote's internal speaker and MotionPlus capabilities without an external attachment. In 2017, the Wii ceased manufacturing. The Wii console only supports analog audio options: mono, stereo, and Dolby Pro Logic II (surround sound). Lacking digital audio options, the Wii lags behind the Xbox 360 and PS3 in terms of audio options. Although the Wii console lacks digital surround sound, the audio of the Wiimote was innovative and rarely duplicated in other gaming systems.

Sources

Flacy, Mike. "Demystifying the Audio Settings on Your PlayStation 3." *Digital Trends*, 9 Sept. 2013, www.digitaltrends.com/home-theater/demystifying-the-audio-settings-on-your-playstation-3.

Kim, Steven. "HD 101: How to Use Dolby TrueHD and DTS-HD with Your PS3." *Engadget*, 21 Apr. 2009, www.engadget.com/2009-04-21-hd-101-how-to-use-dolby-truehd-and-dts-hd-with-your-ps3.html. Accessed 3 June 2020.

Kouno, Tsutomo. "The LocoMotion." Interview by Tom Bramwell. *Eurogamer*, 6 May 2006, www.eurogamer.net/articles/i_locoroco_psp.

Kuchera, Ben. "The Weird Brilliance of the Loco-Roco Theme, 9 Years Later." *Polygon*, 9 Apr. 2015, www.polygon.com/2015/4/9/8376711/the-weird-brilliance-of-the-loco-roco-theme-9-years-later.

Leadbetter, Richard. "Nintendo Wii Mini Review." *Eurogamer.net*, 12 Dec. 2012, www.eurogamer.net/articles/df-hardware-nintendo-wii-mini-review. Accessed 23 Sept. 2020.

Moskovciak, Matthew. "Confirmed: PS3 Slim Bit Streams Dolby TrueHD and DTS-HD Master Audio." CNET, 21 Aug. 2009, www.cnet.com/news/confirmed-ps3-slim-bit-streams-dolby-truehd-and-dts-hd-master-audio/.

Nintendo. "Nintendo Support: What Is the Difference Between the Models of Wii Consoles?" *Nintendo Support*, en-americas-support.nintendo.com/app/answers/detail/a_id/2650/~/what-is-the-difference-between-the-models-of-wii-consoles. Accessed 23 Sept. 2020.

Ohannessian, Kevin. "Nintendo Brings Wii Mini to the U.S.—Should You Buy One?" *Tom's Guide*, 6 Nov. 2013, www.tomsguide.com/us/nintendo-wii-mini-pros-cons,news-17823.html. Accessed 23 Sept. 2020.

"PS3 Specs." PS3Blog.net, www.ps3blog.net/about/ps3-specs/. Accessed 3 Aug. 2018.

Reyes, William. "Rhythm Tengoku FAQ/Walkthrough for Game Boy Advance." *GameFAQs*, 9 Sept. 2006, gamefaqs.gamespot.com/gba/933337-rhythm-tengoku/faqs/44312.

Slec. "Audio and the PS3." 5 Mar. 2008, forum.blu-ray.com/showthread.php?t=40872.

Sony. "PS3 Audio Output Settings." *PlayStation*, manuals.playstation.net/document/en/ps3/current/settings/audiooutput.html. Accessed 3 Aug. 2018.

"Soundvoyager for Game Boy Advance (2006)." *MobyGames*, www.mobygames.com/game/soundvoyager. Accessed 20 Aug. 2018.

"Soundvoyager (Game)." *Giant Bomb*, www.giantbomb.com/soundvoyager/3030-15419/. Accessed 10 Sept. 2018.

Thurrott, Paul. "Xbox 360 Vs. PlayStation 3 Vs. Wii: A Technical Comparison." *IT Pro*, 6 Oct. 2010, www.itprotoday.com/xbox-360-vs-playstation-3-vs-wii-technical-comparison.

Winterhalter, Ryan. "Rhythm Tengoku Review—Review." *Nintendo World Report*, 9 Sept. 2006, www.nintendoworldreport.com/review/12018/rhythm-tengoku-game-boy-advance.

2007 in Review

March 13, 2007—*God of War 2*—PS2

Publisher: Sony. Release Date: March 13, 2007 (NA), April 27, 2007 (EU). Composers: Gerard K. Marino, Ron Fish, Michael Reagan, Cris Velasco. Series: *God of War*. Genre: Action-adventure. Notable musical track: "The End Begins (Main Menu)." Awards: G.A.N.G. 2008 Best Original Vocal Song—Choral, Best Original Soundtrack Album.

The film-like soundtrack of *God of War 2* is not unlike film scores, with its calming sounds of orchestras and choirs. The game's soundtrack features many ominous orchestral pieces, more distinctive than each composer's contributions in the previous *God of War* game. The score is an impressive orchestral accomplishment within the ever-growing and constantly changing arena of videogame composition. The game's music resembles the glorious adventure exhibited by the music of a movie like *The Lord of the Rings*. The notable musical track, "The End Begins (Main Menu)," plays in the game's main menu and second confrontation with Lahkesis. The Greek lyrics include the phrases "The end begins," "I will kill him," and "Olympus will fall." The track achieves epic grandeur through thick vocals, reverbing cymbals and gongs, low brass, deep drums, and frantic strings. The metallic hits sound like the clashing of swords and armor in battle.

June 29, 2007—Apple iPhone 1

Manufacturer: Apple. Release Date: June 29, 2007 (NA), November 9, 2007 (UK, DE). Production Dates: June 29, 2007–July 15, 2008. Launch price: $499.99. Model number: A1203. Audio: Mono.

The iPhone was the first smartphone device with a dedicated app store for instant game downloads. Released by Apple, its compact size and internal storage space for games made it financially competitive in the handheld gaming market. The iPhone was the first cell phone that popularized gaming on cell phones. The iPhone hardware includes either 4GB or 8GB of internal storage, an internal mono speaker, microphone, accelerometer capacitive touchscreen (to detect finger presses), and recessed 3.5mm audio-out port.

With the iPhone, MP3s became the format of choice for music. The iPhone includes a pair of wired earbuds to promote its use as a multimedia device. Even though MP3s are compressed and lossy, they were easy to purchase and listen to within the iTunes Store from Apple. It was convenient to buy MP3s for 99 cents each and have hundreds of songs available on one device for easy listening. All of its games were downloadable through the Apple App Store.

The appeal of the iPhone was its ability to do so much within one compact device and its wireless access to millions of free and paid apps. Apple introduced the Apple App Store on July 10, 2008. The Apple App Store was Apple's quality control for the games available for its iPhone devices. The

smartphone became a popular device for mobile gaming, strengthened with free games and apps from the mobile online marketplace. The most downloaded free game of 2008 from the App Store was *Tap Tap Revenge*, a music game that transferred *Guitar Hero* to a touchscreen. As a result of the iPhone's success, future gaming systems added multimedia features and online marketplaces. Apple released an upgraded iPhone each year, maintaining app compatibility through the iterations of iOS, the operating system for the iPhone and iPad. Although Apple manufactured the iPhone 1 for only one year, it updated the iOS to iOS 3.1.3, released on February 2, 2010.

July 27, 2007—*The World Ends with You*—DS

Publisher: Square Enix. Release Date: July 27, 2007 (JP), April 18, 2008 (EU), April 22, 2008 (NA). Composer: Takeharu Ishimoto. Genre: Action/RPG. Notable musical track: "Lullaby for You (Ending Credits)."

The trance, hip-hop, rap, metal, J-pop, and electronica soundtrack of *The World Ends with You* plays during cutscenes and battles, with songs in English and Japanese. There are 43 songs (the commercial soundtrack includes 14 songs and two unused songs), 19 with vocals. The vocal artists featured in the game include Sawa Kato, Makiko Noda, Leah, Ayuko Tanaka, Mai Matsuda, Wakako, Hanaeryca, Cameron Strother, Andy Kinlay, Nulie Nurly, and Londell "Taz" Hicks. The songs are primarily in English, with some Japanese interspersed. The notable musical track, "Lullaby for You (Ending Credits)," is heard during the game's credits, sung by Japanese pop artist Jyongri. The soundtrack on the game's final version resides in 32 of the 128 total megabytes of the game media. The developers used two techniques to make more room for audio. First, they used CRI Middleware's Kyuseishu Sound Steamer, a compression algorithm generally used for voiceovers, to compress the soundtrack for the game media. Next, they replaced full-motion video cutscenes with Flash-style animations to save more space.

The soundtrack spans many genres, including trance, hip-hop, rap, metal, J-pop, and electronica. The music is prominent throughout the game, heard even during cutscenes and battles.

October 10, 2007—*Portal*—PC

PUBLISHER: Valve. RELEASE DATE: October 10, 2007 (NA), October 18, 2007 (EU). COMPOSERS: Kelly Bailey, Mike Morasky, and Jonathan Coulton. SERIES: *Portal*. GENRE: Puzzle/Platformer. NOTABLE MUSICAL TRACK: "Still Alive (Ending Credits)." AWARDS: G.A.N.G. 2008 Best Original Vocal Song—Pop.

The soundtrack of *Portal* is electronic, employing contemporary synths, chiptunes, 80s sampling techniques, and an iconic robotic voice in the GlaDOS character. Released within *The Orange Box* for Windows 2000, XP, and Vista, *The Orange Box* was a collection of 5 games by Valve: *Half-Life 2*, *Half-Life 2: Episode One*, *Half-Life 2: Episode Two*, *Team Fortress 2*, and *Portal*. The music of *Portal* is a glimpse into the future as seen in different decades. Most of the game's soundtrack is ambient music that reflects the dark and mysterious mood of the game's environments. When the player wanders through the test chambers, the overall sound portrays the future from the perspective of the 1970s. Then later in the game, when the player explores behind the scenes, the overall sound shows the future from the perspective of the 1980s. The notable musical track, "Still Alive," was written by Jonathan Coulton and sung by Ellen McLain as the GLaDOS character in the closing credits. The song's lyrics are displayed on the left side of the screen while the credits scroll on the right side. The lyrics exist as a letter written by GLaDOS to Chell, the game's protagonist. A Latin-style instrumental version of "Still Alive" is used as diegetic music for radios.

November 1, 2007—*Super Mario Galaxy*—Wii

PUBLISHER: Nintendo. RELEASE DATE: November 1, 2007 (JP), November 12, 2007 (NA), November 16, 2007 (EU). COMPOSERS: Mahito Yokota and Koji Kondo. SERIES: *Super Mario Galaxy*. GENRE: Platformer. NOTABLE MUSICAL TRACK: "Gusty Garden Galaxy."

Super Mario Galaxy was the first game in the *Super Mario Bros.* Series with an orchestral soundtrack. The shift in instrumentation represents the expanse of Mario's world to outer space and planetary exploration. The game's soundtrack was composed for a 50-player symphony orchestra. The game's composers requested that the orchestra play each track at different tempos to synchronize well with Mario's movement. The sound effects are supposedly purposed in the same way to fit into the musical score musically. Koji Kondo composed four pieces for the game: "Egg Planet," which plays in the Good Egg Galaxy, and the three "Rosalina in the Observatory" pieces, which play in the Comet Observatory. Mahito Yokota composed the remaining tracks. The music leaves the MIDI-sampled musical programming of previous *Super Mario Bros.* games, favoring live performance to reflect an adventure of enormous scope.

November 16, 2007—*Uncharted: Drake's Fortune*—PS3

PUBLISHER: Sony. RELEASE DATE: November 16, 2007 (NA), December 7, 2007 (EU). COMPOSER: Greg Edmonson. SERIES: *Uncharted*. GENRE: Action-adventure. NOTABLE MUSICAL TRACK: "Nate's Theme."

The soundtrack of *Uncharted: Drake's Fortune* relies on ambient sounds over lush melodies to evoke the sense of adventure in the jungle. The soundtrack's ambient tones reflect the environments of the jungle and caves. The game's plot and characters are reminiscent of the *Indiana Jones* movie series. The game was the first video game project for composer Greg Edmonson, who, before the game, was the composer for the 2002 television sci-fi series *Firefly*. Edmonson was given a sizable budget for an orchestra of 60 musicians for the game's music. The first game in the *Uncharted* series avoids the cinematic sound of *Uncharted 2: Among Thieves*. Instead of varying music through layering, it prioritizes ambient sounds to prevent predictability and repetition upon numerous loops during gameplay. The notable musical track, "Nate's Theme," is the only track in the game with a rousing melody, orchestral flourishes, and film scoring techniques. It accompanies the main menu and is heard at various critical moments throughout the game. The theme is instantly recognizable by its first few notes and unifies the first three *Uncharted* games.

November 20, 2007—*Mass Effect*— Xbox 360

PUBLISHER: Microsoft. RELEASE DATE: November 20, 2007 (NA), December 23, 2007 (EU). COMPOSERS: Jack Wall and Sam Hulick. SERIES: *Mass Effect*. GENRE: Action RPG. NOTABLE MUSICAL TRACK: "Vigil."

Mass Effect has a soundtrack of orchestral and electronic sounds, with musical themes that link the three games in the *Mass Effect* trilogy. The game's soundtrack incorporates the orchestral palette with electronic sounds. Jack Wall, a co-founder of the Game Audio Network Guild and the Video Games Live tour with Tommy Tallarico, was the game's composer. The tone of the soundtrack was influential in the overall design of the game. The soundtrack takes inspiration from the soundtracks of sci-fi movies like *Blade Runner* and *Dune*.

The notable musical track, "Vigil," defines the *Mass Effect* series, appearing during critical moments of the three games in the series. Although not the game's main theme, the track is first heard on the main menu of *Mass Effect*. It uses a drone, a harmonic or monophonic effect or accompaniment where a note or chord lingers throughout most or all of a piece. The track evokes a strong emotional response when the player hears it in the game at Ilos, the game's final planet, when Shepard, the protagonist, learns from Vigil, the Virtual Intelligence in the Prothean vaults on Ilos, of the cyclic plan of the Reapers to harvest all organic life in the universe. *Mass Effect 3* reuses the track on the main menu, in the

War Room of the Normandy SR-2 starship, and during the post-credits scene.

December 20, 2007—*Patapon*—PSP

PUBLISHER: Sony Computer Entertainment America. RELEASE DATE: December 20, 2007 (JP), February 22, 2008 (EU), February 26, 2008 (NA). COMPOSER: Kemmei Adachia and Daisuke Miyake. SERIES: *Patapon*. GENRE: Rhythm. NOTABLE MUSICAL TRACK: "Gyorocchi Theme."

Patapon is a music/rhythm game in which the player selects rhythm to command an army. The game uses rhythmic patterns as commands for the Patapons, tiny army soldiers, to do actions through the battlefield. Throughout the game, there is a steady drumbeat to signify the militaristic march and help the player coordinate the commands. The Patapons regard the player as "Almighty," and the Almighty is the only one to lead them through magical drums. Unlike other rhythm games, which require the player to input a given rhythmic pattern to progress, the player decides which rhythmic patterns to use. Some of the commands are to advance and to attack. The Patapons chant in rhythm in their language based on the button presses. "Pon" is the circle button, "pata" is the square button, and "chaka" is the triangle button. If the player fails to input the correct rhythmic pattern, the Patapons will be confused and aimless, vulnerable to attacks. If the player completes a chain of correct patterns, the Patapons enter Fever mode, making them more powerful and capable of performing "miracles" like summoning rain. *Patapon* creatively incorporates rhythm and music into its story, giving the player some freedom to choose different rhythmic commands and hear other chants from the Patapons.

SOURCES

Arendt, Susan. "Review: Patapon Will Make You a Slave to the Rhythm." *Wired*, 14 Mar. 2008, www.wired.com/2008/03/review-patapon/.
"Can Digital Game Publishing Show Us the Way?" *SXSW Schedule 2014*, 2014, schedule. sxsw.com/2014/2014/events/event_FP27000. Accessed 28 Apr. 2020.

Cowen, Nick. "Uncharted Interview: Greg Edmonson." *Telegraph.co.uk*, 10 Mar. 2011, www.telegraph.co.uk/technology/video-games/8371129/Uncharted-interview-Greg-Edmonson.html. Accessed 29 Apr. 2020.

"Games Review: Patapon Remastered is Gaming's Only Musical Strategy Game." *Metro*, 3 Aug. 2017, metro.co.uk/2017/08/03/patapon-remastered-review-rhythm-of-war-6825390/.

"Mass Effect Original Soundtrack." *Mass Effect Wiki*, 12 June 2017, masseffect.fandom.com/wiki/Mass_Effect_Original_Soundtrack. Accessed 29 Apr. 2020.

Morasky, Mike. Interview. *Game Audio Network Guild*, 23 Feb. 2011, www.audiogang.org/interview-with-valves-mike-morasky/.

Morasky, Mike. Interview. *Podcast 17*, 7 May 2011, podcast17.com/interviews/audio/mike-morasky/.

"Portal Soundtrack." *Combine OverWiki, the Original Half-Life Wiki and Portal Wiki*, 24 May 2018, combineoverwiki.net/wiki/Portal_soundtrack. Accessed 16 Aug. 2018.

Softbank. "SoftBank and Apple to Bring IPhone 3G to Japan on July 11." *SoftBank*, 9 June 2008, www.softbank.jp/en/corp/group/sbm/news/press/2008/20080610_01/. Accessed 1 Feb. 2021.

"Still Alive." *Half-Life Wiki*, 6 June 2018, half-life.wikia.com/wiki/Still_Alive. Accessed 16 Aug. 2018.

Wall, Jack. "Home." *The Official Website of Composer Jack Wall*, jackwall.net. Accessed 6 Aug. 2018.

Wilde, Tyler. "Portal 2's Dynamic Music—an Interview with Composer Mike Morasky, and Five Tracks to Listen to Now!" *Gamesradar*, 14 Apr. 2011, www.gamesradar.com/portal-2s-dynamic-music-an-interview-with-composer-mike-morasky-and-five-tracks-to-listen-to-now/. Accessed 28 Apr. 2020.

2008 in Review

February 15, 2008—*Audiosurf*—PC

PUBLISHER: Audiosurf. RELEASE DATE: February 15, 2008 (WW). COMPOSER: Pedro Macedo de Oliveira Camacho. SERIES: *Audiosurf*. GENRE: Music/Rhythm. NOTABLE MUSICAL TRACK: "Circuit Breakdown (Intro)."

Audiosurf is a music game that algorithmically generates racetracks from audio data through frequency analysis. Released for Steam for Windows, the game's programming includes an algorithm to generate a unique racetrack of colored blocks that matches the audio track's beats and sounds. The gameplay consists of navigating a vehicle on a racetrack. The game's objective is to collect the colored blocks on the track. The colored blocks synchronize with the beats and sounds of the audio track. The game, upon initial release, included MP3 files from *The Orange Box*, a collection of games from Valve, including *Portal* and *Half-Life 2*. The notable musical track, "Circuit Breakdown (Intro)," is almost entirely electronic, reflecting the technological world of the game. A brief moment of acoustic guitar adds a human element to the track.

Each song affects the shape, speed, and mood of each racetrack. Dylan Fitterer, the creator of *Audiosurf*, explained the relationship between music and the racetracks in a 2008 interview. Frequency analysis determines whether the racetrack should be a downward slope for louder music or an uphill slope for softer music. The volumes of music fluctuate, resulting in hills and valleys for the highway. For each sound spike in the music, a block appears on the highway. The color of the block determines how distinct the sound spike is. The distinct sounds are indicated as red blocks, while the subtle sounds are purple.

July 24, 2008—*Korg DS-10*—DS

PUBLISHER: Xseed Games. RELEASE DATE: July 24, 2008 (JP), October 10, 2008 (EU), November 4, 2008 (NA). SERIES: *Korg DS-10*. GENRE: Music creation.

Korg DS-10 was a DS software with a faithful working Korg MS-10 synth with step sequencer, letting the player create music using the DS touchscreen, either live or sequenced. The software takes advantage of the DS's two screens and touchscreen for music composition. Michio Okamiya of The Black Mages, Yasunori Mitsuda of *Chrono Trigger*, and Nobuyoshi Sano (Sanodg) of *Ridge Racer* contributed to the game's development. The user uses the DS stylus to adjust virtual knobs, controlling parameters such as cutoff frequency and waveform shape. The Korg Kaoss Pad is a visual interface to modify volume and panning based on the touchscreen's X and Y axes. The available sounds include two Voltage-Controlled Oscillators (VCOs) for sawtooth, pulse, triangle, noise waveforms, and a four-part drum machine. The user enters pitches on the DS touchscreen from the two-octave keyboard or the Korg Kaoss Pad. The software supports a maximum of six simultaneous sound channels. The user can record 21 sessions with 16 different step patterns of 16 steps, using either live input or a step sequencer. It is possible to compose an entire album of music using only *Korg DS-10* (the DG-10 album).

On September 17, 2009, *Korg DS-10 Plus* was released for the DS in Japan and North America on February 16, 2010. *Korg DS-10 Plus* is *Korg DS-10* with improvements (for the DS and DSi) and exclusive features on the DSi. Players share sounds and songs and play music in real-time simultaneously with up to eight other players wirelessly. When played on the DSi, *Korg DS-10 Plus* supports four dual-oscillator analog synthesizer tracks and eight dedicated drum tracks, 12 total tracks (the DS only supports two analog synthesizer tracks and six total tracks, like the original game). The game includes an improved Song Mode with mute and solo buttons for each track. Other efficiencies include improvements to real-time performance with edit and play buttons for all modes and note entry by touch screen, keyboard screen, and matrix screen.

October 16, 2008—*Wii Music*—Wii

PUBLISHER: Nintendo. RELEASE DATE: October 16, 2008 (JP), October 20, 2008 (NA), November 14, 2008 (EU). COMPOSERS: Kenta Nagata, Toru Minegishi and Mahito Yokota. GENRE: Music. NOTABLE MUSICAL TRACK: "Sebastian's Lesson."

Wii Music is a music game that is easy to pick up and play, where players play music and create music videos by mimicking the playing of instruments with the Wii Remote and Nunchuk. Players are not scored on their performance but are instead encouraged to experiment with different ways to play various songs. The director of *Wii Music* was Kazumi Totaka, who also worked on *Mario Paint* and *Mario Artist: Talent Studio*. In *Wii Music*, the player creates a musical arrangement by selecting a song from classical songs, children's songs, and Nintendo songs and selecting a musical instrument. During the performance, the speed of the player's motions using the Wii Remote and Nunchuk regulates the tempo of the music. In Jam Mode, the player creates music videos with up to six different instruments. The player selects a song, an instrument to control directly, and additional band members to play the other various parts of the music, like the melody, harmony, bass, and drum parts. The game's 50 songs include classical, traditional, Nintendo, and licensed songs. The game is programmed to compensate for poor musical ability, ensuring a decent audio mix in the end. Adding to the creativity, the player can overdub sessions by performing up to six instruments for one music video, each instrument in a separate session which are combined.

The notable musical track, "Sebastian's Lesson," is heard after selecting "Jam Lessons." Sebastian Tute, the music teacher of the tute people, introduces the player to instruments, including the piano, guitar, violin, and trumpet. The music maintains the style of other Wii titles like *Wii Sports* and the Wii system menus. It is in the easy listening genre, using the tambourine, pizzicato strings, glockenspiel, and flutes. *Wii Music* is arguably the most accessible game to play music with little to no experience.

SOURCES

"Audiosurf—Press Kit." *IGDB.com*, 2008, www.igdb.com/games/audiosurf/presskit.

Jeriaska. "Interview: Korg DS-10 Spawns Japanese Album, Concert Series." *Gamasutra*, 18 May 2010, www.gamasutra.com/view/news/119458/Interview_Korg_DS10_Spawns_Japanese_Album_Concert_Series.php. Accessed 26 May 2021.

Totaka, Kazumi. "3. No Score, No Mistakes." Interview by Satoru Iwata. *Nintendo of Europe*,

2008, www.nintendo.co.uk/Iwata-Asks/Iwata-Asks-Wii-Music/Volume-2-Wii-Music-A-First-Time-For-Everyone/3-No-Score-No-Mistakes/3-No-Score-No-Mistakes-238445.html. Accessed 12 May 2020.

Wilburn, Thomas. "Catching Waveforms: Audiosurf Creator Dylan Fitterer Speaks." *Ars Technica*, 11 Mar. 2008, arstechnica.com/gaming/2008/03/catching-waveforms-audiosurf-creator-dylan-speaks/. Accessed 12 May 2020.

2009 in Review

September 29, 2009—*Beaterator*—PSP

PUBLISHER: Rockstar Games. RELEASE DATE: September 29, 2009 (NA), October 2, 2009 (EU). COMPOSER: Timbaland. GENRE: Music Creation.

Beaterator is a DAW (Digital Audio Workstation) with an 8-track sequencer. The player creates music using over 1,700 loops and recorded sounds. The game includes an 8-track sequencer with loops, beats, and sounds, resembling a modern DAW like FL Studio. Timbaland, the successful record producer of R&B and hip-hop artists and a rapper and songwriter, produced the game. He composed approximately 1,700 loops for the game. Alternatively, the player can import WAV files or record sounds using the PSP's microphone to incorporate into new loops. In Live Play mode, an avatar of Timbaland watches the player while the player controls the sounds in real-time using the face buttons of the PSP. Timbaland's involvement in *Beaterator* added credibility to the PSP's first music composition software.

Studio Session mode is where the player combines loops and adjusts the sounds so that they blend well. There is a Melody Crafter and Drum Crafter mode. In Melody Crafter mode, the player adjusts pitches graphically with a piano keyboard positioned vertically. The time signature is restricted to 4/4 with a maximum song length of 240 bars. The tempo range is between 60 and 300 beats per minute. The Song Crafter mode is the mode that pieces the loops, beats, and sounds together in the sequencer.

The gaming software also supports swung-eighth rhythms and time-stretching of loops. Lastly, some of the available audio effects are compressor, chorus, delay, distortion, 3-band EQ, multimode resonant filter, flanger, noise gate, phaser, and tremolo. Besides editing and creating original music with eight simultaneous tracks, the player can save the completed songs as a MIDI or WAV file. The game saves the exported audio file to the Memory Stick Pro or Pro Duo as a WAV of 16-bit, 22.05 kHz stereo audio (88.2 kilobytes per second of uncompressed audio).

October 27, 2009—*DJ Hero*—PS2

PUBLISHER: Activision. RELEASE DATE: October 27, 2009 (NA), October 29, 2009 (EU). DEVELOPER: Harmonix. GENRE: Music/Rhythm.

DJ Hero interacts with an original DJ turntable controller to allow players to remix from master recordings in real-time. The gameplay of *DJ Hero* focuses on the skills of deejaying. *DJ Hero* is another music game by developer Harmonix with inspiration from *Guitar Hero*. *DJ Hero* includes 100 licensed master recordings. Some of the international deejays contributing mixes of the master recordings to the game are DJ Blakey, DJ Z-Trip, DJ AM, and Daft Punk. The development team of DJ Hero programmed the mixes to blend well with the gameplay, never resulting in abrupt or haphazard desynchronization.

The player simulates the role of a disc jockey by creating mashups with a turntable controller. The controller is a wireless deck made up of the essential PS2 buttons for menu navigation, a turntable with a blue, red, and green "stream" button, an effects dial, a crossfader, and a "Euphoria" button. Notes travel in an arc across a spinning record on-screen. The player holds

DJ Hero turntable 2009. It communicates with the PS2 through the controller port (Evan-Amos, "DJ-Hero-Turntable").

down one of the stream buttons to play notes; two stream buttons control the two songs used in that particular mix. The third activates samples to add to the mix, which the player can adjust with the effects dial. The player must also constantly change the crossfader to match on-screen symbols, which alters the relative volume of the songs, placing one song at the forefront of the mix for a short time. There

are objectives to achieve and a final goal to complete the game. *DJ Hero 2* was the only other game to use the turntable controller (using a specific controller for PS3, Wii, and Xbox 360). After the popularity of music games faded in the late 2000s, games offering audio remixing instead used touchscreen input.

SOURCES

"Beaterator™." *PlayStation™Store*, store.playstation.com/en-us/product/UP1004-ULUS 10405_00-RCKSTRBEATERATOR. Accessed 20 Aug. 2018.

"Beaterator—Full Manual—PSP Version." *Internet Archive*, 17 Jan. 2021, archive.org/details/full-manual/mode/2up. Accessed 13 June 2021.

IGN. "Beaterator preview." 2009, www.ign.com/games/beaterator/psp-893429.

Kirn, Peter. "Inside Beaterator, Rockstar Games' New PSP Beat Maker, with Gory Technical Bits." *CDM Create Digital Music*, 3 Sept. 2009, cdm.link/2009/09/inside-beaterator-rockstar-games-new-psp-beat-maker-with-gory-technical-bits/. Accessed 4 June 2020.

2010 in Review

May 18, 2010—*Red Dead Redemption*—PS3

PUBLISHER: Rockstar Games. RELEASE DATE: May 18, 2010 (NA), May 21, 2010 (EU). COMPOSERS: Bill Elm and Woody Jackson. SERIES: *Red Dead Redemption*. GENRE: Action-Adventure. NOTABLE MUSICAL TRACK: "Far Away." AWARDS: G.A.N.G. 2011 Audio of the Year, Music of the Year, Best Interactive Score, Best Dialogue.

The soundtrack of *Red Dead Redemption* evokes the sounds and styles of the spaghetti western films with music by Ennio Morricone. The game's soundtrack includes traditional instruments of the western era of the U.S., like a harmonica, jaw harp, accordion, trumpet, nylon guitar, flute, and ocarina. The harmonica player heard throughout the game is Tommy Morgan, arguably the most recognized harmonica player globally, who has played the harmonica in over 500 movies.

Bill Elm and Woody Jackson composed over 14 hours of music, although only 75 minutes and 18 seconds of music over 20 tracks are found in the game's official soundtrack. The official soundtrack contains representative musical tracks prepared by the composers using the vast musical stems. The notable musical track, "Far Away," is the only musical track with lyrics in the game. The song and its lyrics, distinct to the sounds before this moment in the game, match the emotional response for the specific moment. The song is first heard when riding across Mexico, around a third of the way into the game. The song was written for the game by José González, a Swedish folk singer. The lyrics in English evoke the feeling of desperation and distance: "Step in front of a runaway train, just to feel alive again. Pushing forward through the night, aching chest and blurry sight. It's so far, so far away. It's so far, so far away."

November 4, 2010—*Dance Central*—Xbox 360

PUBLISHER: MTV Games. RELEASE DATE: November 4, 2010 (NA), November 10, 2010 (EU), June 2, 2011 (JP). DEVELOPER: Harmonix. SERIES: *Dance Central*. GENRE: Music/Rhythm. Peripheral Support: Kinect.

Dance Central was the first game to respond to full-body movement with the Kinect. Harmonix, the *Guitar Hero* and *Rock Band* series developer, developed the game. *Dance Central* is a music/rhythm game in which players dance to the master recordings of popular songs. The appeal of the game is the ability to dance naturally to the 30 included songs. The Kinect camera and sensors create and manage skeletal points of up to four players within range of the Kinect. Unlike other dance games before 2010, *Dance Central* is much more accurate in determining whether players match the indicated dance moves. It supports a natural user interface using gestures and spoken commands. Gameplay involves the player physically performing given dance moves tracked by the Kinect and represented on the screen by one of eight in-game avatars. The game features over 650 different dance moves spanning over 90 dance routines. A white silhouette on-screen shows the player's body movements as scanned by the Kinect.

Besides the standard mode, there is a mode to track calories burned, a two-player competitive mode, and a training mode that teaches players how to perform the dance routines in slower sections. The variety of modes makes the game more accessible to more players, whether competitively or leisurely. Players can create new dance routines in the Freestyle section. The Kinect camera takes photos throughout the performance and shows them to the players at the end.

All of the songs are master recordings, not covers. The oldest song is "Jungle Boogie," performed by Kool and the Gane and the newest song is "I Know You Want Me (Calle Ocho)," performed by Pitbull. Lady Gaga has two of her songs in the game: "Just Dance" and "Poker Face" from her debut album *The Fame* in 2008. *Dance Central* contains downloadable content. Players could buy new songs from Xbox Live and store them on the hard drive of the Xbox 360. Thirty-two new songs were offered as downloadable content between November 2010 and September 2011. Using downloadable content, developers support and develop games beyond their release date. With online connectivity, whether to purchase downloadable content or play multiplayer online games, games could be updated and altered beyond the physical media. For *Dance Central*, each downloadable song costs 240 Microsoft Points (the equivalent of $3) from the Xbox Live Marketplace. Buying all of the additional songs would be $64. After the initial purchase, the Xbox 360 automatically adds the additional songs to *Dance Central 2* and *Dance Central 3*.

December 9, 2010—*Ni no Kuni: Dominion of the Dark Djinn*—DS

PUBLISHER: Level-5. RELEASE DATE: December 9, 2010 (JP). COMPOSER: Joe Hisaishi and Rei Kondo. SERIES: *Ni no Kuni*. GENRE: RPG. NOTABLE MUSICAL TRACK: "Kokoro no Kakera—Pieces of a Broken Heart (Main Theme)."

Ni no Kuni: Dominion of the Dark Djinn bears the visual and aural styles of Studio Ghibli and Joe Hisaishi. Released exclusively in Japan, Studio Ghibli, a famous Japanese animation studio, created the game's art and animated cutscenes, which are in the same artistic style as the studio's animated films. Joe Hisaishi, the composer of Studio Ghibli films since 1986, and Rei Kondoh were the game's composers. The Tokyo Philharmonic Orchestra recorded the soundtrack. A 4-gigabit game card (500 MBs) enables the game to fit all of the orchestral music. The notable musical track, "Kokoro no Kakera," is the game's theme song. It was composed by Joe Hisaishi. Mai Fujisawa performed the song in Japanese, while Archie Buchanan performed the song in English. The music reflects the fantasy genre, evoking the elegance and nostalgia of the traditional folk music of Ireland. The sounds of the piano, strings, and pennywhistle, featured prominently in the musical accompaniment, evoke nostalgia. The lyrics evoke the elegance of nature: "Over hills, Green as the springtime, Chasing a lonely cloud, White as snow, Someday soon, I mean to catch it...."

SOURCES

Hisaishi, Joe. Interview. *YouTube*, 8 Jan. 2013, www.youtube.com/watch?v=_Bcf0X7Vlh4.

2011 in Review

February 26, 2011—Nintendo 3DS

MANUFACTURER: Nintendo. RELEASE DATE: February 26, 2011 (JP), March 25, 2011 (EU), March 27, 2011 (NA). MANUFACTURING DATES: February 26, 2011–September 17, 2020. LAUNCH PRICE: $249 (system only). MODEL NUMBER: CTR-001. AUDIO: Stereo with virtual surround sound.

The Nintendo 3DS was a handheld gaming system capable of saving and sending voice recordings and playing music when closed. The 3DS was the first handheld console to display autostereoscopic 3D effects without using 3D glasses or additional accessories. Regarding audio, the 3DS contains a dedicated hardware audio DSP module. The audio output options are pseudo-surround, stereo, or mono. The 3DS outputs audio through either the internal stereo speakers or the headphone jack. Using the system's headphone jack, the 3DS can play music while the console is closed. A set of sound manipulation options is available, as well as several audio filters. The user can record and edit voice recordings at a maximum of 10 seconds in duration.

Nintendo 3DS Sound is a built-in music player and sound recorder in the 3DS handheld gaming system. It can play audio files from an SD card with extensions .mp3, .aac, .m4a or .3gp. The upper screen of the 3DS displays a visualization of the music. The 3DS includes StreetPass, a social feature that uses local Wi-Fi functionality to exchange software content from select games between 3DS systems. Using StreetPass functionality, users exchange song data to form a compatibility chart between users. StreetPass is still active on the 3DS using an ad-hoc network.

Nintendo 3DS 2011. The audio output ports are 3.5mm. The internal speakers are located on the left and right sides of the top panel. The internal microphone is located under the start button on the bottom of the lower panel. The volume slider modulates the internal speakers' volume (Evan-Amos, "Nintendo-3DS-AquaOpen").

Nintendo 3DS XL 2012. The audio output ports are 3.5mm. The internal speakers are located on the left and right sides of the top panel. The internal microphone is located to the right of the start button on the bottom of the lower panel. The volume slider modulates the internal speakers' volume (Evan-Amos, "Nintendo-3DS-XL-angled").

Nintendo 2DS 2013. The audio output ports are 3.5mm. The internal speaker is located on the upper-left corner of the device. The internal microphone is located on the lower-left corner of the lower panel. The volume slider modulates the internal speaker's volume (Evan-Amos, "Nintendo-2DS-angle").

The 3DS series was the last series of handheld gaming systems manufactured by Nintendo. The 3DS XL, released on August 19, 2012, was a 3DS with a larger form factor and screen size. The 2DS, released on October 12, 2013, was a 3DS with a mono internal speaker, tablet design, and lack of the autostereoscopic 3D screen and 3D slider. The New 3DS XL, released on February 13, 2015, maintained the size of the 3DS XL with the addition of an upgraded CPU, 256 megabytes of RAM, three controller buttons, microSD card support, and NFC support for Amiibo (still with internal stereo speakers). The New 3DS, released on September 25, 2015, was the original-sized version of the New 3DS XL with removable faceplates for personalization. The New 2DS XL, released on July 28, 2017, was a 2DS with the upgraded hardware of the New 3DS with the size of the 3DS XL, but with the internal stereo speakers and 3.5mm audio-out port inconveniently situated on the bottom edge of the unit. On September 17, 2020, the New 2DS XL ceased manufacturing, ending the 3DS series of handheld gaming systems. Of the 3DS models, the New 3DS XL has the best audio hardware design. Nintendo then prioritized the Nintendo Switch as a handheld gaming option.

March 24, 2011—*Superbrothers: Sword & Sworcery EP*—iOS

Publisher: Capybara Games. Release Date: March 24, 2011 (WW). Composer: Jim Guthrie. Genre: Action-Adventure. Notable musical track: "And We Got Older."

Superbrothers: Sword & Sworcery EP is a mobile game with puzzles using sound and music and a world hub presented as an EP vinyl disc. Released for the iPad, the soundtrack is a series of moods atmospheric with plenty of creative synths and acoustic sounds. Once the player begins the game, a mysterious character called the Archetype suggests wearing headphones to play the game. The game is presented as an EP vinyl disc in which each audio track on the record represents an episode of the game. The slow gameplay leaves time for the player to listen to the soundtrack while solving the puzzles.

Jim Guthrie, the game's composer, is a Canadian singer-songwriter since the mid–1990s whose credits include the 2003 album *Now More Than Ever* (nominated for a Juno award) and the 2012 documentary *Indie Game: The Movie*. The game design began first with the chiptune/synth music of Jim Guthrie and the pixel art of Craig D. Adams (aka Superbrothers). Some of the game's tracks, such as "Little Furnace," the epilogue track, were composed using *MTV Music Generator* on an original Sony PS1. Adams had contacted Guthrie by postcard in 2003, and Guthrie mailed him a CD with unreleased music composed on an original Sony PS1.

The soundtrack is a series of moods atmospheric with plenty of creative synths and acoustic sounds. A bell tone signifies to continue from the dialogue box or interact with something or someone. In Session 2, the Scythian learns how to perform the "Song of Sworcery," a "consciousness expansion technique that reveals a mystical musical dimension." One of the early puzzles involves tapping on three white orbs ("songbirds") gathered around a nest box to unlock a slumbering Sylvan sprite. Upon revealing the sprite, the player taps on the sprite a total of three times. A vocal "oh" accompanies each tap, collectively forming the song of sworcery. The song is fleshed out as "The Ballad of the Space Babies" on the game's official soundtrack. Upon entering the dream world in Session 3, the Scythian soon meets a man by a crackling fire. He is Jim Guthrie, the game's composer, who plays the notable musical track, "And We Got Older," on guitar. As he performs, the player taps the trees and shrubs to improvise using the musical notes of a minor pentatonic scale.

April 1, 2011—Sony Ericsson Xperia Play

MANUFACTURER: Sony Ericsson. RELEASE DATE: April 1, 2011 (EU), May 26, 2011 (NA). PRODUCTION DATES: April 1, 2011–2012. LAUNCH PRICE: $199.99. MODEL NUMBER: R800a. AUDIO: Stereo.

The Xperia Play was a smartphone designed for gaming with internal stereo speakers. The design of the Xperia Play was a combination of a smartphone and handheld gaming system. Sony Ericsson, a joint venture between Sony and Ericsson, manufactured the Xperia Play. The Xperia Play has two internal speakers for stereo audio (Apple added stereo speakers to the iPhone in 2016 with the iPhone 7). Stereo speakers existed in cell phones as early as 2004 but were not yet a standard feature. The Xperia Play includes a 3.5mm audio-out jack located on the bottom edge, held in landscape orientation (the 3.5mm audio-out port was a standard on all handheld and mobile devices until the iPhone 7 in 2016).

The phone's front resembles the Xperia X10 phone with a large screen and four physical buttons for Back, Home, Menu, and Search. The Xperia Play has a slider that revealed gaming buttons: a D-pad, the four standard PlayStation buttons, a touchpad, a Start button, a Select button, and a Menu button. The L and R shoulder buttons are on the back of the phone. Unlike the PSP series of handheld gaming systems, which stores memory on Sony Memory Sticks, the Xperia Play uses microSD cards. The Xperia Play supports multiplayer gaming via an active mobile 3G network (with a mobile data contract with Verizon) or an

Sony Ericsson Xperia Play 2011. The audio output ports are 3.5mm. The volume rocker modulates the internal speaker's volume (Evan-Amos, "Sony-Xperia-Play-Open-FL").

ad-hoc connection between systems via Wi-Fi.

The Xperia Play is preloaded with *Crash Bandicoot*, a PS classic game. Other pre-installed games were *FIFA 10*, *The Sims 3*, *Star Battalion*, *Bruce Lee Dragon Warriors*, and *Tetris*. The Xperia Play runs on the Android operating system to download and play games from the Google Play Store as a smartphone. Users need to download games from either the Google Play Store, Get Games app, or the PlayStation Pocket app. For a smartphone competing against Apple's iPhone, the Xperia Play offered full pre-installed games of better production value than most iOS and Android games.

June 14, 2011—*Child of Eden*— Xbox 360

PUBLISHER: Ubisoft. RELEASE DATE: June 14, 2011 (NA). Director: Tetsuya Mizuguchi. COMPOSERS: Genki Rockets, Yuki Ichiki, and Shogo Ohnishi. GENRE: Rail Shooter/Music. Peripheral Support: Kinect. NOTABLE MUSICAL TRACK: "Beauty (Stage 3)."

In *Child of Eden*, the player creates sounds to complement the music through motion gestures with the Microsoft Kinect sensor. The game is a spiritual successor to *Rez*, with Tetsuya Mizuguchi as the producer of *Rez* and the director of *Child of Eden*. The notable musical track, "Beauty (Stage 3)," is heard in the third stage as the player navigates a softly colored, garden-like alien world full of bizarre abstract creatures. The track generally has an airy, upbeat feel. The remix of "Beauty" expresses a darker mood than the in-game world depicts. Unlike a Kinect game like *Dance Central*, the player interacts with *Child of Eden* using either a standard controller or the Kinect sensor. The player uses the Kinect to swipe over enemies with a reticule controlled by their right hand and launch attacks by moving the right hand towards the screen. The left hand directs a purple homing laser used to defend against enemy attacks. Raising both hands launches "Euphoria," a powerful attack that clears everything on the screen. Once eight targets are set, the Octa-Lock requires releasing a fully charged shot from the lock-on laser to the beat of the music. The game uses the rumble feature of the standard Xbox 360 controller as a tactile indicator of the beat. The game is a rail shooter that integrates colors and sound in a synesthetic experience.

November 18, 2011—*Minecraft*—PC

PUBLISHER: Mojang Studios. RELEASE DATE: November 18, 2011 (WW). COMPOSER: Daniel Rosenfeld. GENRE: Sandbox/Survival. NOTABLE MUSICAL TRACK: "Alpha."

Minecraft is the best-selling game of all time, playing music after minutes of silence and offering user tools to create music within a 3D world. Released on Windows XP, Vista, and 7, the game's music is heard on the menu and credits screens, aquatic biomes, the Nether, the End, Creative mode, and all other modes. The game does not play music constantly for the many hours of extended play. There are between 10 and 20 minutes of silence between musical tracks. Some locations, like warped forests, are devoid of music. Some areas, like at the credits screen and at the End (while the ender dragon is alive), activate specific musical tracks without delay ("Alpha" and "Boss," respectively). There are five tracks

used in Creative mode, three for aquatic biomes, four for the Nether, and four for the Menu screen. The notable musical track, "Alpha," plays during the credits screen. The credits screen appears after defeating the ender dragon (considered the completion of the game). The track is over 10 minutes and is a medley of different melodies and instrumentations. The tracks that comprise "Alpha" are "Minecraft," "Mice on Venus," "Moog City," and "Sweden."

In *Minecraft*, the 3D world represents musical notation using note blocks and redstone. To create a note, the player places a note block above another block (there must be at least one block of space above the note block to function correctly). The material of the block below determines the instrument sound out of 16 possibilities (for example, most blocks have a harp/piano sound). Right-clicking on the note block raises the pitch by a semitone or begins again at the bottom-most pitch (the pitch range of each instrument is two octaves inclusive, or 25 pitches). When placing the note block, the default pitch is F# (the exact octave varies among instruments). For the player to activate the notes in time, the note blocks are spaced apart and connected with paths of redstone. Each repeater can have between one and four ticks. One redstone tick represents 400 milliseconds. Doing the math, the tempi that offer simple divisions of note values with ticks are 50, 60, 75, 100, and 150 beats per minute. Note blocks do not store volume data. The only way to decrease the volume is to move the player's location away from the activating note block. As the redstone activates the note blocks, the player needs to follow the fuse of the redstone. It is impossible to walk through the musical composition and inspect all of the elements that work together to create a user-created song.

December 17, 2011—Sony PS Vita

MANUFACTURER: Sony. RELEASE DATE: December 17, 2011 (JP), February 22, 2012 (NA, EU). PRODUCTION DATES: December 17, 2011–March 1, 2019. LAUNCH PRICE: $249.99 (Wi-Fi), $299.99 (3G and Wi-Fi). MODEL

NUMBER: PCH-1001 (Wi-Fi only), PCH-1101 (3G and Wi-Fi). AUDIO: Stereo.

The PS Vita was a handheld gaming system with the ability to play user music throughout the system menus and games and to stream video and audio directly from a PS3 or PS4 for portable play. Released by Sony, the PS Vita includes

- front and rear cameras.
- a 5-inch OLED touchscreen display.
- a rear capacitive multi-touch pad.
- internal stereo speakers.
- a 3.5mm audio-out port.
- an internal microphone.

Sony designed the PS Vita's hardware to compete with the mobile smartphone market. There was a PS Vita model sold with 3G network connectivity through AT&T for a monthly subscription rate. It is backward-compatible with PSP games available through the PlayStation Store and most titles from other platforms such as PS one Classics, PlayStation minis, and PlayStation Mobile games. Unlike the PSP, which stored games as UMDs, retail PS Vita games were distributed on PlayStation Vita game cards, resembling an SD card in size and shape (similar to the DS and Switch).

With the PS Vita, users could play music stored on the proprietary PS Vita memory card and listen to music while opening other apps, even while playing a game. By pressing and holding the PS button, users

Sony PS Vita 2011. The audio output ports are 3.5mm. The internal speakers are located on the lower-left and lower-right corners of the device (Evan-Amos, "PlayStation-Vita-1101-FL").

can control the music. The PS Vita's music player operates at the system level, separately from a game's soundtrack. The PS Vita supports audio files in the MP3, MP4, and WAV file formats. The PS Vita can also play music stored on a PC or PS3 via the Remote Play feature.

The PS Vita was one of the first gaming systems with functionality in both a portable and home setting. The PS Vita connects wirelessly with the PS3 and PS4 for added features. Remote Play is a feature that allows the PS Vita to stream PS4 games so players can move around with relative mobility, provided they stay on the same wireless network. The PS3 wirelessly streams the video and audio to the PS Vita. The PS3 still handles the calculations. Some games that support Remote Play show additional content on the PS Vita's screen. The PS Vita can show a radar, maps, alternate camera angles, and playbooks in sports games as a second screen. Another feature is using the PS Vita as a controller with the PS3. Also, players using PlayStation Plus cloud saves could synchronize progress between Sony's home and portable gaming systems. Lastly, the PS Vita's lifespan extended past the PS3 and into the lifespan of the PS4. So, the PS Vita gained support for all of these features when wirelessly connect to the PS4.

The PlayStation TV (VTE-1000), released by Sony on October 14, 2013, in Japan for $99.99, was a small console that played PS Vita game cards and digital downloads from the PlayStation Store on a TV. The PlayStation TV connects wirelessly via Bluetooth to either a DualShock 3 or DualShock 4 (after the 3.10 firmware update). Like the PS Vita, the PlayStation TV supports remote play with a PS4 (the video and audio streams from a PS4 are sent to the PS TV as stereo LPCM). The PS Vita Slim (PCH-2000), released on May 6, 2014, for $199.99, was a thinner and lighter model with better battery life and a 1GB internal hard drive.

Sony ceased manufacturing the PlayStation TV on February 29, 2016. On March 1, 2019, the PS Vita ceased manufacturing. The PS Vita was the first handheld gaming system to support a data plan through

Sony PlayStation TV back 2013. The audio output ports are HDMI (Evan-Amos, "PlayStation-TV-BL").

a mobile phone carrier (only smartphones support this now). It was the first handheld gaming system with two analog sticks. It supports the playback of music files while using other apps or playing a game on the PS Vita. Custom soundtracks are rare on gaming systems nowadays. The PS Vita was the only handheld gaming system to work with a PC, PS3, or PS4. It was also the sole handheld gaming system with a touchpad on the back. Unfortunately for the fate of the PS Vita, Sony gave up on it fairly quickly. The PS Vita uses proprietary memory cards, less compatible when compared with SD cards for the 3DS. There weren't that many must-have games for the system. There were many games from the PlayStation catalog that never were ported to the PS Vita. Also, developers made spinoff games of popular home console franchises on the PS Vita that dumbed down the quality and fun. Unlike many of the systems that fade away into history, the PS Vita still receives new games by independent developers and as part of Cross Buy with PS4 (buy a digital copy of a PS4 game and get the PS Vita or PSN version for free). Despite no longer being manufactured, the PS Vita still has a moderate user base and functionality with the PC, PS3, and PS4.

Sources

Ahmed, Emad. "How Tetsuya Mizuguchi Reinvented Video Games with His Love of Synaesthesia." *New Statesman*, 28 July 2017, www.newstatesman.com/culture/games/2017/07/how-tetsuya-mizuguchi-reinvented-video-games-his-love-synaesthesia.

Ashcraft, Brian. "PlayStation Vita: It's Official, and Here's The Price." *Kotaku*, 6 June 2011, kotaku.com/playstation-vita-its-official-and-heres-the-price-452567453.

Brightman, James. "Nintendo Ends New Nintendo 3DS Production in Japan." *GamesIndustry.biz*, 13 July 2017, www.gamesindustry.biz/articles/2017-07-13-nintendo-ends-new-nintendo-3ds-production-in-japan. Accessed 11 Sept. 2020.

Buchanan, Levi. "Sword & Sworcery EP Micro IPhone Review." *IGN*, 27 Apr. 2011, www.ign.com/articles/2011/04/27/sword-sworcery-ep-micro-iphone-review.

"Does the Psvita Have PS3 Graphics?" *GameSpot*, www.gamespot.com/forums/system-wars-314159282/does-the-psvita-have-ps3-graphics-28766435/. Accessed 7 Sept. 2018.

Fahey, Rob. "Reassessing the Legacy of PlayStation Vita." *GamesIndustry.biz*, 18 May 2018, www.gamesindustry.biz/articles/2018-05-17-reassessing-the-legacy-of-playstation-vita.

Hamilton, Kirk. "The (Actual) Best Game Music of 2011: Superbrothers: Sword & Sworcery EP." *Kotaku*, 29 Dec. 2011, kotaku.com/5871943/the-actual-best-game-music-of-2011-superbrothers-sword—sworcery-ep.

Kuchera, Ben. "How a Song from the 2005 Civilization IV Won a 2011 Grammy." *Ars Technica*, 14 Feb. 2011, arstechnica.com/gaming/2011/02/how-a-song-from-the-2005-civilization-iv-won-a-2011-grammy/. Accessed 2 Sept. 2020.

Margolis, Jason. "A Classical Music Album About Climate Challenges is a Surprise Atop the Charts." *Public Radio International*, 9 July 2014, www.pri.org/stories/2014-07-09/classical-music-album-about-climate-challenges-surprise-atop-charts.

"Minecraft—Volume Beta." *Minecraft Wiki*, 27 Aug. 2020, minecraft.gamepedia.com/Minecraft_-_Volume_Beta. Accessed 4 Sept. 2020.

"Music." *Minecraft Wiki*, 31 Aug. 2020, minecraft.gamepedia.com/Music. Accessed 3 Sept. 2020.

Napolitano, Jayson. "5 Reasons Why Audio on the Nintendo 3DS Should Be Amazing." *Original Sound Version*, 17 Mar. 2011, www.originalsoundversion.com/5-reasons-why-audio-on-the-nintendo-3ds-should-be-amazing.

Nintendo. "Nintendo Support: System Menu Update History." *Nintendo Support*, en-americas-support.nintendo.com/app/answers/detail/a_id/231/~/system-menu-update-history. Accessed 2 Sept. 2020.

Nintendo. "Nintendo 3DS Sound." *Nintendo of Europe*, www.nintendo.co.uk/Nintendo-3DS-Family/Instant-Software/Nintendo-3DS-Sound/Nintendo-3DS-Sound-115638.html. Accessed 3 Aug. 2018.

Nintendo. Nintendo 3DS Sound, 2015. Retrieved from https://www.nintendo.co.uk/Nintendo-3DS-Family/Instant-Software/Nintendo-3DS-Sound/Nintendo-3DS-Sound-115638.html

"PS Vita Tech Specs." *IGN*, 30 Aug. 2013, www.ign.com/wikis/ps-vita/PS_Vita_Tech_Specs. Accessed 9 June 2021.

Savov, Vlad. "Sony Ericsson Xperia Play Review." *Engadget*, 28 Mar. 2011, www.engadget.com/2011-03-28-sony-ericsson-xperia-play-review.html. Accessed 2 Sept. 2020.

Sony. "Using Remote Play Via the Internet | PlayStation®Vita User's Guide." *PlayStation*, manuals.playstation.net/document/en/psvita/ps4link/viainternet.html. Accessed 10 Sept. 2020.

Sylvester, Niko. "How to Play Music on a PS Vita." *Lifewire*, 8 Mar. 2019, www.lifewire.com/play-music-on-ps-vita-2792783. Accessed 4 Sept. 2020.

T., Nick. "Did You Know Which Was the First Phone with Built-in Stereo Speakers?" *Phone Arena*, 17 July 2015, www.phonearena.com/news/Did-you-know-which-was-the-first-phone-with-built-in-stereo-speakers_id71659. Accessed 2 Sept. 2020.

"Tutorials/Redstone Music." *Minecraft Wiki*, 1 Aug. 2020, minecraft.gamepedia.com/Tutorials/Redstone_music. Accessed 3 Sept. 2020.

Webster, Andrew. "Five Years of Sword & Sworcery: The History of a Weird and Beautiful Game." *The Verge*, 24 Mar. 2016, www.theverge.com/2016/3/24/11297534/superbrothers-sword-and-sworcery-retrospective.

2012 in Review

February 16, 2012—*Beat Sneak Bandit*—iOS

PUBLISHER: Simogo. RELEASE DATE: February 16, 2012 (WW). COMPOSERS: Jonathan Eng and Simon Flesser. GENRE: Rhythm/Stealth/Puzzle. NOTABLE MUSICAL TRACK: "Intro."

Beat Sneak Bandit is a mobile game that combines the rhythm and stealth genres with a funky soundtrack. The game's sound design uses household sounds like clocks and phones as instruments. The beat as a regulator of character actions is yet another way to diversify the rhythm genre. Instead of simply pressing buttons based on icons that move across the screen, the player in *Beat Sneak Bandit* aligns inputs with the beat of the music to activate positive actions to the characters on-screen. The gameplay involves tapping on the device screen in rhythm with the music to move the bandit to collect clocks and avoid security guards and spotlights. The puzzles get progressively difficult and require rhythm and logic to complete. A circle at the top of the screen pulsates with the beat of the music, indicating the action that will happen to Beat Sneak Bandit when tapping the finger to the beat. The game consists of five chapters. The first four chapters have 14 stages. The last chapter of the game, "Finale: Duke Clockface's Groovy Disco Machine," is a steep increase in difficulty than the previous chapters (one missed beat makes all the difference). The game's soundtrack includes a baritone sax, flute, vibraphone, glockenspiel, percussion, cowbell, electronic sounds, clock ticks, and a squishy sound. The notable musical track, "Intro," is heard after the player taps the screen on the title logo. The track accompanies the cutscene that establishes the game's plot.

February 22, 2012—*Lumines: Electronic Symphony*—PS Vita

PUBLISHER: Ubisoft. RELEASE DATE: February 22, 2012 (NA, EU), April 19, 2012 (JP). COMPOSER: Makoto Asai. SERIES: *Lumines*. GENRE: Puzzle/Rhythm Music. NOTABLE MUSICAL TRACK: "Never."

Lumines: Electronic Symphony has a soundtrack from prominent electronic music composers and artists and elements of synaesthesia in the sound design. *Lumines: Electronic Symphony* is a puzzle game with gameplay traits like *Tetris* (falling geometric shapes) and *Hexic* (rotating pieces to arrange colors). Q Entertainment, founded by Tetsuya Mizuguchi, developed the game. Mizuguchi also worked on *Rez* and *Child of Eden*. Yoshitaka Asaji was an artist of synaesthesia with Q Entertainment who sought the balance between controller input and audio feedback. The sound design is inspired by the rise and fall of waves, similar to the player's moments of rhythm and calm during the musical journey.

Producer James Mielke requested licensing permissions for 250 songs over six months. He expedited the licensing agreements by requesting songs in WAV format instead of in multi-track data. The game's development team needed time to edit the music files to conform to the game engine. The team's artists designed the game's skins with a tone, pace, and color that somehow reflected the musical tracks. Since its early designs, this entry in the *Lumines* series does not reuse tracks from previous entries, particularly "Shinin" by Mondo Grosso, used in the original *Lumines* for PSP.

The soundtrack includes 34 licensed songs and 10 original songs. The game takes players through a diverse sampling of electronic music. The Master Mode and Stopwatch Mode use the musical tracks composed for this game. The notable musical track, "Never," is a licensed track by Orbit that accompanies the game's credits after completing the 33 licensed tracks in the Voyage game mode. There are 10 original tracks composed by Makoto Asai, accessible in secret bonus skins. The soundtrack was compiled by Makoto Asai, with licensed contributions by active members of the electronic music community, including The Chemical Brothers, Mark Ronson, Underworld, and LCD Soundsystem.

March 13, 2012—*Journey*—PS3

PUBLISHER: Sony. RELEASE DATE: March 13, 2012 (NA), March 14, 2012 (EU). COMPOSER: Austin Wintory. GENRE: Adventure/Art. NOTABLE MUSICAL TRACK: "Apotheosis (Final Level)." AWARDS: D.I.C.E. 2012 Original Music Composition, G.A.N.G 2013 Music of the Year, Best Original Soundtrack Album, Best Interactive Score, Best Original Instrumental, Best Original Vocal Song—Pop.

Journey was the first video game to be nominated for a Grammy award for its soundtrack. The game is a powerful musical and emotional experience with an adaptive sound design when playing alone or with online players. The musical score by Austin Wintory stands out in a game with a silent, faceless protagonist and minimal text. The game is meditative and artistic in its game and art design. The soundtrack is soothing, with memorable moments accentuated

by winds and strings. The main character communicates and interacts through body movement and a musical chime. The chime transforms cloths throughout the world into a free-flowing red fabric that reshapes the world. *Journey* received a nomination at the 2013 Grammy Awards for Best Score Soundtrack for Visual Media. To this day, *Journey* remains the only video game with a soundtrack nominated for this category. The game's soundtrack reached number 116 on the Billboard Sales Charts on April 27, 2012, the second-highest ranking for a video game album.

The instruments act as character motifs in the game's soundtrack. The bass flute represents the ancestors. The harp and viola represent other players. The music has different instrumentation depending on how many players are nearby. The orchestra represents the shooting star. The cello represents the player. The cellist of *Journey* was Tina Guo, who performed on the cello for many films, television series, and video games, including *Inception, Call of Duty: Black Ops II, Family Guy,* and *Batman v. Superman: Dawn of Justice.* The cello melody reflects the isolation and mystery of the game's world. The notable musical track, "Apotheosis (Final Level)," was the most challenging track for composer Austin Wintory to complete because it had to evoke an emotional response fitting for the culmination of the player's journey to the summit of the mountain.

August 7, 2012—*Sound Shapes*— PS Vita

PUBLISHER: Sony Computer Entertainment America. RELEASE DATE: August 7, 2012 (NA), August 15, 2012 (EU), September 27, 2012 (JP). COMPOSERS: Shaw-Han Liem, Jonathan Mak, Jim Guthrie, Deadmau5, and Beck. GENRE: Music/Platformer. NOTABLE MUSICAL TRACK: "Cities."

In *Sound Shapes*, players compose music by constructing interactive levels out of objects with musical properties. Each moving object in each stage contributes to the musical track. The player controls a blob-like entity that rolled and jumped through each stage, collecting musical

notes that become part of the music. All of
the moving elements of each stage react to
the music with unique audio effects. Some
examples include snare drums from lasers,
record scratches from monsters, and hums
from platforms. Other sounds arise from
interactions between the player avatar and
game objects. The sounds caused by the
player naturally aligned well into the musical meter. The further the player advances
in each stage, representing a track on a
record, the more sounds are added to the
music. The game's stages match the musical
styles, rather than the other way around.
Using the included level editor, the player
adds musical notes on a grid. The horizontal axis represents time, and the vertical
axis represents pitch. The player selects an
instrument for each note from a traditional
and electronic collection. Successful musicians, including deadmau5, Beck, and Jim
Guthrie, composed the tracks. Jim Guthrie influenced the industrial office stages,
and deadmau5 influenced the colorful
landscapes.

August 9, 2012—*Orgarhythm*— PS Vita

PUBLISHER: Xseed Games. RELEASE DATE:
August 9, 2012 (JP), November 18, 2012 (NA),
January 16, 2013 (EU). COMPOSER: Ayako
Minami. GENRE: God/Rhythm/RTS. NOTA-
BLE MUSICAL TRACK: "Holy Oratorio."

Orgarhythm combines a rhythm game
with a god game and a real-time strategy
game. The soundtrack blends tribal, rock,
and electric sounds which complement the
rhythm and real-time strategy genres. The
music is dynamic, increasing in complexity
as the player progresses and improves. The
player controls the God of Light, capable
of guiding soldiers through rhythm-based
actions. Progression is based on listening
and tapping to the beat. For example, each
stage starts with the musical track at level
1, a simple beat to tap. By tapping three
times to the beat correctly, the player enters
level 2, and the track adds another musical
instrument or sound. As the game adds new
elements to the track, the track evolves from
its rhythmic essence to dense tribal and rock

songs with electric guitar and vocal chants.
The sound of a clap indicates successful
taps on the beat. The sound of a snare drum
shows unsuccessful taps off the beat.

October 11, 2012—*Bravely Default*—3DS

PUBLISHER: Nintendo of America. RELEASE
DATE: October 11, 2012 (JP), December 6,
2013 (EU), February 7, 2014 (NA). COM-
POSER: Revo. SERIES: *Bravely Default*. GENRE:
RPG. NOTABLE MUSICAL TRACK: "Serpent
Eating the Horizon (Final Boss Theme)."

The soundtrack of *Bravely Default*
includes rock and roll and Celtic genres,
with each character indicated in the music
by a specific instrument. Each of the four
warriors of light has an original musical
theme, which plays at various points during
the game. A solo instrument identifies each
character:

• Tiz's theme has a tin whistle.
• Agnes's theme has a violin.
• Edea has a soprano saxophone.
• Ringabel has an accordion.

The character themes are especially pronounced during combat—the theme
plays whenever a character uses a special
attack to improve the team's stats. The
music indicates which character is summoning the special attack, and the team
stats improve as the music plays. The four
character themes merge in a rock and
electronic setting in the notable musical
track, "Serpent Eating the Horizon," the
medley at the final boss's fifth stage. The
track is a subtle reminder that despite the
battle being epic and final, the moment is
ultimately about the four heroes conquer-
ing all odds.

November 18, 2012—Nintendo Wii U

MANUFACTURER: Nintendo. RELEASE DATE:
November 18, 2012 (NA), November 30, 2012

(EU), December 8, 2012 (JP). Manufacturing Dates: November 18, 2012–January 31,
2017. Launch price: $299.99 (Basic), $349.99
(Deluxe with *Nintendo Land*). Model number: WUP-001 (Basic Set), WUP-101 (Deluxe
Set). Audio: LPCM 5.1.

The Wii U was the first home console to
play games without the TV in Off-TV Play
mode. Released by Nintendo, the Wii U was
the first home console by Nintendo with an
HDMI-out port and high-definition graphics. The Wii U is backward-compatible with
Wii games (in Wii mode) and Wii peripherals (in Wii and Wii U mode), including the
Wii Remote, Wii Nunchuk, Wii sensor bar,
Wii A/V Multi Out cable, and other Wii
peripherals.

The Wii U Gamepad is the Wii U's
unique controller. It is a large controller
with a touchscreen, NFC support (for reading data from Nintendo's Amiibo figures),
built-in IR blaster (for controlling a TV),
volume slider, 3.5mm audio-out port, and
an internal microphone (to the left of the
Home button). The Wii U Gamepad interacts with the Wii U console wirelessly. The
Wii U console streams video and audio to
the Wii U Gamepad wirelessly. However,
the Wii U Gamepad needs to be close to the
Wii U to function. Many Wii U games support Off-TV Play mode, which was the ability to play games entirely from the Wii U
Gamepad without a TV.

Audio from the GamePad can complement the audio that the console sends to

**Nintendo Wii U gamepad 2012. The inter-
nal speakers are located on the lower-left
and lower-right corners of the device. The
internal microphone is located on the bottom of the device (Mariofan13, https://
creativecommons.org/licenses/by-sa/4.0/
legalcode**

the user's television or surround sound system. The Wii U GamePad has two internal
speakers for stereophonic sound and simulates pseudo-surround sound. Multiplayer
games commonly use the internal microphone for voice chat. The microphone also
records voice messages.

The Wii U console has an HDMI-out
port that supports LPCM 5.1 surround
sound, stereo, and mono audio. The Wii U
console contains the same A/V Multi Out
port as the Wii for composite video and
analog stereo audio. So, the Wii U supports
digital and analog audio options. There
are no options for digital surround sound
formats. Firmware 4.0.0 added Dolby Pro
Logic II support to Wii Mode (to play Wii
games on the Wii U). Games for the original Wii supporting DPLII output surround
sound on the Wii U. Otherwise, the system
defaults to stereo audio.

On January 31, 2017, the Wii U ceased
manufacturing. The Wii U had the lowest
sales of hardware and software of all of the
Nintendo systems. The Wii U's name confused consumers who recognized the Wii
U as an upgraded Wii, which was not valid.
Although Nintendo's marketing showed
the Wii U's distinctive feature (the Wii U
Gamepad), consumers could not understand its purpose. Another factor that hurt
the Wii U's sales was the lack of support
from third-party developers, partly due
to the contrasting hardware architecture
from the PS4 and Xbox One.

**Nintendo Wii U back 2012. The audio out-
put ports are A/V (with composite video
and stereo audio RCA adapter) and HDMI
(Evan-Amos, "Nintendo-Wii-U–Console-
BR").**

November 18, 2012—*Disney Epic Mickey 2: The Power of Two*—PS3

Publisher: Disney Interactive. Release Date: November 18, 2012 (NA), November 23, 2012 (EU). Composer: Jim Dooley. Series: *Epic Mickey*. Genre: Action-adventure. Notable musical track: "Help Me Help You (The Mad Doctor's Song)."

Disney Epic Mickey 2: The Power of Two presents the game's sound design as a theatrical presentation of a Disney musical. The Mad Doctor delivers plot points and narratives to the player via melody and lyrics. Lyricist Mike Himelstein drew inspiration from the Broadway musical *The Music Man*. The songs are featured in cinematic sequences, so the player must strategize and pick up clues during the musical numbers sung by the Mad Doctor. The notable musical track, "Help Me Help You (The Mad Doctor's Song)," is heard during the game's introductory cutscene, establishing the plot through song. The Mad Doctor sings to convince the citizens of Wasteland that he has changed his ways from the previous game and that he wants to save them from impending danger. The music could very well fit in a stage musical. Throughout most of the game, three audio tracks run concurrently, with particular instrumentation dropping in or out depending on how much paint Mickey used.

Sources

Beausoleil, Michael. "What Make the Wii U Nintendo's Greatest Failure." *Medium*, 7 Nov. 2019, medium.com/@beausoleil/what-make-the-wii-u-nintendos-greatest-failure-fa758aedbf8. Accessed 10 Sept. 2020.

Davis, Justin. "Beat Sneak Bandit Review." *IGN*, 22 Feb. 2012, www.ign.com/articles/2012/02/22/beat-sneak-bandit-review.

Dyason, Matthew. "Bravely Default's Empowering Music." *YouTube*, 27 Apr. 2017, www.youtube.com/watch?v=COgzJey4EAc.

"Epic Mickey 2: The Power of Two." *Disney Wiki*, 20 May 2021, disney.wikia.com/wiki/Epic_Mickey_2:_The_Power_of_Two. Accessed 9 June 2021.

Kotowski, Don. "Bravely Default—Flying Fairy—Original Soundtrack." *Video Game Music Online*, 1 Aug. 2012, www.vgmonline.net/bravelydefault/.

Magulick, Aaron. "Orgarhythm Review." *BagoGames*, 30 Oct. 2012, bagogames.com/listen-beat-orgarhytm-review/.

Mielke, James. "Lumines Electronic Symphony: Q Entertainment's Love Letter to Electronic Music." *PlayStation.Blog*, 1 Feb. 2012, blog.playstation.com/2012/02/01/lumines-electronic-symphony-q-entertainments-love-letter-to-electronic-music/. Accessed 4 Sept. 2020.

Mielke, James. "Lumines Electronic Symphony: The Untold Story." *Gamasutra—The Art & Business of Making Games*, 30 July 2012, www.gamasutra.com/view/feature/174913/lumines_electronic_symphony_the_.php. Accessed 4 Sept. 2020.

Minotti, Mike. "How Bravely Default's Epic Soundtrack Empowers Players." *VentureBeat*, 27 Apr. 2017, venturebeat.com/2017/04/27/how-bravely-defaults-epic-soundtrack-empowers-players/.

Nintendo. "Disney Epic Mickey 2: The Power of Two for Wii U." 2016, www.nintendo.com/games/detail/D5r6WvYO5Al9w0Pnt_Rbq45_d3Wk2Kcv.

Nintendo. "How to Use Surround Sound on the Wii U." *Nintendo Support*, en-americas-support.nintendo.com/app/answers/detail/a_id/1508/~/how-to-use-surround-sound-on-the-wii-u. Accessed 3 Aug. 2018.

Nintendo. "IR Information: Financial Data—Top Selling Title Sales Units—Wii U Software." *Nintendo Co., Ltd*, 31 Mar. 2020, www.nintendo.co.jp/ir/en/finance/software/wiiu.html. Accessed 10 Sept. 2020.

Nintendo. "Wii U—Technical Specs." *Nintendo*, www.nintendo.com/wiiu/features/tech-specs/. Accessed 3 Aug. 2018.

NintendoFan. "Audio capabilities: Nintendo Wii U (comprehensive post)." 17 Dec. 2012, thewiiu.com/topic/8300-audio-capabilities-nintendo-wii-u-comprehensive-post/.

Pac12345. "Wii U audio FAQ (5.1 surround sound)." 11 Dec. 2012, www.gamefaqs.com/boards/631516-wii-u/64891724.

PlayStation. "Sound Shapes™Level Editor Feature." *YouTube*, 1 Aug. 2012, www.youtube.com/watch?v=Tdm2n_w9BzI. Accessed 5 Sept. 2020.

Polygon. "Why Journey's last song was the hardest to compose." *YouTube*, 18 Nov. 2019, youtu.be/iUaPHTC2TjI. Accessed 4 Sept. 2020.

Stark, Chelsea. "'Sound Shapes' Musical Game Turns Players Into Composers [REVIEW]." *Mashable*, 8 Aug. 2012, mashable.com/2012/08/08/sound-shapes-review/.

Taylor, Jordyn. "How Video Game 'Disney Epic Mickey 2: The Power of 2' Is Like a Musical." *Backstage*, 16 Aug. 2019, www.backstage.com/news/dooley-and-himelstein-disney-epic-mickey-2-power-2/. Accessed 10 Apr. 2021.

"Wii U GamePad Microphone Use (Concept)." *Giant Bomb*, www.giantbomb.com/wii-u-gamepad-microphone-use/3015-7836/. Accessed 29 Sept. 2020.

2013 in Review

June 14, 2013—*The Last of Us*—PS3

PUBLISHER: Sony. RELEASE DATE: June 14, 2013 (WW). COMPOSER: Gustavo Santaolalla. SERIES: *The Last of Us*. GENRE: Action-adventure. NOTABLE MUSICAL TRACK: "Home." AWARDS: D.I.C.E. 2014 Sound Design.

The soundtrack of *The Last of Us* is melancholy in mood, reflecting the isolation and loneliness of the game's characters. The game contains the first video game soundtrack by Gustavo Santaolalla. The soundtrack is not intrusive during gameplay. The player takes control of Joel and Ellie, an adult man and a teenage girl traveling together amidst a version of the United States of America transformed by a fungus that makes humans zombie-like. Although the game contains many moments of terror, the music reflects Joel and Ellie's emotions. Santaolalla matches the intensity of the music to the characters. Most of the game's musical tracks use acoustic guitar in a minimalistic approach. There are only a handful of scenes where the music enters the forefront. Two notable tracks during crucial game scenes are "All Gone (No Escape)" and "The Path (A New Beginning)." During the more stressful and intense moments, Santaolalla uses tribal drum patterns to invoke the fighting spirit. The notable musical track "Home" plays near the game's ending. The track is expressive with a sense of melancholy that matches the gravity of the situation of Joel, who just saved Ellie.

November 15, 2013—Sony PlayStation 4

MANUFACTURER: Sony. RELEASE DATE: November 15, 2013 (NA), November 29, 2013 (EU), February 22, 2014 (JP). PRODUCTION DATES: November 15, 2013—Still in production. LAUNCH PRICE: $399.99. MODEL NUMBER: CUH-1001A. AUDIO: LPCM 7.1.

The PlayStation 4 was the first home console to support 4K resolutions and purely digital audio options. The only A/V ports are HDMI and S/PDIF (optical audio). The 4K resolution support is only for streaming video and video files. The PS4 includes a Blu-ray player. Therefore it couldn't play 4K Ultra Blu-ray discs. Like the PS3, the PS4 integrated with the PS Vita for Remote Play capabilities (the PS4 couldn't integrate with the older Sony PSP). Unlike the PS3, Sony designed the PS4's hardware for Remote Play, so all PS4 games function in Remote Play on the PS Vita.

The PS4's controller is called the DualShock 4. It contains a 3.5mm audio-out port for stereo audio. This port is most commonly used to hook up a headset to talk and play to others during multiplayer matches. Although the PS4 console lacks an analog audio option, the PS4 can be configured to output all system audio through the DualShock 4's headphone port (via the Bluetooth protocol). The headphone port is the only solution for analog audio. The DualShock 4 also contains an internal mono speaker (like the Wii Remote). Some developers creatively used the DualShock 4's speaker and lightbar.

The PS4 contains a dedicated hardware audio module that can support in-game chat with minimal external resources and many MP3 streams for use in in-game audio. The AMD TrueAudio package of user-programmable audio DSPs offloads audio processing from the CPU. Possible effects include 3D audio effects, audio compression and decompression,

Sony PS4 back 2013. The audio output ports are S/PDIF and HDMI (Evan-Amos, "Sony-PlayStation-4-PS4-Console-BR").

reverberation, and voice stream processing. The console defaulted to audio via HDMI; however, the Primary Output Port in the Audio Output settings could also be set to the Digital Out port or headphones connected to a DualShock 4 controller. The Audio Format choices were Linear PCM (maximum 7.1), Bitstream (Dolby), and Bitstream (DTS). The PS4 supports LPCM 7.1, Dolby TrueHD 7.1, DTS-HD Master Audio 7.1, Dolby Digital Plus, Dolby Digital 5.1, and DTS 5.1.

The PS4 Slim, released on September 15, 2016, lacked the optical audio port but added support for USB 3.1, Bluetooth 4.0, and 5Ghz Wi-Fi. The PS4 Pro, released worldwide on November 10, 2016, retains the changes from the PS4 Slim and added more RAM and support for 4K gaming and 4K streaming video (no support for 4K Ultra Blu-ray discs).

November 21, 2013—*Super Mario 3D World*—Wii U

PUBLISHER: Nintendo. RELEASE DATE: November 21, 2013 (JP), November 22, 2013 (NA), November 29, 2013 (EU). COMPOSERS: Mahito Yokota, Toru Minegishi, Koji Kondo, and Yasuaki Iwata. SERIES: *Super Mario Bros.* GENRE: Platformer. NOTABLE MUSICAL TRACK: "Battle on the Great Tower 2 (The Great Tower Showdown 2)."

The soundtrack for *Super Mario 3D World* features music for a big band, including a complete horn section with trumpets and saxophones. The game's soundtrack expanded upon the live instrumentation used in the soundtrack of *Super Mario Galaxy*. The game uses the internal microphone of the Wii U Gamepad like the internal microphone of the Famicom controller. Blowing into the Wii U Gamepad's microphone destroys Blurkers, pink block-like enemies that guard secret passages, for a short time. The game's soundtrack includes live recordings from the Mario 3D World Big Band. The musical track for Shifty Boo Mansion reflects the macabre with pizzicato strings, harpsichord, theremin, and solo strings. All of the tracks used for the moments with Bowser

are arrangements of the track from Bowser's first appearance in the game's introduction ("To the Sprixie Kingdom"). The notable musical track, "Battle on the Great Tower 2 (The Great Tower Showdown 2)," heard in Bowser's Highway Showdown, features the band with electric and harmonic guitars and drums. The final boss encounter with multiple Cat Bowsers (Meowsers) occurs as Mario and friends ascend a tall perilous tower. After Cat Bowser multiplies into more copies, the techno beat kicks in briefly as the musical arrangement resembles "Mars, the Bringer of War" by Gustav Holst.

November 22, 2013—Microsoft Xbox One

MANUFACTURER: Microsoft. RELEASE DATE: November 22, 2013 (NA, EU). PRODUCTION DATES: November 22, 2013—Still in production (Xbox One S). LAUNCH PRICE: $499.99. MODEL NUMBER: 1540. AUDIO: LPCM 7.1 (Dolby Atmos added in update).

The Xbox One was the first home console to support the 3D audio formats Dolby Atmos and DTS:X. Released by Microsoft, the Xbox One was able to control both a cable box and television using an IR blaster and voice commands interpreted by the Microsoft Kinect 2.0. At launch, the Xbox One console included an Xbox One controller and the Kinect 2.0. The Kinect 2.0 improved upon the original Kinect with three times the accuracy, a camera that captures 1080p video, the ability to detect 25 joints, and a microphone that detects voice commands. The Xbox One was the first home console to include an HDMI-in port. This port served to connect a cable box to the Xbox One. The Xbox One can control the cable box and TV via voice commands from the Kinect. The Xbox One had TV features, including OneGuide, a TV guide, and App Channels to access online streaming services. The Xbox One also includes an IR blaster, a device that sends IR signals to a cable box and TV to control them like a remote control. Some of the recognized voice commands are as follows:

- Turn on and off the TV.
- Switch to a channel.
- Take a screenshot of a game.
- Record game footage.
- Turn on or off the Xbox One.
- Sign in and out of Xbox Live.
- Invite friends to a party.
- Switch between apps.

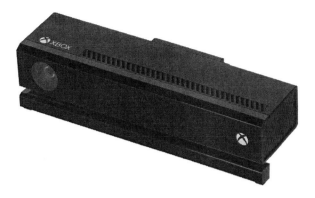

Consumers were greatly concerned about their privacy because the Kinect was always active even when the Xbox One was off. Although Microsoft assured consumers that the Kinect only listened for the Xbox on and off commands, consumers were wary of their private conversations being sent to Microsoft for device improvements. In 2014, Microsoft sold the Xbox One without the Kinect for $399.99. The reduced price and removing the Kinect and its privacy concerns helped sell more Xbox One consoles.

Microsoft Kinect for Xbox One 2013. The microphone array is located at the bottom of the device. The Kinect communicates with the Xbox One through the Kinect port (Evan-Amos, "Xbox-One-Kinect").

The Xbox One supports digital surround sound for games and Blu-ray or DVD movies. The Xbox One included a Blu-ray player. At launch, the available audio options were HDMI (stereo uncompressed, 5.1 uncompressed, 7.1 uncompressed, DTS 5.1 compressed) and optical (stereo uncompressed, DTS 5.1 compressed). The March 2014 system update added a Bitstream Out option over HDMI and optical (DTS 5.1 compressed and Dolby Digital 5.1 compressed), accommodating soundbars and specific surround sound headsets that only support Dolby Digital. The Xbox One does not have an analog A/V output.

The Xbox One S (1681), released worldwide on August 2, 2016, for $299.99, added support for 4K multimedia content either on disc or through select video streaming services (Netflix, Hulu, and Amazon). The Xbox One X (1787), released worldwide on November 7, 2017, for $499.99, was the first home console to support native 4K gaming with visual and audio enhancements for Xbox One X Enhanced games. The Xbox One X shipped at launch with native support for the 3D audio formats of Dolby Atmos and DTS:X. The Xbox One S All-Digital Edition (1681), released worldwide on April 16, 2019, for $249, was the first completely digital home console from Microsoft, lacking a disc drive and a disc eject button.

In a firmware update to the Xbox One and Xbox One S on April 6, 2017, the systems gained support for Dolby Atmos and DTS:X for home theaters via bitstream passthrough via HDMI. On this date, the Xbox One S and Xbox One became the first video gaming systems with support for 3D audio. The first Xbox One games with Dolby Atmos audio were released simultaneously as the Xbox One X in November 2017. Dolby Atmos requires that the user download the Dolby Access app from the Windows

Microsoft Xbox One back 2013. The audio output ports are S/PDIF and HDMI. The audio input ports are HDMI (Evan-Amos, "Xbox-One-Console-BL").

Microsoft Xbox One S back 2016. The audio output ports are S/PDIF and HDMI. The audio input ports are HDMI (Evan-Amos, "Microsoft-Xbox-One-S-Console-BR").

Store on the Xbox One console. Optionally, the player can purchase Dolby Atmos for Headphones functionality from the Dolby Access App for a one-time fee of $15. Also, the player must configure the audio settings on the Xbox One properly. For a home theater setup, set the audio to "Bitstream out" via HDMI audio and the Bitstream format to "Dolby Atmos." For headphones, set the HDMI and Optical audio to Headset format and the Bitstream format to Off.

On July 8, 2020, Xbox One systems received support for DTS:X for home theaters and DTS Headphone:X. Like Dolby Atmos, users need to download the DTS Sound Unbound app from the Xbox Store for DTS:X for home theaters functionality and, optionally, pay the one-time fee of $20 through the app for DTS Headphone:X functionality. As of 2021, Microsoft only supports the Xbox One S, first manufactured in 2016. On July 16, 2020, all other models ceased manufacturing. Microsoft gathered anticipation for its next home console, the Xbox Series X.

SOURCES

Aerisavion. "Gustavo Santaolalla—The Last of Us (album Review)." *Sputnikmusic*, 12 July 2017, www.sputnikmusic.com/review/74256/Gustavo-Santaolalla-The-Last-of-Us/.

Dolby. "How to Get the Best Sound from Your Xbox One." *Dolby*, 14 Apr. 2014, wayback. archive.org/web/20150919074414/blog.dolby. com/2014/04/get-best-sound-xbox-one/.

Dolby. "How to Set Up the PlayStation 4 for Great Game Sound." *Dolby*, 18 Nov. 2013, wayback. archive.org/web/20151210032308/blog.dolby. com/2013/11/set-playstation-4-great-game-sound/.

Kondo, Koji. "Super Mario's Maestro: A Q&A with Nintendo's Koji Kondo." Interview by Bob Mackey. *USGamer.net*, 10 Dec. 2014, www. usgamer.net/articles/koji-kondo-interview-nintendo.

McDonald, Richard. "Super Mario 3D World OST (Review)." *Original Sound Version*, 21 Mar. 2014, www.originalsoundversion.com/super-mario-3d-world-ost-review-2/.

Microsoft. "Choosing Speaker Audio Settings on Xbox One." *Xbox Support*, support.xbox. com/en-US/xbox-one/console/configure-audio-settings. Accessed 3 Aug. 2018.

Napolitano, Jayson. "Super Mario 3D World Soundtrack is Another Masterpiece." *Destructoid*, 15 Nov. 2013, www.destructoid.com/super-mario-3d-world-soundtrack-is-another-masterpiece-265455.phtml.

Pino, Nick. "PS4 Pro Vs Xbox One X: Which 4K Console is Better?" *TechRadar*, 16 Jan. 2019, www.techradar.com/news/ps4-pro-vs-xbox-one-x-how-are-the-mid-generation-consoles-shaping-up. Accessed 20 Sept. 2020.

PlayStation. "Gustavo Santaolalla: The Music of The Last of Us." *YouTube*, 17 May 2013, www. youtube.com/watch?v=Ejdjcun2Jo4.

"PlayStation 4 Secrets." *Edepot*, www.edepot.com/playstation4.html. Accessed 29 Sept. 2020.

"PlayStation3 Super Audio CD FAQ." *PS3SACD. com*, 29 Sept. 2012, www.ps3sacd.com/faq.html. Accessed 22 Apr. 2020.

"PS4 Remote Play." *PlayStation*, www.playstation. com/en-us/explore/ps4/remote-play/. Accessed 31 Aug. 2018.

Sony. "PS4 Audio Output Settings." *PlayStation*, manuals.playstation.net/document/en/ps4/settings/audiooutput.html. Accessed 3 Aug. 2018.

Techno Dad. "Dolby Atmos Setup for Xbox One X | 8 Atmos Titles on Netflix!" *YouTube*, 30 Nov. 2017, youtu.be/Aj6a3JE9DPA. Accessed 21 Sept. 2020.

Whitten, Marc. "Prepare for Titanfall: Marc Whitten Provides Details on Xbox One March Update." *Microsoft*, 5 Mar. 2014, news.xbox. com/en-us/2014/03/05/xbox-one-march-update/.

Willings, Adrian. "Dolby Atmos for Gaming: What is It and Which Games Support It." *Pocket-lint*, 12 Aug. 2020, www.pocket-lint. com/games/news/dolby/141761-dolby-atmos-for-gaming-what-is-it-and-what-games-support-it. Accessed 21 Sept. 2020.

Yokota, Mahito. "Super Mario 3D World Composers Talk Cats, Dogs, and More." Interview by Jayson Napolitano. *Destructoid*, 6 Nov. 2013, www.destructoid.com/super-mario-3d-world-composers-talk-cats-dogs-and-more-264473. phtml.

2014 in Review

April 3, 2014—*Monument Valley*— iOS

PUBLISHER: ustwo Games. RELEASE DATE: April 3, 2014. (WW) COMPOSER: Stafford Bawler. SERIES: *Monument Valley*. GENRE: Puzzle. NOTABLE MUSICAL TRACK: "Amateur Cartography."

The sound design of *Monument Valley* takes influence from the ambient work of composer Brian Eno. The game has a minimalistic soundtrack with ambient, natural sounds. The gameplay involves interacting with the M.C. Escher-inspired puzzles to navigate Ida, the protagonist, around the environment. The music resembles the unique settings. The atmospheric, meditative nature of the music subtly complements the game using bell-like drones alongside the soundscapes. To enhance the dimension of realism, sounds of rain and stormy winds swirl around the music. Other sound design elements help immerse the player in a new world, including shifting stone platforms. The notable musical track, "Amateur Cartography," begins with lo-fi bell-like tones. Then the track adds an electric bass sound and drum beat. Additional percussion layers add more sounds to the track. Each short musical idea is repeated countless times throughout the track. Near the end of the track, the percussion sounds drop out, leaving the melody, echoes, and the bass.

May 20, 2014—*Transistor*—PS4

PUBLISHER: Supergiant Games. RELEASE DATE: May 20, 2014 (WW). COMPOSER: Darren Korb. GENRE: Turn-based strategy. NOTABLE MUSICAL TRACK: "In Circles."

Transistor includes innovative diegetic use of the PS4 controller's audio speaker. The game was the second game by Supergiant Games and the second for composer Darren Korb, who also composed the music for *Bastion* in 2012. Composer Darren Korb describes the musical style of the soundtrack as "old-world electronic post-rock." To fit that genre of music, the instruments used include electric guitars, harps, accordions, mandolins, electric piano, and synth pads. Additionally, the software overlays an EQ (equalization) filter over the music during the pause and "TURN()" menus to have a distant, blurred sound.

Transistor uses the audio speaker of the PS4 DualShock 4 in a creative and diegetic way. In the game, the player controls Red, the woman who carries the sword known as Transistor. Although Red doesn't speak, the sword speaks through the DualShock 4's speaker. Since Red is the closest person to the sword, it makes sense that the player's controller's audio speaker emits the sword's voice. The notable musical track, "In Circles," stands out from the other musical tracks, not just for its use of 5/4 meter, but also for its vocals, provided by singer Ashley Barrett. Korb eases the tension by moving from five beats per measure to three during the track's refrain.

May 29, 2014—*Two Dots*—iOS

PUBLISHER: Betaworks Studio. RELEASE DATE: May 29, 2014 (WW). COMPOSER: Cody Uhler and Ross Wariner. GENRE: Puzzle. NOTABLE MUSICAL TRACK: "Dusty Dots."

Two Dots is a mobile puzzle game with a calm, soothing soundtrack that promotes thinking. The gameplay features interactive sound effects that do not detract from the music. Composers Cody Uhler and Ross Wariner are members of Upright T-Rex Music, a custom music company. Each time that the player connects dots, the game plays harmonizing tones. Each world has matching music, characters, and animations. For example, the winter levels contain a Yeti wearing sunglasses that moves its arms in time with the music. There is also a kraken in the water world and a fox in the desert world. The notable musical track, "Dusty Dots," is the game's main theme. The track's musical style mimics Jewish music, emphasized by the solo trumpet and violin with the double bass plucking the bass line. The bass drum accentuates the bass line. The marimba and guitar fill out the harmony. The pizzicato strings and short sounds add punch to the track. When heard again during gameplay, "Dusty Dots" has more sparse instrumentation. In gameplay, the guitar, bell pads, and organ timbres are more pronounced. The game's audio complements the visuals and gameplay to direct the game's flow and give a sense of direction toward a goal.

September 9, 2014—*Destiny*—PS4

PUBLISHER: Activision. RELEASE DATE: September 9, 2014 (WW). COMPOSERS: Michael Salvatori, C Paul Johnson, Martin O'Donnell, Skye Lewin, Stan LePard, Paul McCartney. SERIES: *Destiny*. GENRE: 1st person shooter. NOTABLE MUSICAL TRACK: "Hope for the Future (Credits)." AWARDS: D.I.C.E. 2015 Original Music Composition, D.I.C.E. 2015 Sound Design., G.A.N.G. 2015 Music of the Year, Best Original Soundtrack Album, Best Original Vocal Song—Choral, Best Original Vocal Song—Pop, Game Awards 2014 Best Score/Soundtrack.

The soundtrack of *Destiny* marks a collaboration with Marty O'Donnell and Sir Paul McCartney. The soundtrack marked Marty O'Donnell's final work for Bungie, after years of composing for the Halo franchise and several games before that. Unlike the Halo series, where musical tracks were only two to three minutes long, O'Donnell has stated that the soundtrack for Destiny has no time restrictions, with the pieces clocking in "as long as they need to be." Michael Salvatori, C Paul Johnson, Martin O'Donnell, Skye Lewin, and Stan LePard composed the soundtrack, with contributions and input from British musician Paul McCartney. O'Donnell reportedly approached McCartney to suggest that writing a video game score could be challenging since the music must change depending on how a player navigates the game. O'Donnell collaborated with Paul McCartney on the soundtrack for the better part of two years, as they traded ideas, melody samples, and themes back and

forth. The notable musical track "Hope for the Future" is heard in the game's ending credits. As Sir Paul McCartney's theme song, the musical track was recorded with a 120-piece orchestra at Abbey Road, with Sir George Martin's son, Giles, conducting, and Madonna and U2 producer Mark Stent producing.

October 21, 2014—*Fantasia: Music Evolved*—Xbox One

PUBLISHER: Disney Interactive Studios. RELEASE DATE: October 21, 2014 (NA). DEVELOPER: Harmonix. COMPOSER: Inon Zur. GENRE: Music/Rhythm. NOTABLE MUSICAL TRACK: "Scout's Song."

Fantasia: Music Evolved is the only Kinect game to allow players to remix music. The game is a Harmonix music/rhythm game that allows players to create remixes, original melodies, and rhythms of classical and pop songs using their bodies and the Microsoft Kinect sensor. The game takes inspiration from Disney's 1940 musical film *Fantasia*, specifically the Sorcerer's Apprentice section. Unlike other music and rhythm games that use the Kinect, this game adds the additional ability to create original melodies and instrumentation using only your hands and arms. The Kinect is required to play the game. It is not surprising that the developer of the game was Harmonix, the developer also responsible for *Guitar Hero*, *Rock Band*, and *Dance Central*. One or two players conduct, create, and remix music using the Kinect sensor.

The song list includes classical and pop songs. The player interacted with the game in *Fantasia: Music Evolved* with swipes, punches, and traces. Rather than respond to a prompt on screen that matches a note in the music, the game encourages movement and music transformation. Numerous times within a piece are "switch cues," which allow the player to swipe toward an instrument group and mix up to three mixes on the fly to create an original remix. Each performance can be saved and played back. After completing objectives in Story Mode, "compositional spells" are unlocked.

A few times during a piece, the player can move his or her hands and body to create an original melodic and rhythmic pattern which the game adds as a layer to the music. The Kinect sensor is accurate in registering a player's response to the visual cues of choreography.

The only original playable track by composer Inon Zur is "Scout's Song" (the remaining playable musical tracks are classical and popular songs). Scout is the former apprentice to Yen Sid, who serves as a guide to the player in how to remix music. Using her power without Yen Sid's teaching, she accidentally infected the realms with the Noise, the antagonistic force in the game. The musical track is accessible near the end of Story Mode. The song is the most challenging song to complete in the game. The musical track features violins, drums, and electronic beats and synths, with Lindsey Sterling as the violin soloist.

December 5, 2014—Game Awards—Event

The Game Awards are the most-watched awards show for video games, with over 45 million viewers watching the Game Awards in 2019. The first Game Awards were held live at the AXIS Theater (now the Zappos Theater) in Las Vegas on December 5, 2014. After Spike TV dropped its own awards show, Geoff Keighley, a Canadian games journalist who produced the Spike Video Game Awards, collaborated with Sony, Microsoft, Nintendo, and game publishers to create a new awards show for games independent of television companies. The Awards ceremony was live-streamed and broadcast through the online networks of the game consoles and Valve's Steam. Gamers are more likely to watch the Game Awards on their gaming machines than on a traditional cable network. Twenty-eight industry experts did the awards by jury voting with nominations by an advisory committee from Microsoft, Sony, Nintendo, AMD, EA, Activision, Rockstar Games, Ubisoft, Valve, and Warner Bros. Interactive Entertainment. The fans also voted for some awards. After the first year, the Awards

were held live at the Microsoft Theater in Los Angeles. In the first year, the only category for audio was "Best Score/Soundtrack," which was awarded to *Destiny*, with *Transistor* as a nominee. The Game Awards in 2017 added "Best Audio Design." These two categories remain in 2021.

Sources

Bilton, Nick. "A Closer Connection for Smartphone Games and Soundtracks." *Bits Blog*, 9 June 2014, bits.blogs.nytimes.com/2014/06/09/for-smartphone-games-attention-for-soundtracks/.

Delahunty-Light, Zoe. "The DualShock 4's Speaker and Lightbar Make These PS4 Games 100% Better." *Official PlayStation Magazine*, 26 Jan. 2018, www.gamesradar.com/games-are-way-cooler-when-played-dualshock-4/. Accessed 23 Sept. 2020.

Good, Owen. "The Winners and Nominees of the 2011 Spike Video Game Awards." *Kotaku*, 11 Dec. 2011, kotaku.com/the-winners-and-nominees-of-the-2011-spike-video-game-a-5867018. Accessed 2 Sept. 2020.

Hill, Katrina. "Two Dots Review." *Arcade Sushi*, 31 May 2014, arcadesushi.com/two-dots-review-ios/.

Jones, Alex. "Monument Valley Game Audio Review." *The Sound Architect*, 28 Mar. 2015, www.thesoundarchitect.co.uk/articlesandreviews/monumentvalleyreview/.

Korb, Darren. "The Holistic Master of Video Game Music: An Interview with Darren Korb." Interview by Juan M. Fontan. *The Indie Game Website*, 9 Mar. 2018, www.indiegamewebsite.com/2018/03/09/interview-darren-korb/.

Korb, Darren. Interview. *The Wayfaring Dreamer*, 5 Mar. 2015, thewayfaringdreamer.com/darren-korb-interview/.

Lomas, Natasha. "Monument Valley, Ustwo's Sumptuous Escher-Inspired IOS Game, Lands Globally on April 3." *TechCrunch*, 26 Mar. 2014, techcrunch.com/2014/03/26/monument-valley-price-and-launch-date/.

Mitroff, Sarah. "TwoDots Review." *CNET*, 2 Dec. 2014, www.cnet.com/products/twodots/review/.

O'Donnell, Martin. "Home." *Marty O'Donnell Music*, martyodonnellmusic.com. Accessed 7 Aug. 2018.

O'Donnell, Martin. "Martin O'Donnell Interview." Interview by Sam Bandah. *UKMusic*, 1 Nov. 2007, web.archive.org/web/20140819090449/www.ukmusic.com/music/martin-o-donnell-interview/.

Zur, Inon. "Home." *Inon Zur*, www.inonzur.com. Accessed 6 Aug. 2018.

Zur, Inon. Interview. *GSoundtracks*, web.archive.org/web/20161211123518/gsoundtracks.com/interviews/zur.htm. Accessed 6 Aug. 2018.

2015 in Review

March 11, 2015—*Ori and the Blind Forest*—Xbox One

PUBLISHER: Microsoft Studios. U.S. RELEASE: March 11, 2015 (WW). COMPOSER: Gareth Coker. SERIES: *Ori*. GENRE: Platformer/ Adventure/Metroidvania. NOTABLE MUSICAL TRACK: "Main Menu." AWARDS: D.I.C.E. 2016 Original Music Composition, G.A.N.G. 2016 Audio of the Year, Best Original Instrumental, Best Audio Mix.

The soundtrack of *Ori and the Blind Forest* harkens back to a mythical world through folk music with Celtic themes. The Nashville Music Scoring Orchestra performed the soundtrack. The music is moderately paced, enough that the player can appreciate its depth and character while playing the game. The piano is featured prominently throughout the game. Solo recorder, alto flute, oboe, bansuri, and vocal sounds add atmosphere to the melodies.

The main menu track, "Main Menu," is not on the official soundtrack as composer Gareth Coker did not realize the track's popularity. The track does not contribute to the game's narrative. The instrumentation consists of piano, solo female voice, strings, oboe, cymbal, and crotales. The voice sings the melody on "ooh," doubled by the high register of the piano. The human voice in the track is Aeralie Brighton. On the second iteration, the strings also play the melody and fill out the sound with lush harmonies. The crotales add a nice ring to the track, suggesting a hint of magic.

May 28, 2015—*Splatoon*—Wii U

PUBLISHER: Nintendo. RELEASE DATE: May 28, 2015 (JP), May 29, 2015 (NA, EU). COMPOSERS: Toru Minegishi and Shiho Fujii. SERIES: *Splatoon*. GENRE: 3rd person shooter. NOTABLE MUSICAL TRACK: "Shiokara-Bushi (Final Boss Phase 2)."

Splatoon incorporates the Japanese tradition of musical icons into its story and universe. The game draws from the Japanese idol musical tradition in the Squid Sisters Callie and Marie, the in-game hosts of the Inkopolis News. Callie and Marie, collectively, are an idol group that sings and performs in the Inkling language. The techno music in Octo Valley was composed (within the game world) by DJ Octavio, the leader of the Octarians, broadcasted to control the minds of the Octarians. During the final boss of Hero Mode, the Squid Sisters assist the player, overriding the boss music with their music. The notable musical track, "Shiokara-Bushi (Final Boss Phase 2)," is also known as "Calamari Inkantation." The vocals for Callie are by keity. pop, and the vocals for Marie are by Mari Kikuma. The lyrics use the Inkling language. The official soundtrack includes the hiragana lyrics of the track, although the lyrics are without meaning in Japanese. Outside the game, the Squid Sisters were so popular in Japan that there have been Squid Sisters concerts since 2016 with digital 3D projections of Callie and Marie singing and dancing to their songs.

The Inkling Squid Amiibo is required to unlock Squid Beatz, a rhythm-based minigame. Using the Inkling Squid Amiibo first unlocks the Ravenous Octomaw Amiibo challenge. Completing the challenge unlocks Squid Beatz, a rhythm game in the style of *Guitar Hero*. The player uses the Wii U Gamepad buttons to match the visual icons. There are 31 musical tracks to select from, with four additional tracks added from the 2.0.0 update. The sounds vary between the normal and hard modes. Some of the sounds include drums, cymbals, claps, and inkling voices and chants.

September 15, 2015—*Undertale*—PC

PUBLISHER: Toby Fox. RELEASE DATE: September 15, 2015 (WW). COMPOSER: Toby Fox. GENRE: RPG. NOTABLE MUSICAL TRACK: "Megalovania."

Undertale is an independent game with witty dialogue, thought-provoking decisions, and many ways to play. Released on Steam for Windows and Mac, the game was an instant success, with visual and aural styles evoking nostalgia for gaming's past. The game was self-published by Toby Fox, the developer, publisher, designer, and composer. Before becoming a programmer, Fox began as a music composer. He composed all of the tracks with FL Studio. The music reflects Fox's experience writing SNES music for hacks of *Earthbound*. Each prominent character in *Undertale* has a leitmotif, many of which appear in other musical tracks. There are three endings to the game. The player achieves the True Pacifist Route when the player doesn't kill any monsters on the game's first playthrough. The player achieves the Neutral Route when the player kills at least one but not all of the monsters. The player reaches the Genocide Route when the player kills every monster. The notable musical track "Megalovania" plays during the final boss battle with Sans on the Genocide Route.

SOURCES

"Arcade Machine." *Inkipedia, the Splatoon Wiki*, 17 Dec. 2018, splatoonwiki.org/wiki/Arcade_Machine. Accessed 22 Dec. 2018.

Coker, Gareth. "Ori And the Blind Forest—Main Menu (feat. Aeralie Brighton)." *SoundCloud*, 18 Mar. 2015, soundcloud.com/garethcoker/ori-and-the-blind-forest-main-menu-feat-aeralie-brighton.

FrostyMac. "The Meaning Behind Megalovania." *Aminoapps.com*, 7 Jan. 2017, aminoapps.com/c/toby-fox-amino/page/blog/the-meaning-behind-megalovania/kwm5_q0btGupDdQQY7j4mvP4rzo66oPReZB. Accessed 9 Sept. 2020.

"MEGALOVANIA." *Undertale Wiki*, 7 Sept. 2020, undertale.fandom.com/wiki/MEGALOVANIA. Accessed 9 Sept. 2020.

"Music Used on the Menu Screen? Ori and the Blind Forest General Discussions." *Steam Community*, 12 Mar. 2015, steamcommunity.com/app/261570/discussions/0/617330227200090656/.

Oxford, Nadia. "Note Block Beat Box: Listening to Hopes and Dreams from Undertale." *USgamer.net*, 21 Apr. 2016, www.usgamer.net/articles/note-block-beat-box-listening-to-hopes-and-dreams-from-undertale. Accessed 9 Sept. 2020.

2016 in Review

October 10, 2016—*Thumper*—PS4

PUBLISHER: Drool LLC. RELEASE DATE: October 10, 2016 (WW). COMPOSER: Brian Gibson. GENRE: Music/Rhythm. NOTABLE MUSICAL TRACK: "Level 8."

Thumper is a music/rhythm game with abstract horror elements that combines a fast-paced frenzy of rhythmic pulses with an electric energy of suspense and surprise. A soundtrack of industrial musical tracks complements the game's frantic gameplay with quick responses, each musical track with sharp, abrasive sounds. The player controls Junebug Joe, a silver metallic space beetle racing on a track floating in a void. The player, moving through levels and defeating the boss Crakhed, a giant spiky head boss, reacts to the music's rhythm to progress and prevent collisions. As the player successfully clears obstacles, each musical track gradually morphs with musical layers to the constant noise. If the player misses the glowing track elements, the game briefly removes the beat. There are nine levels in the game with many checkpoints. The number of beats in a measure corresponds to the number of the level. For example, the musical track of level 4 is in 4/4 meter while the music of level 7 is in 7/8 meter.

SOURCES

Sprixim. "Thumper Time Signatures." *Steam Community*, 9 Dec. 2017, steamcommunity.com/app/356400/discussions/0/1500126447393849303/.

Wiltshire, Alex. "How Turns Make Thumper Feel Physical." *Rock Paper Shotgun*, 25 Nov. 2016, www.rockpapershotgun.com/2016/11/25/thumper-music-game/.

2017 in Review

March 3, 2017—Nintendo Switch

MANUFACTURER: Nintendo. RELEASE DATE: March 3, 2017 (WW). PRODUCTION DATES: March 3, 2017—Still in production. LAUNCH PRICE: $299.99. MODEL NUMBER: HAC-001. AUDIO: LPCM 5.1.

The Nintendo Switch was the first home console with native portability. Released by Nintendo, players can use the Switch either in docked mode (the Switch console placed in the Switch Dock with A/V from television) or portable mode (Switch console not in Switch Dock with A/V on Switch's screen). Other home consoles' portability solutions that used multiple devices were the PS4 and PS Vita, Xbox Play Anywhere game support, and the Xbox One and PC with the Xbox app. The Wii U Gamepad, to stream games, needed to be close to the Wii U console to maintain a steady wireless connection.

The Switch contains the Realtek ALC5639 audio codec on the back of its motherboard. There is a 3.5mm audio-out port on the top edge of the Switch console. At the time, Apple's iPhone 7 was the first smartphone in the iPhone series to remove the 3.5mm headphone port. The Switch console includes two internal stereo speakers underneath the screen facing the player for LPCM 2.0 audio (the 3.5mm audio-out port also supports LPCM 2.0).

Nintendo Switch console with Joy-Cons 2017. The internal speakers are located on the lower-left and lower-right corners of the Switch console. The audio output ports are 3.5mm (Evan-Amos, "Nintendo-Switch-wJoyCons-BlRd-Standing-FL").

The software creates a pseudo-surround in the stereo mix. When the Switch console is in the dock, the audio improves to LPCM 5.1 audio. There aren't any options for 7.1 surround sound on the docked Switch nor other 5.1 surround sound formats. The 3.5mm headphone jack is active in handheld and docked modes but only outputs in stereo. The 4.0.0 system update supports wireless headphones with a USB receiver plugged into the dock of the Switch. There is no support for Bluetooth audio and audio connections via other cables or surround sound formats.

Unlike the Wii Remote, the Switch's Joy-Cons do not include internal speakers. Despite this, Switch developers cleverly used the HD rumble of the Left and Right Joy-Cons and the Switch Pro controller to create sound effects without a speaker using the haptic motors to create vibrations that match the sounds. The HD Rumble of the Switch consists of linear resonant actuators that function in theory like a loudspeaker. For example, *Mario Part 8 Deluxe* uses the HD Rumble for the sound of speed boosts and coin collecting (for more games using the HD Rumble as a speaker, check out *ARMS*, *1–2-Switch*, *Golf Story*, and *Super Mario Odyssey*).

The Switch Lite (HDH-001), released worldwide by Nintendo on September 20, 2019, at a launch price of $199.99, was a cheaper model that removed the video and audio output to a TV, detachable Joy-Cons, the IR camera sensor, and HD rumble features. Regarding audio, the Switch Lite retains a 3.5mm audio-out port on the top edge of the unit. However, the internal stereo speakers are placed at the unit's bottom edge, facing downward to the player. The Switch Lite functions as a handheld gaming system for Switch games.

February 23, 2017—*Nier: Automata*—PS4

PUBLISHER: Square Enix. RELEASE DATE: February 23, 2017 (JP), March 7, 2017 (NA),

March 10, 2017 (EU). Composers: Keiichi Okabe and Keigo Hoashi. Series: *Nier*. Genre: Action/RPG. Notable musical track: "Weight of the World the [E]nd of YoRHa." Awards: Game Awards 2017 Best Score/Music.

Nier: Automata explores existentialism through its minimalistic and melancholic soundtrack. The game's plot revolves around an endless war between robots and androids. Both sides show human qualities through lasting relationships and human-like actions, although devoid. The instruments representing the human qualities are vocals, chants, guitar, strings, and piano. The instruments representing the mechanical qualities are synthesizers, xylophones, bells, and metallic sounds. The piano, commonly used as a solo instrument, reflects isolation through minimalist textures. Musical tracks transition seamlessly into another version based on the location and level of intensity. The music especially stands out during the amusement park scenes, a city in shambles, and a city buried by sand. The notable musical track, "Weight of the World the [E]nd of YoRHa," plays at the ending credits of Ending E after the player chooses to save YoRHa's data.

September 29, 2017—*Cuphead*— Xbox One

Publisher: StudioMDHR. Release Date: September 29, 2017 (WW). Composer: Kristofer Maddigan. Genre: Run and gun. Notable musical track: "Floral Fury." Awards: D.I.C.E. 2018 Original Music Composition, G.A.N.G. 2018 Audio of the Year.

Cuphead has the aesthetic visual and audio style of animated shorts from the 1930s, popularized by Fleischer Studios and Walt Disney Animated Studios. The soundtrack is jazz with traditional big band orchestration. The big band instruments include trumpets, saxophones, trombones, clarinet, tuba, piano, bass, drum kit, and vocals. Many of the songs sound like traditional early film era chase music. The soundtrack (*Selected Tunes from Cuphead*) is the only video game soundtrack to reach number 1 on the Billboard Jazz charts on September 14, 2019.

The theme song for Cuphead, which explains the game's plot, was sung by a barbershop quartet called Shoptimus Prime. The quartet personified in the game as four Barber's poles also sang "Quick Break," a song that breaks the fourth wall. After Cuphead retrieves the missing fourth member of the quartet, the quartet persuades the player in song to take a break from the video game. The notable musical track, "Floral Fury," accompanies the battle of Cuphead with Cagney Carnation, the flower. The track is a samba with trumpets, saxophones, and percussion instruments. The track begins with solo trumpet and bongo hits. Then the tambourine and another percussion sound play. The percussion continues as the trumpets and saxophones play the melody. Then the piano plays an improvised solo with percussion accompaniment.

Sources

"Barbershop Quartet." *Cuphead Wiki*, 14 July 2020, cuphead.fandom.com/wiki/Barbershop_Quartet. Accessed 9 Sept. 2020.

Bell, Larryn. "Full List of Xbox One X Enhanced Games at Launch." *AllGamers*, 7 Nov. 2017, ag.hyperxgaming.com/article/3365/full-list-of-xbox-one-x-enhanced-games-at-launch. Accessed 21 Sept. 2020.

Billboard. "Jazz Albums Chart—The Week of September 14, 2019." *Billboard*, www.billboard.com/charts/jazz-albums/2019-09-14. Accessed 9 Sept. 2020.

Evans, Emi. *Twitter*, 2 Apr. 2018, twitter.com/emirevans/status/980820204274855936. Accessed 14 Sept. 2020.

Frank, Allegra. "Nintendo Switch Update Also Adds Wireless Headset Support." *Polygon*, 19 Oct. 2017, www.polygon.com/2017/10/19/16504088/nintendo-switch-wireless-headphones-headset-update.

Gerblick, Jordan. "Cuphead Has the First Video Game Soundtrack to Hit Number 1 on Billboard's Jazz Charts." *Gamesradar*, 18 Sept. 2019, www.gamesradar.com/cuphead-has-the-first-video-game-soundtrack-to-hit-number-1-on-billboards-jazz-charts/. Accessed 9 Sept. 2020.

Jarman, Casey. "High Scores: Kristofer Maddigan's Big Band Soundtrack for 'Cuphead.'" *Bandcamp Daily*, 18 Jan. 2018, daily.bandcamp.com/high-scores/cuphead-soundtrack-interview. Accessed 9 Sept. 2020.

Nintendo. "Buy Now—Nintendo Switch—Bundles,

What's Included." *Nintendo—Official Site*, www.nintendo.com/switch/buy-now/. Accessed 10 Sept. 2020.

Nintendo. "IR Information: Sales Data—Dedicated Video Game Sales Units." *Nintendo Co., Ltd*, 30 June 2020, www.nintendo.co.jp/ir/en/finance/hard_soft/. Accessed 10 Sept. 2020.

Nintendo. "Technical Specs—Nintendo Switch." *Nintendo*, www.nintendo.com/switch/features/tech-specs/. Accessed 6 Aug. 2018.

Porter, Jon. "Meet the Minds Behind Nintendo Switch's HD Rumble Tech." *TechRadar*, 7 Feb. 2017, www.techradar.com/news/meet-the-minds-behind-nintendo-switchs-hd-rumble-tech. Accessed 19 Sept. 2020.

Rawmeatcowboy. "The Subtle Sound Effects of the Switch's HD Rumble (with Audio Examples)." *GoNintendo*, 28 May 2017, gonintendo.com/stories/281248-the-subtle-sound-effects-of-the-switch-s-hd-rumble-with-audio-ex. Accessed 19 Sept. 2020.

Signor, Jeremy. "Weight of the World." *First Person Scholar—Weekly Critical Essays, Commentaries, and Book Reviews on Games*, 7 Mar. 2018, www.firstpersonscholar.com/weight-of-the-world/. Accessed 14 Sept. 2020.

Studio MDHR. "The Music of Cuphead: Recording Floral Fury." *YouTube*, 18 Sept. 2017, youtu.be/CG5RdWnUVlc. Accessed 9 Sept. 2020.

2018 in Review

January 25, 2018—*Celeste*—PC

PUBLISHER: Matt Makes Games. RELEASE DATE: January 25, 2018 (WW). COMPOSER: Lena Raine. GENRE: Platformer. NOTABLE MUSICAL TRACK: "Mirror Temple (Mirror Magic Mix)." AWARDS: G.A.N.G. 2019 / MAGFEST People's Choice Award.

Celeste is a game with a soundtrack of electronic sounds and a commentary on mental illness. Released worldwide on Steam for Windows and Mac, within each of the game's eight chapters is a cassette room that contains a B-Side cassette tape. Madeline, the protagonist, must navigate pink and blue walls that activate and deactivate to reach the cassette tape. Obtaining the cassette unlocks a B-Side level, a modified level with more complex challenges, and a remix of the level's music. Guest artists remixed all of the B-Side musical tracks except Chapter 7. The hidden cassette room of each B-Side level uses an 8-bit arrangement of the level's music, arranged either by Lena Raine or by Keven Regamey. Electronic sounds and chiptunes reflect the game's visual style of pixels and sprites. The notable musical track "Mirror Temple (Mirror Magic Mix)" is a remix by 2 Mello of "Mirror Temple." The musical style is in contrast with the original musical style for the track for Mirror Temple.

April 20, 2018—*Nintendo Labo: Toy-Con 01—Variety Kit—* Switch

PUBLISHER: Nintendo of America. RELEASE DATE: April 20, 2018 (JP, NA), April 27, 2018 (EU). SERIES: *Nintendo Labo*. GENRE: Party/Minigame. NOTABLE MUSICAL TRACK: "The Toy-Con Garage Song."

Nintendo Labo: Toy-Con 01—Variety Kit is a video game and pieces of cardboard used to build a working piano that operates with the Nintendo Switch. The kit includes enough cardboard to create five projects. The Toy-Con is one of the five projects that the user can make with the variety kit. When assembled, the player interacts with the 13-key piano (one octave) through the right Joy-Con's infrared sensor. The Switch console fits in the music holder of the piano. The keyboard contains 13 keys within one octave. The four included knobs allow the user to change the sounds from the normal piano. Knob 1 sets various cat noises. Knob 2 sets various singing voices. Knob 3 sets various groans, moans, and yawns. The final knob replaces the sounds with the Joycon's HD Rumble vibrations. The lever on the left side of the piano makes the pitch go up or down. The play/pause button plays some preset songs, including Happy Birthday in the key of F major.

The IR sensor of the right Joy-Con recognizes piano key presses. The right Joy-Con is placed in the back of the piano facing inward. The variety kit includes reflective stickers placed around each key and knob. The IR sensor of the right Joy-Con recognizes the corresponding sticker at the press of a key or the turn of a knob. Each key has a bent piece of cardboard that acts as a spring to reset the position of each key upon being pressed.

In Studio Mode for advanced features, the player can play and record songs using five sets of one-octave keyboard settings and sounds. When the left Joy-Con is placed into the Toy-Con Baton, the user can wave it like a baton to control the playback speed of the recording. Lastly, a user activates new waveforms by sliding the four included Frequency cards into a slot at the top of the constructed piano. The Switch scans each card to change the waveform used with the piano. The user can use the square Frequency card to create a customized waveform by cutting a unique shape. The Switch console even recognizes original shapes from a piece of paper.

The game contains some preset songs, but the song unique to the kit is "The Toy-Con Garage Song." The cardboard includes the sheet music to the Toy-Con Garage song from Part 3 of Nintendo's Toy-Con Garage online videos.

May 1, 2018—*Beat Saber*—PC with VR

PUBLISHER: Beat Games. RELEASE DATE: May 1, 2018 (WW). COMPOSER: Jaroslav Beck. GENRE: Rhythm. REQUIRED PERIPHERALS: Oculus Rift, HTC Vive. NOTABLE MUSICAL TRACK: "Beat Saber."

Beat Saber was the first successful rhythm game for VR devices. Released worldwide on May 1, 2018, the game began in early access on Steam for PC with a VR headset. At its release, *Beat Saber* supported the Oculus Rift and HTC Vive. The game is exclusive to gaming systems with VR support. The gameplay combines the music-rhythm association of *Guitar Hero* with the gestures of *Fruit Ninja* and the lightsabers of *Star Wars*. The player wields red and blue lightsabers marking the left

Facebook Oculus Rift. The player wears the headset and hears the audio in both ears. It communicates to the PC through the USB port (Evan-Amos, "Oculus-Rift-CV1-Headset-Front").

and right hands in the game, respectively. While wearing the VR headset, the player alters the placement and rotation of the lightsabers using the VR system's two controllers. The player earns points by slicing matching colored blocks with the lightsabers and dodging walls by turning the head away from them. Most blocks show either an arrow to indicate a precise direction of a slice or a dot to indicate any direction.

The developer added the level editor (only for PC) and practice mode (select the mortarboard icon with each song to adjust the speed of the song) when version 1.0 was officially released on May 21, 2019 (to coincide with the release of the Oculus Quest and the game on the PS4 with PS VR). In the level editor, the player can import any OGG audio file. The game creates a beatmap that marks the obstacles with the timing in the musical track. Standalone VR systems lack the official level editor or the ability to import audio.

The base game included 10 original songs by Jaroslav Beck. The soundtrack is entirely electronic dance music and techno. This aural aesthetic matches with the CGI geometric shapes and flashes of light. Additional songs were added to *Beat Saber* since its early access release every one to four months. As of 2020, there are music packs from Monstercat (a Canadian independent electronic music label), Imagine Dragons, Camellia, Panic! At the Disco, Monstercat X Rocket League (licensed EDM from the game *Rocket League*), Green Day, Timbaland, and Linkin Park. Thirty-one songs are now part of the base game, with the remaining songs as DLC.

The notable musical track, "Beat Saber," is the third track in the game and lasts almost two minutes. The game's full release includes the musical track in OGG format. The track, set at 166 BPM (beats per minute), begins with an introduction the establish the beat. During the track, the blocks reflect the melody line, then the drum part, and then the beats. After the first instance of the melody, a section begins in which the drum hits take the lead with ornamentation from the melodic instrument and rapping vocals.

December 7, 2018—*Super Smash Bros. Ultimate*—Switch

PUBLISHER: Nintendo. RELEASE DATE: December 7, 2018 (WW). COMPOSER: Hideki Sakamoto. SERIES: Super Smash Bros. GENRE: Fighting. NOTABLE MUSICAL TRACK: "Lifelight."

Super Smash Bros. Ultimate is a triumph of the *Smash Bros.* series and a celebration of first and third-party games, some never appearing on a Nintendo system. The game is a fighting game featuring characters from many game series. The game has the most extensive soundtrack of any game. DLC continuously adds new tracks. The initial release included 876 tracks (some need to be unlocked) and now contains 986 tracks. The musical tracks include the original versions and new arrangements. This game includes the most extensive assortment of the best musical tracks of video game history. Some of the games and series represented in music in *Super Smash Bros. Ultimate* are *Super Mario Bros.* Series, *The Legend of Zelda* series, *Metroid* series, *Pokémon* series, *F-Zero* series, *Kid Icarus* series, *Splatoon* series, *Metal Gear* series, *Sonic* series, *Mega Man* series, *Pac-Man* series, *Street Fighter* series, *Castlevania* series, *Fatal Fury* series (includes *The King of Fighters* series and *Samurai Shodown* series), *Final Fantasy VII*, *Tetris*, *Electroplankton*, *Undertale*, and *Cuphead*.

As a result of licensing agreements from the contributing composers, the game locks the songs from each game series to the stages based on the same series. After the 8.1.0 software update on August 5, 2020, the Battlefield, Small Battlefield, Big Battlefield, and Final Destination stages can use all of the songs. The Sounds menu contains all of the unlocked musical tracks and the unlocked characters' voice clips. In-game challenges, song purchases on the Nintendo eShop, and free and paid character DLC unlock additional musical tracks (for example, "Megalovania" and "Floral Fury" are added as musical tracks with the purchase of the Sans and Cuphead Mii costumes, respectively). The notable musical track, "Lifelight," is the game's main theme, with English vocals by Abby Trott. Composed by Hideki Sakamoto, the game's original musical tracks, including "Menu," "Battlefield," and the Mii Fighters' victory theme, are remixes of "Lifelight."

SOURCES

Assumma, Mike. "Review: Beat Saber Gets Your Blood Pumping and Feet Moving." *Gamecrate*, 22 May 2018, gamecrate.com/reviews/review-beat-saber-gets-your-blood-pumping-and-feet-moving/19331. Accessed 9 Sept. 2020.

Baird, Scott. "The Latest Smash Bros Update Required Permission from All IP Holders Involved with the Game." *TheGamer*, 11 Sept. 2020, www.thegamer.com/smash-bros-ultimate-patch-update-final-destination-music/. Accessed 24 Sept. 2020.

"Lifelight." *SmashWiki*, 22 May 2021, www.ssbwiki.com/Lifelight. Accessed 27 May 2021.

Martin, Garrett. "The Nintendo Labo Piano Is a Surprisingly Useful Little Synthesizer." *Pastemagazine.com*, 3 May 2018, www.pastemagazine.com/games/nintendo-labo/what-ive-learned-about-the-nintendo-labo-piano/. Accessed 17 Sept. 2020.

"Music (SSBU)." *SmashWiki*, 1 Sept. 2020, www.ssbwiki.com/Music_(SSBU). Accessed 24 Sept. 2020.

Nintendo. "Buy Now—Nintendo Labo Official Site—What's Included, Where to Buy." *Nintendo Labo™ for the Nintendo Switch™ Home Gaming System—Official Site*, labo.nintendo.com/kits/variety-kit/. Accessed 17 Sept. 2020.

"Toy-Con Piano—Nintendo Labo Wiki Guide." *IGN*, 3 June 2018, www.ign.com/wikis/nintendo-labo/Toy-Con_Piano. Accessed 6 Aug. 2018.

2019 in Review

November 8, 2019—*Death Stranding*—PS4

PUBLISHER: Sony Interactive Entertainment. RELEASE DATE: November 8, 2019 (WW). COMPOSER: Ludvig Forssell. GENRE: Action. NOTABLE MUSICAL TRACK: "BB's Theme." AWARDS: Game Awards 2019 Best Score/Music, D.I.C.E. 2020 Outstanding Achievement in Audio Design. G.A.N.G. 2020 Audio of the Year, Sound Design of the Year, Best Cinematic/Cutscene Audio, Best Dialogue, Best Original Soundtrack Album, Best Audio Mix.

The game's soundtrack favors texture and feel over melody and harmony. The player controls Sam Bridges, a respected porter who makes deliveries between isolated cities in a post-apocalyptic world in which the worlds of the pre-afterlife and living became intertwined with positive and negative effects. The soundtrack combines synths with unique audio effects by manipulating acoustic instruments for unconventional sounds, like a prepared piano. The audio design uses the PS4 Dualshock controller's internal speaker to play the cries of Lou, Sam's bridge baby who he carries within a pod on his travels. The game uses bird sounds to express the condition of the world in the opening and ending cutscenes.

The soundtrack includes 27 licensed songs, 22 from Low Roar and 2 from Silent Poets. The player traverses long distances by walking, and the game breaks up the monotony by playing the licensed songs. The notable musical track, "BB's Theme," links Sam to his father Cliff and to Lou, who detects hostile beached things, deceased souls stranded in the world of the living. The lyrics, sung by Jenny Plant, reflect the emotional connection between someone and a bridge baby, respecting the baby as more than just equipment but with tenderness and parental care. The song appears in the game in three instances. Cliff introduces the song's lyrics to Sam, and both men whistle the melody together. While resting or walking with Lou, Sam whistles the melody. After receiving a harmonica, Sam plays the melody on the harmonica while resting with Lou.

SOURCES

Alwani, Rishi. "The Music of Death Stranding: Every Licensed Song, Original Soundtrack, and More." *The Mako Reactor*, 11 Nov. 2019, themakoreactor.com/features/death-stranding-music-list-soundtrack-download-itunes-spotify-low-roar-ludvig-forssell/7663/. Accessed 28 May 2021.
"BB's Theme." *Death Stranding Wiki*, 8 Feb. 2021, deathstranding.fandom.com/wiki/BB's_Theme. Accessed 28 May 2021.
Garst, Aron. "Playing Piano with a Sledgehammer: Creating Death Stranding's Unidentifiable Score." *The Verge*, 8 Nov. 2019, www.theverge.com/2019/11/8/20954112/death-stranding-score-music-interview-joel-corelitz-ludvig-forssell. Accessed 28 May 2021.

2020 in Review

November 10, 2020—Microsoft Xbox Series S and X

MANUFACTURER: Microsoft. RELEASE DATE: November 10, 2020 (WW). PRODUCTION DATES: November 10, 2020—Still in production. LAUNCH PRICE: $299 (S), $499 (X). MODEL NUMBER: RRS-00001 (S), RRT-00001 (X). AUDIO: 3D audio.

The Xbox Series S and X support Dolby Vision and Atmos. The two models are the Xbox Series S and the Xbox Series X. The Xbox Series S, the cheaper model, lacks a disc drive. The Xbox Series X, the expensive model, has a 4K Ultra HD drive and supports a video output of 4K resolution at 60 frames per second. Regarding audio outputs, the Xbox Series S and X support digital audio output via the HDMI-out and USB 3.1 ports. The audio formats are stereo, Dolby TrueHD 7.1, DTS-HD 7.1, DTS:X, Dolby Atmos, and Windows Sonic for Headphones. The Xbox Series S and X natively support Dolby Atmos for Home Theater (Bitstream format). To enable Dolby Atmos for Headphones and DTS Headphone:X, the user must purchase the license via the Dolby and DTS apps in the Microsoft Store on the Xbox Series S or X.

Xbox Series S with controller 2020. The audio output ports are HDMI (Asmodean-Underscore, CC-BY-SA-4.0)

Xbox Series X with controller 2020. The audio output ports are HDMI (Der. Bellemer, CC-BY-SA-4.0).

November 12, 2020—Sony PlayStation 5

MANUFACTURER: Sony. RELEASE DATE: November 12, 2020 (WW). PRODUCTION DATES: November 12, 2020—Still in production. LAUNCH PRICE: $400 (Digital Edition), $500 (Standard). MODEL NUMBER: CFI-1015A (Standard), CFI-1015B (Digital). AUDIO: 3D audio.

The PlayStation 5 was the first home console to support Tempest 3D AudioTech. The PS5 (PlayStation 5) was released in two models: one without and one with a disc drive. Besides the disc drive, both models have the same hardware specs, including the graphics card, hard drive, and video output. Unlike the PS4, the PS5 lacks the optical audio port, the only audio out ports being the HDMI-out and the three USB 3.1 Gen 2 ports (two Type A and one Type C). The available audio formats on the PS5

Sony PS5 Digital Edition with controller 2020. The audio output ports are HDMI (Wfrmsf, CC-BY-SA-4.0).

are stereo, Dolby Digital 5.1, DTS 5.1, Tempest 3D AudioTech, and Sony 360 Reality Audio for headphones. Unlike the Xbox Series S and X, the PS5 models lack support for Dolby Atmos for 3D surround sound. Instead, the PS5 models support Tempest 3D AudioTech, Sony's proprietary format for 3D audio. Sony's 3D audio uses the Tempest 3D audio engine to place audio sources within a 360-degree mix. At launch, the only way to hear the 3D audio as intended was with Sony's Pulse 3D wireless headset. Television and device manufacturers were slow to support the Tempest Engine. The PS5 DualSense controller has a headphone port, helpful in connecting older headphones. The PS5 DualSense controller also included an internal microphone, which the Xbox Series X controller lacked. The internal microphone of the PS5 DualSense is a beneficial feature, but it isn't essential when using a headset with a microphone.

SOURCES

Moore-Colyer, Roland. "PS5 and 3D Audio: Everything You Need to Know." *Tom's Guide*, 30 Aug. 2020, www.tomsguide.com/features/ps5-and-3d-audio-everything-you-need-to-know. Accessed 16 Sept. 2020.

CHAPTER 3

The Expanded Universe
of Video Game Audio

Where to Listen to Video Game Music

The most authentic way to experience video game audio is in the context of the original video game release. As the years go by, retro games and game systems are scarcer to find, let alone in working condition. Furthermore, to hear most of the game's music, one must successfully complete the game, which can take many hours of play. Still, modern video game music adapts the music in real-time to create a unique aural experience. Next to playing the original games, playing official game rereleases offers a similar aural experience. Many games are available through the digital marketplaces of Steam, iOS, Android, and modern gaming systems still supported by the manufacturers. Nintendo, Commodore, Sony, Sega, and NEC released retro dedicated consoles of their most popular gaming machines (NES Classic Edition, C64 Mini, PlayStation Classic, Sega Genesis Mini, and TurboGrafx-16 Mini). For a quicker listening experience, one can locate a game's official soundtrack, released on audio cassette, CD, vinyl, digital download, or internet streaming. iam8bit is a publisher that releases vinyl of video game soundtracks, including *Uncharted: Drake's Fortune*, *Monument Valley*, *Undertale*, *Cuphead*. Sumthing Else Music Works is a publisher that released CD sets of video game soundtracks, including *Journey* and *Fantasia: Music Evolved*. Bandcamp is an online website that composer and game developers use to promote and sell video game soundtracks. *Minecraft*'s two official soundtracks are available on the Bandcamp page of composer David Rosenfeld.

Selected Audio Exploration

An effective musical track relays valuable information to the player, heightening the senses and promoting player engagement. A common function of video game music is to establish the scene's mood. Another function is to indicate changes in the characters or setting, sometime without a corresponding graphic.

1981—*Donkey Kong*

The first background music plays when the game gives the control of Jumpman, an early version of Mario, to the player. The musical track consists of a repeating pattern of five notes using four pitches. A squeaking sound effect indicates Jumpman's footsteps and Jumpman climbing a ladder. Another thump represents the barrels that Donkey Kong rolls falling off one platform and landing on the one below. A high-pitched sound effect indicates when Jumpman retrieves an item from the stage. When Jumpman enters hammer mode, the hammer jingle supersedes the background music. When wielding the hammer, Jumpman can break the incoming barrels for points. The hammer is in use for a limited time. A warbling sound indicates that Jumpman has destroyed a barrel with the hammer. While wielding the hammer, Jumpman cannot jump or climb ladders. A spring sound represents Jumpman jumping up or jumping over objects. A brief jingle plays when Jumpman reaches the platform of Pauline, the girl in distress. The laughter sound effect plays as Donkey Kong snatches Pauline and ascends upward.

The background music that accompanies the first 50m stage (the stage at 50m changes as the game progresses) is less engaging than the first stage. It only consists of a three-note pattern using only two pitches. The game reuses the ground thumping sound that Donkey Kong used in the first stage as Donkey Kong shakes his fists. A new sound effect plays when Mario removes the last rivet from the second stage. A variant of the 50m stage background music plays briefly as Donkey Kong pounds his chest to no avail. A descending slide sound matches the downward fall of Donkey Kong as he is defeated. The thumping sound plays when Donkey Kong hits his head on the lower platform. A short victory jingle plays as Jumpman and Pauline are reunited with a heart that Donkey Kong does not break.

The second 50m stage has magenta platforms with a column of ascending and descending platforms. There is no background music to accompany this stage. A sound effect indicates the bouncing of a pogo-stick type obstacle and removing the pogo-stick type obstacle from the stage. The third 50m stage has orange platforms, and Donkey Kong slides horizontally across the top platform. The background music is less interesting than the earlier tunes. It is a three-note pattern of long-short-short on one pitch. In an arcade setting, the stage music conveys the current player's skill to him or herself and nearby players.

1993—*Alone in the Dark*

The game's background music builds up through orchestral layering. The track "I'm Not Afraid ... I Think" uses these build-ups to add suspense to the game. The music creates a false lull in the player that all is well. As the player explores the surroundings, the music fills in what would otherwise be a disturbingly quiet experience. The game's menu music has jazz elements, including the use of the pipe organ. The game's sound effects are convincing, including footsteps, door creaks, and chest opening. The narrations of all of the literary contents (Book, Letter, Diary) are voices of sound clarity and character. When the player switches from exploration to combat, the orchestration changes to a more heroic tone with a sense of imminent danger. The player receives hints to the safety of the environment based on the shifts of the musical mood.

1995—*The Adventures of Batman and Robin*

A highlight of the soundtrack is the notable musical track, "Space Boss," accompanying the Mad Hatter boss fight of Level 3. The track shifts in its mood while the scene unfolds. It builds up as Batman and Robin stand on a checkered ribbon in what looks to be outer space or another dimension. Then the Mad Hatter floats down in a giant floating top hat, throwing explosive nutcrackers and rabbits at the heroes. Shortly after his arrival, the track shifts into dubstep as the ribbon ground moves toward the screen in 3D fashion, sending obstacles toward the heroes at a brisk pace. As a game released late in the lifespan of the Genesis, the game exhibits detailed knowledge and application of FM synthesis on the Genesis in its techno music of long tracks and shifting moods.

1996—*Real Sound: Kaze no Regret*

The notable musical track, "A New Nostalgia," has a simple melody, first played on the acoustic guitar and then matched with human whistling. The guitar employs pitch-bending liberally. The narration of the opening scene uses words to describe an array of sounds (English translation by Dr. Christopher Hopkins):

時を刻み、時計がかちかちと鳴っている。
Tick-tock, there is a ringing clock marking the hour.
主人公、野々村博司のモノローグがかぶさる。
The monologue of our protagonist, Hiroshi Nonomura, is covered.
博司 (M)「時に人と人との出会いが
Hiroshi (M) "People meet each other sometimes.
はじめてじゃないような気がするのは、
I feel that it's not like the first time,
何も前世なんて言葉で解決するようなことでは無いのかもしれない。
Nothing in the past life could be solved by words.
幼いころ、まるでそれが世界のすべてかのように愛した、
When I was young, I loved it as if it were all in the world.
自転車や虫かごや学校の裏山も、
Bicycles, bug cages, and the mountains behind the school,

今では何も思い出せず、
I can't remember anything now,
遠い霧の向こうに音もたてずに隠れている。
The distant fog over there obscures the sounds.
けれど記憶喪失の人間が自転車の乗り方は忘れないように、それは決して消えてなくなったわけではなく、
But as a person with amnesia does not forget how to ride a bicycle, it is not because the sounds have ever faded away,
ある日突然、霧は晴れる」
Suddenly one day, the fog clears away"
蝉の鳴き声。
The sounds of the cicada's cry.
小学校の始業ベルが鳴り響く。
The elementary school opening bell rings out.
廊下を走り抜ける何人もの子供たちの足音。
The footsteps of many children running through the hallways.
黒板を打つチョークの音が聞こえる。
The sound of chalk hitting the blackboard can be heard.
教室内で算数の授業が行われており、
Math classes are held in the classroom,
先生が簡単な計算式について教えている。
The teacher is teaching about an easy calculation.
扉が開く。
The door is opened.

2011—*Minecraft*

The notable musical track, "Alpha," begins with a slow, melodic piano line. The piano rings with reverberation. While the track plays, an extended poem scrolls upward on the screen. String pads then accompany the piano, adding sonorous harmonies and musical intensity. After three minutes and five seconds (3:05), the second melody begins on the clarinet with accompaniment of strings, low brass, and snare drums. The string section repeats the theme with louder accompaniment and more forceful hits on the snare drums. The piano returns a minute and 35 seconds later (4:40) briefly for a delicate phrase. After the string swell, the piano absorbs the intensity and tones it down. After a minute and five seconds (5:45), the piano plays a short and slow passage alone. Unlike the first minutes of the track, electronic sounds and string pads accompany the piano. This section is minimalistic; the game adds and removes layers. The intensity develops after a minute and 55 seconds (7:40) with the reintroduction of the snare drums and strings. The piano concludes softly and delicately after 35 seconds (8:15). The piano plays softly and slowly in the final section. And the poem finally concludes after nine minutes. Now the game credits begin. This section continues with string pads taking over from the piano. The musical track ends at a little over 10 minutes. However, the credits continue without music until a random track begins.

2012—*Beat Sneak Bandit*

The notable musical track, "Intro," is heard after the player taps the screen on the title logo. The track accompanies the cutscene that establishes the game's plot. The track begins with a plucked double bass, finger snaps, and drum rim shots. The music changes rhythm to mimic a news report when the TV appears. An electronic harpsichord plays the melody when the cutscene switches to the villain, dressed like a classical composer. The ringing of a clock coordinates with the musical beats. The track has a funky groove with a lead baritone sax, accentuated by interjections of warped sounds and DJ scratches. The track establishes the harmonic progression used by all of the game's musical tracks.

2012—*Sound Shapes*

The notable musical track, "Cities," was one of three composed by Beck (the other were "Touch the People" and "Spiral Staircase"). Each object on the screen, at any given time, moves in time with the notes of one of the instruments. The track begins with a maraca and bass drum hits. Then an electric guitar enters. When the voice enters, the word "AHHHHHHHHH" appears on the screen. The player's circle can attach to the letters while they are visible. Later, steel drums, represented on-screen by the explosion of a nuclear bomb, join the other instruments. When the lyrics begin, they appear on the screen like smoke. The entire harmonic progression is 16 beats, repeated for the whole track. When the lyrics sing "turn a little" and "move a little," platforms move and rotate to the lyrics. The track evolves at the pace of the player's progress navigating the screen's obstacles (stay on a screen longer to hear the current collection of instruments longer). On some screens, the bass guitar or the melody drops out. Near the end of the track, a closed hi-hat adds percussion, visualized by the bulldozer's engine.

2012—*Journey*

The notable musical track, "Apotheosis (Final Level)," was the most challenging track for composer Austin Wintory to complete because it had to evoke an emotional response fitting for the culmination of the player's journey to the summit of the mountain. Before the track plays in the game, the player dies from exhaustion in the snow, then reborn with the ability to fly. As the player explores this newfound ability to advance to the summit with haste, the musical track combines a cello melody with high-energy violins playing in triplets. It is not yet intense; it reflects the tone of the previous musical tracks. Later, the flute enters briefly. The strings play the melody as the triplet rhythm continues in the violins. Then choir aahs enter as the player ascends ever higher. Near the very top, a tubular bell rings. When the player reaches the final stretch of snow toward the light, the triplet rhythm concludes. The track ends with the cello playing alone until the sound softens and fades away. The track's conclusion matches the game's conclusion, as the player too reaches the mountaintop and fades out into pure white light.

2015—*Undertale*

The notable musical track "Megalovania" plays during the final boss battle with Sans on the Genocide Route. Toby Fox previously used the track in Radiation's Halloween Hack of *Earthbound* in 2009 as "Dr. Ardonut's Rage," in the Flash animation "[S] Wake" for the webcomic *Homestuck*, and on the album *Homestuck Vol. 6: Heir Transparent* from 2011. When the player battles Sans and hears this track in *Undertale*, the player is, in fact, the final boss who defends against Sans. The track uses electronic and orchestral synths, square tones, electric guitar, and drum kit, emulating the N64 musical style. The track matches the fast and energetic for the game's final boss in the Genocide Route with a BPM of 230. Over a quarter into the battle, the track abruptly switches to a calmer tempo after Sans spares you. If the player does not accept, then the track begins again, and Sans attacks. The track pauses and then starts again with the abrupt changes of San's attacks. As Sans prepares for his special attack, the music fades out to silence. The rest of the battle consists of the text sound while Sans bores the player without further attacks.

2017—*Nier: Automata*

The notable musical track, "Weight of the World the [E]nd of YoRHa," plays at the ending credits of Ending E after the player chooses to save YoRHa's data. Within the context of the game's plot, the sacrifice of save data will help other players to escape the programming loop to become autonomous. In this particular ending, the song blends three different versions of the tracks. The version for this ending is in three languages: English, Japanese, and Chaos. The vocalists are J'Nique Nicole, Marina Kawano, and Emi Evans (who wrote and sang the songs for *Nier*). Chaos is a language constructed by Emi Evans designed as the result of a thousand years of evolution of modern languages.

Along with sounds from English, German, French, and Japanese, she included words from Chamicuro, an endangered language. The song speaks from the perspective of 2B. The track begins with a chiptune arrangement to accompany the *Asteroids*-like minigame. As the track continues, the English vocals begin over the chiptune accompaniment.

Soon, strings, percussion, and piano replace the chiptune sounds. The player still shoots the incoming names from the ending credits that drop orange and magenta orbs. If the player's ship gets destroyed, the player must then determine whether it is worth saving the data. After much persistence, the player receives a rescue offer. Other ships gather around the player's ship upon acceptance, musically represented by the presence of a choir. The choir entrance is a decisive moment not just in the track but in the game. In a game of existentialism and isolation, hearing human voices in a world devoid of humans gives a glimpse of a world without war. Perhaps the androids can become autonomous and be the very humans they seek. The ensemble is made up of director and writer Yoko Taro and members of the PlatinumGames development team.

2018—*Celeste*

The notable musical track "Mirror Temple (Mirror Magic Mix)" is a remix by 2 Mello of "Mirror Temple." The musical style is in contrast with the original musical style for the track for Mirror Temple. The original track is mysterious, dark, and sad. The mood matches the actions of the Mirror Temple. Madeline helps Theo confront his problems. By doing so, she learns how to cope with her own issues. The musical track expresses Madeline's depression even as she attempted to bring Theo to approach his problems head-on. The track is sparse, with small crescendos

and electronic distortion. The player can hear composer Lena Raine speak about her struggle with depression by listening to the musical track in reverse. The B-Side remix, however, discards the mysterious mood for acid jazz and smooth funk. The track uses electronic instruments and choir voices, piano, violins, and vibraphone. Near the end of the B-Side stage, Madeline encounters Theo, an explorer encased in crystal. Theo breaks the fourth wall and says directly to the player, "It's the temple remix, featuring your box Mix Master Theo!"

Composer Interviews

Due to the growing interest in video game studies and the 40-year history of

the commercial video game industry, the sound engineers and composers of the video game industry have shared count-less documents and interviews in print and multimedia.

Collins, Karen, and Chris Greening. *Beep: Documenting the History of Game Sound.* ePUB, Ehtonal, 2016.

Dwyer, Nick, and Tu Neill. "Diggin' in the Carts." *Red Bull Music Academy*, 2014, www.redbull.com/us-en/shows/diggin-in-the-carts. Accessed 31 May 2021.
Marie, Meagan. *Women in Gaming: 100 Professionals of Play.* Prima Games, 2018.

Other Histories of Video Game Audio

There have been many attempts to create a history of video game audio. Most are brief, outdated, or inaccurate, or the history is intertwined within a more extensive exploration of video game music.

Campbell, Bruce D. "History of Video Game Music." *Bruce Donald Campbell [bdcampbell. net]*, 2016, bdcampbell.net/music/. Accessed 25 Jan. 2020.
Chang, Kyusik, et al. "Video Game Console Audio: Evolution and Future Trends." Sept. 2007. *Computer Graphics, Imaging and Visualisation.* www.researchgate.net/publication/4270536_Video_Game_Console_Audio_Evolution_and_Future_Trends.
Collins, Karen. *Game Sound: An Introduction to the History, Theory, and Practice of Video Game Music and Sound Design.* MIT P, 2008.
"The Evolution of Video Game Music." *NPR.org*, 13 Apr. 2008, www.npr.org/templates/story/story.php?storyId=89565567. Accessed 25 Jan. 2020.
Fritsch, Melanie. "History of Video Game Music." *Music and Game: Perspectives on a Popular Alliance*, Springer Science & Business Media, 2012, pp. 11–40.
Joe. "History of Video Game Soundtracks." *T.blog*, 29 July 2019, www.thomann.de/blog/en/history-of-video-game-soundtracks/. Accessed 25 Jan. 2020.
Kalata, K. "Best video game music of all time–2011." 25 Oct. 2011, www.hardcoregaming101.net/vgm/bestvgm2011.htm.

McDonald, Glenn. "A History of Video Game Music." *GameSpot*, 28 Mar. 2005, www.gamespot.com/articles/a-history-of-video-game-music/1100-6092391/. Accessed 25 Jan. 2020.
Mera, Miguel, et al. "Dimensions of Game Audio History." *The Routledge Companion to Screen Music and Sound*, Taylor & Francis, 2017, pp. 139–152.
Purves, Robert. "A Video Game Odyssey—a Brief History of Video Game Music." *Music Files*, www.mfiles.co.uk/video-game-music-history.htm. Accessed 25 Jan. 2020.
Seabrook, Andrea. "The Evolution of Video Game Music." *NPR.org*, 13 Apr. 2008, www.npr.org/templates/story/story.php?storyId=89565567.
Service, Tom. "The Evolution of Video Game Music." *BBC*, 19 Apr. 2018, www.bbc.co.uk/programmes/articles/4cFwfytTrrg439K8t t1ffcG/the-evolution-of-video-game-music. Accessed 25 Jan. 2020.
Summers, Tim. "Dimensions of Game Music History." *The Routledge Companion to Screen Music and Sound*, Taylor & Francis, 2017, pp. 139–152.
Sweet, Michael. "Video Game Composition Over the Past 40 Years." *Writing Interactive Music for Video Games: A Composer's Guide*, Pearson Education, 2014, pp. 85–108.
Weir, William. "From the Arcade to the Grammys: The Evolution of Video Game Music." *The Atlantic*, 10 Feb. 2011, www.theatlantic.com/entertainment/archive/2011/02/from-the-arcade-to-the-grammys-the-evolution-of-video-game-music/71082/. Accessed 25 Jan. 2020.

Video Game Music Composition

Today, more than ever, there are many accessible tools and digital audio workstations to create and implement music for video games. Multimedia composers share their workflow and the musical requirements necessary for implementation in a video game.

Brandon, Alexander. *Audio for Games: Planning, Process, and Production.* New Riders Pub, 2005.
Hoffert, Paul, and Jonathan Feist. *Music for New Media: Composing for Videogames, Web Sites, Presentations, and Other Interactive Media.* Berklee Publications, 2007.
Hopkins, Christopher. *Chiptune music: An exploration of compositional techniques as found*

in *Sunsoft Games for the Nintendo Entertainment System and Famicom from 1988–1992.* Five Towns College, PhD Dissertation. *ProQuest Dissertations and Theses.* Accessed 25 Jan. 2020.

Phillips, Winifred. *A Composer's Guide to Game Music.* MIT P, 2014.

Thomas, Chance. *Composing Music for Games: The Art, Technology and Business of Video Game Scoring.* CRC P, 2016.

Other Information

Other sources explore video game history, audio hardware, and music's impact within video games.

Goodwin, Simon N. "Chapter 2: Early Digital Audio Hardware and Chapter 3: Sample Replay." *Beep to Boom: The Development of Advanced Runtime Sound Systems for Games and Extended Reality,* Routledge, 2019.

Hildenbrand, Jerry. "Does My Phone Have a DAC? Explaining DACs and Amps in Smartphones Today." *Android Central,* 31 Oct. 2017, www.androidcentral.com/does-my-phone-have-dac-explaining-dacs-and-amps-smartphones-today.

Poh, Michael. "Evolution of Home Video Game Consoles: 1967–2011." *Hongkiat,* 2011, www.hongkiat.com/blog/evolution-of-home-video-game-consoles-1967-2011/. Accessed 3 Aug. 2018.

Rubin, Peter. "Check Out This Glorious, Colorful History of Arcade Games." *WIRED,* 13 May 2014, www.wired.com/2014/05/arcade-history/.

Summers, Tim. *Understanding Video Game Music.* Cambridge UP, 2016.

Théberge, Paul, et al. "Stereo Timeline." *Living Stereo: Histories and Cultures of Multichannel Sound,* Bloomsbury Academic, 2015, p. 270.

Wardyga, Brian J. "Chapter 2: Behind the Technology." *The Video Games Textbook: History • Business • Technology,* CRC Press, 2018.

Weske, Jörg. "History." *Digital Sound and Music in Computer Games,* Dec. 2000, 3daudio.info/gamesound/history.html.

Zehnder, S. M., and S.D. Lipscomb. "The Role of Music in Video Games." *Playing Video Games: Motives, Responses, and Consequences,* Lawrence Erlbaum Assoc, 2006, pp. 241–258.

Honorable Mention

In conclusion, there will always be more games and more great audio to listen to and share. Check out these games and their notable musical tracks for an expanded history of video game audio.

Apple iOS

• *Super Hexagon*

PUBLISHER: Terry Cavanagh. RELEASE DATE: August 31, 2012 (WW). COMPOSER: Niamh Houston. GENRE: Action. NOTABLE MUSICAL TRACK: "Courtesy."

Atari Jaguar

• *Wolfenstein 3D*

PUBLISHER: Atari. RELEASE DATE: May 1994 (NA). COMPOSER: Bobby Prince. SERIES: *Castle Wolfenstein.* GENRE: 1st person shooter. NOTABLE MUSICAL TRACK: "Get Them Before They Get You (Episode 1 Mission 1)."

Atari Lynx

• *Chip's Challenge*

PUBLISHER: Atari. RELEASE DATE: September 1989 (NA). COMPOSERS: Lx Rudis and Robert Vieira. GENRE: Puzzle. NOTABLE MUSICAL TRACK: "Title Screen."

• *Toki*

PUBLISHER: Atari. RELEASE DATE: 1991 (NA). COMPOSER: Matt Scott. GENRE: Platformer. NOTABLE MUSICAL TRACK: "Labyrinth of Caves (Stage 1,3,4,5,6)."

ColecoVision

• *Popeye*

PUBLISHER: Parker Bros. RELEASE DATE: 1983 (NA). GENRE: Platformer. NOTABLE MUSICAL TRACK: "Intro Theme."

• *Subroc*

PUBLISHER: Coleco. RELEASE DATE: 1983 (NA). GENRE: Action.

COMMODORE AMIGA

• *Cannon Fodder*

PUBLISHER: Virgin. RELEASE DATE: December 1993 (NA). COMPOSERS: Richard Joseph and Jon Hare. GENRE: Shmup. NOTABLE MUSICAL TRACK: "War! (Never Been So Much Fun)."

• *Turrican II: The Final Fight*

PUBLISHER: Rainbow Arts. RELEASE DATE: 1991 (EU). COMPOSER: Chris Huelsbeck. SERIES: *Turrican*. GENRE: Run-and-gun. NOTABLE MUSICAL TRACK: "Freedom (Ending Theme)."

COMMODORE 64

• *Myth: History in the Making*

PUBLISHER: System 3. RELEASE DATE: 1989 (NA). COMPOSER: Jeroen Tel. GENRE: Platformer. NOTABLE MUSICAL TRACK: "Title Theme."

MATTEL INTELLIVISION

• *Deep Pockets: Super Pro Pool and Billiards*

PUBLISHER: Mattel. RELEASE DATE: 2010. Development: 1990. SOUND DESIGNER: David Warhol. NOTABLE MUSICAL TRACK: "Billiard Blues (Title Theme)."

MICROSOFT XBOX ONE

• *Guitar Hero Live*

PUBLISHER: Activision. U.S. RELEASE DATE: October 20, 2015. DEVELOPER: Harmonix. GENRE: Music/Rhythm.

• *Halo 5: Guardians*

PUBLISHER: Microsoft Studios. RELEASE DATE: October 27, 2015. COMPOSER: Kazuma Jinnouchi. SERIES: *Halo*. GENRE: 1st person shooter. NOTABLE MUSICAL TRACK: "The Trials."

MICROSOFT XBOX 360

• *Eternal Sonata*

PUBLISHER: Namco Bandai Games. RELEASE DATE: June 14, 2007. COMPOSER: Motoi Sakuraba. GENRE: RPG. NOTABLE MUSICAL TRACK: "Raindrop (Prelude Op. 28, No. 15)."

• *Fez*

PUBLISHER: Microsoft. RELEASE DATE: April 13, 2012. COMPOSER: Rich Vreeland. GENRE: Puzzle/Platformer. NOTABLE MUSICAL TRACK: "Reflection."

NEC TURBOGRAFX-16

• *Air Zonk*

PUBLISHER: Hudson Soft. RELEASE DATE: 1992 (NA). COMPOSERS: Daisuke Morishima and Hisashi Matsushita. SERIES: *Air Zonk*. GENRE: Shmup.

• *Champions Forever Boxing*

PUBLISHER: NEC. RELEASE DATE: 1991 (NA). COMPOSERS: Michael J. Sokyrka and Krisjan Hatlelid. GENRE: Boxing.

NINTENDO FAMICOM/NES

• *Castlevania III: Dracula's Curse*

PUBLISHER: Konami. RELEASE DATE: December 22, 1989 (JP), September 1990 (NA), December 10, 1992 (EU). COMPOSERS: Hidenori Maezawa, Jun Funahashi, Yukie Morimoto, and Yoshinori Sasaki. SERIES: *Castlevania*. GENRE: Platformer. NOTABLE MUSICAL TRACK: "Beginning."

• *Gimmick!*

PUBLISHER: Sunsoft. RELEASE DATE: January 31, 1992 (JP), May 19, 1993, as *Mr. Gimmick* (NO). COMPOSER: Matashi Kageyama. GENRE: Platformer. NOTABLE MUSICAL TRACK: "Happy Birthday (Stage 1)."

NINTENDO GAME BOY

• *Castlevania II: Belmont's Revenge*

PUBLISHER: Konami. RELEASE DATE: August 1991 (NA). COMPOSER: Hidehiro Funauchi. SERIES: *Castlevania*. GENRE: Platformer.

• *Tetris*

PUBLISHER: Nintendo. RELEASE DATE: June 14, 1989 (JP), July 31, 1989 (NA), September

28, 1990 (EU). COMPOSER: Hirokazu Tanaka. SERIES: *Tetris*. GENRE: Puzzle. NOTABLE MUSICAL TRACK: "Korobeiniki (Type A)."

NINTENDO GAME BOY COLOR

• *Shantae*

PUBLISHER: Capcom. RELEASE DATE: June 2, 2002 (NA). COMPOSER: Jake Kaufman. SERIES: *Shantae*. GENRE: Platformer. NOTABLE MUSICAL TRACK: "Labyrinths."

• *The Smurf's Nightmare*

PUBLISHER: Infogrames Europe. RELEASE DATES: February 28, 1999 (NA), 1999 (EU). COMPOSER: Alberto José González. SERIES: Smurfs. GENRE: Platformer. NOTABLE MUSICAL TRACK: "The Mysterious Planet 1 and 2."

NINTENDO GAMECUBE

• *F-Zero GX*

PUBLISHER: Nintendo of America. RELEASE DATE: July 25, 2003. COMPOSER: Hidenori Shoji. SERIES: *F-Zero*. GENRE: Racing. NOTABLE MUSICAL TRACK: "Mute City."

• *Metroid Prime*

PUBLISHER: Nintendo. RELEASE DATE: November 17, 2002 (NA), February 28, 2003 (JP), March 21, 2003 (EU). COMPOSERS: Kenji Yamamoto and Kouichi Kyuma. SERIES: *Metroid, Metroid Prime*. GENRE: Action-adventure. NOTABLE MUSICAL TRACK: "Phendrana Drifts."

NINTENDO 64

• *Jet Force Gemini*

PUBLISHER: Rare. RELEASE DATES: October 11, 1999 (NA), October 29, 1999 (EU), 1999 (JP, as *Star Twins*). COMPOSERS: Robin Beanland, Alistair Lindsay, and Graeme Norgate. GENRE: 3rd person shooter. NOTABLE MUSICAL TRACK: "Water Ruin."

NINTENDO 3DS

• *Kid Icarus: Uprising*

PUBLISHER: Nintendo of America. RELEASE DATE: March 22, 2012. COMPOSERS: Motoi Sakuraba, Yuzo Koshiro, Masafumi Takada, Noriyuki Iwadare, Takahiro Nishi, and Yasunori Mitsuda. SERIES: *Kid Icarus*. GENRE: 3rd Person Shooter. NOTABLE MUSICAL TRACK: "Dark Pit's Theme."

NINTENDO WII

• *Bit.Trip Complete*

PUBLISHER: Aksys Games. RELEASE DATE: September 13, 2011. SERIES: *Bit.Trip*. GENRE: Action/Music. NOTABLE MUSICAL TRACK: "Credits (Mermaid ft. Anamanaguchi)."

• *No More Heroes*

PUBLISHER: Ubisoft. RELEASE DATE: December 6, 2007. COMPOSERS: Masafumi Takada and Jun Fukuda. SERIES: *No More Heroes*. GENRE: Action-adventure. NOTABLE MUSICAL TRACK: "We Are Finally Cowboys."

NOKIA N-GAGE

• *Super Monkey Ball*

PUBLISHER: Sega of America. RELEASE DATE: October 7, 2003 (NA, EU). COMPOSER: Martin Goodall. SERIES: *Super Monkey Ball*. GENRE: Platformer. NOTABLE MUSICAL TRACK: "Jungle."

PERSONAL COMPUTER

• *VVVVVV*

PUBLISHER: Nicalis. RELEASE DATE: January 11, 2010. COMPOSER: Magnus Pålsson. GENRE: Platformer. NOTABLE MUSICAL TRACK: "Potential for Anything."

SEGA CD/MEGA CD

• *Night Trap*

PUBLISHER: Sega. RELEASE DATE: October 15, 1992 (NA), May 1993 (EU), November 19,

1993 (JP). COMPOSERS: Sunny BlueSkyes and Martin Lund. GENRE: Interactive movie.

SEGA GAME GEAR

• *The GG Shinobi*

PUBLISHER: Sega of America. RELEASE DATE: 1991 (NA). COMPOSER: Yuzo Koshiro. SERIES: *Shinobi*. GENRE: Hack-and-slash. NOTABLE MUSICAL TRACK: "Highway Stage."

SEGA GENESIS/MEGA DRIVE

• *Castle of Illusion Starring Mickey Mouse*

PUBLISHER: Sega. RELEASE DATE: November 21, 1990 (JP), December 1990 (NA), March 1991 (EU). COMPOSER: Shigenori Kamiya. SERIES: *Illusion*. GENRE: Platformer. NOTABLE MUSICAL TRACK: "Teacup Library."

• *Sonic the Hedgehog*

PUBLISHER: Sega. RELEASE DATE: June 23, 1991 (NA, EU), July 26, 1991 (JP). COMPOSER: Masato Nakamura. SERIES: *Sonic the Hedgehog*. GENRE: Platformer. NOTABLE MUSICAL TRACK: "Green Hill Zone."

SEGA MASTER SYSTEM

• *Ghouls 'n' Ghosts*

PUBLISHER: Sega of America. RELEASE DATE: March 1990 (NA). COMPOSERS: Chris Huelsbeck and Darius Zendeh. SERIES: *Ghouls 'n' Ghosts*. GENRE: Platformer. NOTABLE MUSICAL TRACK: "Stage 1 Theme."

• *R-Type*

PUBLISHER: Sega. RELEASE DATE: October 1, 1988 (JP), December 1988 (NA), 1988 (EU). COMPOSER: Masato Ishizaki. GENRE: Horizontal-scrolling shooter.

• *Wonder Boy III: The Dragon's Trap*

PUBLISHER: Sega. RELEASE DATE: September 1989 (NA), 1989 (EU). COMPOSER: Shinichi Sakamoto. SERIES: *Wonder Boy*. GENRE: Platformer.

SEGA SATURN

• *Panzer Dragoon Saga*

PUBLISHER: Sega. RELEASE DATE: January 29, 1998 (JP), April 30, 1998 (NA), June 5, 1998 (EU). COMPOSERS: Saori Kobayashi and Mariko Nanba. SERIES: *Panzer Dragoon*. NOTABLE MUSICAL TRACK: "Sona Mi Areru Ec Sancitu (Ending Credits)."

• *Sonic 3D Blast*

PUBLISHER: Sega. RELEASE DATE: November 20, 1996 (NA), February 14, 1997 (EU), October 14, 1999 (JP). COMPOSER: Richard Jacques. SERIES: *Sonic the Hedgehog*. GENRE: Platformer. NOTABLE MUSICAL TRACK: "You're My Hero (Ending Credits)."

SEGA 32X

• *Kolibri*

PUBLISHER: Sega. RELEASE DATE: November 1995 (NA), November 30, 1995 (EU). COMPOSER: Zsolt Dvornik. GENRE: Shooter. NOTABLE MUSICAL TRACK: "Dark Obstruction (Stage 14)."

SONY PS4

• *Dying Light*

PUBLISHER: Techland. RELEASE DATE: January 28, 2015. COMPOSER: Pawel Blaszczak. SERIES: *Dying Light*. GENRE: Survival horror. NOTABLE MUSICAL TRACK: "Main Menu Theme."

SONY PS2

• *Crash Twinsanity*

PUBLISHER: Vivendi Universal Games. RELEASE DATE: September 28, 2004. COMPOSER: Spiralmouth. SERIES: *Crash Bandicoot*. GENRE: Platformer. NOTABLE MUSICAL TRACK: "Totem Hokum (Bee Chase)."

• *Kingdom Hearts*

PUBLISHER: Square Electronic Arts. RELEASE DATE: March 28, 2002 (JP), September 17, 2002 (NA), November 15, 2002 (EU). COMPOSER: Yoko Shimomura. SERIES: *Kingdom Hearts*. GENRE: Action RPG. NOTABLE MUSICAL TRACK: "Hicari."

Appendix

Commercial Video Game Music Soundtracks

After Burner 20th Anniversary Box. Catalog Number WM-0581–6. Published by Wave Master. 6 Discs. November 29, 2007. https://vgmdb.net/album/4992

Azel: Panzer Dragoon RPG Complete Album. Catalog Number MJCA-10009. Published by Marvelous Entertainment. 2 Discs. February 4, 1998. https://vgmdb.net/album/1038

Beat Saber Original Game Soundtrack. Catalog Number N/A. Published by Epic Music Productions. Digital Download. May 1, 2018. https://vgmdb.net/album/77397

Bit.Trip Runner Original Soundtrack. Catalog Number N/A. Published by Gaijin Games. Digital Download. August 3, 2010. https://vgmdb.net/album/20554

The Bouncer Original Soundtrack. Catalog Number SSCX-10049–50. Published by DigiCube. 2 Discs. March 23, 2001. https://vgmdb.net/album/82

Bravely Default Flying Fairy Original Soundtrack. Catalog Number SQEX-10333~4. Published by Square Enix. 2 Discs. October 10, 2012. https://vgmdb.net/album/33726

Capcom Music Generation Famicom Music Complete Works Rockman 1–6. Catalog Number CPCA-1064~6. Published by Suleputer. 3 Discs. September 20, 2002. https://vgmdb.net/album/255

Castlevania III: Dracula's Curse—Original Video Game Soundtrack. Catalog Number MOND-073. Published by Mondo. 2 Discs. March 22, 2017. https://vgmdb.net/album/66716

Celeste Original Soundtrack. Catalog Number STS-028. Published by Ship to Shore PhonoCo. 2 Discs. May 2018. https://vgmdb.net/album/76301

Chrono Trigger Original Sound Version. Catalog Number PSCN-5021–3. Published by NTT Publishing. 3 Discs. March 25, 1995. https://vgmdb.net/album/18

Crash Twinsanity Original Videogame Soundtrack. Catalog Number N/A. Published by Vivendi Universal. Digital Download. 2004. https://vgmdb.net/album/9343

Cuphead Deluxe Vinyl Soundtrack. Catalog Number 8BIT-8064. Published by iam8bit.

4 Discs. September 2017. https://vgmdb.net/album/68904

Death Stranding Original Score. Catalog Number 19439727722. Published by Sony Classical. 3 Discs. March 13, 2020. https://vgmdb.net/album/95928

Destiny Original Soundtrack. Catalog Number N/A. Published by Bungie Music Publishing. Digital Download. September 26, 2014. https://vgmdb.net/album/48297

Donkey Kong Country 2: Diddy's Kong Quest The Original Donkey Kong Country2 Soundtrack. Catalog Number N/A. Published by Nintendo of America. 1 Disc. November 1, 1995. https://vgmdb.net/album/469

Dying Light Soundtrack. Catalog Number N/A. Published by Techland. Digital Download. February 4, 2015. https://vgmdb.net/album/51251

ecco SONGS OF TIME: A MUSICAL JOURNEY BENEATH THE WAVES. Catalog Number 697–124–126–2. Published by Sega Music Group. 1 Disc. October 1, 1996. https://vgmdb.net/album/353

Epic Mickey 2: The Power of Two Original Game Score. Catalog Number D001837502. Published by Walt Disney Records. 1 Disc. November 19, 2012. https://vgmdb.net/album/36368

F-Zero GX/AX Original Soundtracks. Catalog Number SCDC-00358–9. Published by Scitron Digital Contents. 2 Discs. July 22, 2004. https://vgmdb.net/album/411

Fantasia: Music Evolved Original Soundtrack. Catalog Number SE-3124–2. Published by Sumthing Else Music Works. 1 Disc. October 21, 2014. https://vgmdb.net/album/48248

Fez Original Soundtrack. Catalog Number PO050001. Published by Polytron. 2 Discs. November 26, 2015. https://vgmdb.net/album/55857

Final Fantasy VI Original Sound Version. Catalog Number PSCN-5001–3. Published by NTT Publishing. 3 Discs. March 25, 1994. https://vgmdb.net/album/40

Final Fantasy VII Original Sound Track. Catalog Number SSCX-10004. Published by DigiCube. February 10, 1997. https://vgmdb.net/album/3407

Fire Emblem: Awakening—Fire Emblem: Kaku-sei Original Soundtrack. Catalog Number TSCM-0008–12. Published by Symphony No.5 / Tablier Communications. 5 Discs. March 27, 2013. https://vgmdb.net/album/37510

Gitarooman Original Soundtrack. Catalog Number KECH-1190. Published by KOEI. 1 Disc. July 4, 2001. https://vgmdb.net/album/854

God of War II Official Soundtrack. Catalog Number SYS-1128. Published by System Recordings. 1 Disc. April 10, 2007. https://vgmdb.net/album/4731

Grand Theft Auto—The Soundtrack. Catalog Number 76896 428682 1. Published by BMG Interactive. 1 Disc. 1997. https://vgmdb.net/album/72819

Halo 5: Guardians Original Soundtrack. Catalog Number 34300005. Published by Microsoft Studios / 343 Industries. 2 Discs. October 30, 2015. https://vgmdb.net/album/54792

Halo Original Soundtrack. Catalog Number SE-2000–2. Published by Sumthing Else Music Works. 1 Disc. June 11, 2002. https://vgmdb.net/album/190

Jet Set Radio Future Original Sound Tracks. Catalog Number SCDC-00166. Published by Scitron Digital Contents. 1 Disc. March 20, 2002. https://vgmdb.net/album/290

Journey Original Soundtrack. Catalog Number SE-3009–2. Published by Sumthing Else Music Works. 1 Disc. October 9, 2012. https://vgmdb.net/album/34267

The King of Fighters '96. Catalog Number PCCB-00223. Published by Scitron / Pony Canyon. 1 Disc. August 21, 1996. https://vgmdb.net/album/1567

Kingdom Hearts Original Soundtrack. Catalog Number 7243–5–80453–21. Published by Walt Disney Records. 2 Discs. November 25, 2002. https://vgmdb.net/album/5059

The Last of Us Soundtrack. Catalog Number 88765 49315 2. Published by Masterworks. 1 Disc. June 11, 2013. https://vgmdb.net/album/39075

The Legend of Zelda: Ocarina of Time Original Sound Track. Catalog Number PCCG-00475. Published by Pony Canyon. 1 Disc. December 18, 1998. https://vgmdb.net/album/293

The Legend of Zelda—Takt of Wind—Original Sound Tracks. Catalog Number SCDC-00250–1. Published by Scitron Digital Contents. 2 Discs. March 19, 2003. https://vgmdb.net/album/418

LocoRoco's Song: LocoRoco Original Soundtrack. Catalog Number COCX-33981. Published by Columbia Music Entertainment. 1 Disc. October 18, 2006. https://vgmdb.net/album/1094

The Lost World: Jurassic Park Original Soundtrack from the PlayStation and Saturn Games. Catalog Number SID-8803. Published by Sonic Image Records. February 10, 1998. https://vgmdb.net/album/2548

Lumines Remixes. Catalog Number BRST-0001–2. Published by Brainstorm. 2 Discs. May 27, 2005. https://vgmdb.net/album/2541

Mass Effect Original Soundtrack. Catalog Number SE-2041–2. Published by Sumthing Else Music Works. 1 Disc. November 20, 2007. https://vgmdb.net/album/5380

Metal Gear Solid Original Game Soundtrack. Catalog Number KICA-7895. Published by Konami. 1 Disc. September 23, 1998. https://vgmdb.net/album/130

Metal Slug Complete Sound Box. Catalog Number SCDC-00542–9. Published by Happinet. 8 Discs. September 6, 2006. https://vgmdb.net/album/1113

Metroid Prime & Fusion Original Soundtracks. Catalog Number SCDC-00276–7. Published by Scitron Digital Contents. 2 Discs. June 18, 2003. https://vgmdb.net/album/412

Minecraft—Volume Alpha. Catalog Number GI-243. Published by Ghostly International. 1 Disc. August 21, 2015. https://vgmdb.net/album/78759

Monument Valley Official Game Soundtrack Volumes 1 & 2. Catalog Number 8BIT-8009. Published by iam8bit. 2 Discs. May 18, 2016. https://vgmdb.net/album/56893

Music from Ys III Wanderers from Ys. Catalog Number 276A-7715. Published by Falcom. 1 Disc. October 21, 1989. https://vgmdb.net/album/1277

The Music of Grand Theft Auto V [Limited Edition]. Catalog Number N/A. Published by Mass Appeal Records and Rockstar Games. 3 Discs. December 9, 2014. https://vgmdb.net/album/49022

Ni No Kuni: Dominion of the Dark Djinn—Ni no Kuni: Wrath of the White Witch—The Original Soundtrack. Catalog Number WAYO-003–4. Published by Wayô Records. 2 Discs. March 29, 2013. https://vgmdb.net/album/37618

NieR: Automata Original Soundtrack. Catalog Number SQEX-10589~91. Published by Square Enix Co. 3 Discs. March 29, 2017. https://vgmdb.net/album/65091

No More Heroes Original Sound Track. Catalog Number MJCD-20108. Published by Marvelous Entertainment. 3 Discs. January 23, 2008. https://vgmdb.net/album/5585

The Orange Box Original Soundtrack. Catalog Number N/A. Published by Valve. 1 Disc. November 1, 2007. https://vgmdb.net/album/6194

Ori and the Blind Forest Original Soundtrack. Catalog Number 8BIT-8023. Published by iam8bit. 2 Discs. February 2017. https://vgmdb.net/album/58390

PaRappa The Rapper Original Soundtrack. Catalog Number SRCL-3742. Published by Sony Records. December 12, 1996. https://vgmdb.net/album/701

Patapon Original Soundtrack. Catalog Number N/A. Published by Sony Computer Entertainment Inc. 1 Disc. July 13, 2011. https://vgmdb.net/album/27335

Radiant Silvergun Soundtrack. Catalog Number TYCY-5613. Published by Futureland / Toshiba

EMI. 1 Disc. August 7, 1998. https://vgmdb.net/album/2156

Red Dead Redemption Original Soundtrack. Catalog Number 36886–1. Published by Rockstar Games. 1 Disc. August 23, 2010. https://vgmdb.net/album/20838

Rez / Gamer's Guide to…. Catalog Number IDCT-1001. Published by Third-Ear/Musicmine. 1 Disc. January 23, 2002. https://vgmdb.net/album/386

Shantae Original Soundtrack. Catalog Number N/A. Published by Limited Run Games. 1 Disc. November 11, 2016. https://vgmdb.net/album/62508

Shenmue chapter 1—yokosuka—Original Sound Track. Catalog Number TYCY-10034–5. Published by Futureland/Toshiba EMI. 2 Discs. March 23, 2000. https://vgmdb.net/album/595

Sonic the Hedgehog 1 & 2 Soundtrack. Catalog Number POCS-21032–4. Published by DCT Records. 3 Discs. October 19, 2011. https://vgmdb.net/album/26814

Splatoon Original Soundtrack—Splatune. Catalog Number EBCD-10001~2. Published by Enterbrain. 2 Discs. October 21, 2015. https://vgmdb.net/album/54591

Streets of Rage 2 Original Soundtrack. Catalog Number MCM-10106–2. Published by Mars Colony Music. 1 Disc. February 18, 2000. https://vgmdb.net/album/2134

Subarashiki Kono Sekai Original Soundtrack. Catalog Number SQEX-10100. Published by Square Enix. 1 Disc. August 22, 2007. https://vgmdb.net/album/4630

Super Hexagon EP. Catalog Number 8BIT-8004. Published by iam8bit. 1 Disc. November 2015. https://vgmdb.net/album/54339

Super Mario Galaxy Official Soundtrack. Catalog Number NTDO-17239. Published by Nintendo of America. 1 Disc. October 23, 2011. https://vgmdb.net/album/35008

Super Mario 64 Original Sound Track. Catalog Number N/A . Published by Nintendo of America. 1 Disc. November 1996. https://vgmdb.net/album/4869

Super Mario 3D World Original Sound Track. Catalog Number NTDT-17289–90. Published by Nintendo. 2 Discs. January 2014. https://vgmdb.net/album/42692

Super Metroid "Sound in Action." Catalog Number SRCL-2920. Published by Sony Records. 1 Disc. June 22, 1994. https://vgmdb.net/album/883

Sword & Sworcery LP—Ballad of the Space Babies. Catalog Number DF-001. Published by Capybara Games. 1 Disc. April 2011. https://vgmdb.net/album/62536

Tempest 2000: The Soundtrack. Catalog Number J8909. Published by Atari. 1 Disc. 1995. https://vgmdb.net/album/1916

Thumper. Catalog Number N/A. Published by Thrill Jockey Records. 1 Disc. October 14, 2016. https://vgmdb.net/album/62422

Thumper Official Soundtrack. Catalog Number N/A. Published by Limited Run Games. 1 Disc. https://vgmdb.net/album/88372

Tommy Tallarico Virgin Games Greatest Hits Volume One. Catalog Number 7243–8-28445–2-5. Published by Capitol. 1 Disc. June 14, 1994. https://vgmdb.net/album/1984

Transistor Original Soundtrack. Catalog Number N/A. Published by Supergiant Games. 1 Disc. May 20, 2014. https://vgmdb.net/album/45769

Trusty Bell—Chopin no Yume—Original Score. Catalog Number KICA-1445–8. Published by King Records. 4 Discs. July 25, 2007. https://vgmdb.net/album/4631

Two Dots, Vol. 1–3 (Original Soundtrack). Catalog Number DM-006. Published by Dots Music. 2 Discs. November 17, 2016. https://vgmdb.net/album/63051

Uncharted: The Nathan Drake Collection. Catalog Number 8BIT-8010. Published by iam8bit. 3 Discs. March 2016. https://vgmdb.net/album/55286

Undertale Vinyl Soundtrack. Catalog Number 8BIT-8048. Published by iam8bit. 2 Discs. December 2016. https://vgmdb.net/album/61074

Wander and the Colossus Original Soundtrack: Roar of the Earth. Catalog Number KICA-1379. Published by King Records. 1 Disc. December 7, 2005. https://vgmdb.net/album/96

Glossary of Terms

ADPCM: Short for adaptive differential pulse-code modulation.

ADSR: Short for Attack Decay Sustain Release, describing the four stages of a sound. Programmers manipulate the ADSR envelope to adjust a sound's pitch, timbre, and volume at each stage of production.

AES: Short for SNK Neo Geo Advanced Entertainment System, the home counterpart to the MVS.

AM: Short for amplitude modulation, a form of sound generation used in the Atari Jaguar

Ambiance: In music, a structure that emphasizes mood over melody and rhythm. Ambient music uses elongated tones, natural sounds, and slow melodies.

Audio channel: An audio output stream to a designated sound source. The number of audio channels is described as monophonic, stereophonic, or surround audio. In contrast with sound channel.

A/V: Short for audiovisual. It refers to the device ports for audio and video output. In contrast with separated audio and video ports.

AY-3–8910: The preferred soundchip of arcade games in the early 1980s. A variant of the series appears within the Intellivision.

Basic waveform: An unaltered waveform. Some examples are square, sine, sawtooth, triangle, and pulse. Basic waveforms are combined in audio generation such as FM and AM synthesis.

BIOS: Short for Basic Input/Output System. It consists of initialization programs for when a system first boots up. The BIOS is needed to know how to load the system OS or game.

BPM: Short for beats per minute, a measure of musical tempo. A BPM of 60 represents one beat per second.

CD-DA: Short for CD-Digital Audio, an audio standard for audio tracks on an audio CD recognized by a CD player. The audio standard supports audio with a bit depth of 16 bits and a sampling rate of 44.1 kHz. CD-DA tracks on a game CD begin at track 2, leaving track 1 for game data.

CD-quality audio: An audio standard matching CD-DA. Unlike CD-DA, CD-quality audio does not have to be stored as an audio track on an audio CD.

Cover: A recording of a song other than from the original artist. Covers have alterations in the vocals and instrumentation while retaining the original melody.

CPU: Short for central processing unit, the microprocessor that performs the majority of calculations. Specialized microprocessors like the GPU and APU offload calculations from the CPU.

C64: Short for Commodore 64.

Cutscene: A non-interactive game sequence, used to direct the player to pivotal plot and character elements. Cutscenes can be either cinematic, played as a pre-rendered video file, or in-game, rendered in real-time through the game engine.

DAC: Short for Digital-to-Analog converter, used to convert digital audio streams, like PCM, to an analog stream sent to an audio output channel.

DC: Short for Sega Dreamcast.

DD5.1: Short for Dolby Digital 5.1.

DDR: Short for Dance Dance Revolution, a series of arcade and home console games with dance as the primary gameplay element.

DLC: Short for downloadable content.

DMA: Short for direct memory access, the ability for a hardware chip to access main system memory independently of the CPU. It is commonly used to send audio sample data to a soundchip or DSP.

DPC: Short for Display Processor Chip, an enhancement chip used for *Pitfall 2: Lost Caverns* (1984) for the Atari 2600.

DPCM: Short for differential pulse-code modulation, a form of PCM.

DPLII: Short for Dolby Pro Logic II, an analog surround sound solution.

Drum kit: A particular set of percussion instruments including snare drum, hi hats, crash cymbal, high tom, kick drum, mid-tom, ride cymbal, and floor tom.

DS: Short for Nintendo DS.

DSP: Short for Digital Signal Processor, used to add audio effects to audio and manipulate game data.

DTS: Short for Digital Theater Sound, a digital encoding format for surround sound.

DVD-quality audio: An audio standard of 16-bit depth and 48 kHz sampling rate.

EAD: Short for Nintendo Entertainment Analysis and Development

ECS: Short for Entertainment Computer System, an enhancement module for the Intellivision used for *Melody Blaster* (1983).

EQ: Short for equalization, a method of adjusting volumes of specific frequencies of audio

Famicom: Short for Family Computer.

FDS: Short for Famicom Disk System.

5B: Short for Sunsoft 5B, an enhancement chip used in the Famicom version of *Gimmick!* (1992).

FM: Short for frequency modulation, a form of sound generation.

FMV: Short for full-motion video. It was used frequently in early CD-based games to showcase the extra memory.

FPS: Short for first-person shooter, a genre of video games in which the player shoots targets from a first-person viewing perspective.

Game: A software for a computer or gaming system with a win condition. In contrast with business applications.

GB: Short for Game Boy, a handheld gaming system manufactured by Nintendo.

GBA: Short for Game Boy Advance, a handheld gaming system manufactured by Nintendo.

GBC: Short for Game Boy Color, a handheld gaming system manufactured by Nintendo.

GEMS: Short for Genesis Editor for Music and Sound Effects, a popular sound engine used by Genesis developers.

GEN: Short for Sega Genesis/Mega Drive.

GG: Short for Sega Game Gear.

Handheld gaming system: A device capable of reading games that is held comfortably within the hands. It is not heavy nor large and is portable.

Home console: A device capable of reading games that connects to a screen and speakers. It can be heavy and large. It is designed to remain in one place when in use.

HuCard: A card-sized ROM cartridge playable on the TurboGrafx-16. Its U.S. equivalent is the TurboChip.

HuC6280A: Short for Hudson Soft HuC 6280A, the soundchip of the Turbo Grafx-16.

iOS: The operating system for mobile devices manufactured by Apple including the Apple iPad and iPhone.

Jerry: The soundchip of the Atari Jaguar.

Jingle: A musical track of short duration without looping, used to signal a status change in a game, like success, failure, or game start.

LFE: Short for low-frequency effects. The

subwoofer of a surround sound speaker system emits them.

Live: An extended recording of a live performance, usually of many instruments and/or voices. In contrast to orchestral soundtracks using instrument samples.

LR35902: Short for Sharp LR35902, the soundchip of the Game Boy.

Master recording: The original recording of a piece or song by the original artist.

MCPX: Short for NVIDIA Media Communications Processor, the audio processor of the Microsoft Xbox.

MD: Short for Sega Mega Drive/Genesis.

Microprocessor: A computer chip containing an integrated circuit, the brains of a computer or gaming system. A microprocessor can be dedicated to one particular function, like audio, or multiple functions, like the CPU and graphics.

MIDI: Short for Musical Instrument Digital Interface.

Mikey: The chip of the Atari Lynx.

Mixing: The process of combining multiple sound channels into an audio channel.

MMC5: Short for Nintendo Memory Management Controller 5, an enhancement chip for the NES.

MOD: A music data format first used on the Commodore Amiga and also by the Lynx.

Musical track: A complete musical piece, not to be confused with a track in a racing game. A musical track can have vocals.

MP3: An audio file format based on compression. It was popularized with the rise of file-sharing applications like Napster and Limewire.

MSM5205: Short for Oki MSM5205, the soundchip of the Turbo-Grafx-CD.

MT-32: Short for Roland MT-32.

MVS: Short for SNK Multi Video System, the arcade counterpart to the AES.

NES: Short for Nintendo Entertainment System.

N64: Short for Nintendo 64.

Official soundtrack: A collection of musical tracks either taken directly from a video game or prepared by the game's composers or audio contributors with support from the game's publisher. An official soundtrack is distributed either on physical media for audio (audio cassette, CD, vinyl) or through digital distribution (streaming, download). An official soundtrack can lack musical tracks from the game soundtrack. For games in which musical tracks are highly adaptive to game statuses, the official soundtrack contains representative tracks that recreate one possible version.

PCM: Short for pulse-code modulation

Periodic noise: A signal with a regular period added to white noise.

POKEY: Short for Potentiometer and Keyboard Integrated Circuit, an enhancement chip used in *Ballblazer* (1987) and *Commando* (1987) for the Atari 7800.

PS Vita: Short for PlayStation Vita.

PS1: Short for Sony PlayStation.

PS2: Short for Sony PlayStation 2.

PS3: Short for Sony PlayStation 3.

PS4: Short for Sony PlayStation 4.

PS5: Short for Sony PlayStation 5.

PSG: Short for programmable sound generator, a type of soundchip for primitive sound production.

PSP: Short for PlayStation Portable, the first handheld system by Sony.

QSound: An analog encoding format to approximate 3D sounds in a stereo audio signal.

QTE: Short for quick-time event, a moment in a game requiring the player to press a button quickly to progress.

RAM: Short for random-access memory. Some CD-based games transfer their game data to system RAM to use the CD drive to read music from audio CDs.

RCP: Short for Reality Coprocessor, the chip in the N64 that manipulates the graphics and audio.

RDP: Short for Reality Display Processor, the chip in the N64 that handles pixel rasterization and Z-buffer computations.

Real-time: In video games, the ability to process calculations at the time of request. In contrast with pre-processed media and cutscenes.

Redbook: Another term for CD-Digital Audio.

RF Adapter: Short for radio frequency adapter. A device to modulate an A/V signal to an RF signal over coaxial cable to a television.

ROM: Short for read-only memory. It commonly refers to the game data within a game cartridge.

RP2C33: Short for Ricoh RP2C33, the soundchip of the Famicom Disk System

RSP: Short for Reality Signal Processor, the chip in the N64 that performs transform, clipping and light calculations, and triangle setup.

SCD: Short for Sega CD.

SCSP: Short for Saturn Custom Sound Processor, the soundchip of the Sega Saturn.

SG-1000: Short for the Sega Game 1000, an earlier model of the Sega Master System.

64DD: Short for Nintendo 64 Disk Drive.

SMPS: Sample Music Playback System, a common sound engine used by Genesis developers.

SMS: Short for Sega Master System.

SNES: Short for Super Nintendo Entertainment System or Super NES.

SN76489: Short for Texas Instruments SN76489, the soundchip of the Sega Master System and Game Gear.

SN76489A: The soundchip of the ColecoVision and the PSG soundchip of the Sega Genesis/Mega Drive.

Software: A program or application for a computer or gaming system. It lacks a win condition. In contrast to game.

Song: A musical track with vocals.

Sound channel: An audio stream of one sound at a time with musical parameters. Sound channels are mixed at output delivery to audio channels. In contrast to audio channel.

Soundchip: A microprocessor with audio functions. A soundchip can also have functions for other systems, but is understood primarily for dedicated audio microprocessors.

Soundtrack: The collection of all musical tracks included within a video game. A game soundtrack excludes sound effects. In contrast with official soundtrack.

SPC: A file type containing music data from a SNES or Super Famicom cartridge. The name references the soundchip of the SNES.

SPC700: Short for Sony SPC700, the soundchip of the SNES.

Speaker: The destination of an audio channel. The speaker can be installed in a television or monitor or can be a dedicated device. In contrast with a speaker, a character or person who speaks in a game.

Speech: A digital audio sample representing sounds or words in a verbal language.

SPL: Short for sound programming language, sound software by Epyx for the Atari Lynx based on sounds similar to the Atari 2600 or TG-16.

SPU: Short for Sony Sound Processing Unit, the soundchip of the Sony PlayStation.

SPU1: Short for Sound Processing Unit 1, the CPU of the PS2.

SPU2: Short for Sound Processing Unit 2. It functions similarly to the SPU of the PS1.

SSG: Short for software sound generator, a type of soundchip for primitive sound production.

Surround sound: An output of three or more audio channels, configured for an arrangement of audio speakers around the listener.

TG-CD: Short for Turbo-Grafx CD.

TG-16: Short for Turbo-Grafx 16.

3DO: A set of standards for a gaming system developed by 3DO Systems and manufactured by numerous vendors.

TIA: Short for Television Interface Adapter, the chip that generates the graphics, audio, and input of the Atari 2600.

TurboChip: A card-sized ROM cartridge playable on the TurboGrafx-16. Its Japanese equivalent is the HuCard.

2A07: Short for Ricoh 2A07, the soundchip of the NES for PAL televisions.

2A03: Short for Ricoh 2A03, the soundchip of the Famicom and NES for NTSC televisions.

USB: Short for Universal Serial Bus.

VCS: Short for Atari Video Computer System, the original name for the Atari 2600.

VLM: Short for Virtual Light Machine, the music visualizer on the Jaguar CD.

VRC6: Short for Konami Virtual ROM Controller 6, an enhancement chip used in the Famicom version of *Castlevania III: Dracula's Curse* (1989).

VRU: Short for Voice Recognition Unit, a peripheral for the N64 that converts audio input from the N64 microphone into data interpreted in software.

White noise: A signal with random frequencies from all frequencies heard by the human ear. It sounds like the static from an old television set.

WMA: Short for Windows Media Audio, a lossy audio file format developed by Microsoft.

YM2413: Short for Yamaha YM-2413, the soundchip of the Japanese Sega Master System.

YM2612: Short for Yamaha YM2612, the FM soundchip of the Sega Mega Drive/Genesis.

Bibliography

"AdLib Visual Composer." *The Game Maker Archive*, 1 Feb. 2016, www.aderack.com/game-maker/index.php?title=AdLib_Visual_Composer. Accessed 29 Sept. 2020.

"AdLib Visual Composer." *Video Game Music Preservation Foundation Wiki*, 19 Feb. 2020, www.vgmpf.com/Wiki/index.php?title=AdLib_Visual_Composer. Accessed 29 Sept. 2020.

Aerisavion. "Gustavo Santaolalla—The Last of Us (album Review)." *Sputnikmusic*, 12 July 2017, www.sputnikmusic.com/review/74256/Gustavo-Santaolalla-The-Last-of-Us/.

Ahmed, Emad. "How Tetsuya Mizuguchi Reinvented Video Games with His Love of Synaesthesia." *New Statesman*, 28 July 2017, www.newstatesman.com/culture/games/2017/07/how-tetsuya-mizuguchi-reinvented-video-games-his-love-synaesthesia.

AIAS. "23rd Annual D.I.C.E. Awards Panelists." *The Academy Of Interactive Arts & Sciences*, 6 Feb. 2020, www.interactive.org/awards/23rd_diceawards_panelists.asp. Accessed 6 Feb. 2020.

"Al Alcorn Interview—Page 2." *IGN*, 10 Mar. 2008, www.ign.com/articles/2008/03/11/al-alcorn-interview?page=2.

Alwani, Rishi. "The Music of Death Stranding: Every Licensed Song, Original Soundtrack, and More." *The Mako Reactor*, 11 Nov. 2019, themakoreactor.com/features/death-stranding-music-list-soundtrack-download-itunes-spotify-low-roar-ludvig-forssell/7663/. Accessed 28 May 2021.

"Amiga Hardware Reference Manual." *The Evergreen State College*, ada.evergreen.edu/~tc_nik/files/AmigaHardRefManual.pdf. Accessed 3 Aug. 2018.

Apple. "IPad Pro—Technical Specifications." *Apple*, www.apple.com/ipad-pro/specs/. Accessed 3 Aug. 2018.

Apple. (2016). iPad Pro—Design. Retrieved from http://www.apple.com/ipad-pro/design/

"Arcade Machine." *Inkipedia, the Splatoon Wiki*, 17 Dec. 2018, splatoonwiki.org/wiki/Arcade_Machine. Accessed 22 Dec. 2018.

"Architecture of the Atari Lynx." *Diary of an Atari Lynx Developer*, 20 Sept. 2010, atarilynxdeveloper.wordpress.com/2010/09/20/architecture-of-the-atari-lynx/.

Arendt, Susan. "Review: Patapon Will Make You a Slave to the Rhythm." *Wired*, 14 Mar. 2008, www.wired.com/2008/03/review-patapon/.

Ashcraft, Brian. "PlayStation Vita: It's Official, and Here's The Price." *Kotaku*, 6 June 2011, kotaku.com/playstation-vita-its-official-and-heres-the-price-452567453.

Assumma, Mike. "Review: Beat Saber Gets Your Blood Pumping and Feet Moving." *Gamecrate*, 22 May 2018, gamecrate.com/reviews/review-beat-saber-gets-your-blood-pumping-and-feet-moving/19331. Accessed 9 Sept. 2020.

Atari History Museum. "2600/7800 development kit." www.atarimuseum.com/ahs_archives/archives/pdf/videogames/7800/7800_devkit.pdf.

"Atari Jaguar System Info." *The Video Game Museum*, www.vgmuseum.com/systems/jaguar/. Accessed 3 Aug. 2018.

"Atari Pong History." *Atari Gaming Headquarters*, www.atarihq.com/dedicated/ponghistory3.php. Accessed 27 May 2021.

"Atari 2600 specifications." problemkaputt.de/2k-6specs.htm. Accessed 3 Aug. 2018.

"Audio Hardware—3DO." altmer.arts-union.ru/3DO/docs/DevDocs/ppgfldr/mgsfldr/mpg-fldr/02mpg002.html. Accessed 28 Sept. 2020.

"Audiosurf—Press Kit." *IGDB.com*, 2008, www.igdb.com/games/audiosurf/presskit.

Auffret, Dominique. "Designing 2D Graphics in the Japanese Industry." *Video Game Densetsu*, 1 Nov. 2018, vgdensetsu.tumblr.com/post/179656817318/designing-2d-graphics-in-the-japanese-industry.

B, Michelle. "Vib Ribbon." *Pioneer Project*, www.pioneerproject.net/games/vib-ribbon/. Accessed 12 Sept. 2018.

Baird, Scott. "The Latest Smash Bros Update Required Permission from All IP Holders Involved with the Game." *TheGamer*, 11 Sept. 2020, www.thegamer.com/smash-bros-ultimate-patch-update-final-destination-music/. Accessed 24 Sept. 2020.

"Barbershop Quartet." *Cuphead Wiki*, 14 July 2020, cuphead.fandom.com/wiki/Barbershop_Quartet. Accessed 9 Sept. 2020.

Barry. "SEGA Retrospective: Jet Set Radio Future and the Latch Brothers." *Sega Bits*, 21 Apr. 2015, segabits.com/blog/2015/04/

21/sega-tunes-jet-set-radio-future-and-the-latch-brothers/.

Base Media. "Sega Dreamcast." *Console Database,* www.consoledatabase.com/consoleinfo/segadreamcast/. Accessed 3 Aug. 2018.

Bateman, Selby. "The Summer Consumer Electronics Show." *Compute,* Aug. 1984, p. 32, www.atarimagazines.com/compute/issue51/176_1_Software_Power.php. Accessed 10 Apr. 2020.

"BB's Theme." *Death Stranding Wiki,* 8 Feb. 2021, deathstranding.fandom.com/wiki/BB's_Theme. Accessed 28 May 2021.

"Beaterator—Full Manual—PSP Version." *Internet Archive,* 17 Jan. 2021, archive.org/details/full-manual/mode/2up. Accessed 13 June 2021.

"Beaterator™." *PlayStation™Store,* store.playstation.com/en-us/product/UP1004-ULUS10405_00-RCKSTRBEATERATOR. Accessed 20 Aug. 2018.

Beausoleil, Michael. "What Make the Wii U Nintendo's Greatest Failure." *Medium,* 7 Nov. 2019, medium.com/@beausoleil/what-make-the-wii-u-nintendos-greatest-failure-fa758aedbf8. Accessed 10 Sept. 2020.

"A Beginner's Guide to Digital Signal Processing (DSP)." *Analog Devices,* www.analog.com/en/design-center/landing-pages/001/beginners-guide-to-dsp.html. Accessed 29 Nov. 2018.

Bell, Larryn. "Full List of Xbox One X Enhanced Games at Launch." *AllGamers,* 7 Nov. 2017, ag.hyperxgaming.com/article/3365/full-list-of-xbox-one-x-enhanced-games-at-launch. Accessed 21 Sept. 2020.

Benfield, Lee. "Gitaroo Man." *Hardcore Gaming 101,* 23 Aug. 2017, www.hardcoregaming101.net/gitaroo-man/.

Billboard. "Jazz Albums Chart—The Week of September 14, 2019." *Billboard,* www.billboard.com/charts/jazz-albums/2019-09-14. Accessed 9 Sept. 2020.

Bilton, Nick. "A Closer Connection for Smartphone Games and Soundtracks." *Bits Blog,* 9 June 2014, bits.blogs.nytimes.com/2014/06/09/for-smartphone-games-attention-for-soundtracks/.

Bittencourt, Ricardo. "YM2413 FM Operator Type-LL (OPLL) Application Manual." *SMS Power!,* 2003, www.smspower.org/maxim/Documents/YM2413ApplicationManual. Accessed 16 Nov. 2018.

Blue Sky Rangers. "Intellivoice Speech Synthesis Module #3330." *Blue Sky Rangers Intellivision History,* history.blueskyrangers.com/hardware/intellivoice.html. Accessed 22 Apr. 2021.

Blue Sky Rangers. "Melody Blaster." *Blue Sky Rangers Intellivision History,* history.blueskyrangers.com/mattelelectronics/games/melodyblaster.html. Accessed 10 Apr. 2021.

Boris, Dan. "The Atari 7800 ProSystem." 2013, www.atarihq.com/danb/a7800.shtml.

Boris, Dan. "Atari 7800 Tech Page." *Atari Gaming Headquarters,* www.atarihq.com/danb/a7800.shtml. Accessed 3 Aug. 2018.

Boris, Dan. "ColecoVision Sound Generation Hardware." *Atari Gaming Headquarters,* www.atarihq.com/danb/files/CV-Sound.txt. Accessed 3 Aug. 2018.

Bramwell, Tom. "Golden Sun." *Eurogamer.net,* 21 Feb. 2002, www.eurogamer.net/articles/r_goldensun_gba.

Brandon, Alexander. *Audio for Games: Planning, Process, and Production.* New Riders Pub, 2005.

Brannon, Charles. "Magic Voice Speech For The 64." *COMPUTE!,* Oct. 1984, p. 102, www.atarimagazines.com/compute/issue53/036_2_REVIEWS_Magic_Voice_Speech_For_The_64.php. Accessed 16 Nov. 2018.

Brence, C. "Sid Meier's C.P.U. Bach - 3DO (1994)." 20 Sept. 2015, www.hardcoregaming101.net/cpubach/cpubach.htm.

Brennan, Martin, et al. "Technical Reference Manual: Tom & Jerry." *Emu-Docs,* 28 Feb. 2001, emu-docs.org/Jaguar/General/jag_v8.pdf.

Brightman, James. "Nintendo Ends New Nintendo 3DS Production in Japan." *GamesIndustry.biz,* 13 July 2017, www.gamesindustry.biz/articles/2017-07-13-nintendo-ends-new-nintendo-3ds-production-in-japan. Accessed 11 Sept. 2020.

Buchanan, Levi. "Sword & Sworcery EP Micro IPhone Review." *IGN,* 27 Apr. 2011, www.ign.com/articles/2011/04/27/sword-sworcery-ep-micro-iphone-review.

Byrne, Brian C., and Console G. Magazine. *History of The Nintendo 64: Ultimate Guide to the N64's Games & Hardware.* Console Gamer Magazine, 2017.

Campbell, Bruce D. "History of Video Game Music." *Bruce Donald Campbell [bdcampbell.net],* 2016, bdcampbell.net/music/. Accessed 25 Jan. 2020.

Campbell, J. "Audio Hardware." 2010, hackipedia.org/Platform/3DO/html,%203DO%20SDK%20Documentation/Type%20A/ppgfldr/mgsfldr/mpgfldr/02mpg002.html.

Campbell, Keith. "Corruption: Adventure Reviews." *Computer and Video Games,* July 1988, pp. 92–93.

"Can Digital Game Publishing Show Us The Way?" *SXSW Schedule 2014,* 2014, schedule.sxsw.com/2014/2014/events/event_FP27000. Accessed 28 Apr. 2020.

Caprani, Ole. "The Pong Game." *Aarhus University,* 27 Sept. 2014, cs.au.dk/~dsound/DigitalAudio.dir/Greenfoot/Pong.dir/Pong.html.

"Carnival." *Blue Sky Rangers Intellivision History,* history.blueskyrangers.com/coleco/carnival.html. Accessed 18 Jan. 2021.

Chang, Kyusik, et al. "Video Game Console Audio: Evolution and Future Trends." Sept. 2007. *Computer Graphics, Imaging and Visualisation.* www.researchgate.net/publication/4270536_Video_Game_Console_Audio_Evolution_and_Future_Trends.

Charnock, Tom. "Jag Star." *Do The Math,* Apr. 2014, www.atarijaguar.co.uk/2014/04/jag-star.html.

Chilly Willy. "Tell Me About the 32X Sound Chip."

12 June 2012, forums.sonicretro.org/index. php?showtopic=29056.

Chowning, John M. "The Synthesis of Complex Audio Spectra by Means of Frequency Modulation." *Journal of the Audio Engineering Society*, vol. 21, no. 7, Sept. 1973, pp. 526–534, people. ece.cornell.edu/land/courses/ece4760/Math/ GCC644/FM_synth/Chowning.pdf. Accessed 27 Nov. 2018.

"Chris Grigg." *Video Game Music Preservation Foundation Wiki*, 18 Jan. 2021, www.vgmpf. com/Wiki/index.php?title=Chris_Grigg. Accessed 30 May 2021.

Christensen, Ken. "Monkey Island 2 Walkthrough." *World of Monkey Island*, www.world ofmi.com/gamehelp/walk/monkey2.php. Accessed 16 Aug. 2018.

Coker, Gareth. "Ori and the Blind Forest—Main Menu (feat. Aeralie Brighton)." *SoundCloud*, 18 Mar. 2015, soundcloud.com/garethcoker/ori-and-the-blind-forest-main-menu-feat-aeralie-brighton.

ColecoVision sound generation hardware. (n.d.). Retrieved from ftp://ftp.komkon.org/pub/ EMUL8/Coleco/Docs/CV-Sound.txt

"ColecoVision Technical." *A Danish ColecoVision Site*, 17 Sept. 2015, www.colecovision.dk/ technical.htm.

Coleman, J. "Atari Jaguar CD." 8 June 2004, www. gamefaqs.com/jaguarcd/916378-jaguar-cd/ reviews/74108.

Collins, Karen. *Game Sound: An Introduction to the History, Theory, and Practice of Video Game Music and Sound Design*. MIT P, 2008.

Collins, Karen, and Chris Greening. *Beep: Documenting the History of Game Sound*. ePUB, Ehtonal, 2016.

Commodore. "Commodore Magic Voice Speech Module." *Cubic Team & $eeN and Other Demo Scene Related Stuff*, www.cubic.org/~doj/c64/ magic.html. Accessed 16 Nov. 2018.

"Commodore 64–1872." *Obsolete Technology*, 21 July 2014, www.oldcomputers.net/c64.html.

"Computer Space." *Media Fandom*, 13 Feb. 2017, media.fandom.com/wiki/Computer_Space. Accessed 22 Jan. 2021.

"Console wars system specifications." 2006, wars. locopuyo.com/cwsystemspecsold.php.

Copetti, Rodrigo. "Sega Master System Architecture." *Rodrigo's Stuff*, 28 Nov. 2020, www. copetti.org/writings/consoles/master-system/. Accessed 24 Apr. 2021.

"Corruption : Hall Of Light." *Hall Of Light—The Database of Amiga Games*, 13 May 2017, hol. abime.net/3094. Accessed 31 Jan. 2020.

Cowen, Nick. "Uncharted Interview: Greg Edmonson." *Telegraph.co.uk*, 10 Mar. 2011, www. telegraph.co.uk/technology/video-games/837 1129/Uncharted-interview-Greg-Edmonson. html. Accessed 29 Apr. 2020.

Cvxfreak. "PSone LCD Screen FAQ." *GameFAQs*, 8 Apr. 2007, gamefaqs.gamespot.com/ps/916392-playstation/faqs/15131. Accessed 31 Mar. 2020.

"Dance Dance Revolution—Videogame by

Konami." *International Arcade Museum*, www. arcade-museum.com/game_detail.php?game_ id=7489. Accessed 16 Aug. 2018.

Davis, Justin. "Beat Sneak Bandit Review." *IGN*, 22 Feb. 2012, www.ign.com/articles/2012/02/ 22/beat-sneak-bandit-review.

DeBoer, Clint. "Understanding the Different HDMI Versions (1.0 to 2.0)." *Audioholics*, 11 Sept. 2013, www.audioholics.com/hdtv-formats/understanding-difference-hdmi-versions. Accessed 27 Apr. 2020.

De Feo, Teresa. "Who Is Toshio Iwai?" *Digicult*, 9 Feb. 2016, digicult.it/design/who-is-toshio-iwai/.

Deku. "Sound on the Gameboy Advance." deku. gbadev.org/program/sound1.html.

Delahunty-Light, Zoe. "The DualShock 4's Speaker and Lightbar Make These PS4 Games 100% Better." *Offical PlayStation Magazine*, 26 Jan. 2018, www.gamesradar.com/games-are-way-cooler-when-played-dualshock-4/. Accessed 23 Sept. 2020.

Deleon, Nicholas. "Confirmed: Michael Jackson Composed the Music for Sonic The Hedgehog 3." *TechCrunch*, 3 Dec. 2009, techcrunch. com/2009/12/03/confirmed-michael-jackson-composed-the-music-for-sonic-the-hedge hog-3/.

DePapier. "SEGA: 'SEGA 3D Classics Collection Developer's Interview.'" *NintendObserver*, 2 May 2016, nintendobserver.com/2016/05/ sega-sega-3d-classics-collection-developers-interview/. Accessed 30 Sept. 2020.

"D.I.C.E. Awards (Concept)." *Giant Bomb*, www. giantbomb.com/dice-awards/3015-4604/. Accessed 6 Feb. 2020.

"Difference Between a DSP & a DAC." *The Emotiva Lounge*, 3 Feb. 2013, emotivalounge.proboards. com/thread/28801.

"Difference Between PAM, PWM, and PPM—Comparison of PWM and PAM." *Electronic Projects for Engineering Students*, 23 Aug. 2017, www.elprocus.com/difference-between-pam-pwm-ppm/.

"Does the Psvita Have PS3 Graphics?" *GameSpot*, www.gamespot.com/forums/system-wars-314159282/does-the-psvita-have-ps3-graphics-28766435/. Accessed 7 Sept. 2018.

Dolby. "11.1.8 Mounted / Overhead Speaker Setup." *Dolby.com—Dolby*, www.dolby.com/about/ support/guide/speaker-setup-guides/11.1.8-mounted-overhead-speakers-setup-guide/. Accessed 21 Sept. 2020.

Dolby. "How to Get the Best Sound from Your Xbox One." *Dolby*, 14 Apr. 2014, wayback. archive.org/web/20150919074414/blog.dolby. com/2014/04/get-best-sound-xbox-one/.

Dolby. "How to Set Up the PlayStation 4 for Great Game Sound." *Dolby*, 18 Nov. 2013, wayback. archive.org/web/20151210032308/blog.dolby. com/2013/11/set-playstation-4-great-game-sound/.

Dolby Laboratories. "Dolby TrueHD Audio Coding for Future Entertainment Formats."

Dolby Laboratories, 2008, www.dolby.com/uploadedFiles/Assets/US/Doc/Professional/TrueHD_Tech_Paper_Final.pdf. Accessed 3 June 2020.

Dreamcast Technical Pages. "Nintendo's Gamecube technical overview." 2004, www.segatech.com/gamecube/overview/.

Dreamcast Technical Pages. "Saturn Overview." 2004, segatech.com/technical/saturnspecs/index.html.

Dwyer, Nick, and Tu Neill. "Diggin' in the Carts." *Red Bull Music Academy*, 2014, www.redbull.com/us-en/shows/diggin-in-the-carts. Accessed 31 May 2021.

Dyason, Matthew. "Bravely Default's Empowering Music." *YouTube*, 27 Apr. 2017, www.youtube.com/watch?v=COgzJey4EAc.

Eckster. "Hey You, Pikachu! Voice Command List (Duplicates Merged)." *Pastebin*, 6 Apr. 2015, pastebin.com/NaPmSBuR. Accessed 31 Mar. 2020.

Eckster. "Hey You, Pikachu! Voice Command List." *Pastebin*, 6 Apr. 2015, pastebin.com/ZRkdZQgy. Accessed 31 Mar. 2020.

Eggebrecht, Julian. "What's Wrong With Music On the N64?" *IGN*, 24 Feb. 1998, www.ign.com/articles/1998/02/25/whats-wrong-with-music-on-the-n64.

"Electroplankton." *IGN*, 10 Jan. 2006, www.ign.com/articles/2006/01/11/electroplankton.

"Electroplankton—Press Kit." *IGDB.com*, www.igdb.com/games/electroplankton/presskit. Accessed 20 Aug. 2018.

"Entertainment Computer System." *Intellivision Productions*, www.intellivisionlives.com/bluesky/games/credits/ecs.shtml. Accessed 16 Nov. 2018.

"Epic Mickey 2: The Power of Two." *Disney Wiki*, 20 May 2021, disney.wikia.com/wiki/Epic_Mickey_2:_The_Power_of_Two. Accessed 9 June 2021.

Evans, Emi. *Twitter*, 2 Apr. 2018, twitter.com/emirevans/status/980820204274855936. Accessed 14 Sept. 2020.

"The Evolution of Video Game Music." *NPR.org*, 13 Apr. 2008, www.npr.org/templates/story/story.php?storyId=89565567. Accessed 25 Jan. 2020.

Explained.Today. "Mega Man 2 Explained." 2016, everything.explained.today/Mega_Man_2/.

Fahey, Rob. "Reassessing the Legacy of PlayStation Vita." *GamesIndustry.biz*, 18 May 2018, www.gamesindustry.biz/articles/2018-05-17-reassessing-the-legacy-of-playstation-vita.

"Famicom Disk System: The More You Play It, the More You'll Want to Play [Disk 2]." *Metroid Database*, Sept. 2004, wayback.archive.org/web/20160723015114/www.metroid-database.com:80/m1/fds-interview2-p0.php. Accessed 14 Aug. 2018.

"Famicom Expansion Audio Overview." *Nerdly Pleasures*, 4 Aug. 2017, nerdlypleasures.blogspot.com/2017/08/famicom-expansion-audio-overview.html. Accessed 30 Sept. 2020.

Famitracker Wiki. "Sound hardware." 28 Mar. 2015, famitracker.com/wiki/index.php?title=Sound_hardware. Accessed 30 Jan. 2016.

Fatnick. "IRQ: 7"—The Complicated World of Early MS-DOS Sound Options." *Fatnick Industries*, 3 Sept. 2018, mechafatnick.co.uk/2018/09/03/irq-7-the-complicated-world-of-early-ms-dos-sound-options/. Accessed 29 Sept. 2020.

Fayzullin, Marat. "GameBoy Technical Information." *Home Page of Marat Fayzullin*, fms.komkon.org/GameBoy/Tech/. Accessed 3 Aug. 2018.

Fielder, Lauren. "MTV Music Generator Review." *GameSpot*, 10 Dec. 1999, www.gamespot.com/reviews/mtv-music-generator-review/1900-2548503/.

Flacy, Mike. "Demystifying the Audio Settings on Your PlayStation 3." *Digital Trends*, 9 Sept. 2013, www.digitaltrends.com/home-theater/demystifying-the-audio-settings-on-your-playstation-3.

Fletcher, JC. "Rocksmith Also Available in $200 Epiphone Guitar Bundle." *Engadget*, 9 June 2011, www.engadget.com/2011/06/09/rocksmith-also-available-in-200-epiphone-guitar-bundle/.

Ford, Brody. "Trent Reznor Soundtrack For Video Game Quake To Be Released On Vinyl." *Mxdwn Music*, 12 June 2017, music.mxdwn.com/2017/06/12/news/trent-reznor-soundtrack-for-video-game-quake-to-be-released-on-vinyl/.

Foss, Christopher. "F-Zero X: EXpansion Kit—Red Canyon." *YouTube*, 24 Aug. 2007, www.youtube.com/watch?v=EfxO7lht5-Y. Accessed 1 Apr. 2020.

"Four Player Games & Expansion Audio Games." *Analogue*, 25 June 2018, support.analogue.co/hc/en-us/articles/225770047-Four-Player-Games-Expansion-Audio-Games.

Frank, Allegra. "Nintendo Switch Update Also Adds Wireless Headset Support." *Polygon*, 19 Oct. 2017, www.polygon.com/2017/10/19/16504088/nintendo-switch-wireless-headphones-headset-update.

Frey, Angelica. "Video Game Music: Focus on Nobuo Uematsu." CMUSE, 21 Mar. 2015, www.cmuse.org/video-game-music-focus-on-nobuo-uematsu/.

Fries, Bruce, and Marty Fries. "Digital Audio Formats." *Digital Audio Essentials*, O'Reilly Media, Inc., 2005, pp. 155–166.

Fritsch, Melanie. "History of Video Game Music." *Music and Game: Perspectives on a Popular Alliance*, Springer Science & Business Media, 2012, pp. 11–40.

FrostyMac. "The Meaning Behind Megalovania." *Aminoapps.com*, 7 Jan. 2017, aminoapps.com/c/toby-fox-amino/page/blog/the-meaning-behind-megalovania/kwm5_q0btGupDdQQY-7j4mvP4rzo66oPReZB. Accessed 9 Sept. 2020.

"Gameboy Advance Direct Sound." *BeLogic Software*, belogic.com/gba/directsound.shtml. Accessed 29 Nov. 2018.

"Gameboy Sound Hardware." *Gameboy Development*, 9 May 2008, gbdev.gg8.se/wiki/articles/

Gameboy_sound_hardware. Accessed 24 Apr. 2021.

"GameCube Spec Sheet." *GameCubicle.com,* 2001, www.gamecubicle.com/system-gamecube-specs.htm. Accessed 3 Aug. 2018.

"Games Review: Patapon Remastered is Gaming's Only Musical Strategy Game." *Metro,* 3 Aug. 2017, metro.co.uk/2017/08/03/patapon-remastered-review-rhythm-of-war-6825390/.

Gantayat, Anoop. "PSP-2000 Tops 100,000 in Japan." *IGN,* 22 Sept. 2007, www.ign.com/articles/2007/09/22/psp-2000-tops-100000-in-japan. Accessed 19 Jan. 2021.

Gardner, Matt. "The End of the Battle (Shadow of the Colossus) Review." *GameTripper,* 5 Feb. 2018, www.gametripper.co.uk/games/music/shadow-of-the-colossus-end-battle/.

Garst, Aron. "Playing Piano with a Sledgehammer: Creating Death Stranding's Unidentifiable Score." *The Verge,* 8 Nov. 2019, www.theverge.com/2019/11/8/20954112/death-stranding-score-music-interview-joel-corelitz-ludvig-forssell. Accessed 28 May 2021.

"Gau of the Veldt." "SPC-700 Programming Information." *Emulator Review,* emureview.ztnet.com/developerscorner/SoundCPU/spc.htm. Accessed 3 Aug. 2018.

George, G. D. "Atari 7800 vs. Nintendo NES." 19 Mar. 2014, www.ataritimes.com/?ArticleIDX=632.

Gerblick, Jordan. "Cuphead Has the First Video Game Soundtrack to Hit Number 1 on Billboard's Jazz Charts." *Gamesradar,* 18 Sept. 2019, www.gamesradar.com/cuphead-has-the-first-video-game-soundtrack-to-hit-number-1-on-billboards-jazz-charts/. Accessed 9 Sept. 2020.

Giacchino, Michael. "Exclusive: Interview...Film Composer Michael Giacchino." Interview by Mark Ciafardini. *GoSeeTalk.com,* 14 May 2012, goseetalk.com/interview-film-composer-michael-giacchino/.

Giacchino, Michael. "An Interview with Michael Giacchino." Interview by Peter Van der Lugt. *ScreenAnarchy,* 11 Aug. 2009, screenanarchy.com/2009/08/an-interview-with-michael-giacchino.html.

Giant Bomb. "Last Game Released on a Console." 5 Oct. 2015, www.giantbomb.com/last-game-released-on-a-console/3015-3262/. Accessed 29 Jan. 2016.

Giant Bomb. "Neo Geo (Platform)." 10 Mar. 2015, www.giantbomb.com/neo-geo/3045-25/. Accessed 30 Jan. 2016.

Giant Bomb. "TurboGrafx-CD (Platform)." 13 June 2014, www.giantbomb.com/turbografx-cd/3045-53/. Accessed 28 Jan. 2016.

"Golden Sun / Awesome Music." *TV Tropes,* 26 July 2018, tvtropes.org/pmwiki/pmwiki.php/AwesomeMusic/GoldenSun.

Goninon, Mark. "Where Are They Now? - Michael Z. Land." Choicest Games, 3 Dec. 2014, www.choicestgames.com/2014/12/where-are-they-now-michael-z-land.html.

Good, Owen. "The Winners and Nominees of the 2011 Spike Video Game Awards." *Kotaku,* 11 Dec. 2011, kotaku.com/the-winners-and-nominees-of-the-2011-spike-video-game-a-5867018. Accessed 2 Sept. 2020.

Goodwin, Simon N. "Chapter 2: Early Digital Audio Hardware and Chapter 3: Sample Replay." *Beep to Boom: The Development of Advanced Runtime Sound Systems for Games and Extended Reality,* Routledge, 2019.

"Got Lag? Got Latency? READ THIS FIRST." *Ubisoft Forums,* 29 Oct. 2011, forums.ubi.com/showthread.php/282374-Got-Lag-Got-Latency-READ-THIS-FIRST?s=8c689cfb3d8ae47737537188776914dd.

Govoni, Jim. "Frequency FAQ/Walkthrough for PlayStation 2." *GameFAQs,* 28 Jan. 2003, gamefaqs.gamespot.com/ps2/516506-frequency/faqs/21435.

"The Great Giana Sisters (Rainbow Arts, 1987)." *Finnish Retro Game Comparison Blog,* 20 Sept. 2013, frgcb.blogspot.com/2013/09/the-great-giana-sisters-rainbow-arts.html. Accessed 24 Jan. 2021.

Greening, Chris. "Koji Kondo Profile." *Video Game Music Online,* 30 Dec. 2012, www.vgmonline.net/kojikondo/.

Greening, Chris. "Nobuo Uematsu Profile." *Video Game Music Online,* 18 Mar. 2013, www.vgmonline.net/nobuouematsu/.

"GTA3 + VC Xbox—Custom Soundtracks?" *AVForums,* 16 Dec. 2003, www.avforums.com/threads/gta3-vc-xbox-custom-soundtracks.107903/.

"Guide To: The Super Game Boy." *Ancientelectronics,* 16 May 2015, ancientelectronics.wordpress.com/2015/05/16/guide-to-the-super-game-boy/. Accessed 1 June 2020.

Hamilton, Kirk. "The (Actual) Best Game Music of 2011: Superbrothers: Sword & Sworcery EP." *Kotaku,* 29 Dec. 2011, kotaku.com/5871943/the-actual-best-game-music-of-2011-superbrothers-sword—sworcery-ep.

Harley, Trevor. "The Different Iterations of the Super Game Boy." *Snail Tooth Gaming,* 5 Feb. 2017, www.snailtoothgaming.com/articles/the-different-iterations-of-the-super-game-boy/. Accessed 1 June 2020.

Harris, C. "Electroplankton." 10 Jan. 2006, www.ign.com/articles/2006/01/11/electroplankton.

Hildenbrand, Jerry. "Does My Phone Have a DAC? Explaining DACs and Amps in Smartphones Today." *Android Central,* 31 Oct. 2017, www.androidcentral.com/does-my-phone-have-dac-explaining-dacs-and-amps-smartphones-today.

Hill, Katrina. "Two Dots Review." *Arcade Sushi,* 31 May 2014, arcadesushi.com/two-dots-review-ios/.

Hisaishi, Joe. Interview. *YouTube,* 8 Jan. 2013, www.youtube.com/watch?v=_Bcf0X7Vlh4.

"History and Memories of the IBM PCjr and Tandy 1000." *The Oldskool Shrine to the IBM PCjr and Tandy 1000,* 10 Oct. 2015, www.oldskool.org/shrines/pcjr_tandy/.

Hoffert, Paul, and Jonathan Feist. *Music for New Media: Composing for Videogames, Web Sites, Presentations, and Other Interactive Media.* Berklee Publications, 2007.

Hopkins, Christopher. *Chiptune music: An exploration of compositional techniques as found in Sunsoft games for the Nintendo Entertainment System and Famicom from 1988–1992.* Five Towns College, PhD Dissertation. *ProQuest Dissertations and Theses.* Accessed 25 Jan. 2020.

Hopkins, Christopher. "Mario Paint: An Accessible Environment of Musical Creativity and Sound Exploration." *Journal of Literature and Art Studies*, vol. 5, no. 10, Oct. 2015, pp. 847–858.

Horowitz, Ken. "GEMS Shine on the Genesis." *Playing at the Next Level: A History of American Sega Games*, McFarland, 2016, pp. 66–68.

"How to Make Sega Genesis Music (in 1994)." *YouTube*, 16 Aug. 2017, www.youtube.com/watch?v=WEvnZRCW_qc.

Hubbard, Rob. "Interview with Rob Hubbard." Interview by Warren Pilkington. SID, www.sidmusic.org/sid/rhubbard.html. Accessed 6 Aug. 2018.

Hubbard, Rob. Interview. *C64.com*, www.c64.com/interviews/hubbard.html. Accessed 8 Aug. 2018.

Hüelsbeck, Chris. "Giana Sisters: Twisted Dreams—Original Soundtrack, by Chris Huelsbeck, Fabian Del Priore." *Chris Huelsbeck Productions*, 14 Nov. 2012, chrishuelsbeck.bandcamp.com/album/giana-sisters-twisted-dreams-original-soundtrack.

Iggy. "The Official Famicom Switch Controller's Microphone Actually Works." *NintendoSoup*, 24 Mar. 2019, nintendosoup.com/the-official-famicom-switch-controllers-microphone-actually-works/. Accessed 30 Sept. 2020.

IGN. "Beaterator preview." 2009, www.ign.com/games/beaterator/psp-893429.

IGN. "PSP Specs revealed." 29 July 2003, www.ign.com/articles/2003/07/29/psp-specs-revealed.

"(Incomplete) List of GB/GBC Games to Use PCM Samples (Page 1)." *ChipMusic.org*, 7 July 2015, chipmusic.org/forums/topic/16824/incomplete-list-of-gbgbc-games-to-use-pcm-samples/.

Inns, Simon. "Commodore SID 6581 Datasheet." *Waiting for Friday*, 26 Mar. 2010, www.waitingforfriday.com/?p=661.

"Intellivision Master Component #2609." *Intellivision Productions*, www.intellivisionlives.com/bluesky/hardware/intelli_tech.html. Accessed 3 Aug. 2018.

"Intellivoice." *Retro Consoles Wiki*, 28 May 2013, retroconsoles.fandom.com/wiki/Intellivoice. Accessed 31 Jan. 2020.

"Jake Kaufman." *Video Game Music Preservation Foundation Wiki*, 13 Jan. 2016, www.vgmpf.com/Wiki/index.php?title=Jake_Kaufman. Accessed 6 Aug. 2018.

Jarman, Casey. "High Scores: Kristofer Maddigan's Big Band Soundtrack for "Cuphead."" *Bandcamp Daily*, 18 Jan. 2018, daily.bandcamp.com/high-scores/cuphead-soundtrack-interview. Accessed 9 Sept. 2020.

Jeepyurongfu. "The classics: Carnival." 2016, www.jeepyurongfu.com/86155946-the-classics-carnival/.

Jeriaska. "Interview: Korg DS-10 Spawns Japanese Album, Concert Series." *Gamasutra*, 18 May 2010, www.gamasutra.com/view/news/119458/Interview_Korg_DS10_Spawns_Japanese_Album_Concert_Series.php. Accessed 26 May 2021.

"Jesper Kyd: Music Transcends All Platforms." *Plarium*, plarium.com/en/blog/jesper-kyd/. Accessed 14 Aug. 2018.

Joe. "History of Video Game Soundtracks." *T.blog*, 29 July 2019, www.thomann.de/blog/en/history-of-video-game-soundtracks/. Accessed 25 Jan. 2020.

Jones, Alex. "Monument Valley Game Audio Review." *The Sound Architect*, 28 Mar. 2015, www.thesoundarchitect.co.uk/articlesandreviews/monumentvalleyreview/.

"Journey (1983)/Walkthrough." *StrategyWiki*, 29 Oct. 2014, strategywiki.org/wiki/Journey_(1983)/Walkthrough. Accessed 15 Aug. 2018.

"The Journey of the 'PCjr./Tandy Sound Chip.'" *Nerdly Pleasures*, 10 Oct. 2015, nerdlypleasures.blogspot.com/2015/10/the-journey-of-pcjrtandy-sound-chip.html.

"Journey—Videogame by Bally Midway." *International Arcade Museum*, www.arcade-museum.com/game_detail.php?game_id=8242.

Kalata, K. "Best video game music of all time - 2011." 25 Oct. 2011, www.hardcoregaming101.net/vgm/bestvgm2011.htm.

Kaufman, Jake. Interview. *Experimental Gamer Studios*, 16 Jan. 2014, www.experimentalgamer.com/interview-boot-hill-heroes-composer-jake-kaufman-download-3-tracks/.

Kaufman, Jake. Interview. *Gamasutra*, 27 Feb. 2015, www.gamasutra.com/view/news/237629/Road_to_the_IGF_Yacht_Club_Games_Shovel_Knight.php.

Kaufman, Jake. Interview. *Nintendo World Report*, 16 Oct. 2011, www.nintendoworldreport.com/interview/28011/nwr-interview-jake-kaufman.

"Kenji Yamamoto." *Kyoto Report*, 16 Sept. 2017, kyoto-report.wikidot.com/kenji-yamamoto. Accessed 14 Aug. 2018.

"Kenji Yamamoto." *Video Game Music Preservation Foundation Wiki*, 25 June 2016, www.vgmpf.com/Wiki/index.php?title=Kenji_Yamamoto. Accessed 14 Aug. 2018.

Kim, Steven. "HD 101: How to Use Dolby TrueHD and DTS-HD with Your PS3." *Engadget*, 21 Apr. 2009, www.engadget.com/2009-04-21-hd-101-how-to-use-dolby-truehd-and-dts-hd-with-your-ps3.html. Accessed 3 June 2020.

Kinder, Jeff, and Dave Hallock. "Dragon's Lair Cinematronics 1983." *The Dragon's Lair Project*, www.dragons-lair-project.com/games/pages/dl.asp. Accessed 6 Dec. 2018.

Kinder, Jeff, and Dave Hallock. "Dragon's Lair Manual." *The Dragon's Lair Project*, 9 Jan. 1984, www.dragons-lair-project.com/tech/manuals/lair/. Accessed 23 Apr. 2021.

"King Arthur's World (Europe) SNES ROM." *CDRomance*, 23 May 1993, cdromance.com/snes-rom/king-arthurs-world-europe/. Accessed 18 Jan. 2021.

"King's Quest IV: The Perils of Rosella: Making of." *The Sierra Chest*, www.sierrachest.com/index.php?a=games&id=4&fld=making. Accessed 16 Aug. 2018.

Kirn, Peter. "Inside Beaterator, Rockstar Games' New PSP Beat Maker, with Gory Technical Bits." *CDM Create Digital Music*, 3 Sept. 2009, cdm.link/2009/09/inside-beaterator-rockstar-games-new-psp-beat-maker-with-gory-technical-bits/. Accessed 4 June 2020.

"Koji Kondo." *Famous Composers*, www.famouscomposers.net/koji-kondo. Accessed 6 Aug. 2018.

"Koji Kondo." *Video Game Music Preservation Foundation Wiki*, 21 Jan. 2018, www.vgmpf.com/Wiki/index.php?title=Koji_Kondo. Accessed 6 Aug. 2018.

Kondo, Koji. Interview. *Shmuplations.com*, 1990, shmuplations.com/supermarioworld. Accessed 6 Aug. 2018.

Kondo, Koji. "Super Mario's Maestro: A Q&A with Nintendo's Koji Kondo." Interview by Bob Mackey. *USGamer.net*, 10 Dec. 2014, www.usgamer.net/articles/koji-kondo-interview-nintendo.

Korb, Darren. "The Holistic Master of Video Game Music: An Interview with Darren Korb." Interview by Juan M. Fontan. *The Indie Game Website*, 9 Mar. 2018, www.indiegamewebsite.com/2018/03/09/interview-darren-korb/.

Korb, Darren. Interview. *The Wayfaring Dreamer*, 5 Mar. 2015, thewayfaringdreamer.com/darren-korb-interview/.

Kortink, J. "SN76489." 11 Dec. 2005, www.smspower.org/Development/SN76489.

Kotowski, Don. "Bravely Default -Flying Fairy- Original Soundtrack." *Video Game Music Online*, 1 Aug. 2012, www.vgmonline.net/bravelydefault/.

Kouno, Tsutomo. "The LocoMotion." Interview by Tom Bramwell. *Eurogamer*, 6 May 2006, www.eurogamer.net/articles/i_locoroco_psp.

Krotz, Scott A. "Michel Buffa's 3DO FAQ WWW Page." *Polytech Nice Sophia*, users.polytech.unice.fr/~buffa/videogames/3do_faq2.4.html. Accessed 3 Aug. 2018.

Kuchera, Ben. "How a Song from the 2005 Civilization IV Won a 2011 Grammy." *Ars Technica*, 14 Feb. 2011, arstechnica.com/gaming/2011/02/how-a-song-from-the-2005-civilization-iv-won-a-2011-grammy/. Accessed 2 Sept. 2020.

Kuchera, Ben. "Remembering One of the Best Songs in Gaming History." *Polygon*, 29 Mar. 2017, www.polygon.com/2017/3/29/15106794/gitaroo-man-legendary-theme-acoustic.

Kuchera, Ben. "The Weird Brilliance of the LocoRoco Theme, 9 Years Later." *Polygon*, 9 Apr. 2015, www.polygon.com/2015/4/9/8376711/the-weird-brilliance-of-the-loco-roco-theme-9-years-later.

Kyd, Jesper. "Home." *The Official Website of Jesper Kyd*, www.jesperkyd.com. Accessed 14 Aug. 2018

Kyd, Jesper. "Interview with Jesper Kyd: Award Winning Games Composer." Interview by Steven Wiliamson. *Hexus*, 13 Apr. 2006, hexus.net/gaming/features/industry/5268-jesper-kyd-unreal-tournament-2007/.

Kyd, Jesper. "Sound Byte: Meet the Composer—Assassin's Creed's Jesper Kyd." Interview by Sophia Tong. *GameSpot*, 19 Nov. 2010, www.gamespot.com/articles/sound-byte-meet-the-composer-assassins-creeds-jesper-kyd/1100-6284304/.

Lakawicz, Steve. "Fidelity Concerns: The Lost Sound Expansion Chips of the NES." *Classical Gaming*, 27 Feb. 2011, classicalgaming.wordpress.com/2011/02/27/fidelity-concerns-the-lost-sound-expansion-chips-of-the-nes/.

Land, Michael. Interview. *GSoundtracks*, web.archive.org/web/20170815193359/www.gsoundtracks.com/interviews/land.htm. Accessed 6 Aug. 2018.

Langshaw, Mark. "Feature: The History Of Mobile Gaming." *Digital Spy*, 10 Apr. 2011, www.digitalspy.com/gaming/news/a313439/feature-the-history-of-mobile-gaming/.

Langston, Peter S. "Six Techniques for Algorithmic Music Composition." 2 Nov. 1989, *International Computer Music Conference*. Columbus, OH. peterlangston.com/Papers/amc.pdf.

Leadbetter, Richard. "Nintendo Wii Mini Review." *Eurogamer.net*, 12 Dec. 2012, www.eurogamer.net/articles/df-hardware-nintendo-wii-mini-review. Accessed 23 Sept. 2020.

Lee. "Best Super Game Boy Games." *Pug Hoof Gaming*, 28 Sept. 2018, www.pughoofgaming.com/videos/best-super-game-boy-games/. Accessed 1 June 2020.

Lee. "Super Game Boy Commander—The Definitive Guide." *Pug Hoof Gaming*, 15 Dec. 2016, www.pughoofgaming.com/videos/super-game-boy-commander/. Accessed 1 June 2020.

"Lifelight." *SmashWiki*, 22 May 2021, www.ssbwiki.com/Lifelight. Accessed 27 May 2021.

Linneman, John. "DF Retro: Revisiting Sega's Nomad—the Original Switch?" *Eurogamer.net*, 13 May 2018, www.eurogamer.net/articles/digitalfoundry-2018-retro-revisiting-sega-nomad-the-original-switch.

"List of AES and MVS Version Differences." *Neo-Geo.com*, 8 Dec. 2016, www.neo-geo.com/forums/showthread.php?269243-List-of-AES-and-MVS-Version-Differences.

"List of Every GBC Black Cart (dual Compatibility) Game." *RetroGaming with Racketboy*, www.racketboy.com/forum/viewtopic.php?f=6&t=48882. Accessed 11 Feb. 2020.

"Listening to the Music of Turing's Computer." BBC News, 1 Oct. 2016, www.bbc.com/

news/magazine-37507707. Accessed 26 May 2021.

Lomas, Natasha. "Monument Valley, Ustwo's Sumptuous Escher-Inspired IOS Game, Lands Globally On April 3." *TechCrunch*, 26 Mar. 2014, techcrunch.com/2014/03/26/monument-valley-price-and-launch-date/.

Loughrey, Clarisse. "Turns out Michael Jackson Definitely Composed Music for Sonic the Hedgehog 3." *The Independent*, 26 Jan. 2016, www.independent.co.uk/arts-entertainment/music/news/michael-jackson-confirmed-to-have-composed-music-in-secret-for-sonic-the-hedgehog-3-a6835121.html.

Lyon, Tony. "Monty on the Run." *Retro Video Game Systems*, 10 Oct. 2013, retrovideogamesystems.com/monty-on-the-run/.

"Macintosh User." "Jaguar CD Review for Jaguar CD." *GameFAQs*, 8 June 2004, www.gamefaqs.com/jaguarcd/916378-jaguar-cd/reviews/74108.

Magulick, Aaron. "Orgarhythm Review." *Bago Games*, 30 Oct. 2012, bagogames.com/listen-beat-orgarhytm-review/.

Maher, Jimmy. "Wing Commander II." *The Digital Antiquarian*, 2 Mar. 2018, www.filfre.net/2018/03/wing-commander-ii/.

"Manami Matsumae." *Video Game Music Preservation Foundation Wiki*, 3 Oct. 2019, vgmpf.com/Wiki/index.php/Manami_Matsumae. Accessed 10 Apr. 2020.

Manes, Stephen. "Lights! Cameras! Music! Insects!" *The New York Times*, 29 Apr. 1997, www.nytimes.com/1997/04/29/science/lights-cameras-music-insects.html.

Manikas, Pantelis. "Atari Home Pong." *Game Medium*, gamemedium.com/console/pong. Accessed 26 May 2021.

Mantione, Philip. "The Fundamentals of AM Synthesis." *Pro Audio Files*, 5 Sept. 2018, theproaudiofiles.com/the-fundamentals-of-am-synthesis/.

Mantione, Philip. "Introduction to FM Synthesis." *Pro Audio Files*, 26 June 2017, theproaudiofiles.com/fm-synthesis/.

"Marble Madness (ARC)." *Video Game Music Preservation Foundation Wiki*, 16 Jan. 2018, www.vgmpf.com/Wiki/index.php/Marble_Madness_(ARC). Accessed 15 Aug. 2018.

Margolis, Jason. "A Classical Music Album About Climate Challenges is a Surprise Atop the Charts." *Public Radio International*, 9 July 2014, www.pri.org/stories/2014-07-09/classical-music-album-about-climate-challenges-surprise-atop-charts.

Marie, Meagan. *Women in Gaming: 100 Professionals of Play*. Prima Games, 2018.

Martin, Garrett. "The Nintendo Labo Piano Is a Surprisingly Useful Little Synthesizer." *Pastemagazine.com*, 3 May 2018, www.pastemagazine.com/games/nintendo-labo/what-ive-learned-about-the-nintendo-labo-piano/. Accessed 17 Sept. 2020.

"Mass Effect Original Soundtrack." *Mass Effect Wiki*, 12 June 2017, masseffect.fandom.com/wiki/Mass_Effect_Original_Soundtrack. Accessed 29 Apr. 2020.

"Master Component #2609." *Blue Sky Rangers Intellivision History*, history.blueskyrangers.com/hardware/2609.html. Accessed 9 June 2021.

"Master System." *Sega Corporation*, sega.jp/fb/segahard/master/data.html. Accessed 3 Aug. 2018.

Mastrapa, Gus. "Elite Beat Agents." *The A.V. Club*, 11 Dec. 2006, games.avclub.com/elite-beat-agents-1798210323.

Mathurin, Jeff. "Welcome to the Xbox FAQ." *Biline.ca*, www.biline.ca/xbox-faq.htm. Accessed 3 Aug. 2018.

Matsumae, Manami. "Mega Man Theme Song Composer Still Jamming Over 20 Years Later." Interview by Mary-Ann Lee. *Tech in Asia*, 14 Dec. 2014, www.techinasia.com/manami-matsumae-video-game-music.

Matsumae, Manami. Interview. *USgamer.net*, 20 Jan. 2016, www.usgamer.net/articles/manami-matsumae.

Mattel. "Handheld Game Manual: Auto Race (Mattel)." *Internet Archive*, 1976, archive.org/details/manuals-handheld-games-Mattel-AutoRace/page/n1/mode/2up. Accessed 29 Jan. 2020.

McCrea, Nick. "Retired Developer Who Created 'NHL '94' Video Game in Maine Barn Reflects on Career." *Bangor Daily News*, 21 Feb. 2015, bangordailynews.com/2015/02/21/living/retired-developer-who-created-nhl-94-video-game-in-maine-barn-reflects-on-career/. Accessed 6 Apr. 2020.

McDonald, Glenn. "A History of Video Game Music." *GameSpot*, 28 Mar. 2005, www.gamespot.com/articles/a-history-of-video-game-music/1100-6092391/. Accessed 25 Jan. 2020.

McDonald, Richard. "Super Mario 3D World OST (Review)." *Original Sound Version*, 21 Mar. 2014, www.originalsoundversion.com/super-mario-3d-world-ost-review-2/.

"Mega Drive/Genesis Sound Engine List." *Game Developer Research Institute*, 24 Dec. 2017, gdri.smspower.org/wiki/index.php/Mega_Drive/Genesis_Sound_Engine_List. Accessed 18 Nov. 2018.

"MEGALOVANIA." *Undertale Wiki*, 7 Sept. 2020, undertale.fandom.com/wiki/MEGALOVANIA. Accessed 9 Sept. 2020.

Mera, Miguel, et al. "Dimensions of Game Audio History." *The Routledge Companion to Screen Music and Sound*, Taylor & Francis, 2017, pp. 139–152.

"Metal Gear Solid 2: Making of The Hollywood Game." *YouTube*, 20 Aug. 2012, www.youtube.com/watch?v=2B7yLQV70e0.

Microsoft. "Choosing Speaker Audio Settings on Xbox One." *Xbox Support*, support.xbox.com/en-US/xbox-one/console/configure-audio-settings. Accessed 3 Aug. 2018.

Microsoft. "Connect and Configure Digital Audio

On Xbox 360." *Xbox Support,* support.xbox.com/en-US/xbox-360/console/configure-audio-settings. Accessed 3 Aug. 2018.

Microsoft. "Video and Audio Playback on Xbox 360 FAQ." *Xbox Support,* support.xbox.com/en-US/xbox-360/console/audio-video-playback-faq. Accessed 3 Aug. 2018.

Midway Mfg. Co. "Midway's Rally-X Parts and Operating Manual." *Internet Archive,* Jan. 1981, archive.org/details/ArcadeGameManualRallyx/mode/2up. Accessed 26 May 2021.

Mielke, James. "Lumines Electronic Symphony: The Untold Story." *Gamasutra—The Art & Business of Making Games,* 30 July 2012, www.gamasutra.com/view/feature/174913/lumines_electronic_symphony_the_.php. Accessed 4 Sept. 2020.

Mielke, James. "Lumines Electronic Symphony: Q Entertainment's Love Letter to Electronic Music." *PlayStation.Blog,* 1 Feb. 2012, blog.playstation.com/2012/02/01/lumines-electronic-symphony-q-entertainments-love-letter-to-electronic-music/. Accessed 4 Sept. 2020.

"Minecraft—Volume Beta." *Minecraft Wiki,* 27 Aug. 2020, minecraft.gamepedia.com/Minecraft_-_Volume_Beta. Accessed 4 Sept. 2020.

Minotti, Mike. "How Bravely Default's Epic Soundtrack Empowers Players." *VentureBeat,* 27 Apr. 2017, venturebeat.com/2017/04/27/how-bravely-defaults-epic-soundtrack-empowers-players/.

Mitroff, Sarah. "TwoDots Review." *CNET,* 2 Dec. 2014, www.cnet.com/products/twodots/review/.

Mitsuda, Yasunori. "Music (Chrono Trigger)." *Chrono Compendium,* 21 Jan. 1995, www.chronocompendium.com/Term/Music_(Chrono_Trigger).html#Chrono_Trigger_Arranged_Version:_The_Brink_of_Time.

Mitsuda, Yasunori. Interview. *The Official Homepage of Yasunori Mitsuda,* Nov. 1999, www.procyon-studio.com/profile/biog.html.

"MMCA Chairman's Award—Toshio Iwai (Media Artist)." *Multimedia Grand Prix '97,* wayback.archive.org/web/20090609223028/www.dcaj.org:80/oldgp/97awards/english/person/person01.htm. Accessed 6 Aug. 2018.

Moore-Colyer, Roland. "PS5 and 3D Audio: Everything You Need to Know." *Tom's Guide,* 30 Aug. 2020, www.tomsguide.com/features/ps5-and-3d-audio-everything-you-need-to-know. Accessed 16 Sept. 2020.

Morasky, Mike. Interview. *Game Audio Network Guild,* 23 Feb. 2011, www.audiogang.org/interview-with-valves-mike-morasky/.

Morasky, Mike. Interview. *Podcast 17,* 7 May 2011, podcast17.com/interviews/audio/mike-morasky/.

Morton, Philip. "Xbox 360 Tech Specs." *Thunderbolt,* 20 Apr. 2005, www.thunderboltgames.com/feature/xbox-360-tech-specs.

"MOS Technology 6502." *Gunkies.org,* 28 Apr. 2016, gunkies.org/wiki/MOS_Technology_6502. Accessed 22 Jan. 2021.

Moskovciak, Matthew. "Confirmed: PS3 Slim Bit Streams Dolby TrueHD and DTS-HD Master Audio." *CNET,* 21 Aug. 2009, www.cnet.com/news/confirmed-ps3-slim-bit-streams-dolby-truehd-and-dts-hd-master-audio/.

MSX Resource Center. "4 Channels of 8-bit Sound + 2 Original Sounds on Standard C64. Why Not MSX?" *MSX Resource Center,* 30 May 2010, www.msx.org/forum/development/msx-development/4-channels-8-bit-sound-2-original-sounds-standard-c64-why-not-msx.

"MT-32." *SynthMania,* www.synthmania.com/mt-32.htm. Accessed 24 Jan. 2021.

"Music." *Minecraft Wiki,* 31 Aug. 2020, minecraft.gamepedia.com/Music. Accessed 3 Sept. 2020.

"Music (SSBU)." *SmashWiki,* 1 Sept. 2020, www.ssbwiki.com/Music_(SSBU). Accessed 24 Sept. 2020.

"Music Used on the Menu Screen? Ori and the Blind Forest General Discussions." *Steam Community,* 12 Mar. 2015, steamcommunity.com/app/261570/discussions/0/617330227200090656/.

"N-CT FM." *GTA Wiki,* Fandom, 19 Mar. 2021, gta.fandom.com/wiki/N-CT_FM. Accessed 10 Apr. 2021.

"N64 Hardware Specifications." *Angelfire,* digitalfantasy.angelfire.com/n64-hardware-specifications.html. Accessed 3 Aug. 2018.

Napolitano, Jayson. "5 Reasons Why Audio on the Nintendo 3DS Should Be Amazing." *Original Sound Version,* 17 Mar. 2011, www.originalsoundversion.com/5-reasons-why-audio-on-the-nintendo-3ds-should-be-amazing.

Napolitano, Jayson. "Super Mario 3D World Soundtrack Is Another Masterpiece." *Destructoid,* 15 Nov. 2013, www.destructoid.com/super-mario-3d-world-soundtrack-is-another-masterpiece-265455.phtml.

NEC. "TurboGrafx-16 Unit Service Manual." *Console5,* Dec. 1989, console5.com/techwiki/images/b/bc/TurboGrafx-16_Unit_Service_Manual_-_SMTG16.pdf. Accessed 28 Sept. 2020.

"Neo Geo (Platform)." *Giant Bomb,* 10 Mar. 2015, www.giantbomb.com/neo-geo/3045-25/.

Newsfield. "Monty on the Run." *ZZap!64,* Oct. 1985, pp. 16–17, archive.org/details/zzap64-magazine-006/page/n15/mode/2up. Accessed 28 May 2021.

Nintendo. "Buy Now—Nintendo Labo Official Site—What's Included, Where to Buy." *Nintendo Labo™ for the Nintendo Switch™ Home Gaming System—Official Site,* labo.nintendo.com/kits/variety-kit/. Accessed 17 Sept. 2020.

Nintendo. "Buy Now—Nintendo Switch—Bundles, What's Included." *Nintendo—Official Site,* www.nintendo.com/switch/buy-now/. Accessed 10 Sept. 2020.

Nintendo. "Disney Epic Mickey 2: The Power of Two for Wii U." 2016, www.nintendo.com/

games/detail/D5r6WvYO5Al9w0Pnt_Rbq45_d3Wk2Kcv.

"Nintendo DS NTR-001." *TechInsights,* www.techinsights.com/DeviceProfileSF_Austin Parts.aspx?TeardownId=222. Accessed 3 Aug. 2018.

"Nintendo DSi Sound." *Nintendo Fandom,* 29 Apr. 2020, nintendo.fandom.com/wiki/Nintendo_DSi_Sound. Accessed 23 Sept. 2020.

Nintendo. "Family BASIC Manual." *Famicom World,* 1984, famicomworld.com/Personal/uglyjoe/FamilyBasicManual.pdf. Accessed 17 Jan. 2021 English translation from Japanese.

Nintendo. "Game Boy Programming Manual Version 1.1." 3 Dec. 1999, ia803208.us.archive.org/9/items/GameBoyProgManVer1.1/GameBoyProgManVer1.1.pdf. Accessed 21 Apr. 2021.

Nintendo. "How to Use Surround Sound on the Wii U." *Nintendo Support,* en-americas-support.nintendo.com/app/answers/detail/a_id/1508/~/how-to-use-surround-sound-on-the-wii-u. Accessed 3 Aug. 2018.

Nintendo. "IR Information: Financial Data—Top Selling Title Sales Units—Wii U Software." *Nintendo Co., Ltd,* 31 Mar. 2020, www.nintendo.co.jp/ir/en/finance/software/wiiu.html. Accessed 10 Sept. 2020.

Nintendo. "IR Information : Sales Data—Dedicated Video Game Sales Units." *Nintendo Co., Ltd,* 30 June 2020, www.nintendo.co.jp/ir/en/finance/hard_soft/. Accessed 10 Sept. 2020.

Nintendo. "Majesco Ships first "Game Boy Advance Video" Titles." *Game Boy Advance Video,* 5 May 2004, web.archive.org/web/20040623124828/www.gba-video.com/pressrelease2.html. Accessed 31 Mar. 2020.

"Nintendo Music Format (N-SPC)." *Super Famicom Development Wiki,* wiki.superfamicom.org/nintendo-music-format-(n-spc). Accessed 24 Nov. 2018.

Nintendo. "Nintendo Support: System Menu Update History." *Nintendo Support,* en-americas-support.nintendo.com/app/answers/detail/a_id/231/~/system-menu-update-history. Accessed 2 Sept. 2020.

Nintendo. "Nintendo Support: What Is the Difference Between the Models of Wii Consoles?" *Nintendo Support,* en-americas-support.nintendo.com/app/answers/detail/a_id/2650/~/what-is-the-difference-between-the-models-of-wii-consoles. Accessed 23 Sept. 2020.

"Nintendo 64 Technical Specifications." *Video Game Review,* videogamereview.tripod.com/n64/specs.html. Accessed 3 Aug. 2018.

Nintendo. "Technical Specs—Nintendo Switch." *Nintendo,* www.nintendo.com/switch/features/tech-specs/. Accessed 6 Aug. 2018.

Nintendo. "Nintendo 3DS Sound." *Nintendo of Europe,* www.nintendo.co.uk/Nintendo-3DS-Family/Instant-Software/Nintendo-3DS-Sound/Nintendo-3DS-Sound-115638.html. Accessed 3 Aug. 2018.

Nintendo. (2016). Nintendo 3DS Sound. Retrieved from https://www.nintendo.co.uk/Nintendo-3DS-Family/Instant-Software/Nintendo-3DS-Sound/Nintendo-3DS-Sound-115638.html

Nintendo. "Wii U—Technical Specs." *Nintendo,* www.nintendo.com/wiiu/features/tech-specs/. Accessed 3 Aug. 2018.

NintendoFan. "Audio capabilities: Nintendo Wii U (comprehensive post)." 17 Dec. 2012, thewiiu.com/topic/8300-audio-capabilities-nintendo-wii-u-comprehensive-post/.

"Nobuo Uematsu." *Video Game Music Preservation Foundation Wiki,* 24 June 2016, www.vgmpf.com/Wiki/index.php?title=Nobuo_Uematsu. Accessed 6 Aug. 2018.

Nokia. "Nokia N-Gage Extended User's Guide." *Archive.org,* 2003, ia800402.us.archive.org/20/items/nokia-n-gage/nokia-n-gage.pdf. Accessed 5 Apr. 2021.

North, Dale. "Play Your PS1 Discs on Your PSP Via PS3's Remote Play." *Destructoid,* 18 Dec. 2007, www.destructoid.com/stories/play-your-ps1-discs-on-your-psp-via-ps3-s-remote-play-60261.phtml. Accessed 22 Sept. 2020.

O'Donnell, Martin. "Home." *Marty O'Donnell Music,* martyodonnellmusic.com. Accessed 7 Aug. 2018.

O'Donnell, Martin. "Martin O'Donnell Interview." Interview by Sam Bandah. *UKMusic,* 1 Nov. 2007, web.archive.org/web/20140819090449/www.ukmusic.com/music/martin-o-donnell-interview/.

Ohannessian, Kevin. "Nintendo Brings Wii Mini to the U.S.—Should You Buy One?" *Tom's Guide,* 6 Nov. 2013, www.tomsguide.com/us/nintendo-wii-mini-pros-cons,news-17823.html. Accessed 23 Sept. 2020.

Orth, Steven A. "Melody Blaster." *INTV Funhouse,* www.intvfunhouse.com/games/melo.php. Accessed 24 Jan. 2021.

"Otocky/Music Maker Mode." *StrategyWiki,* 12 June 2009, strategywiki.org/wiki/Otocky/Music_Maker_Mode. Accessed 12 Sept. 2018.

"OutRun (ARC)." *Video Game Music Preservation Foundation Wiki,* 31 Jan. 2017, www.vgmpf.com/Wiki/index.php?title=OutRun_(ARC). Accessed 15 Aug. 2018.

Oxford, Nadia. "Note Block Beat Box: Listening to Hopes and Dreams from Undertale." *USgamer.net,* 21 Apr. 2016, www.usgamer.net/articles/note-block-beat-box-listening-to-hopes-and-dreams-from-undertale. Accessed 9 Sept. 2020.

Pac12345. "Wii U audio FAQ (5.1 surround sound)." 11 Dec. 2012, www.gamefaqs.com/boards/631516-wii-u/64891724.

Parish, Jeremy. "Last of the Line: Game Boy Advance Ended One Legacy As It Began Another." *USgamer.net,* 25 Mar. 2016, www.usgamer.net/articles/last-of-the-line-game-boy-advance-ended-one-legacy-while-beginning-another/page-2.

"Pathway to Glory—NG—Review." *GameZone,* 4 May 2012, www.gamezone.com/reviews/pathway_to_glory_ng_review/.

"PC Engine/Turbografx-16 Music for Beginners

(Page 1)." *ChipMusic,* 21 Feb. 2010, chipmusic. org/forums/topic/790/pc-engineturbografx16-music-for-beginners/.

"PC Speaker." *OSDev Wiki,* 27 June 2020, wiki. osdev.org/PC_Speaker. Accessed 26 May 2021.

"PC Speaker." *OSDev Wiki,* 27 June 2020, wiki. osdev.org/PC_Speaker. Accessed 22 Jan. 2021."Who Had a Trademark on "Mega Drive" in 1989?" *Sega-16,* 13 May 2012, www.sega-16. com/forum/showthread.php?20946-Who-had-a-trademark-on-quot-Mega-Drive-quot-in-1989.

Phillips, Winifred. *A Composer's Guide to Game Music.* MIT P, 2014.

Phillips, Yoh. "How a PlayStation Music-Making Game Inspired a Generation of Producers."*DJ-Booth,* 19 May 2017, djbooth.net/features/2017–05–19-mtv-music-generator-history.

Pino, Nick. "PS4 Pro Vs Xbox One X: Which 4K Console is Better?" *TechRadar,* 16 Jan. 2019, www.techradar.com/news/ps4-pro-vs-xbox-one-x-how-are-the-mid-generation-consoles-shaping-up. Accessed 20 Sept. 2020.

Plasket, Michael. "Magician Lord." *Hardcore Gaming 101,* 13 Sept. 2017, www.hardcoregaming101. net/magician-lord/.

"Player [1]—Space Invaders." *Discogs,* www. discogs.com/Player-1-Space-Invaders/release/ 944745. Accessed 23 Jan. 2021.

PlayStation. "Gustavo Santaolalla: The Music of The Last of Us." *YouTube,* 17 May 2013, www. youtube.com/watch?v=Ejdjcun2Jo4.

PlayStation. "Sound Shapes™Level Editor Feature." *YouTube,* 1 Aug. 2012, www.youtube.com/ watch?v=Tdm2n_w9BzI. Accessed 5 Sept. 2020.

"PlayStation 4 Secrets." *Edepot,* www.edepot.com/ playstation4.html. Accessed 29 Sept. 2020.

"PS3 Specs." *PS3Blog.net,* www.ps3blog.net/about/ ps3-specs/. Accessed 3 Aug. 2018.

"PlayStation3 Super Audio CD FAQ." *PS3SACD. com,* 29 Sept. 2012, www.ps3sacd.com/faq.html. Accessed 22 Apr. 2020.

Plunkett, Luke. "So THAT'S What They're Saying In Civ IV's Intro." *Kotaku,* 19 Aug. 2014, kotaku. com/so-thats-what-theyre-saying-in-civ-ivs-intro-1624242582.

Poh, Michael. "Evolution of Home Video Game Consoles: 1967–2011." *Hongkiat,* 2011, www. hongkiat.com/blog/evolution-of-home-video-game-consoles-1967-2011/. Accessed 3 Aug. 2018.

Polygon. "Why Journey's last song was the hardest to compose." *YouTube,* 18 Nov. 2019, youtu.be/ iUaPHTC2TjI. Accessed 4 Sept. 2020.

"Portal Soundtrack." *Combine OverWiki, the Original Half-Life Wiki and Portal Wiki,* 24 May 2018, combineoverwiki.net/wiki/Portal_ soundtrack. Accessed 16 Aug. 2018.

Porter, Jon. "Meet the Minds Behind Nintendo Switch's HD Rumble Tech." *TechRadar,* 7 Feb. 2017, www.techradar.com/news/meet-the-minds-behind-nintendo-switchs-hd-rumble-tech. Accessed 19 Sept. 2020.

"The Price of PC Sound (and Some Other Stuff)." *Nerdly Pleasures,* 24 May 2013, nerdlypleasures.

blogspot.com/2013/05/how-much-do-we-pay-for-sound-hardware.html. Accessed 29 Sept. 2020.

"PS Vita Tech Specs." *IGN,* 30 Aug. 2013, www. ign.com/wikis/ps-vita/PS_Vita_Tech_Specs. Accessed 9 June 2021.

"PS4 Remote Play." *PlayStation,* www.playstation. com/en-us/explore/ps4/remote-play/. Accessed 31 Aug. 2018.

"PS1 Ridge Racer Insert Music CD While Playing?" *Digital Press,* 8 Dec. 2008, forum.digitpress. com/forum/showthread.php?125450-PS1-Ridge-Racer-insert-music-CD-while-playing.

"PSP Specs Revealed." *IGN,* 29 July 2003, www.ign. com/articles/2003/07/29/psp-specs-revealed.

"PSX Specifications." *NO$FUN,* problemkaputt. de/psx-spx.htm. Accessed 3 Aug. 2018.

Purves, Robert. "A Video Game Odyssey—a Brief History of Video Game Music." *Music Files,* www.mfiles.co.uk/video-game-music-history. htm. Accessed 25 Jan. 2020.

QSound Labs, Inc. "OEM Guide to QSound Q3D Positional 3D Audio." *QSound Labs, Inc,* Oct. 1998, www.qsound.com/2002/library/Q3d1_5. pdf. Accessed 11 Feb. 2020.

"Quake." *Quake Fandom,* 2 Jan. 2021, quake.fan-dom.com/wiki/Quake. Accessed 18 Jan. 2021.

"Rally-X Arcade Video Game by NAMCO (1980)." *Gaming History,* www.arcade-history.com/?n=-rally-x&page=detail&id=2171. Accessed 15 Aug. 2018.

Rawmeatcowboy. "The Subtle Sound Effects of the Switch's HD Rumble (with Audio Examples)." *GoNintendo,* 28 May 2017, gonintendo. com/stories/281248-the-subtle-sound-effects-of-the-switch-s-hd-rumble-with-audio-ex. Accessed 19 Sept. 2020.

Red Bull Music Academy. "Hirokazu Tanaka on Nintendo Game Music, Reggae and Tetris." *YouTube,* 22 Nov. 2014, www.youtube.com/ watch?v=F7J5GlE3YLQ. Accessed 9 Apr. 2020.

Redifer, Joe. "Did Any 32X Games Take Advantage of the Enchanced Sound?" *Sega-16,* 24 Feb. 2013, www.sega-16.com/forum/showthread.php? 23425-Did-any-32X-games-take-advantage-of-the-enchanced-sound.

Redifer, Joe. "32X PWM Sound." *Sega-16,* 7 Oct. 2007, www.sega-16.com/forum/showthread. php?3317-32X-PWM-sound.

Reed, Kristan. "E3 2003: Nokia N-Gage." *Euro gamer.net,* 14 May 2003, www.eurogamer.net/ articles/news140503nokiae3. Accessed 17 Jan. 2021.

Reese, Emily, and Nora Huxtable. "Top Score: Robyn Miller and the Story of Myst." *Classical MPR,* 25 Aug. 2014, www.classicalmpr.org/ story/2014/07/31/robyn-miller-myst-top-score.

Regel, Julian. "Inside Nintendo 64." *Nintendo 64 Tech,* 21 June 1999, n64.icequake.net/mirror/ www.white-tower.demon.co.uk/n64.

Retropete. "Sony PlayStation 2 (PS2)." 2016, www. 8-bitcentral.com/sony/playStation2.html.

Reyes, William. "Rhythm Tengoku FAQ/Walk-through for Game Boy Advance." *GameFAQs,*

9 Sept. 2006, gamefaqs.gamespot.com/gba/
933337-rhythm-tengoku/faqs/44312.

ReyVGM. "Super Game Boy Borders." *The Video Game Museum*, www.vgmuseum.com/features/ sgb/. Accessed 1 June 2020.

Rick. "Nintendo DS Specs." *GameCubicle.com*, Aug. 2004, www.gamecubicle.com/hardware-nintendo_ds_spec_sheet.htm.

Ritz, Eric J. "An Introduction to Mode 7 on the SNES." *One More Game-Dev and Programming Blog*, 16 July 2013, ericjmritz.wordpress.com/2013/07/15/an-introduction-to-mode-7-on-the-snes/.

"Rob Hubbard." *Video Game Music Preservation Foundation Wiki*, 5 Aug. 2017, www.vgmpf.com/Wiki/index.php/Rob_Hubbard. Accessed 6 Aug. 2018.

"Rock'n Rouge." *Wikipedia*, Wikimedia Foundation, Inc, 20 Dec. 2020, ja.wikipedia.org/wiki/Rock%27n_Rouge. Accessed 22 Jan. 2021.

Roland Corporation. "Roland MT-32 Multi-Timbre Sound Module Owner's Manual." *Archive.org*, 1987, ia800709.us.archive.org/17/items/synthmanual-roland-mt-32-owners-manual/rolandmt-32ownersmanual.pdf. Accessed 29 Sept. 2020.

"Roland MT-32." *Vintage Synth Explorer*, www.vintagesynth.com/roland/mt32.php. Accessed 29 Sept. 2020.

Ronspies, Wade. "REVIEW: 'Amplitude' Gifts Players with Simpler, Cheaper 'Rock Band.'" *The Daily Nebraskan*, 30 Jan. 2018, www.dailynebraskan.com/culture/review-amplitude-gifts-players-with-simpler-cheaper-rock-band/article_2092bf86-0568-11e8-9dfd-cf464005e2d6.html.

Rubin, Peter. "Check Out This Glorious, Colorful History of Arcade Games." *WIRED*, 13 May 2014, www.wired.com/2014/05/arcade-history/.

Saed, Sherif. "Rockstar Plans to Replace Music Removed from GTA 4 Due to Expired Licenses." *VG 24/7*, 11 Apr. 2018, www.vg247.com/2018/04/11/gta-4-soundtrack-songs-removed-expired-music-licenses/.

Saucedo, Kaylyn. "Dance Dance Revolution Retrospective: Arcade Machines." *YouTube*, 5 Apr. 2016, www.youtube.com/watch?v=Nec-a_EddxQ.

Savov, Vlad. "Sony Ericsson Xperia Play Review." *Engadget*, 28 Mar. 2011, www.engadget.com/2011-03-28-sony-ericsson-xperia-play-review.html. Accessed 2 Sept. 2020.

Schilling, Chris. "Gitaroo Man Retrospective." *Eurogamer.net*, 8 Apr. 2013, www.eurogamer.net/articles/2013-08-04-gitaroo-man-retrospective.

Score, Avery. "Pathway to Glory Review." *GameSpot*, 8 Dec. 2004, www.gamespot.com/reviews/pathway-to-glory-review/1900-6114566/.

"Script for Real Sound: Regret of the Wind." *OneSwitch.org.uk Blog*, 17 Oct. 2018, switchgaming.blogspot.com/2018/10/script-for-real-sound-regret-of-wind.html. Accessed 2 June 2020.

Seabrook, Andrea. "The Evolution of Video Game Music." *NPR.org*, 13 Apr. 2008, www.npr.org/templates/story/story.php?storyId=89565567.

Sega Corporation. "Master System." sega.jp/fb/segahard/master/data.html.

"Sega Dreamcast's Samba De Amigo." *The Game Goldies*, 15 July 2009, wayback.archive.org/web/20130625002520/www.gamegoldies.org/samba-de-amigo-sega-dreamcast/.

"Sega Master System." *Sega Retro*, 29 Jan. 2016, segaretro.org/Sega_Master_System.

Sega Retro. "Sega Master System." 29 Jan. 2016, segaretro.org/Sega_Master_System. Accessed 30 Jan. 2016.

"Sega Saturn System Info." *The Video Game Museum*, www.vgmuseum.com/systems/saturn/. Accessed 3 Aug. 2018.

"Sega Saturn Tech Specs." *Dave's Sega Saturn Page*, 13 Apr. 2021, www.sega-saturn.com/saturn/other/satspecs.htm. Accessed 9 June 2021.

"Sega 32X." *Sega Retro*, 29 Jan. 2016, segaretro.org/Sega_32X.

"SEGA Tunes: Sonic Triple Trouble's Sunset Park Act 3." *Sega Bits*, 13 Mar. 2012, segabits.com/blog/2012/03/13/tuesday-tunes-sonic-triple-troubles-sunset-park-act-3/.

Service, Tom. "The Evolution of Video Game Music." *BBC*, 19 Apr. 2018, www.bbc.co.uk/programmes/articles/4cFwfytTrrg439K8tt1ffcG/the-evolution-of-video-game-music. Accessed 25 Jan. 2020.

"7800 Compared to the NES." *Atari 7800 Programming, Google Sites*, sites.google.com/site/atari7800wiki/7800-compared-to-the-nes. Accessed 3 Aug. 2018.

"Sid Meier's C.P.U. Bach." *Hardcore Gaming 101*, 4 May 2017, www.hardcoregaming101.net/sid-meiers-c-p-u-bach-3do-1994/.

Signor, Jeremy. "Weight of the World." *First Person Scholar—Weekly Critical Essays, Commentaries, and Book Reviews on Games*, 7 Mar. 2018, www.firstpersonscholar.com/weight-of-the-world/. Accessed 14 Sept. 2020.

Simpson, Martin P. "The First King Arthur, and Dolby Surround." *Martin P Simpson*, 17 Sept. 2011, www.martinpsimpson.com/2011/09/first-king-arthur-and-dolby-surround.html. Accessed 21 Apr. 2021.

"SimTunes." *PC Gaming Wiki*, 12 Jan. 2020, www.pcgamingwiki.com/wiki/SimTunes. Accessed 27 May 2021.

"The 64DD: Nintendo's Disk Drive." *IGN*, 29 Jan. 1998, www.ign.com/articles/1998/01/29/the-64dd-nintendos-disk-drive. Accessed 31 Mar. 2020.

Slec. "Audio and the PS3." 5 Mar. 2008, forum.blu-ray.com/showthread.php?t=40872.

Snail Tooth Gaming. "Super Game Boy 1 and 2 Comparison." *YouTube*, 5 Feb. 2017, youtu.be/7YVw1–3QRfU. Accessed 1 June 2020.

"SNK Neo-Geo 101: A Beginner's Guide." *Racketboy*, 20 May 2011, www.racketboy.com/retro/snk-neo-geo-101-a-beginners-guide.

Softbank. "SoftBank and Apple to Bring IPhone 3G to Japan on July 11." *SoftBank,* 9 June 2008, www.softbank.jp/en/corp/group/sbm/news/press/2008/20080610_01/. Accessed 1 Feb. 2021.

Sony. "PS4 Audio Output Settings." *PlayStation,* manuals.playstation.net/document/en/ps4/settings/audiooutput.html. Accessed 3 Aug. 2018.

Sony. "PS3 Audio Output Settings." *PlayStation,* manuals.playstation.net/document/en/ps3/current/settings/audiooutput.html. Accessed 3 Aug. 2018.

Sony. "SPU2 Overview." *Dropbox,* Apr. 2002, www.dropbox.com/s/87xwmydprwubmyh/SPU2_Overview_Manual.pdf.

Sony. "Using Remote Play Via the Internet | PlayStation®Vita User's Guide." *PlayStation,* manuals.playstation.net/document/en/psvita/ps4link/viainternet.html. Accessed 10 Sept. 2020.

"Sony PlayStation 2 (PS2)." *8-Bit Central,* www.8-bitcentral.com/sony/playStation2.html. Accessed 3 Aug. 2018.

Sorrel, Charlie. "PS2 Still Outselling PS3 by Four to One." *WIRED,* 24 Aug. 2007, www.wired.com/2007/08/ps2-still-outse/. Accessed 21 Sept. 2020.

"Sound Hardware." *Famitracker Wiki,* 28 Mar. 2015, famitracker.com/wiki/index.php?title=Sound_hardware. Accessed 3 Aug. 2018.

"Sound on the Gameboy Advance—Day 1." *Deku's Tree of Art,* deku.gbadev.org/program/sound1.html. Accessed 3 Aug. 2018.

"Soundtrack (Civ4)." *Civilization Wiki,* 17 Mar. 2018, civilization.wikia.com/wiki/Soundtrack_(Civ4). Accessed 16 Aug. 2018.

"Soundvoyager (Game)." *Giant Bomb,* www.giantbomb.com/soundvoyager/3030-15419/. Accessed 10 Sept. 2018.

"Soundvoyager for Game Boy Advance (2006)." *MobyGames,* www.mobygames.com/game/soundvoyager. Accessed 20 Aug. 2018.

"SPC Hacking Guide." *SMW Central,* 30 Aug. 2010, www.smwcentral.net/?p=viewthread&t=38116.

Sprixim. "Thumper Time Signatures." *Steam Community,* 9 Dec. 2017, steamcommunity.com/app/356400/discussions/0/1500126447393849303/.

"SSG." *NeoGeo Development Wiki,* 11 Feb. 2017, wiki.neogeodev.org/index.php?title=SSG. Accessed 26 Nov. 2018.

Stark, Chelsea. "'Sound Shapes' Musical Game Turns Players Into Composers [REVIEW]." *Mashable,* 8 Aug. 2012, mashable.com/2012/08/08/sound-shapes-review/.

"Still Alive." *Half-Life Wiki,* 6 June 2018, half-life.wikia.com/wiki/Still_Alive. Accessed 16 Aug. 2018.

Stone, Dan. "What Is PCM Audio?" *Techwalla,* www.techwalla.com/articles/what-is-pcm-audio. Accessed 25 Nov. 2018.

Stridsberg, Douglas. "XBOX Hardware Specifications." *Thy Old XBOX—Tips, Tweaks and Guides,* xbox.douglasstridsberg.com/xbox-hardware-specifications/. Accessed 3 Aug. 2018.

Studio MDHR. "The Music of Cuphead: Recording Floral Fury." *YouTube,* 18 Sept. 2017, youtu.be/CG5RdWnUVlc. Accessed 9 Sept. 2020.

Summers, Tim. "Dimensions of Game Music History." *The Routledge Companion to Screen Music and Sound,* Taylor & Francis, 2017, pp. 139–152.

Summers, Tim. *Understanding Video Game Music.* Cambridge UP, 2016.

"Super Game Boy Enhancement." *Giant Bomb,* www.giantbomb.com/super-game-boy-enhancement/3015-4804/. Accessed 1 June 2020.

"Super Game Boy 2." *Nintendo Fandom,* 4 Dec. 2020, nintendo.fandom.com/wiki/Super_Game_Boy_2. Accessed 18 Jan. 2021.

Sweet, Michael. "Video Game Composition Over the Past 40 Years." *Writing Interactive Music for Video Games: A Composer's Guide,* Pearson Education, 2014, pp. 85–108.

Sylvester, Niko. "How to Play Music on a PS Vita." *Lifewire,* 8 Mar. 2019, www.lifewire.com/play-music-on-ps-vita-2792783. Accessed 4 Sept. 2020.

T., Nick. "Did You Know Which Was the First Phone with Built-in Stereo Speakers?" *Phone Arena,* 17 July 2015, www.phonearena.com/news/Did-you-know-which-was-the-first-phone-with-built-in-stereo-speakers_id71659. Accessed 2 Sept. 2020.

Talbot-Watkins, Richard. "Sega Master System Technical Information." *SMS Power!,* 10 June 1998, www.smspower.org/uploads/Development/richard.txt.

Tallarico, Tommy. "Interview: Tommy Tallarico (Composer)." Interview by Ken Horowitz. *Sega-16,* 1 June 2005, www.sega-16.com/2005/06/interview-tommy-tallarico/.

Taylor, Brad. "2A03 Technical Reference." *Nes-Dev,* 23 Apr. 2004, nesdev.com/2A03%20technical%20reference.txt.

Taylor, Jordyn. "How Video Game 'Disney Epic Mickey 2: The Power of 2' Is Like a Musical." *Backstage,* 16 Aug. 2019, www.backstage.com/news/dooley-and-himelstein-disney-epic-mickey-2-power-2/. Accessed 10 Apr. 2021.

Techno Dad. "Dolby Atmos Setup for Xbox One X | 8 Atmos Titles on Netflix!" *YouTube,* 30 Nov. 2017, youtu.be/Aj6a3JE9DPA. Accessed 21 Sept. 2020.

TecToy. "Master System Evolution Com 132 Jogos Na Memória." *Tec Toy,* www.tectoy.com.br/master-system-evolution-com-132-jogos-na-memoria-995020351822-p186. Accessed 24 Apr. 2021.

"That Police Dispatch Noise. You Know. That One." *Giant Bomb,* 5 July 2010, www.giantbomb.com/forums/off-topic-31/that-police-dispatch-noise-you-know-that-one-429586/. Accessed 9 Apr. 2021.

Theìberge, Paul, et al. "Stereo Timeline." *Living Stereo: Histories and Cultures of Multichannel Sound,* Bloomsbury Academic, 2015, p. 270.

"32X." *Sega Wiki,* 13 Oct. 2020, sega.wikia.com/wiki/Sega_32X. Accessed 9 June 2021.

Thomas, Chance. *Composing Music for Games: The Art, Technology and Business of Video Game Scoring*. CRC P, 2016.

Thurrott, Paul. "Xbox 360 Vs. PlayStation 3 Vs. Wii: A Technical Comparison." *IT Pro*, 6 Oct. 2010, www.itprotoday.com/xbox-360-vs-playstation-3-vs-wii-technical-comparison.

Tiberio, David. "Famous Amiga Uses." *Amiga Report Magazine*, 1993, www.amigareport.com/ar134/p1-12.html.

"Tommy Tallarico." *Video Game Music Preservation Foundation Wiki*, 28 May 2018, www.vgmpf.com/Wiki/index.php?title=Tommy_Tallarico. Accessed 6 Aug. 2018.

"Toshio Iwai 'From Flipbooks to Media Art.'" *MIT Media Lab*, www.media.mit.edu/events/talk-iwai.html. Accessed 7 Aug. 2018.

Totaka, Kazumi. "3. No Score, No Mistakes." Interview by Satoru Iwata. *Nintendo of Europe*, 2008, www.nintendo.co.uk/Iwata-Asks/Iwata-Asks-Wii-Music/Volume-2-Wii-Music-A-First-Time-For-Everyone/3-No-Score-No-Mistakes/3-No-Score-No-Mistakes-238445.html. Accessed 12 May 2020.

"Toy-Con Piano—Nintendo Labo Wiki Guide." *IGN*, 3 June 2018, www.ign.com/wikis/nintendo-labo/Toy-Con_Piano. Accessed 6 Aug. 2018.

Truax, Barry. "Tutorial for Frequency Modulation Synthesis." *Simon Fraser University*, www.sfu.ca/~truax/fmtut.html. Accessed 27 Nov. 2018.

Turboboy215. "(Incomplete) List of GB/GBC Games to Use PCM Samples." *ChipMusic.org*, 7 July 2015, chipmusic.org/forums/topic/16824/incomplete-list-of-gbgbc-games-to-use-pcm-samples/. Accessed 21 Sept. 2020.

"TurboGrafx-CD (Platform)." *Giant Bomb*, 13 June 2014, www.giantbomb.com/turbografx-cd/3045-53/.

"TurboGrafx-16 101: The Beginner's Guide." *Racketboy*, 12 Dec. 2014, www.racketboy.com/retro/turbografx-16/tubrografix-16-tg16-101-beginners-guide.

"Tutorials/Redstone Music." *Minecraft Wiki*, 1 Aug. 2020, minecraft.gamepedia.com/Tutorials/Redstone_music. Accessed 3 Sept. 2020.

"2600/7800 Development Kit." *The Atari Museum*, www.atarimuseum.com/ahs_archives/archives/pdf/videogames/7800/7800_devkit.pdf. Accessed 3 Aug. 2018.

Tyson, Jeff. "How Dreamcast Works." *HowStuffWorks*, 19 Oct. 2000, electronics.howstuffworks.com/dreamcast.htm.

"Ultimate SoundTracker V1.21 (Amiga Soundeditor)." janeway.exotica.org.uk/release.php?id=17706. Accessed 18 Jan. 2021.

"Unused/underused Solutions to Limitations of the Genesis/MD." *Sega-16*, 25 Oct. 2010, www.sega-16.com/forum/showthread.php?14476-Unused-underused-solutions-to-limitations-of-the-Genesis-MD.

Vaskelis, Darius. "Atari Lynx FAQ." *AtariAge*, 3 Aug. 2003, atariage.com/Lynx/faq/index.html.

The Video Game Museum. "Technical Specs." www.vgmuseum.com/systems/jaguar/.

Wall, Jack. "Home." *The Official Website of Composer Jack Wall*, jackwall.net. Accessed 6 Aug. 2018.

Wardyga, Brian J. "Chapter 2: Behind the Technology." *The Video Games Textbook: History • Business • Technology*, CRC Press, 2018.

"Wavetable Archive." *GbdevWiki*, 16 Jan. 2017, gbdev.gg8.se/wiki/articles/Wavetable_Archive. Accessed 26 Nov. 2018.

Webster, Andrew. "Five Years of Sword & Sworcery: The History of a Weird and Beautiful Game." *The Verge*, 24 Mar. 2016, www.theverge.com/2016/3/24/11297534/superbrothers-sword-and-sworcery-retrospective.

Weir, William. "From the Arcade to the Grammys: The Evolution of Video Game Music." *The Atlantic*, 10 Feb. 2011, www.theatlantic.com/entertainment/archive/2011/02/from-the-arcade-to-the-grammys-the-evolution-of-video-game-music/71082/. Accessed 25 Jan. 2020.

Wenz, John. "End of an Era: The Last Games for 12 Iconic Consoles." *Popular Mechanics*, 17 June 2015, www.popularmechanics.com/culture/gaming/g2071/last-video-games-for-12-consoles/.

Weske, Jörg. "History." *Digital Sound and Music in Computer Games*, Dec. 2000, 3daudio.info/gamesound/history.html.

"What Is LPCM - Linear Pulse Code Modulated Audio." *AppGeeker*, www.appgeeker.com/audio/what-is-lpcm.html. Accessed 25 Nov. 2018.

Whitaker, Jed. "Review: Superbeat: Xonic." *Destructoid*, 30 Nov. 2015, www.destructoid.com/review-superbeat-xonic-323291.phtml.

Whitten, Marc. "Prepare for Titanfall: Marc Whitten Provides Details on Xbox One March Update." *Microsoft*, 5 Mar. 2014, news.xbox.com/en-us/2014/03/05/xbox-one-march-update/.

"Wii U GamePad Microphone Use (Concept)." *Giant Bomb*, www.giantbomb.com/wii-u-gamepad-microphone-use/3015-7836/. Accessed 29 Sept. 2020.

Wilburn, Thomas. "Catching Waveforms: Audiosurf Creator Dylan Fitterer Speaks." *Ars Technica*, 11 Mar. 2008, arstechnica.com/gaming/2008/03/catching-waveforms-audiosurf-creator-dylan-speaks/. Accessed 12 May 2020.

Wilde, Tyler. "Portal 2's Dynamic Music—an Interview with Composer Mike Morasky, and Five Tracks to Listen to Now!" *Gamesradar*, 14 Apr. 2011, www.gamesradar.com/portal-2s-dynamic-music-an-interview-with-composer-mike-morasky-and-five-tracks-to-listen-to-now/. Accessed 28 Apr. 2020.

Willings, Adrian. "Dolby Atmos for Gaming: What Is It and Which Games Support It." *Pocket-lint*, 12 Aug. 2020, www.pocket-lint.com/games/news/dolby/141761-dolby-atmos-for-gaming-what-is-it-and-what-games-support-it. Accessed 21 Sept. 2020.

Wiltshire, Alex. "How Turns Make Thumper Feel Physical." *Rock Paper Shotgun*, 25 Nov.

2016, www.rockpapershotgun.com/2016/11/25/thumper-music-game/.

"Wind Waker (Item)." *Zelda Wiki,* 9 Aug. 2017, zelda.gamepedia.com/Wind_Waker_(Item). Accessed 7 Aug. 2018.

Winterhalter, Ryan. "Rhythm Tengoku Review—Review." *Nintendo World Report,* 9 Sept. 2006, www.nintendoworldreport.com/review/12018/rhythm-tengoku-game-boy-advance.

Wittel, Greg. "Sega Genesis: Specs." *Digital Extremes,* dextremes.com/genesis/gen-spec.html. Accessed 3 Aug. 2018.

"Xbox 101: A Beginner's Guide to Microsoft's Original Console." *Racketboy,* 2 Mar. 2014, www.racketboy.com/retro/microsoft/xbox/xbox-101-a-beginners-guide-to-microsofts-original-console.

"Yamaha DX7 FM Synthesis Tutorial: Algorithms Explained." *YouTube,* 3 May 2017, www.youtube.com/watch?v=Y1xPT5D7Oc0.

"Yasunori Mitsuda." *Square Enix Music Online,* www.squareenixmusic.com/composers/mitsuda.html. Accessed 10 Aug. 2018.

"Yasunori Mitsuda." *Video Game Music Preservation Foundation Wiki,* 4 Dec. 2017, www.vgmpf.com/Wiki/index.php?title=Yasunori_Mitsuda. Accessed 14 Aug. 2018.

Yokota, Mahito. "Super Mario 3D World Composers Talk Cats, Dogs, and More." Interview by Jayson Napolitano. *Destructoid,* 6 Nov. 2013, www.destructoid.com/super-mario-3d-world-composers-talk-cats-dogs-and-more-264473.phtml.

"Yukio Kaneoka." *Video Game Music Preservation Foundation Wiki,* 4 May 2018, www.vgmpf.com/Wiki/index.php?title=Yukio_Kaneoka. Accessed 15 Nov. 2018.

Zdyrko, Dave. "LCD Screen (for PS One) Review." *IGN,* 13 Dec. 2001, www.ign.com/articles/2001/12/13/lcd-screen-for-ps-one-review.

Zehnder, S. M., and S. D. Lipscomb. "The Role of Music in Video Games." *Playing Video Games: Motives, Responses, and Consequences,* Lawrence Erlbaum Assoc, 2006, pp. 241–258.

Zur, Inon. "Home." *Inon Zur,* www.inonzur.com. Accessed 6 Aug. 2018.

Zur, Inon. Interview. *GSoundtracks,* web.archive.org/web/20161211123518/gsoundtracks.com/interviews/zur.htm. Accessed 6 Aug. 2018.

Index